FROM THE SEA END

Also by Christopher Lee
Nicely Nurdled, Sir (edited)

FROM THE SEA END

THE OFFICIAL HISTORY OF
SUSSEX COUNTY
CRICKET CLUB

CHRISTOPHER LEE
Foreword by Ted Dexter

PARTRIDGE PRESS

LONDON · NEW YORK · TORONTO · SYDNEY · AUCKLAND

TRANSWORLD PUBLISHERS LTD
61–63 Uxbridge Road, London w5 5sa

TRANSWORLD PUBLISHERS (AUSTRALIA) PTY LTD
15–23 Helles Avenue, Moorebank, NSW 2170

TRANSWORLD PUBLISHERS (NZ) LTD
Cnr Moselle and Waipareira Aves,
Henderson, Auckland

Published 1989 by Partridge Press
a division of Transworld Publishers Ltd
Copyright © Christopher Lee 1989
All pictures kindly supplied by Sussex CCC
except where otherwise credited

British Library Cataloguing in Publication Data

Sussex county cricket club
From the sea end: the official history of sussex
County cricket club.
1. East Sussex. West Sussex. East & West Sussex.
County cricket. Clubs. Sussex County cricket club
1988
I. Title   II. Lee, Christopher, 1941–
796.35'863'094225

ISBN 1–85225–083–6

Printed in Great Britain
by Mackays of Chatham PLC, Chatham, Kent

Acknowledgements

I would like to thank R. M. Leadley, the Sussex CCC Chairman, and the Club's Committee for the encouragement given for this official history. Also, thanks must be expressed to the Secretary, Nigel Bett, and to the Marketing Manager, Jim Parks, for his fund of modern cricketing knowledge. To Ted Dexter go special thanks for his foreword. Nor should the good humour and wise advice of my editor, Dick Douglas-Boyd, be ignored, even if he is a member of Surrey. Above all, it would be impossible to thank enough the research and enthusiasm of Ossie Osborne, the Sussex CCC's Hon. Librarian. His memory of dates and quick access to information seemingly make the whole world of computer technology redundant. Finally a special thanks to Ossie Osborne's assistant, David Dickinson, particularly for the moments when he clambered through a shuttered and dank pavilion in search of pictures, and to Phillip Bailey and Norman Epps for their special gift of compiling statistics. May I also thank Alan Ross for allowing me to quote his poem 'J. M. Parks at Tunbridge Wells.'

Christopher Lee
Cambridge, 1989

Foreword by E.R. Dexter

When I led the side in the first Gillette Cup Final, I said to myself, 'At last, Sussex has won something.' We did it again, and there were other successes. But we never quite managed to win the County Championship, although we were not the only county side without a Championship pennant. Today there are more competitions than some ever imagined there could be and, while one-day games have been criticised, they have undoubtedly revived public interest in the sport, and incidentally the standard of fielding and therefore public enjoyment. If there is no public enjoyment, there is no public, and eventually less cricket.

For those who remain unhappy at the new styles of play, the revolution of the seventies should be put into context. It is almost nothing compared with many of the other changes since the game went from two stumps to three. Too much money involved? Read the moaners of the nineteenth century when the game was supposed to be full of 'average mongering and money making'. The one-day game has been part of the inevitable evolution of entertainment and trophy hunting, nothing more. Sussex has had its share of success in these trophies, but the ultimate crown remains the Championship. While this is so, then cricket, for all its faults, is in good health. Sussex cricket throughout its long history reflects this.

If one were to ask the average cricketer where the game began, then in all probability the reply would be Hambledon. Some might even remember the names of famous players of the time: Newland, Nyren, 'Silver' Billy Beldham, John Small and Lambert. (Though whether they batted or bowled would be another matter.) Yet the answer would be wrong. For, although no one should doubt the rightful fame of Nyren's Hambledon, its great playing years were few and clustered towards the close of the eighteenth century. You might say that that is history and tradition enough. But the truth is that cricket is much older. Its references date from at least as far back as the sixteenth century and, less surely, from earlier times. It does not matter what origins we claim for the game. It could have evolved from stool-ball, or even from a form of rounders. What we know for sure is that by the sixteen hundreds cricket was being played in Sussex, a hundred years and more before Hambledon became famous.

A predecessor of mine as captain of Sussex, Arthur Gilligan, called Sussex the 'cradle of cricket'. A quick glance at the records of the great families of the county and the parish ledgers will show how right he was. From Brightling, Ninfield and the Dickers in the eastern part of Sussex to Chichester, Slindon and the estates of the Dukes of Richmond in the west, cricket was a thriving sport almost three hundred years ago. One of the first great cricket grounds was laid out in Brighton in the 1790s by the then Prince of Wales. The patronage given to Sussex cricket reads like something from the pages of *Burke's Peerage* and *Who's Who*.

With such a history, and a keen following, it was inevitable that the game should have developed in the county and that some of the most important changes should have been associated with Sussex. For example, the first bowlers to persevere with round-arm, as opposed to underarm, were Sussex men. And in 1827 it was the Sussex side, with these bowlers, who played the three 'trials' against an All-England team to judge the rights and wrongs of the style that was to lead to modern overarm.

And with this fine pedigree came great Sussex characters. There was the Lillywhite family, who produced wonderful cricketers including the first captain of an England Test side and the name of one of the most famous sports stores. Wisden, a startlingly good player who eventually went into business and gave his name to the yellow-coloured 'bible'. And what about Ranjitsinhji? He was the first, some say the greatest, of the Indian princes to play. At the same time, C. B. Fry was the most dominating of batsmen, while Maurice Tate was said by some to be one of the finest bowlers ever to play. The families of Coxes, Parkses and Langridges claim their places in the roll of honour. And there have been very many others in that Hove dressing room, including, in post-war years, Billy Griffith, David Sheppard, Robin Marlar, Ken Suttle, Ian Thomson, John Snow and Imran Khan. Such talent has meant great highs in the club's fortunes but also, it has to be said, quite a few lows.

But, for this oldest of first-class sides, the way the game is played matters most of all. Few would deny that Sussex, even when they are down the table, are rarely in the dumps. Their cricket shows a remarkable resilience that has survived the most humiliating drubbings to bounce back within a season or two to a whisker of the County Championship. What's more, even in its worst moments, Sussex is rarely a dull team to play with or to watch, and throughout its whole history has been known as one of the finest fielding sides on the county circuit. Sussex has played its way through 150 years of first-class cricket without forgetting for one moment that, above all things, cricket is a game, a sport. That single sentiment has made its mark on whoever has played for the team or watched from the pavilion, the striped deckchairs, the cowshed or from the sea end.

Arthur Gilligan was right. Sussex is the cradle in which cricket was nursed, and this history of the first 150 years of Sussex County Cricket Club is not simply a bucket of statistics and a record of who did what to make them. It is even more than a celebration of the game. For cricket is part of this land's social history, and Sussex is one of its cornerstones.

Ted Dexter
April 1989

Preface

The story of Sussex cricket is a tale of the game itself. Certainly as far back as the seventeenth century, men brought bat and ball to the villages and meadows of the downs and levels of the east and west of the county. By the seventeen hundreds the players of Sussex were ranked high and fortunate among patron and onlooker as cricket began to establish itself as part of the eighteenth-century rural landscape. By the next century it had matured to become part of our way of life. Its origins are in the men who shouldered curved bat then straight, hard ball, sported unguarded blood-stained stockings, and crossed the county of Sussex to bring scores and wickets and a folklore that has survived, although it is rarely told. So the celebration of 150 years of Sussex county cricket does not find its true beginning in 1839. This would be like coming to a Test match on the fourth day without having seen, or heard of, the drama of the previous three. For, above all, cricket is a great theatre of pathos, drama, comedy and even farce. Its players are as colourful as any who trod Garrick's firmer boards; its uncertainties just as treacherous. And so the risen curtain reveals not a series of scorecard-dotted nineteenth- and twentieth-century games, but a prelude in which the pastel memories of times past set themselves in place. It is then that the theatrical feast of Sussex cricket can be enjoyed.

FROM THE SEA END

Chapter 1

There is a dream. Across a meadow elms and oaks stand sturdy testament to a time gone before, while martins dive and swoop by distant slate spire. Peg and tile roofs, baked warm in the afternoon sun, squat silently, aloof from the lane's dust and dandelion verge. By the meadow's rim, children scampering and tumbling, parents lolling on favoured rugs with scattered picnics and old men, creased and big-knuckled, nodding and murmuring from dark green and peeling benches. To one side a slatted hut leans on its tired frame hung with square black clattering tins, their white pitted numbers calling 130 for 5 and tea not yet taken. And in front, in striped curved canvas chairs, lounge pale flannelled heroes, padded and awaiting their turn at the crease to bring bat to ball. In the middle meadow, cut square and rolled true, the baker with rolled shirt-sleeves and braces swings hard and runs, calling 'Yes!' to the round, red-faced parson – Trinity-tied girth free from font, pew and pulpit for the greatest game of all. There is a dream.

And why not? Cricket is about dreams. It is blessed with every sensation of beauty, grace and joy that might be conjured into the sweetest of slumbers; it is cursed with every anguish and unspeakable horror that tosses the sleeping body through black night's hell. Its gifts are moments never to be forgotten when eye, hand, bat and ball come together; when master, journeyman and apprentice have their way and skills bring a delight that cannot be explained. Its scorn is unbending when too slow, fumbling hands best be left in prayer, wayward arm brings captain's glare and batsman's smirk, and leaden feet retrace the way to the pavilion's mutters – capped, gloved, padded and all

1

for nought. Then, why should grown man risk such misery? So few moments of imagined bliss, which only he will remember beyond closing time and factory's siren. What power has this game that ridicule and fame can so easily bat side by side? The essayist E. V. Lucas pondered as much when he wrote in *English Leaves*, fifty years and more ago:

> How to explain the fascination that cricket exerts? It is not simple. That it should attract the proficients is understandable, though they are liable to continual mischances and mortifications such as no other game presents; but the curious thing is that it attracts the incompetents as well; those who never make a run and cannot bowl, and yet, doomed only to dreary waiting in the pavilion, and to fatiguing fielding, they turn up punctually on every occasion, hoping for the best, and even (such is the human heart's buoyancy) expecting it. There is no other game at which the confirmed duffer is so persistent and so undepressed. It is for the experts, victims of misfortune, that depression awaits: it is they who chew the cud of bitterness.
>
> The phrase about 'the glorious uncertainty of cricket' applies to the individual as much as to the fortunes of the struggle. For there is no second chance: the batsman who is out first ball must retire to the pavilion and brood on his ill-luck until it is time to field and forget it – when, as likely as not, he will miss the catch and enter purgatory again . . . perhaps, when all is said, the secret of the spell of cricket lies in the possibilities of every ball. The bat awaiting the ball is indeed an implement of destiny, but the ball which the bat awaits is more fateful. In its flight through the air, after it has left the bowler's hand and before it reaches the batsman, the spectator can live a lifetime . . .

A strange communion indeed – for some almost a cult. As C. B. Fry wrote:

> To some people cricket is a circus show upon which they may or may not find it worth while to spend sixpence; to others it is a pleasant means of livelihood; to others a physical fine art full of plot, interest and enlived by difficulties; to others in some sort it is a cult and a philosophy, and these last will never be understood by the *profanum vulgus*, nor by the merchant-minded, nor by the unphysically intellectual.

Perhaps, then, the dream is simply that. Romantic visions settle fine muslin over truth, yet cricket's friend stands no more pious

2

than music's, or letters'. True, those who would debunk its cant are sound and reasonable; cant is to be scoffed at wherever found. Maybe the dream is an English dream, let and learned so that this game for boys may be played by men wherever they may be. In the nineteenth century, Edward Cracroft Lefoy remarked that 'The whole edifice of the Christian virtues could be raised on a basis of good cricket'. Hubert Phillips was a little more earthy: 'An Englishman's crease is 'is castle.' Note: an *Englishman*'s crease. The early nineteenth-century essayist William Hazlitt clearly believed that cricket was English, and so it was then.

> The very names of a cricket-bat and ball make English fingers tingle. What happy days must 'Long Robinson' have passed in getting ready his wickets and mending his bats, who, when two of the fingers of his right hand were struck off by the violence of a ball, had a screw fastened to it to hold the bat, and with the other hand still sent the ball thundering against the boards that bounded old Lord's cricket ground! What delightful hours must have been his in looking forward to the matches that were to come, in recounting the feats he had performed in those that were passed! I myself have whiled away whole mornings in seeing him strike the ball (like a countryman mowing with a scythe) to the farthest extremity of the smooth, level, sun-burnt ground; and with long awkward strides count the notches that made victory sure.

A curious, almost macabre scene from Hazlitt, but the like of which appears again and again as lore and tale are recounted. It is a picture of a manly game, totally unforgiving, its origins obscure, its characters unbending, single-minded as a Saracen, its followers knowledgeable, fervent and fickle as the fortune that hovers by hand, by bat, by ball. So where did it all begin? There are those who say it started in Hambledon, in the middle or the second half of the eighteenth century. They would be wrong. Cricket's line is to be found in the fifteen hundreds.

It is a natural pastime to hit and to throw. The test of arm and eye may be as old as man himself. To club and to hurl brought reputation and food; to strike and to fend was the basis of the oldest tourney. Some say that cricket's seed was scattered in the Middle Ages. Certainly there was a pastime of bat and ball. In the southern villages, especially in Sussex, a stool was set to be guarded by one with a club or bat while another lobbed or bowled a ball at it. This game of stool-ball is played today, now with a square board on a stand at shoulder height as the target. The rules are similar to the laws of cricket; indeed, there is a 'stool' at either end, two batsmen,

3

one bowler, overs, fours and sixes, wides and byes and no-balls galore. Yet have not these been learned from cricket's parliament? There is eager argument that stool-ball foreran cricket; that its own ancient origins were found with villagers in Kent, Sussex and Hampshire where men and women, boys and their girls, would play up with paddle bat and bound and strung ball. Very likely to be true. Then runs one claim that some, more manly, played a faster game where ball with hardened centre was no longer lobbed in gentle play, but bowled hard, true and swiftly. To defend the stump or tiny wicket against the speedily bowled ball, a longer bat was needed, one that could be swung from shoulder to skim the ground, predictably and perfectly to strike and dominate the new skills shown by countrymen with centuries-bred cunning. This, too, may be true. Yet similar is not same, and stool-ball's issue perhaps is stool-ball, not cricket, whatever the hopes of well-meaning historians of the game.

It is said that in the late thirteenth century there was a game called creag. The Reverend James Pycroft, writing in the 1850s, suggested that creag was derived from Criece, the Saxon name for a crooked stick 'which we see in old pictures of cricket' by which he meant the early 1300s. Perhaps. An aside which Pycroft never sought to invoke was that some medievalists might point to a similar-sounding work of the Middle Ages – creak, which was sometimes used to describe the noise of the insect, the cricket. Sadly, Mr Pycroft's Victorian scholarship was sometimes less sure than his delightful eye-witness accounts of the nineteenth-century game, especially as played at Oxford.

Joseph Strutt, in his *Sports and Pastimes of the People of England*, has a drawing suggesting some form of bat and ball game being played in the Middle Ages. More interesting is a section of an illustrated manuscript, thought to originate from 1340. There are six characters – nuns and monks. To the right, four stand with hands shaped as if waiting to catch a ball. To the left, a nun holds a ball, while a tonsured monk has in his left hand a curved stick, about the size and shape of an eighteenth-century cricket bat. The manuscript is called 'Romance of Alexander'. The section with monkish bat and nunnish ball forms but part of the illumination.

It would be easy to pore over detail and amusing to enquire into meaning. Many cricket historians have done just that. But dull scholarship is full of expectations and hopes satisfied by the flimsiest of evidence and grasped supposition which, if stated firmly enough, will acquire an authority beyond belief. And because there are those who long for mysterious reason, romantic history and forebears of quite another age, there is a ready audience for that willed conclusion.

Would it not complete the glory given to this greatest game if it were found that in some thirteenth-century monastery, monk tossed ball to bucket or stump, while brother novice defended with bat and father confessor stood, soft of cheek and eye, at distant cloister to see fair play at cricks, or croaks, or creag? How noble would be cricket's pedigree. But there is no real evidence. What of the 'Romance of Alexander' and brothers and sisters waiting, hands outstretched, to catch that chance mis-hit? Might they not have been in prayer? We don't really know. And does it really matter?

Yet some seek still through record and dialect for grander ancestry. Could there be faded testimony in a Sussex vestry, spared by mice and indolence? Might brown copperplate of long-forgotten clerk one day delight *Wisden*'s browser so that an even more honourable lineage could be established? Might those with a curiosity for the fifteenth century show handyn and handoute to be the true parent of the modern game, or cite Edward IV as seen in some obscure chapel painting, lean, batted and striking while varlet fetches and monarch stares, bandanas at waist and throat (red and gold, of course)? There is always an interpretation of history that will show heritage where none exists. Eric Parker in his *History of Cricket* has an apt summary of origins:

> Take the words crick, creek, cricket, crook, crooked, croquet. All of them carry with them the same essential, underlying meaning – something with a twist or curve in it, something out of the straight. A crick in the neck comes from a twist, something irregular. A creek is a winding inlet. A crook is a curved stick used by shepherds. Crocket is another form of the word crochet, which is the diminutive of the word *croc* (or *croche*), a crook – a game played with a crooked stick. And so we get two words allied in meaning, cricket, a diminutive of the work crick, and crooked. As to sound, cricket, crooked – is there much difference? Cricket is a game played with a crooked stick.
>
> When once you reach that simple conclusion, other questions vanish. They become side-issues. Club-ball remains club ball, just a game with a club and a ball. Cat and dog is – cat and dog. Whatever hand-in-and-hand-out may have been, there is nothing to show that it was a game with a stick or a ball.

The truth is that cricket's beginnings are obscure and those who would wish for fourteenth-century origins must wait. Disappointment should not dull pride of history, for most certainly records of cricket are to be found from the sixteenth century, fully two hundred years before those of Hambledon.

Chapter 2

By the mid-sixteenth century, at a time when Sebastian Cabot was created Grand Pilot of England and those English-speaking peoples were sailing to adventure, cricket was being played in villages and towns of the south, certainly by small boys. There's no evidence that it was organised as a team game, but it was accepted as a game. In Guildford at the Royal Grammar School is had been played for many a year, perhaps even in the early sixteenth century. In the Guildford Borough Records there is a document in the Court Book, dated 17 January 1598, that is treasured by cricket's chroniclers:

> Court Leet held there Monday next after the Feast of St Hilary the fortieth year of the reign of our Lady Elizabeth, Queen of England, France and Ireland, Defender of the Faith etc.
>
> Memo, that att this day came John Derrick of Guldeford aforesaid gent one of the Queenes Majestes Coroners of the County of Surrey beinge of the age of fyfty and nyne yeeres or thereabouts and vuluntarily sworne and examined saith upon his oath that he hath known the parcell of land lately used for a garden and sometymes in the occupacon of John Parrishe late of Guldeford aforesaid Inhoulder deceased lyinge in the parishe of the Holy Trinity Guldeford aforesaid betweene the garden sometymes Thomas Northall on the north parte and the high way leadinge through the North Towne ditch of the said Towne of Guldeford on the south parte for the space of fyfty yeeres and more. And did knowe the same lay waste and was used and occupied by the Inhabitantes of Guldeford

7

aforesaid to lay Timber in for sawpittess and for makinge of frames of Timber for the said Inhabitantes. And that ould Butler a carpenter deceased dwellinge in the Towne aforesaid did commonly use to make frames of Timber there. And also this deponent saith that hee being a scholler in the free Schoole of Guldeford hee and divers of his fellowes did runne and play there at Creckett and other Plaies. And also that the same was used for the Baytinge of Beares in the said Towne untill the said John Parrishe did inclose the said parcell of land.

So one John Derrick, perhaps a schoolboy in and around 1550, did runne and play at Guldeford at Creckett. Perhaps, but only perhaps, Creckett had been played for fifty years by then, maybe one hundred. Again we can guess, some may hope, but nothing more. However, if we accept that Creckett was a form of the game we play today, then this must be its earliest record. And by documents alone, admittedly fragile and vulnerable windows of our histories, for one hundred and fifty years or so cricket would appear to have been peculiar to England's southern peoples, especially those of Kent, Surrey, Hampshire and Sussex. Certainly it did not have the universal recognition of, say, stool-ball, by then a more established pastime. Again this is a guess, yet from an early seventeenth-century pamphlet, probably written by Samuel Rowlands in about 1610, we find laid the fun and games of a merry England:

> Man, I dare challenge thee to throw the sledge
> To jumpe or leape over ditch or hedge
> To wrestle, play at stooleball, or to runne,
> To pitch the cane, or shoot off a gunne.
> To play at loggets, nine holes, or ten pinnes
> To try it out at football by the shinnes.
> At tick-tacke, Irish noddie, man and ruffe,
> At hot cockles, leap frogge, or blindman buffe.
> To drink half pots, or deale at the whole can,
> To play at base, or pen and inkhorne, Sir Jhan.
> To daunce the morris, play at barley brake,
> At all exploytes a man can think or speake,
> At shove-groate, venter point, or cross and pile,
> At beshrow him that's last at yonder style,
> At leaping ore a midsummer bonfire,
> Or at the drawing Dan out of the myre.
> At any of those, or all those presently

8

Wagge but your finger, I am for you,
I scorne that any youngster of our toune
Should for the Bow-bell cockney put me downe.

There is some temptation to read Rowlands' doggerel and wonder how cricket was missed from more than a score of pastimes. Surely there was space and time for willow bat and ball by 'tick-tacke, Irish noddie, man and ruffe'? After all, the Guldeford Court Leet Book owned that cricket had been played in about 1550, a full sixty years before Samuel Rowlands' list of throwings, pitchings, leaping, runninge and hits. It could be that he never thought to include the game because it was unknown to him, although not to others. Rowlands wrote in London. Guildford, by today's notion of distance, is but a close-by commuter city. During the late sixteenth century and early seventeenth century, however, the goings-on in Guldeford, the villages of Surrey and the hamlets of Sussex, Hampshire and Kent may not have attracted the pen of Rowlands, nor his friends for whom a mighty fear was 'that any youngster of our toune/Should for the Bow-bell cockney put me downe'.

Equally sad for those who would find a place for this game of ours in the most distant and ancient ledgers is the lack of coherent mention in verse and prose. References to cricket, usually 'the cricket', and bowlers, usually those at nine-pins, are easily come by, yet there is no description of the game to which they refer. Unusual? Perhaps, considering the manliness and excitement found by other writers when cricket was well established in the eighteenth century. It might be argued that after James I had attempted to spin the people giddy with a cry to sport there was a reaction that cast damp and clammy clouds over the game. To some extent this is probably true, but not so much that writers who, after all, were quick to seize a fashion as if it were their very own notion – would have failed to tell and tell again of cricket's exploits. Burton's *Anatomy* of Melancholy, published in the early 1600s, speaks of 'keelpins, tronks, quoits, pitching of bars, hurling, wrestling, wasters, foils, football, balowne, quintance, and many such, which are the common recreations of the country folk'. Nothing of cricket.

Then, towards the end of the seventeenth century, cricket emerged from its age of mystery and faint reference. Its footprint in literature and record had up to this point, with one or two exceptions, been obscure and of doubtful origin. Only the hopes of later cricket historians drew conclusions from the yeti-like sightings floating through pamphlet, ledger and log. But by the 1680s the animal was in captivity. The nineteenth-century cricket historian Charles Box noted:

> Better evidence is afforded of the progress of the game in 1685, where, in a work entitled the 'Mysteries of Love and Eloquence', a bumpkin is made to address his betrothed in these words, 'Will you not, when you have me, throw stools at my head and cry, "Would my eyes have been beat out by a *cricket-ball* the day before I saw thee?" '

With the dawn of the eighteenth century, the reign of silence ended and 'the clouds that loured around the art', such as it was, vanished. Whether the oracle then proclaimed itself, and in what way, is still a mystery; but in a very limited space of time cricket, as a game, became the subject of correspondence, material for law-suits, and a theme for censors. It had spread into the centre of the kingdom. Among many cases which might be cited is that which records a match played at Birmingham during the battles with rebels at Preston.

In an age of poetry, it is somewhat remarkable that the imagination of the Muse was not stretched a little in portraying a subject both novel and inviting. Here a stanza, and there a line, are all the contributions as yet gathered up, none of which throws the least light upon the principles and practices of the game, at this time evidently put into rough shape. The humble classes were not the only sections of the community to mature it. Laws were framed and these, though comparatively crude, had in them the elements of order, which implied a design and intelligence not likely to be found among a class of persons devoid of education and social status.

Why this should have been is yet another subject for guesswork and surmise. During this period there were close communities where fashions and amusements travelled easily through the four southern counties, but not very much further. Similar games such as stool-ball seemingly never greatly attracted the villagers of the Midlands and northern counties; indeed, stool-ball remains very much a southern amusement. But eventually spread it did, especially with gambling and patronage, and probably because it assumed a certain fashion and therefore something approaching gentility. However, like so many pastimes of gentlemen in the seventeenth and eighteenth centuries, cricket existed alongside bear-baiting and other spectacles

10

of socially acceptable savagery. The seventeenth-century chronicler George Swinnocke, quoting the somewhat puritanical and sometimes forthright parson Thomas Wilson, records the game played in Kent's county town: 'Maidstone was formerly a very prophane town, insomuch that I have seen morris-dancing, cudgel-playing, stool-ball, crickets, and many other sports openly and publikly on the Lord's Day.'

Play on the Sabbath was indeed unacceptable to many of Wilson's orders, who were often openly opposed to the edicts of the *King's Book of Sports*, which was eventually burned by the public executioner. Gerald Brodribb notes in *The English Game* an extract from a broadsheet dated 1712, which suggests that even the Duke of Marlborough should not have played at cricket but should instead have been about his devotions:

As the Devil never is wanting in his own cause, so he had taken all imaginable care to second the Duke's inclinations; for, as the Devil wou'd have it, the Duke and Lord found several boys ready to their Hands playing at Cricket. Quoth the Lord, 'When I went to Eaton School I understood this game better than my book.' – 'And I' (says the Duke) 'lov'd it better than Moral Philosophy'. – 'I'll play with you for Twenty Guineas' (says the Lord). – 'A match,' cries the Duke; and so the Game begun.

The Nobles agreed to chuse the two best boys at Cricket for each a partner, and promis'd 'em Crowns a piece for their pains when the Match was Won or Lost, and Twelvepence to a third Boy to knotch the Game down exact.

The Boy that was Partner against the Duke whispers my Lord and tells him, 'Sir, I can play ten times better than t'other Boy, and if you'll make my Crown ten Shillings, I'll catch them both out in three or four stroaks.' The Lord readily agreed to't, and the Boy performed his promise, and won him Twenty Guineas, but not so easily as imagin'd, for the Duke gave 'em several Master stroaks before he was outed.

I had this information from the Mouth of Justice, and it's question'd whether or no these Sabbath-Breakers will long escape the Hands of Justice: for the Reformers of Manners, and many Conscientious Dissenters, are strangely alarmed at this Princely Way of Sabbath-Breaking.

And in Sussex itself there is record of disgraceful play on one Sunday in May in the year 1622. It appears among the Bills of Presentment of parishioners to the Right Reverend Bishop of Chichester:

11

I present Ralphe West, Edward Hartley, Richard Slaughter, William Martin, Richard Martin jun. together with others in their company whose names I have no notice of, for playing at cricket in the churchyard on Sunday the fifth of May, after sufficient warnings given to the contrary to the 7th Article, secondly that they used to breake the church windows with the ball and, thirdly, for that a little childe had like to have her braynes beaten out with a cricket bat.

And also I present Richard Martin sen. and Thomas West, the old churchwardens for defending and mayntayning them in it and Edward Hartley, for playing at cricket in evening prayer tyme on Sunday the XXVII of April.

Who was this little childe so nearly left without her braynes? We know not; though we do know that twenty-five years later one Henry Brand, hardly a little child, suffered a similar calamity which sadly had a more dramatic end. In 1647, at the West Sussex Quarter Sessions, record was made in the sitting at Arundel that Margaret Brand of Selsey had been told by her brother, Henry, that he had been coshed by 'Thomas Latter, of the sayd parish with a cricket batt'. Henry Brand died. The horrifying tale is to be found lodged in the archive of the West Sussex Record Office:

Sussex: The examinacyon of Margarete Brand of the parish of Rumbolsweeke taken on oath the 13 of December 1647 before William Cawley Esquire one of His Maiestyes Justice of Peace for the sayd County.

Whoe deposeth that her Brother henry brand of the parish of Selsey tolde her this Examinant aboubt a month before he dyed, that he had aboubt 6 weekes before that time received a wound in the head given him by one Thomas Latter of the sayd parish with a Cricket batt, and that her sayd Brother tolde her he would cause Thomas Latter aforesayd to be brought before Mister Cawley that soe he might give him some allowance towards the charge he was at while his wound was in cure, that he tolde this examinant farder that he felt noe payne in his head about a month before his death, but she deposeth that she being with him what time he dyed, observed both his head, and face to be much swollen, and that Thomas Laters [sic] Mother, and Goodwife Holoway, who dressed his wound, came to her this examinant aboubt 14 days after her brothers death, the mother earnestly desyring her with teare's, to take 26s in moneys in recompense of such charges as she and her brother had beene at, which summe of moneys this Deponent accepted, and farder sayth not.

The marke of Margaret Brand

12

Our records of early cricket are rich in amazing incident. In Sussex, though death by cricket batt was rare, the keenness was often more than the simple joy of tussle and skill, of idyllic scene set by breeched and buckled yeomen testing carved willow and sewn leather. The noble and manly game owed its early, and perhaps continuing, popularity to betting. For hundreds of years champions had been put up to win handsome purses, sometimes whole estates and even fairytale hands of princesses. Cricket was a chance for side bets and huge wagers.

One of the earliest recorded organised games was in East Sussex in 1677, probably at Upper Dicker where now close by stands the Plough Inn. The Earl and Countess of Essex were putting up at Herstmonceux, a less than exciting time which apparently tested greatly her ladyship's good nature. She was said to be 'tired of the prevailing amusements – hunting, hawking, ninepins, cricket'. The exchequer note records during that period: 'Pd. to my Lord when his lordship went to the creckitt match at ye Dicker £3.00.00.' The £3 would have been a reasonable wager in the second half of the seventeenth century, although not at all unusual. In 1700, the sheet the *Post Boy* carried the following notice:

> These are to inform Gentlemen, or others, who delight in Cricket playing, That a Match at Cricket, of 10 Gentlemen on each side, will be play'd on Clapham Common, near Fox-Hall, on Easter Monday next, for £10, a Head each Game (five being design'd) and £20 the Odd one.

The following May, in 1701, there was born at Goodwood, Charles Lennox, Earl of March, heir to the first Duke of Richmond. As a child, he came by cricket almost as he did hunting, for by that time it was an established sport in the county and among his friends. The first Duke is remembered as having supplied much brandy to his team to celebrate their win over an Arundel side in 1702. The second Duke's biographer, John Marshall (*The Duke Who Was Cricket*, 1961) des- cribed him as the father of cricket in Sussex. 'The team he built up became the strongest in the country; it was virtually Sussex and England too . . .' Others, notably the cricket historian Dr H. F. Squire, have suggested at least a joint pretender to the founder's chair. He was Sir William Gage, who was born in 1695 and lived across the county from the young Duke at Firle, still no more than a small village lying south and east from Lewes. As Mr Marshall records:

13

In 1725 the Duke challenged the knight to play a cricket match against him, undoubtedly for a substantial stake as was the usual custom. Sir William took up the challenge and replied to it in this fashion:

'From Sir William Gage
My Lord Duke,
   I received this moment your Grace's letter and am extremely happy your Grace intends us ye honour of making one a Tuesday, and will without fail bring a gentleman with me to play against you, One that has played very seldom for these several years.
   I am in great affliction from being shamefully beaten Yesterday, the first match I played this year. However I will muster up all my courage against Tuesday's engagement. I will trouble your Grace with nothing more than that I wish you Success in everything but ye Cricket Match and that I am etc. etc.

W. Gage

Firle July ye 16th 1725.'

So we do know that Sir William lost his first match of the season. Unfortunately we do not know how he fared against his principal rival, the Duke of Richmond, or even where the match was played. From the wording of the letter it would seem likely that Sir William journeyed across the county from Firle to Goodwood, which would have been the best part of a day's ride. Doubtless he was entertained by the Duke and Duchess and slept in Goodwood House both before and after the contest.

The Duke appears to have been one of the greatest patrons of cricket in the whole of the land and there is much to support Mr Marshall's notion that his team was the most powerful in existence. As he points out:

His enthusiasm for the game influenced his choice of servants for the estate. Where possible, good cricket players were hired and they were, in addition to serving in such capacities as gardeners and coachmen, the Duke's own professionals. They were almost certainly the first real professional cricketers and therefore the 'ancestors' of all professional cricketers today.

This patronage was to maintain the game at a fashionable level for many years and attracted the likes of the Duke of Dorset, Lord

14

Frederick Beauclerk, Lord Sandwich and the Prince of Wales who was to become George IV. The Duke of Richmond was also joint author of the first recorded *Laws of Cricket*, although they were really articles of play rather than laws for all time. These articles were drawn up with a gentleman of Surrey, a Mr A. Brodrick of Pepperharowe, in 1727:

Articles of Agreement by & between His Grace the Duke of Richmond and Mr Brodrick (for two Cricket Matches) concluded the Eleventh of July 1727.

Imprimis. 'Tis by the aforesaid Parties agreed that the first Match shall be played some day of this Instant July in the County of Surrey; the Place to be named by Mr Brodrick; the second Match to be played in August next in the County of Sussex, the Place to be named by the Duke of Richmond.

2nd. That the Wickets shall be pitched in a fair and even Place, at twenty three yeards distance from each other.

3rd. A ball caught, cloathed or not cloathed the Striker is out.

4th. When a Ball is caught out, the Stroke counts nothing.

5th. Catching out behind the Wicket is allowed.

6th. That 'tis lawful for the Duke of Richmond to choose any Gamesters, who have played in either of his Graces two last matches with Sir William Gage; and that 'tis lawful for Mr Brodrick to choose any Gamesters within three miles of Pepperharowe, provided they actually lived there last Lady Day.

7th. That twelve Gamesters shall play on each side.

8th. that the Duke of Richmond & Mr Brodrick shall determine the Ball or Balls to be played with.

9th. if any of the Gamesters shall be taken lame or sick after the Match is begun, their Places may be supplied by any One chose conformably to the Sixth Article, or in Case that can not be done, the other side shall be obliged to leave out one of their Gamesters, whomsoever they please.

10th. that each Match shall be for twelve Guineas of each Side; between the Duke and Mr Brodrick.

11th. that there shall be one Umpire of each Side; & that if any of the Gamesters shall speak or give their opinion, on any point of the Game, they are to be turned out & voided in the Match; this not to extend to the Duke of Richmond and Mr Brodrick.

12th. If any Doubt or Dispute arises on any of the aforemd. Articles, or whatever else is not settled therein, it shall be determined by the Duke of Richmond and Mr Brodrick on their Honours; by whom the Umpires are likewise to be determined on any Difference between Them.

13th. The Duke of Richmond's Umpire shall pitch the Wickets

when they play in Sussex; and Mr Brodrick's when they play in Surrey; & Each of Them shall be obliged to conform Himself strictly to the Agreements contained in the second Article.

14th. The Batt Men for every One they count are to touch the Umpires Stick.

15th. that it shall not be lawful to fling down the wickets, and that no Player shall be deemed out by any wicket put down, unless with the Ball in Hand.

16th. that both Matches shall be played upon, and determined by these Articles.

Richmond
A. Brodrick

Diaries and family records are about the only evidence to be found of the outcome of matches of this period. Indeed, there is little idea of the results of even the most grand games, including the early years of formal and regional challenges. This is partly because many documents have perished since the days of the second Duke of Richmond. Equally, it may be remembered that there was no scorebook or scorecard at these events. The scores were notched on strips of wood, which were described by Charles Box:

> . . . every time a run was effected the parties in charge of the piece of wood made a notch on the edge, and upon accomplishment of ten the notch was cut deeper to facilitate the reckoning of the total. Now, as this method lumped the runs, without specifying by whom they were obtained, recourse was in time had to putting down the names of the parties who headed the respective sides, and the remaining ten were presented by figures in the order of going in; thus 1 had his runs marked against it, say 20, and so to the last man.

At the end of the match, the notched sticks were given to each side. Consequently, few scores remain and often the only idea of the players' identities are the names of the 'owners', the captains of the opposing teams.

The first official result of a Sussex match that has survived dates to 1728. Although the side was called Sussex, it should not be thought of as an official county team as we know them today. Teams still owed their identity to patrons, even if they might carry with them descriptions as 'Eleven of Sussex'. The two young men who were the

16

strongest enthusiasts and patrons to the east and to the west of the county remained Sir William Gage of Firle and the Second Duke of Richmond.

In this match, it was the Duke's side and pride that were dented by the men from both banks of the Medway. It was one of three believed to have been played that year against Kent. On 24 June the Duke raised a Sussex side to play a team formed by Mr Edwin Stead from Maidstone. The game was played at Coxheath. If the scores exist, they remain hidden, although we do know that Kent won, as indeed they are thought to have won the next two matches. The second game was played a month later in the victorious county, at the family seats of the Earls of Leicester, Penshurst Park. On the third occasion that the two counties met, it was Sir William Gage's side which returned to Penshurst Park to do battle with Mr Stead's men. The change of Sussex leader did Kent little harm: they won by 7 runs.

The following year, Kent, often considered the most consistently strong side in the region, took on a side made up of Sussex, Hampshire and Surrey, although it seems as if the side was known simply as Sussex. From what little is known of the game, Kent went down, probably by an innings: 'Sussex got within three, in one hand as the former [Kent] did in two hands so the Kentish men threw it up . . .' One of the Duke of Richmond's grooms 'signalised himself by such extraordinary agility and dexterity to the surprise of all the spectators, which were some thousands, and 'tis reckoned he turned the scale of victory which for some years past has generally been on the Kentish side'.

It should be no surprise to learn that thousands gathered to watch the two teams. Cricket was by then a sport of great spectacle with kudos and purse equally tempting to those who played up and to those who watched the game. So keen was interest, and so influential its patrons, that on one occasion it cast its spell over the politics of the county.

The noble gentlemen of influence in Sussex politics were also keen cricketers. Again the Richmond name was in the thick of things, as was the Duke of Dorset, another patron of the game; and intrigue and manipulation came about during an important election. Sussex was a very political county, with twenty-eight Members of Parliament. In 1741 James Butler was one of two Members elected to Parliament, the other being Henry Pelham, the younger brother of the Duke of Newcastle. Unfortunately, Butler died eleven days after the May election. The politicking began, and the tale is taken up by Timothy J. McCann:

17

The dominant interest in the county was that of the Duke of Newcastle, who had managed the elections with a combination of personal and family connections, and the liberal use of money. . . . Newcastle suggested that Charles Sackville, Earl of Middlesex and son of the Duke of Dorset, should succeed Butler in the county seat. Dorset and Newcastle had long been political associates, and Dorset, who lived just outside the county in Kent, was Newcastle's political ally in the east of the county, as Richmond was in the west. However, Middlesex had certain defects as a candidate. He was indiscreet, and, more important, he did not live in the county.

It was a tradition that one county member should come from the east of the county, and one from the west. The Duke of Somerset, in particular, was incensed that Butler was not to be succeeded by a 'Western Gentleman', and gave his support to Thomas Sergison of Cuckfield who had emerged as the leader of the opposition to the Newcastle interest . . . The voting qualification for the county seat was the forty shilling freehold, and, since cricket was now enthusiastically followed by the 'better' class of people, Sergison was determined to make his first move at a cricket match in the western half of the county. There would be gathered the people of influence in the county, who would not otherwise meet in such numbers except at the Assizes or Quarter Sessions; or at Lewes Races, which were very much dominated by Newcastle. Newcastle's chief political ally in the western half of the county was the Duke of Richmond, and the Duke was the most enthusiastic cricketer of his day.

The Duke by this time was acting as sponsor to the team representing Slindon, and several members of the team found employment on the Duke's estate in Goodwood, and in his service in London . . . His correspondence includes a letter from Lord John Sackville dated 14th September, 1745, describing a cricket match in which the Duke's team evidently took part, and one from John Fuller of Uckfield, dated 18 August, 1746, which is important for being the first reference to 'capping', and which suggested the formation of clubs rather than just local teams.

On 14 June, 1741, the 2nd Duke of Richmond wrote to the Duke of Newcastle, 'Sergison was expected last night at Westdean, and 'tis believed he will go to a great cricket match in Standstead Parke tomorrow between Slyndon and Portsmouth.' Richmond was already alive to the importance of cricket matches in the electoral campaign, and had written to the Duke of Dorset on 10 June, 1741:

'My Steward is now going about the parishes, he has been at a Crickett match today where he found the greatest part almost all hearty for us, two or three of Sr John Peachys tenants were

18

there & one Parson Powel sayd they must go with Sr John, butt did not say that he had yett apply'd to them, however a malster that I employ one Caleb Chitty assures that Sr John has ask'd him in London for Sergison, but he told him he was engagaed to us . . . the discourse of the Crickett match today was that the Duke of Somersett would be neuter, with what foundation I can't tell.'

Three letters have survived which give an account of the electioneering at the cricket match at Standstead, the seat of James Lumley, the sitting member for Arundel. Richmond wrote to Dorset on 16 June, that Sergison:

'. . . has been at these three days at Sr John Peachys at Westdean, where he is very busy butt has mett with hardly any thing butt negatives except at Midhurst where to be sure he'l beat us five to one; butt there and Westdean are the only two places where he can do anything in this Rape . . . I was at a great Crickett match yesterday, where there were above 5000 people, Sergison just made his appearance; he was attended by Lisbon Peckham, & four or five of the Chichester Torys . . .'

Later the same evening, Richmond reported to Newcastle:

'Sergison was at the cricket match attended by Lisbon Peckham, old Eastgate the hatter, Ludgator and two or three more of the Chichester Torys. He did not venture to aske a vote, nor could he have got one I do really believe. Tanky was there ready to puff his cheeks at him, butt he never appeared before us, butt quietly stole away, as soon as we came. All our friends seemed mighty hearty, & were in great spirits especially as Slyndon beat Portsmouth, & had none men to go in.'

Richmond, having removed Sergison from the west, set about arranging the western tour of Lord Middlesex . . . The tour seemed to go well, and Richmond wrote letters to Newcastle confident of victory. He organised a public dinner at Goodwood for the freeholders in the area, but made the mistake of choosing a date in July which clashed with a cricket match. Two days after the match he told Newcastle: 'The reasons for the thinness of the meeting were, a great cricket match at Green, the sessions at Horsham, and the assizes at Winchester, all happening upon that day, which was very unlucky for me.'

Sergison made his next move when Slindon played another cricket match, this time at Portslade, and then a fracas punctured the hitherto quiet and inevitable campaign, Richmond described

19

the event to Newcastle: 'Have you heard that Sergison treated his people the night of the cricket match at Portslade & that there was a bloody battle between them and Slyndoners? butt the last came off victorious tho with some broken heads.'

The cause of the battle was a reference to the notorious night in 1735, when Middlesex and some friends gathered at the Golden Eagle in Suffolk Street in London, and, forgetting that it was the anniversary of the execution of King Charles I, lit a bonfire in the street, in their drunken stupor. The crowd who gathered with memories of republican meetings, rioted, and the incident was not forgotten. Sir William Gage gave more details of the battle at Portslade in his letter to Newcastle of 5 August. He wrote:

'. . . the county is at this time quieter and better humoured than for this seven years past. Tis true the night of the cricket match after yr Grace left the field, there was a bustle occassioned by the cry of Calves head being resented by some of yr Graces friends, and some hearty blows were given, and our friends had ye worse the battell att first. But the western Cricketers that had left the hearing of it returned with their Crickett Batts and dealt some heavy blows wch carried the victory on our side. I am glad the cricket match was over before this happened.'

Even Sergison's staunchest supporters such as the Peacheys at West Dean wondered why he persisted in his determination to continue the fight. It was clear that his support in the west was derisory, and Richmond was writing victorious letters to Newcastle promising the biggest vote yet for Newcastle's candidate. Richmond showed his confidence by watching cricket rather than attending a meeting with Newcastle. He wrote to the Duke: 'I can't be with you till late, because I shall see a crickett match I have made of poor little Slyndon, against almost your whole county of Surrey, it is to be play'd at the basin upon merroe down.' On the following day he wrote again: 'Wee have beat Surrey almost in one innings.'

Sergison made one final effort to attract the voters. He made a cricket match for forty guineas to be played in his own park at Cuckfield. The match was advertised in all the neighbouring parishes and attracted a large crowd, but once again Sergison surprised his guests. John Board of Paxhill, another of Newcastle's agents, described the match in a letter to his master.

'Sergison . . . at his own house, made a cricket match for 40 guineas, to be played for in his Park on monday last was sevennight, and by crying it all the neighbouring parishes, on the sunday next

20

before, having drawn a great concourse of people to his door, I look'd upon it as a strategem design'd to give him a fresh and better opportunity of applying to the people there the invitation to his own house had procured him; but that he might not have the whole field to himself, I took care to despatch several proper agents to the cricket match, with orders to be all times on the ground, to keep a strict watch on all the motions of the enemy, and to use their utmost art & diligence in the service of Lord Middlesex, whose interest your Grace has so much at heart. But I believe I wronged my neighbour by entertaining these injurious thoughts of him, for it was it seems so very careful of avoiding all imputations of being guilty of any indirect practices of carrying on his own interest, that he did not, as I can hear, sollicite or so much as to ask any of the gamsters who won his money for him (several of whom were from Lindfield) or of the company at the conclusion of the game, either to eat or drink with him, who all, judging as I did, his intention of calling them to him, in the manner aforesaid, to be for that very purpose, were, at that, and some other omissions he was then guilty of, I am inform'd, much disappointed & highly disobliged.'

The campaign gradually petered out, and on 23 December, Sergison wrote to Dorset and threw up the contest, much to Somerset's fury. Three weeks later Middlesex was returned unopposed for the county seat, and Newcastle gathered a large number of his political friends, such as Henry Pelham, Richmond, Dorset, Sir John Miller and others, to show the county the support Middlesex would have had, had it come to a contest. It has been suggested that the battle of Waterloo was won on the playing fields of Eton; it can certainly be argued now, that the county by-election of 1741 was won on the cricket fields of Sussex.

Many names that lolloped through the intrigue and connivings of 1741 appear in most of the early reports of cricket matches. Villages put up teams, although not with the exclusively local membership that might be imagined. A gentleman landowner became owner of the team and brought in friends to guarantee his cricketing reputation. The big matches, in terms of money changing hands and therefore of spectators, were to be found at the contests between the oldest cricketing rivals, Kent and Sussex. Sir John Sackville and the Earl of Middlesex played for a Kent side against Sussex in September 1734, which Kent won in spite of Sir William Gage leading the men of Sussex. By the time a return game had been fixed to be played at Lewes, Sussex had to forfeit the chance of satisfaction. This, remember, was the early eighteenth century; the fashionable had decamped to Bath. But revenge was at hand and, by scant account, sweet. The following 10 August, the two sides met once more. Again, Sir William Gage led the side at home near Lewes, and Middlesex and Sir John Sackville played for Kent. John Whaley, writing to Horace Walpole, noted:

> . . . have spent the whole day at a Cricket match at Lewes between the Gentlemen of Kent and Sussex, which was won by the latter, at which they seemed as much pleas'd as if they had got an Election. We have been at supper with them all, and have left them at this one O'clock in the morning, laying betts about the next match. Lord Midlesex and Sir William Gage are the rivals of the Bat.

The doings of the August weeks were recorded in the *London Evening Post* of the twenty-sixth of that month in 1735:

> Last week we play'd at Sevenoaks, in Kent, a great Cricket Match between the Earl of Middlesex, the Lord John Sackville, and nine other Gentlemen of the County of Kent, and Sir William Gage, and ten other Gentlemen of the County of Sussex, when the Kentish Gentlemen beat; but the week before, when they play'd on the Downs, near Lewes, the Sussex Gentlemen beat considerably, so that its thought the Conqueror will be play'd in a few days.

When so much was at stake, little wonder they were teasing, joshing and odds-laying to the early hours in Lewes. It had perhaps become a noble game, but once more there was the clear notion that the ethics of cricket in Sussex, and anywhere else, were in the early eighteenth century clearly tied to society's intrigue for gambling and wager-mongering. Cricket was simply something else to bet on. An editorial in the *Gentleman's Magazine* of 1743 commented that 'all diversion at exercise have certain bounds as to expense, and when they exceed this, it is an evil in itself and justly liable to censure'. The writer went on in the most scathing tones:

> . . . I have heard of cricket matches, which I own, however, to be so strange and incredible that if I had not received them from eye-witnesses I could never have yielded to them any belief. Is it not a very wild thing to be as serious making such a match as in the most material occurrences of life? Would it not be extremely odd to see lords and gentlemen, clergymen and lawyers, associating

themselves with butchers and cobblers in pursuit of their diversions? or can there be anything more absurd than making such matches for the sake of profit, which is to be shared mong so remote in their quality and circumstances? Cricket is certainly a very innocent and wholesome exercise, yet it may be abused if either great or little people make it their business. It is grossly abused when it is made the subject of public advertisements, to draw together great crowds of people who ought all of them to be somewhere else. Noblemen, gentlemen, and clergymen have certainly a right to divert themselves in what manner they think fit – nor do I dispute their priviliege of making butchers, cobblers, or tinkers, their companions, provided they are gratified to keep their company; but I very much doubted whether they have any right to invite thousands of people to be spectators of their agility at the expense of their duty and honesty. The time of people of fashion may be indeed of very little value, but in a trading country the time of the meanest man ought to be of some worth to himself and the community. The diversion of cricket may be proper in holyday-time and in the country; but upon days when men ought to be busy and in the neighbourhood of a great city, it is not only inproper but mischievous in a high degree. It draws numbers of people from their employments to the ruin of their families. It brings together crowds of apprentices and servants whose time is not their own. It propagates a spirit of idleness at a juncture when, with the utmost industry, our debts, taxes, and decay of trade will scarce allow us to get bread. It is a most notorious breach of the laws, as it gives the most open encouragement to gaming, the advertisements most impudently reciting that great sums are laid, so that some people are so little ashamed of breaking the laws that they had hand in making, that they give public notice of it.

A year later, in June 1744, cricket did indeed once again draw people by their thousands to witness innocent and wholesome exercise, and maybe more than a little scampering between those who would make and those who would wager hold. Sackville issued a challenge from his gentlemen of Kent to play against an England eleven. The game was set for the Artillery Grounds in London's Finsbury Square, 18 June. It was a fashionable affair with the young Frederick, Prince of Wales and his court in attendance. The Prince was a keen player as well as spectator. Sadly, he is thought to have died because of his enthusiasm for the game. A ball struck him on his chest; an abscess developed which later perforated, and that was the lot of George II's son. The importance of the game from Sussex's point of view was the fact that eight of the eleven were from the county, including the three Newland brothers in the England side. They came from the village of Slindon, whose patron was the cricketing and politicking Duke of Richmond.

Chapter 3

Slindon was the most famous of Sussex sides in the mid-seventeen hundreds. Its players were celebrated, as by and by were those of Hambledon. On 2 June 1744, a team which appears to have been Slindon played a side which appears to have been London. Vagueness and expectation are bad bedfellows; only hearsay embroidered by reasonable assumption can build a picture of the match's origin. The game was played in London, and the Sussex side certainly included Slindoners, but there is no written record of the nature of the challenge. This may appear relatively unimportant except for two points: sketch evidence is one of history's traps which are set for would-be theorists; and, sadly, it would have been very agreeable if more precise record were at hand, because this game left one important relic – the earliest complete cricket scorecard so far discovered, now cherished in the archives of the cricketing Dukes of Richmond at Goodwood.

Play'd ye 2nd June 1744
London

	1st hands	2nd hands		1st hands	2nd hands
Cuddy	5	0	Howlet	1	5
Bryan	5	10	Dingate	0	19
R. Newland	0	0	Sawyer	4	4
A. Newland	0	22	Maynard	8	6
Ridgeway	6	not in	Bennet	11	7

25

Josh Harris	13	14	Fawkener	1	0
Jackson	19	1	Weymark	13	16
Jno Harris	18	47	Butler	18	0
Norris	13	not in	Green	11	12
Andrews	7	4	Hoder	6	0
Smith	8	not in	Collins	2	1
Saved by	8	4	They run'd	4	–
Bye-Balls			Bye-Balls		
	102	102		79	70
	102			70	
	204			149	
	149	the other side			
	55	notches beat by and three men to go in			

In spite of this woeful performance, no score in either innings, Richard Newland was the most formidable cricketer of his day. A fortnight later, with his two brothers Adam and John in the side, Newland captained the Slindon side against an eleven from Kent. No ordinary match this. Slindon was truly an All-England side, and the men of Kent the most powerful team of batters and bowlers under Lord John Sackville. And they triumphed, though not easily, before a right royal and gallant crowd which included the Prince of Wales, his brother the Duke of Cumberland, Admiral Vernon and, of course, the Duke of Richmond. The deeds were set down in verse by a man called Dance, a former Oxford scholar, who wrote under the name James Love and must have been about twenty-two when the match was played out. Years later, Love, who lived in Surrey, sent his epic (for it was hundreds of lines long) to the Richmond Cricket Club of Surrey with the following remarks:

> The following little poem, which near thirty years ago, was the effusion of a youthful mind, is reprinted for your amusement. The greatest circumstance in its favur is that it is founded upon fact, and may serve to entertain the true lovers of cricket by a recollection of many particulars at the time when the game was cultivated with the utmost assiduity, and patronised by the personal appearances and management of some of the most capital people in the kingdom. If the admirers of a manly British exercise should, in a vacant hour, receive the least entertainment from the production, it will amply satisfy the author's untmost ambition, who, as an inhabitant of Richmond, would ever be happy to contribute his mite to the

26

pleasure of his friends and neighbours, and as their most obedient and humble servant,

James Love

It began with a great herald of the game above all games, or so Love supposed:

Hail!
While others, soaring on a loft wing,
Of dire Bellona's cruel triumph sing,
Sound the shrill clarion, mount the rapid car,
And rush delighted through the ranks of war,
My tender muse in humbler, milder strains,
Presents a bloodless conquest on the plains,
Where vigorous youth in life's fresh bloom resort
For pleasing exercise and healthy sport;
Where emulation fires, where glory draws,
And active sportsmen struggle for applause,
Expert to bowl, to run, to stop, to throw
Each nerve collected at each mighty blow.

Hail cricket! glorious, manly, British game!
First of all Sports! be first alike in fame!
To my fir'd Soul thy busy transports bring,
That I may feel thy raptures, while I sing!
And thou, kind Patron, of the mirthful play,
Sandwich, the Country's friend, accept the Lay!
Tho' mean my Verse, my Subject yet approve
And look propitious on the Game you love!

When the returning sun begins to smile,
And sheds its glories round the sea-girt isle
When new-born nature, deck'd in vivid green,
Chases dull winter from the charming scene
High painting with delight he jovial swain
Trips it exulting o'er the flower-strewn plain;
Thy pleasures, Cricket, all his heart control,
Thy eager transports dwell upon his soul;
He weighs the well-turned Bat's experienced force,
And guides the Ball's impetuous, rapid course;
His supple limb, with nimble labour plies,
Nor bends the grass beneath him as he flies;
The joyous conquests of the late flown year
In fancy's paint, with all their charms appear,
And now again he views the long wished season near.

O thou, sublime Inspirer of my Song!

27

What matchless Trophies to thy Worth belong!
Look round the Globe, inclined to Mirth, and see
What daring Sport can claim the Prize from thee!

Obviously, not everyone was smitten by the manly and British game. Yet, as the anonymous writer in the *Gentleman's Magazine* tells us, in the 1740s 'thousands of people' were only too willing to be drawn to witness the agility practised as men of varied breeding brought bat and ball. But the serene landscape could not hide the sometimes radical social and political change in the artist's and lyricist's green and pleasant land; with it faded the round of many simple games and amusements. By the middle of the seventeenth century there was hardly a coin in the land that had not at some time ridden on the outcome of stance and contest.

Cricket, too, survived the sporting revolution; Richmonds, Dorsets *et al.* ensured its reputation. Cudgelling and skimming artisans were hired for their skills to guarantee noble victory and clinking purse (and what is more noble than clinking purse?), thereby amusing its wider audience and, attracting ne'er-do-wells, gamblers, tricksters and shallow fellows, arousing fear for the morals of sons fallen among the growing brotherhood of cricketers. Yet, even as late as the 1750s, still the northern counties had little time for its attractions.

> The athletic division of cricket is still kept up in the southern and western parts of England, and is sometimes practised by people of the highest rank. It is performed by a person who, with a clumsy wooden bat, defends a wicket raised by two slender sticks with one across, which is attacked by another person, who endeavours to beat it down with a hard leather ball from a certain stand. The farther the distance is to which the ball is driven, the oftener the defender is able to run between the wicket and the stand. This is called gaining so many notches, and he who gets the most is the victor.

On many occasions, the victory was guided to its patron's purse by the notches of Richard Newland. If the Duke of Richmond was the father of Sussex cricket, Newland was the elder statesman. He batted, so it is said, left-handed and with enormous power. As Love described the team against Kent, Newland appeared omnipotent:

> On the adverse party, towering o'er the rest,
> Left-handed Newland fires each arduous breast;

From many a bounteous crop the foodful grain,
With swelling stores rewards his useful pain,
While the glad Farmer, with delighted eyes,
Smiles to behold his close-crammed granaries rise.

Many years later, when John Nyren wrote his famous *Cricketers of My Time*, he recorded the origins of his most worthy father, Richard Nyren, one of the founders of the Hambledon Club in the late eighteenth century. Although Hambledon is in Hampshire, Richard Nyren spent his youth in Slindon and was there wed to Frances Pennicud, remembered as a young lady of Quaker origin who 'went out only to church and on errands of mercy', and who was more than ninety years when she died and who, it was said, 'blushed like a young girl up to that time'. Nyren was somewhat less retiring than his bride and became one of cricket's most awesome practitioners, under his venerable tutor Richard Newland, of whom John Nyren wrote:

Although a very stout man (standing about five feet nine) he was uncommingly active. He owed all the skill and judgement he possessed to an old uncle, Richard Newland, of Slindon, in Sussex, under whom he was brought up – a man so famous in his time, that when a song was written in honour of the Sussex Cricketers, Richard Newland was especially and honourably signalised. No one man ever dared to play him. When Richard Nyren left Hambledon, the club broke up, and never resumed from that day.

It is said also that, when Newland left the village to live in Chichester, Slindon, too, fell silent as the clarion of Sussex and English cricket, and settled as comfortable memory by autumn's grate.

Not that cricket itself fell into fashionable slumber. In fact, it was so acceptable a pastime among all but the easily scandalised that eventually young ladies took the notion that, as earnest as the game was, there was no sound reason for them to be excluded from this sport of princes, dukes, gentlemen and waggoners. The *Lewes Journal* of 13 July 1747 gave notice:

On Monday next there will certainly be played in the Artillery Ground, London, the match at cricket that has been so long talked of between the women of Charlton & Singleton, in Sussex, against the women of West Dean and Chalgrove in the same county.

29

It appears from this that the ladies of Sussex had 'for some time' talked not only of playing cricket, but of having their own sides. It is possible – even likely – that gentlemen, considerate of course for the safety of their ladies, would never have entertained them as members of a male team. Nothing for it but to gather stumps and bails, bats and balls and skirts, and set wickets at the most fashionable ground in England, the Artillery in the centre of London, where more than two hundred years later gentlemen, especially those of the City, still weekend at honourable soldiering complete with pikes, and where cricket is still played.

The ladies' efforts were not without cost, both financial and to their very safety. The hiring of the ground is said to have been a full eighty pounds, and the ladies of Sussex asked sixpence of each of those who came to watch. Forty sixpences to the pound called for many spectators, yet it seems there may have been fully sufficient to cover eighty pounds and more. A correspondent to the *General Advertiser* reported that: 'There were present the greatest number of spectators of both sexes ever seen at any public diversion.' Quite possibly some went as friends, others from curiosity. But the social history of the times suggests that many went for utter spectacle, an eighteenth-century version of women mud wrestling, and to bet large sums on who might fall and who might win.

Indeed, the outcome had little to do with skills at underarm skimmers or flexed wrists, full drives or cupped hands and taken chances.The only laws to decide the game were those that rule the odds, the abode of all the demons, and pandemonium was let loose: the betting went wrong. Whether there was an umpiring decision that caught all but the bet-makers' imagination is uncertain. Perhaps the game was simply going against all the odds, and suspicion, greed and anger stepped in to put matters right, or at least to express frustration. Whatever the reason, the easy-going course of wager-mongering was that day interrupted. The crowds at the 'public diversion' tumbled on to the pitch. It is imagined there were scuffles; certainly it is reported that some of the ladies from Sussex were injured and not a little put out by such goings-on at this manly and British sport. Match Abandoned.

The general guidelines and understandings of the way in which cricket might be played had been reasonable for many a long year. The articles set down by duke and commoner had never been doubted, and inherited learning went from game to game. But cricket was on the move and interpretation was its baggage, sometimes loading it down with objection and argument as some thought the game should be played one way while others thought another. Cricket had become

30

serious, and sometimes presented anxious moments for its growing brotherhood. If the scale of seriousness might be judged on the basis of formality, then the establishment of cricket as what R. C. Robertson-Glasgow thought to be a sometimes solemn and calculating old bloke, no longer a simple pastime, may be dated to the year 1774. A group of ennobled and gentle men, a parson in their number, gathered in Pall Mall at the Star and Garter, and with firm mind wrote not rules, but the first universally accepted *Laws of Cricket*.

Ye Laws at 1774

The pitching ye first Wicket is to be determined by ye cast of a piece of money. When ye first Wicket is pitched and ye popping Crease Cut which must be exactly 3 Foot 10 Inches from ye Wicket ye Other Wicket is to be pitched directly opposite at 22 yards distance and ye other popping crease cut 3 Foot 10 Inches before it. The Bowling Creases must be cut in a direct line from each stump. The Stumps must be 22 Inches long and ye Bail 6 Inches. The Ball must weight between 5 and 6 Ounces. When ye Wickets are both pitched and all ye Creases Cut The party that wins the toss up may order which side shall go in first at his Option.

Laws For Ye Bowlers 4 Balls And Over

The Bowler must deliver ye Ball with one foot behind ye Crease even with ye Wicket and When he has Bowled one Ball or more shall Bowl to ye number 4 before he Changes Wickets and he Shall Change but once in ye Same Innings. He may order ye Player that is in his wicket to Stand on which side of it he Pleases at a reasonable distance. If he delivers ye Ball with his hinder foot over ye Bowling crease the Umpire Shall Call no Ball though she be struck or ye Player is Bowled out Which he shall do without being asked and no Person shall have any right to ask him.

Laws For Ye Strikers, Or Those That Are In

If ye Wicket is Bowled down its out. If he Strikes or treads down or falls himself upon ye wicket in Striking (but not in over running) its out. A Stroke or Nip over or under his Batt or upon his hands (but not his arms) if ye Ball be held before She touches ye Ground though She be hugged to the Body its out. If in Striking both his feet are over ye Popping Crease and his Wicket put down except his Batt is down within its out. If he runs out of his Ground to hinder a Catch its out. If a Ball is nipped up and he Strikes her again Wilfully before she comes to ye Wicket its out. If ye Players have crossed each other he that runs for the Wicket that is put down is out. If they are not Crossed he that returns is out. If in running a Notch ye Wicket is struck down by a throw before

31

his Foot Hand or Batt is over ye Popping Crease or a Stump be hit by ye Ball though ye Bail was down its out. But if ye Bail is down before he that catches ye Ball must strike a Stump out of ye Ground Ball in Hand then its out. If the Striker touches or takes up ye Ball before she is lain quite still unless asked by ye Bowler or Wicket-keeper its out.

Batt Foot Or Hand Over Ye Crease

When ye Ball has been in Hand by one of ye Keepers or Stopers and ye Player has been at home He may go where he pleases till ye next Ball is bowled. If Either of ye Strikers is crossed in his running Ground designedly which design must be determined by the Umpires   NB The Umpires may order that notch be Scored When ye Ball is hit up   either of the Strikers may hinder ye catch in his running Ground or if She is hit directly across ye Wickets ye Other Player may Place his Body any where within ye Swing of his Batt so as to hinder ye Bowler from catching her but he must neither Strike at her nor touch her with his hands. If a Striker nips a Ball up just before him he may fall before his Wicket or pop down his Batt before She comes to it to Save it. The Bail hanging on one Stump though ye Ball hit ye Wicket is not out.

Laws For Wicket Keepers

The Wicket Keepers shall stand at a reasonable distance behind ye Wicket and shall not move till ye Ball is out of ye Bowler's Hands and shall not by any noise incommode ye Striker and if hands knees or foot or head be over or before his Wicket though the Ball hit it it shall not be out.

Laws For Ye Umpires

To allow 2 minutes for each man to come in when one is out and 10 Minutes between Each Hand to mark ye Ball that it may not be changed. They are sole judges of all outs and ins of all fair and unfair Play of frivolous delays of all hurts whether real or pretended and are discretionally to allow what time they think Proper before ye Game goes on again. In case of real hurt to a Striker they are to allow another to come in and the Person hurt to come in again But are not to allow a fresh Man to Play on either side on any Account They are sole judges of all hindrances crossing ye Players in running and Standing unfair to Strike and in case of hindrance may order a Notch to be Scored. They are not to order any man out unless appealed to by one of ye players. These Laws are to ye Umpires Jointly. Each Umpire is ye Sole Judge of all Nips and Catches Ins and Outs good or bad runs at his own Wicket and his determination shall be absolute and he shall not be changed for another Umpire without ye Consent of both Sides. When ye 4 Balls are Bowled he is to call over. These

Laws are separately. When both Umpires shall call Play 3 Times 'tis at ye Peril of giving ye Game from them that refuse to Play.

Thanks to the likes of the Duke of Richmond, Richard Newland, Sir William Gage in Sussex and similar fanciers of the game in neighbouring counties, the game was established not by general proxy, but by firm agreement of the *Laws*. Hambledon was born a strong and healthy infant. The Earl of Winchilsea and Charles Lennox, the future 4th Duke of Richmond, were offering financial guarantees to Thomas Lord if he would set down a new and private cricket ground, the first of three. Cricket was to have a world headquarters, for it had come of age – a sturdy watchman of code and character, of cant and nonsense, of manners and empire.

Chapter 4

In the early 1770s Hambledon became a club to be reckoned with; Richard Nyren, brought up and tutored by his Slindon uncle, its backbone. The chronicler John Nyren remembered that he was left-handed and, along with Thomas Brett, the most capital bowler in England. 'He had a high delivery, always to the length, and his balls were provokingly deceitful.' In or around 1778, another man of Sussex joined the band of Hambledon brothers. He was Noah Mann, a batsman of great renown and a fielder of fine speed and agility.

Mann was born near Petworth at North Chapel on 15 November 1756. As a lad he learned the trade of shoe and boot maker and later kept an alehouse in North Chapel, in which he met a grizzly and very early end. He was a short, stocky and swarthy individual, 'swarthy as a gipsy' said one. He did not move to Hambledon, but remained most days at his taps. So every Tuesday he rode the forty miles to Hambledon and back for practice. A very remarkable character during an era of the game full of characters, and perhaps one of the first swing bowlers. For some idea of Noah Mann of Sussex among those mighty men of Hambledon we had best turn to John Nyren, for then we have a sketch of a fine cricketer of his day, and of the game itself as played in the 1770s, the years that set the way for the formation of the first county side, sixty years on. Of Noah Mann, Nyren wrote:

> He was a fellow of extraordinary activity, and could perform clever feats of agility on horseback. For instance, when he has

35

been seen in the distance coming up the ground, one or more of his companions would throw down handkerchiefs, and these he would collect, stooping from his horse while it was going at full speed. He was a fine batter, a fine field, and the swiftest runner I ever remember: indeed, such was his fame for speed, that whenever there was a match going forward, we were sure to hear of one being made for Mann to run against some noted competitor; and such would come from the whole country around. Upon these occasions he used to tell his friends, 'If, when we are half-way, you see me alongside of my man, you may always bet your money upon me, for I am sure to win.' And I never saw him beaten. He was a most valuable fellow in the field; for besides being very sure of the ball, his activity was so extraordinary that he would dart all over the ground like lightning. In those days of fast bowling they would put a man behind the long-stop, that he might cover both long-stop and slip: the man always selected for this post was Noah. Now and then little George Lear (. . . so fine a long-stop) would give Noah the wink to be on his guard, who would gather close behind him: then George would make a slip on purpose, and let the ball go by, when, in an instant, Noah would have it up, and into the wicket-keeper's hands, and the man was put out. This I have seen done many times, and this nothing but the most accomplished skill in fielding could have achieved.

Mann would, upon occasion, be employed as a change-bowler, and in this department he was very extraordinary. He was left-handed, both as bowler and batter. In the former quality his merit consisted in giving a curve to the ball the whole way. In itself it was not the first-rate style of bowling, but so very deceptive that the chief end was frequently attained. They who remember the dexterous manner with which the Indian jugglers communicated the curve to the balls they spun round their heads, by a twist of the wrist or hand, will at once comprehend Noah's curious feat in bowling. Sometimes when a batter had got into his hitting, and was scoring more runs than pleased our general, he would put Mann in to give him eight or twelve balls, and he almost always did so with good effect.

Noah was a good batsman, and a most severe hitter; by the way I have observed this to be a common quality in left-handed men. The writer of this was in with him at a match on Windmill-down, when, by one stroke from a toss that he hit behind him, we got ten runs.

At a match of the Hambledon Club against All England, the club had to get in to get the runs, and there was a long number of them. It became quite apparent that the game would be closely fought. Mann kept on worrying old Nyren to let him go in, and although he became quite indignant at his constant refusal, our general knew what he was about in keeping him back. At length, when the last but one was out, he sent Mann in, and there were then ten runs to get. The sensation now all over the ground was greater than anything of the kind I witnessed before or since. All knew the state of the game, and many thousands were hanging upon this narrow point. There was Sir Horace Mann [of Kent, and no relation], walking about, outside the ground, cutting down the daisies with his stick – a habit with him when he was agitated; the old farmers leaning forward upon their tall old staves, and the whole multitude perfectly still. After Noah had had one or two balls, Lumpy [this would have been Lumpy Stevens with Harris, one of the supreme bowlers of the day] tossed one a little too far, when our fellow got in, and hit it out in his grand style. Six of the ten were gained. Never shall I forget the roar that followed this hit. Then there was a dead stand for some time, and no runs were made; ultimately, however, he gained them all, and won the game. After he was out, he upbraided Nyren for not putting him in earlier. 'If you had let me go in an hour ago,' said he, 'I would have served them in the same way.' But the old tactician was right, for he knew Noah to be a man of such nerve and self-possession, that the thought of so much depending upon him would not have the paralysing effect that it would upon many others.

Poor Noah! his death was a very deplorable one. Having been out shooting all day with some friends, they finished their evening with a free carouse, and he could not be persuaded to go to bed, but persisted in sleeping all night in his chair in the chimney-corner. It was, and still is, the custom in that part of the country, to heap together the ashes on the hearth, for the purpose of keeping the fire in till next day. During the night my poor playmate fell upon the embers, and being unable to help himself, burned his side so severely that he did not survive twenty-four hours.

Throughout Sussex, cricket thrived. Where great men had called bailiff to bowl and waggoner to long-stop, villages now put up their own to play for reputation, good crack and beer, and not a little silver. From Lewes to Mayfield, Brightling to Hastings, Chailey to Warbleton, Newick and Hamsey, Rottingdean and old Brighton, Brighthelmstone, cricket settled itself in roughly cut meadow and shaved park as villagers and townspeople played and watched a perfect afternoon slip by.

This is to Aquaint the Public
That on Wednesday, July 28, 1758, will be
play'd at Rottingdean, near Lewes,
A GREAT MATCH AT CRICKET

For a Guinea a Man
NEWICK, CHAILEY, LINDFIELD and HAMSEY
against
LEWES, BRIGHTHELMSTONE and
ROTTINGDEAN
The Wickets to be Pitch'd at Twelve o'clock
and the Game to be Play'd out

The Gamesters to be chosen out of the
undermentioned:–
Newick: James Burt, Henry Kennard
Chailey: Thomas Hoather, John Turle
Lindfield: Richard Harland, Francis Blaker,
    Edward Fain, John Tabb, George Haynes
    Thomas Blaker, Thomas Finch
Hamsey: William Howell, Henry Smith
Lewes: Nicholas Groves, Richard Winter
    John Postle, Thomas Godsmith, Stephen
    Eager
Brighthelmstone: George Barnham, John Howell
    Thomas Baker
Rottingdean: John Newington, Stenning Beard, Thomas
    Clare, Phillip Emery

As is so often the case with that time, there is no record of the result. The interest, of course, is that established villages (and Brighthelmstone, not yet Brighton, a fishing village of perhaps fifteen hundred souls and yet to become a spa town sipping chalybeate water and catering to royalty's whims) were coming together to play each other and combining to bring more competition to the game. While a duke's side might be called 'men of Sussex', the instinct towards a larger and more powerful team came also from the villages, especially because the size of wagers and odds was growing and more, literally, was at stake; in short, the origins of the county side.

In 1759, Brighthelmstone and Rottingdean took on Battle and Eastbourne, and for good reason: 'A great many bets are depending' declared the notice of play. Much was placed and much was drunk at

38

these outings where edge and carnival paraded easily side by side. In 1763, or perhaps 1764, a festival at East Hoathly included a single-wicket cricket match played for half a crown's worth of fine punch. One of the gamesters, a Mr Turner, is recorded as saying, 'We won very easy, but it was very hot, and we drinking a pretty deal of punch, it got into my head, so that I came home not sober.' Not that a dull head clouded Mr Turner's enthusiasm. In a letter his wife, Mrs Mary Turner, wrote:

> Last Munday your Father was at Mr. Payn's and plaid at Cricket and came home please enuf for he struck the best ball in the game and whished he had not anny thing else to do, he would play at Cricket all his Life.

The 1760s were indeed lively times in the county. In 1766 there took place the first recorded match between Sussex and Hampshire sides, although the county titles are misleading. The teams tended to be those of some great patron together with 'given men', that is, imported players who may be seen as the professionals of their time. And in 1768 the first noted game between a Sussex eleven and the Hambledon Club was played. The men of Sussex were really the Duke of Richmond's, but the game is worthy of note because it suggested that the Duke's reputation and players were sufficiently sound to challenge Hambledon, by that time the finest side in the country. Hambledon – lauded by men of letters, not the first but surely the most famous of the clubs that played during those closing afternoons of the eighteenth century. And what names! They were now long dead, as Andrew Lang remembered, but what names!

Ballade of Dead Cricketers

Ah, where be Beldham now, and Brett,
Barker, and Hogsflesh, where be they?
Brett, of all bowlers fleetest yet
That drove the balls in disarray?
And Small that would, like Orpheus, play
Till wild bulls follow his minstrelsy?
Booker, and Quiddington, and May?
Beneath the daisies, there they lie!

And where is Lambert, that would get
The stumps with balls that broke astray?
And Mann, whose balls would ricochet
In almost an unholy way

(So do baseballers 'pitch' today);
George Lear, that seldom let a bye,
And Richard Nyren, grave and gray?
Beneath the daisies, there they lie!

Tom Sueter, too, the ladies' pet,
Brown that would bravest hearts affray;
Walker, invincible when set,
(Tom, of the spider limbs and splay);
Think ye that we could match them, pray,
These heroes of Broad-halfpenny,
With Buck to hit, and Small to stay?
Beneath the daisies, there they lie!

An indulgence for our wander through Sussex history, yet it was among these long-lived heroes that the game would unfurl like some great standard. And what a right royal banner it was that reminded how patrons cared and tended the game, and how a century later a prince from another land, not yet empire, would be sung in fine praise. At about the time of the fledgling Hambledon Club, an unblest prince of the sport was born in Sussex. He was John Hammond of Storrington, the village in which he died seventy-five years later. Alfred J. Gaston, 'Leather Hunter' in so many Sussex cricketing chronicles, recalled him as:

. . . one of the greatest and most successful players that has ever appeared, as he was eminent for his skill in batting, bowling, and wicket-keeping. Born at Pulborough, in 1769, he went into Kent at the age of 18 or 19, and lived near Dartford till about 1799, when he went to live at Storrington, where he resided till his death in 1844. He was one of the hardest hitters of his day, and, as he had an awkward habit of running out to the slow bowlers, and driving them forward, he was considered rather an unpleasant opponent when at the wicket (this practice was introduced by him), and he once drove back a ball to Lord Beauclerk, who was bowling to him, with such tremendous force that he nearly killed him. The ball hummed close to his head and frightened him almost out of his senses, so much so, indeed, that he could scarcely go on bowling. Hammond was a thoroughly independent John Bull, and yet extremely courteous and pleasant in manner, and an excellent general, so that he was very much liked by the gentlemen with whom he played, and his services were in constant requisition. The first match of any importance in which his name is found was played at Lord's in June 1790. The following year at

40

Brighton, in September, 1791, between Brighton and Middlesex, Hammond got 13 wickets, besides contributing 50 runs to the score in one innings. From the Brighton list we learn the names of the players of that day. It comprises Borrer and Marchant, both of Hurst, and mighty batsmen in their time; Streeter, an excellent bowler, known by the name of 'The Honest Miller'; Jutten, a well-known, fast, daisy-cutting bowler, who had a special knack of hitting his adversaries on the shins when they stopped in too long to please him; the Vallances, even then a great Brighton family; and Gregory, a capital long-stop, and a fair bat. Brighton however, was defeated by 21 runs. Next year the match was played again at Lord's, when Brighton won by nine wickets, Hammond getting 34 runs and nine wickets.

And so by the 1790s Brighton appeared a greensward court in which the skilful and fashionable players danced minuet and gavotte to an increasingly elegant and gartered game. For by this time royalty had shown itself well pleased to play at cricket.

Chapter 5

Brighthelmstone in the middle of the eighteenth century was scarcely more than a village. It was a coastal community with little romantic legend along a shore that was flat-faced, uninteresting and passed by. Any beauty lay in the folds and slopes of the Downs rather than in the clawing Channel, indifferent to the fortunes of those fishing hard livings from the offshores of what was to become Brighton. It comprised some four hundred families, perhaps two thousand souls, in 1761. But slowly the bracing air and suggestion of health-giving mineral water attracted fashion and favour. Pace of the town's growth may be judged by the appointment in 1773 of sixty-four commissioners, whose purpose was:

> . . . for lighting and cleansing the streets, lanes and other places within the town of Brighthelmstone, as also for removing and preventing nuisances, holding and regulating a daily market there, and building and repairing groins, in order to render the coast more safe and commodious for vessels to unload and land sea-coal, culm and other coal for the use of the town; and in order to enable the said Commissioners to accomplish these public and serviceable ends, they were allowed by the Act a duty of Sixpence on every chaldron of coals or culm landed.

To this growing and pleasant seaside village came nobility. The Duke and Duchess of Marlborough set up home for salt-sprayed summers, and the Duke of Cumberland took up almost permanent residence in the south-coast town. Indeed, it was Cumberland who suggested that his high-born nephew take the pleasant airs, fifty miles to the south of London. As the official history of Sussex noted:

> In the year 1782 his late Majesty George IV, then Prince of Wales, and 21 years of age, paid a visit to his illustrious uncle, the Duke of Cumberland. The visit was repeated in the following year, when so much attached became the young prince to the rising town, to its thymy downs and clean sea, that he signified his intention of making it the place of his summer residence. The determination of His Royal Highness decided the fate of Brighton. It was no longer to be a second or third rate watering place; but with the stimulus of princely patronage, was rapidly to rise from its condition of mediocrity, and in a few years to become the first and most splendid marine abode in Europe.

The next year, 1784, work started on the most ornate pavilion in all England alas – without dank locker for winter's stumps, bails and beaten ball. However, the prince brought with him an enthusiasm for the game that was far more than fashionable and elegant bystanding. The future king was a well-known player in the eighteenth century. He was closely associated with the Je ne sais quoi Club in London. Its members, not necessarily cricketers, attended for their different amusements, and in 1782 a few of them gathered to form the White Conduit Cricket Club. As A. D. Taylor, in his *Annals of Lord's and History of the MCC*, described it, 'the acorn that blossomed into the gigantic oak known as the Marylebone Club', so it was. Its members, among whom numbered Charles Lennox, by all accounts a fine bat and wicket-keeper and soon to be the 4th Duke of Richmond, played many games in London and emerged towards the end of 1787 as the Marylebone Cricket Club.

As mentioned earlier, Lennox along with the 9th Earl of Winchilsea, who played for Brighton, underwrote Thomas Lord to set up a private ground. Lord, a keen cricketer and a native of Yorkshire, was the lessee of the Allsop Arms, and the first Lord's Cricket Ground was on land next to the inn. A plan of London, published ten years later, described the playing field as the 'Prince of Wales's Cricket Ground'. What a fine sporting pedigree travelled to Cumberland's invitation and set up summer home in Brighton. Mr F. S. Ashley-Cooper, the cricket historian, noted:

> As to the vitality he infused into the life of Brighthelmstone, as it was then generally called, it is not our province on the present

occasion to tell; suffice to say that amusements were indulged in to an extent never known there before, and that the town, from being a sleepy hollow, became a centre of revelry, and a rendez-vous of many of the highest personages in the land. The Prince frequently played cricket there, and a contemporary chronicler has left it on record that 'he would be often engaged in this manly game with the noblemen and gentlemen of his suite, and was esteemed a very excellent player'.

An excellent player he may have been, but his excellence or otherwise was obviously in the eye of the beholder as, in August 1785, when the Prince took bat, ball and court to the delight of all in warm summer sun:

> The Prince of Wales, on Monday last, the 29th of August, at Brighthelmstone, engaged in a game of cricket, with many noblemen and gentlemen there. His Royal Highness played with great condescension and affability through the whole game which lasted several hours; and though he was not so expert at it as some others who had a greater share of practice, yet he displayed as much alertness and activity as the best of them, and appeared highly pleased with the diversion. A great number of spectators of both sects were present and expressed great satisfaction at the engaging deportment of the Prince.

This was no passing fancy; the prince was of a mind to make the game his sport of summer and, as one report noted, 'the Prince and his friends make a party at cricket almost every day, and generally dine on the ground in a marquee, having a temporary kitchen at a small distance to warm the victuals that have been prepared at the pavilion'. It is not recorded if ladies-in-waiting did the teas.

That same year, 1788, according to one record, cricket indirectly caused the death of the melancholic Duke of Manchester. But not from flying ball, or loutish swung bat. The Duke had 'laboured under rheumatic fever, which was so invigorated by a cold that his Grace received from sitting on the grass to see a cricket match, that it baffled all the power of medicine, and after four days ardent illness caused his death'.

By 1790 Brighton had blossomed into a glorious spa, sweet scented with the lazy, regal fun of fine summer. For some, at least, 'This place has never been more full than it has been this season, and at present not a bed is to be had in the town. The visitors are, however, chiefly confined to the circles of the Prince's acquaintances, and but few families are here.'

But let not it be imagined that the locals fawned and giggled over the sporting antics of the Prince's 'acquaintances'. Not all were popular. And some of the ill-feeling peeped through, as on the occasion in 1791 when the Lewes newspaper reported the loutish behaviour of Lord Barrymore, who lived in Brighton and was, by most accounts, a good cricketer.

> It seems his Lordship, on his return to his phaeton from the cricket-ground where he had dined with the Prince, thought proper to lay his whip over the shoulders of a gentleman who was driving a one-horse chair, merely because it was out of his power to get soon enough out of the way of this modern Jehu.
> Lord Barrymore was saved from the possibility of a thrashing by the interference of Bully Hooper, a notorious prize-fighter, who for neither the first nor the last time got his Lordship out of a tight corner . . .

Ah, what sport would the modern popular press have had. But Barrymore got his come-uppance before life's harshest bench – the cricket field. And the importance of the report in tracing the history of Sussex is the reference to the cricket-ground, on which it was that his lordship got a duck in both innings. Moreover, the match itself had great significance for cricket in the county.

First, the ground: until 1791, cricket was played in Brighton on a patch between the race-course and what became known as The Level. But the future king felt a finer wicket should be laid out, one that could be fenced and tended and one upon which marquee and trappings might be pitched to play and entertain in high and whimsical style. And so, to a large field just to the north of what is today Brighton's second landmark, the imposing St Peter's church, the Prince sent surveyor, turfsman and labourer. The field was cut, grazed, fenced, and wicket measured. Sussex, not yet a formal side although often called that by name, now had womb and nursery for the Brighton Cricket Club, out of which came the county side. The enclosed field was known as the Prince of Wales Ground and then The Prince's Gardens, and it survived the Prince (who, in later years, became distracted by the war with France) to become the first home of the Sussex County Cricket Club. But we are hardly done with 1791.

The game in which convenient retribution for Barrymore's boorish manners was cast took place on the new ground over four days in

September 1791. A Middlesex side travelled to play Brighton and brought with it such leading players as the Hon. Edward Bligh, an early member of the MCC and ancestor of Ivo Bligh, to whom in 1882 ladies of Melbourne gave an urn containing the ashes of English cricket. Playing for Middlesex also were William Fennex and Thomas Lord. Fennex was said to be the first man to play forward. The batsmen of the late eighteenth century chose to wait in their crease for the skimming ball to reach them. But with the tendency of a new breed of bowlers to pitch and bounce Fennex invented the strategy of going out to meet it. Lord's name was to become the most famous in cricket and, although the man was remembered by relatively few, the majority would never forget the cricket ground that has carried his name from generation to generation.

MIDDLESEX v BRIGHTON
September 19, 20, 21, 22, 1791
at
BRIGHTON

Middlesex

Hon. E. Bligh	run out	9	b.Hammond	3
Hon. H. Fitzroy	run out	10	not out	11
Harvey Aston Esq.	b.Streeter	3	c.Jutten	4
G. Louch Esq.	b.Hammond	6	b.Streeter	6
J. Goldman	b.Hammond	8	b.Hammond	3
T. Lord	b.Hammond	6	c.Hammond	17
W. Fennex	b.Hammond	90	c.Hammond	0
– Butler	c.Jutten	50	b.Hammond	13
W. Bedster	c.Hammond	0	b.Streeter	5
– Cantrell	b.Hammond	2	b.Hammond	20
– Turner	not out	3	b.Hammond	6
	Byes	10		0
		197		88

Brighton

Lord Barrymore	c.Fennex	0	c.Louch	0
– Living	b.Fennex	9	c.Aston	4
– Hyde	run out	9	b.Lord	5
– Borrer	not out	12	run out	20
– Merchant	b.Fennex	36	c.Fennex	20
– Streeter	c.Bligh	3	b.Lord	1
P. Valence	b.Fennex	39	c.Butler	5
J. Hammond	b.Fennex	0	c.Butler	50

– Gregory	b.Lord	0	run out	1
– Jutten	b.Lord	0	c.Louch	23
J.Valence	b.Fennex	3	not out	10
	Byes	5		9
		116		148

Middlesex won by 21 runs

It can be seen from the scoresheets that Hammond took at least ten wickets for the Sussex side. It may have been three more, because in those days the bowler was not mentioned if a catch was taken off his bowling; only the catcher was noted in the scorecard. Also, he made fifty runs in the second innings, or 'hand', as it was then called. It might be wondered if he scored freely off the slower bowlers by his technique of advancing down the wicket to them. According to the Reverend John Mitford, who spent many years watching cricket in Sussex, he was told that 'Hammond, on one occasion, hit back a slow ball to Lord F. (Frederick) Beauclerk with such frightful force that it just skimmed his Lordship's unguarded head, and he had scarcely nerve to bowl after'. Although they lost, the Brighton men arranged a return game with the London side, to be played at Lord's the following year, 1792.

While the unpopular Barrymore and his men were playing Middlesex at Brighton, another Sussex side were on Windmill Down, facing the famous Hambledon team. There are two points of particular interest in this game. First, this was the year that Hambledon broke up and it was the last recorded match of the famous Hambledon wicketkeeper, Tom Sueter, the 'ladies' pet'. Furthermore, in the scoresheet we see that John Small, Snr, played for the Sussex team, while John Small, Jnr, played for Hambledon.

John Small (1737–1826)

> Here lies, bowled out by Death's unerring ball,
> A Cricketer renowned, by name John Small.
> But though his name was Small, yet great his fame,
> For nobly did he play the noble game;
> His life was like his innings, long and good,
> Full ninety summers he had death withstood.
> At length the ninetieth winter came, when (fate
> Not leaving him one solitary mate)
> This last of Hambledonians, old John Small,
> Gave up his bat and ball, his leather, wax and all.
> Pierce Egan (1772–1849)

48

Second, the Sussex team was described as Sussex West of Arundel, a reminder that, although teams were occasionally known as Sussex sides, they were not county teams in the sense that we were to find them a few years later. This one was led by the Earl of Winchilsea and his friend, the Hon. George Lennox from Goodwood. And they beat the Hambledonians, a much paler side than that fielded in earlier years, by 11 runs.

May 1792 found the Earl of Winchilsea playing for Marylebone against the Brighton men who had lost the year before. Interestingly, position and patronage appear to have been gently set aside for talent and determination. In the match at Lord's, Bligh and Fitzroy gave up their right as 'owners' to open the batting as they had done, 'without great distinction', the previous September. Fennex, who had scored 90 at Brighton, opened with Bedster. Lord Barrymore, perhaps remembering his shaming ducks at the previous meeting, chose to bat at number ten instead of opening. The gentlemen of Marylebone scored 180 in the first hand, with Thomas Lord getting 11 and the Earl of Winchilsea 39. Brighton batted and could make no more than 155 in spite of a sturdy 34 from Hammond before he was bowled by Lord. But in the second hand, all was changed. Marylebone knocked up 105 with Hammond bowling and catching eight men. Then in went Brighton and got the runs for the loss of but one wicket.

In August of the same year, Marylebone returned to the Prince of Wales Ground at Brighton, complete with Bligh, Winchilsea, Louch and Fitzroy, to face Brighton without Barrymore, but still with Hammond, perhaps the most notable Sussex cricketer of his day, whose son Charles came to play for the 'proper' county side in 1842. Seven more wickets and 35 runs for him and Brighton trotted home in three days to win by three wickets. When, the next day, the sides met again, Brighton proved their worth when they won by an innings and 44 runs.

The next meeting between the two was most curious indeed. The game started in September 1792 and ended in May 1793. As so often in the noble game, the weather had a say in the course of the match. Stumps were pitched at the Prince of Wales Ground on 5 September 1792 and Middlesex batted first through somewhat inclement weather for 74. Brighton made 34. But this first innings had taken three days. The likes of the Earl of Winchilsea, the Hon. Edward Bligh and, for Sussex, Shelley, Vallence and, of course, John Hammond agreed that the game should be abandoned for the winter and continued when spring should come. And so the two sides returned on 27 May the following year; Hammond took six wickets for hardly anything at all, and Brighton won by five wickets. Here indeed was testimony to Brighton's right to be the nucleus of the county's representative side. In most of the matches of this period, the names of Marchant and Borrer are recorded with quiet honour. They are reminders that village cricket was the solid heartbeat for the more fashionable and grandly staged matches.

C. F. Trower, the author of *Sussex Cricket: Past and Present*, wrote in the 1870s of the archaeology of Sussex cricket. Under the pseudonym 'An Old Sussex Cricketer', he dwelt on the history and love of villages for this game of inspiration and fortune, and in particular on the Oakendene Club, which probably took its name from Ockenden Farm, and on Borrer, Marchant, Voice and the Wood brothers, all of whom played for the side.

> From about 1790 to 1815, there was a very strong club at Oakendene, near Cowfold. Three brothers named Wood, Marchant of Hurst, Borrer of Ditchling, Voice of Hand-Cross, were the chief players. William Wood, though he never played in great matches, was reckoned the best bowler in Sussex. He used to carry a ball as he walked about his farm, and trained a dog to pick it up and bring it back. He was always bowling at some object. Borrer and Marchant were great batsmen and hard hitters. Vallance of Brighton also belonged to this club. He and Borrer won a great match at Lord's, in 1792, for Brighton against Marylebone, the former making 68 and the latter 60 in the second innings, both 'not out'. The betting was heavy against Sussex, when they began their second innings, as they had 131 to get; and the spectators actually staked their watches and rings at last, but Brighton won by nine wickets . . . Jutten also played; he was a sort of tramp, but a very fast bowler, who always bowled *at* his man, when he could not get a wicket, and so *frightened* many batsmen 'out'!

The records are littered with such tittle-tattle, which reminds us that there is little new under the cricketing sun. Even the notion of gifted athletes to play where the sport was keen and the prizes great is hardly a modern phenomenon, as the good John Hammond showed.

When Hammond returned from living in Kent, to take up his craft as plumber in Sussex, he gave much effort to organising cricket matches in his village of Storrington. With his reputation he was able to attract fine teams to play the village and good players to bat and ball alongside him. In one game, in July 1800, Storrington played Sussex and both Silver Billy Beldham and John Wells of Hambledon turned

(Captions read from top of picture and from left to right)

1867 Killick, Ewbank, Stubberfield, CH Smith, Ellis, H Charlwood, Wells, Jas, Lillywhite, Southerton, John Lillywhite, C Payne

1876 R Fillery, G Humphreys, CA Brown, J Phillips, J Lillywhite, H Killick, H Charlwood, JM Cotterill, FJ Greenfield, A Smith, WB Weighell, H Phillips

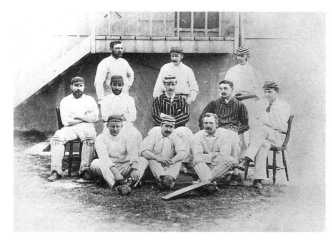

1884 J Hide, Tester, Juniper, H Phillips, RT Ellis, H Whitfield, W Newham, W Blackman, A Hide, Payne, Humphreys

1895 Parris, Bean, Marlow, F Tate, WA Bettesworth, Fry, Newham, Murdoch, Brann, KS Ranjitsinhji, Killick, Butt

1905 J Vine, RA Young, G Leach, HP Chaplin, EH Killick, G Cox, Joe Clayton (coach), CLA Smith, AE Relf, CB Fry, H Butt, KO Goldie

1908 RR Relf, J Vine, G Leach, EB Dwyer, EH Killick, AE Relf, HR Butt, CLA Smith, CB Fry, KS Ranjitsinhji, G Cox (snr)

1911 G Leach, JH Vincett, R Relf, J Vine, G Cox, AE Relf, WH Edwards,
KD Goldie, EH Killick, HP Chaplin, H Butt, CLA Smith

1914 E Bowley, Roberts, V Jupp, JH Vincett, G Street, R Relf, HL Wilson,
HP Chaplin, N Holloway, G Cox, J Vine AE Relf

1920 WL Cornford, HF Roberts, KA Higgs, MW Tate, G Stannard,
G Street, JE Frazer, G Cox, AER Gilligan, AHH Gilligan, AC Watson

1922 Reeves (umpire), J Byrne (sec), T Cook, HE Roberts, E Bowley, MW Tate, JS Stannard
G Street, J Vine, R Young, AER Gilligan, G Cox, AHH Gilligan, Chester (umpire)

1926 WL Knowles (sec), W Cornford, EH Bowley, AF Wensley, MW Tate, TE Cook, J Parks,
J Langridge, AH Isaacs (scorer), AHH Gilligan, AC Watson, AER Gilligan, G Cox, CH Gibson

1929 W Cornford, TER Cook, AF Wensley, RL Holdsworth, GS Grimston,
RA Hollingdale, HW Parks, Jas Langridge, MW Tate, VS Duleepsinhji,
AHH Gilligan, AER Gilligan, Sir Home Gordon, EH Bowley

1932 RGS Scott, HE Hammond, Jas Langridge, HW Parks, TE Cook, MW Tate
AER Gilligan, KS Duleepsinhji, EH Bowley, AF Wensley, W Cornford

1933 TER Cook, HW Parks, Jas Langridge, John Langridge, J Cornford, JH Parks, G Cox,
MW Tate, Sir Home Gordon, EH Bowley, RS Scott, AER Gilligan, W Cornford, AF Wensley

1934 JH Parks, HW Parks, HE Hammond, John Langridge, Jas Langridge,
J Cornford, TEF Cook, MW Tate, A Melville, AF Wensley, W Cornford

1937 EH Killick, H Parks, G Cox, John Langridge, J Cornford, C Oakes, JH Parks, MW Tate, AJ Homes, W Cornford, TEF Cook, Jas Langridge

1947 AK Wilson, C Oakes, G Cox, John Langridge, J Nye, DN Fell (umpire), Jas Langridge, HT Bartlett, SC Griffith, EE Harrison, HW Parks

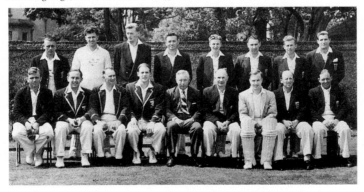

1953 DJ Wood, NI Thomson, ASM Oakman, DV Smith, JM Parks, AE James, KG Suttle, RT Webb, RG Marlar, SC Griffith, Jas Langridge, DS Sheppard, Duke of Norfolk, John Langridge, GHG Doggart, G Cox, C Oakes

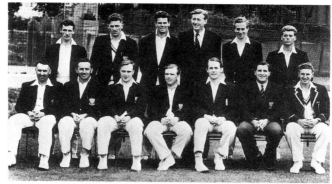

1957 G Cogger, NI Thomson, D Bates, ASM Oakman, L Lenham, D Mantell, AE James, DV Smith, GHG Doggart, RG Marlar, DS Sheppard, RT Webb, JM Parks

1960 KG Suttle, LJ Lenham, NI Thomson, DL Bates, A Buss, RV Bell, GC Cooper DJ Mordaunt, DS Sheppard, ER Dexter, DV Smith, JM Parks.
Picture: S & G Press Agency Ltd

1963 GC Cooper, RJ Langridge, DL Bates, A Buss, JA Snow, LJ Lenham, NI Thomson, JM Parks, ER Dexter, ASM Oakman, KG Suttle

1978 Second XI Championship Winners: A Buss (manager) C Wells, M Carter, A Pigott, C Fletcher, SP Hoadley, J Hayward, A Green, R Marshall (coach), K Churchward, K Smith, C Waller, J. Groome, I Greig, T Head

1982 I Greig, A Green, C Wells, G Le Roux, A Wells, A Pigott, L Chandler (scorer) S Storey, G Mendis, P Parker, J Barclay, C Waller, I Gould, P Phillipson

1986 S Storey (coach), N Lenham, A Green, A Babington, D Reeve, R Alikhan, A Jones, A Wells, C Wells, G Le Roux, I Gould, A Pigott, P Parker, P. Phillipson. (Not shown Imran Khan, J Barclay)

out for the village. John Nyren described Beldham as the finest batter of his own or perhaps of any age. 'No one within my recollection could stop a ball better, or make more brilliant hits all over the ground. Wherever the ball was bowled, there she was hit away, and in the most severe, venomous style.' And Wells? He was known as 'Honest' John Wells, a baker by trade. Nyren remembered: 'He was a short, thick, well-set man; in make like a cob-horse, proportionately strong, active, and laborious. As a bowler he had a very good general field, and a steady batter – in short, an excellent servant of all work.'

Such men were attracted to play in Sussex village cricket for good crack, reputation and not a little silver to the side. Wells, Beldham and Hammond hit between them 136 of Storrington's 213 runs and then disposed of thirteen Sussex batsmen. The village won by 19 runs. Hammond's success with ball suggests the all-round skill of this Storrington man, for although the surviving scoresheets show him as an exceptional bowler John Nyren remembers him also as one of the finest wicket-keepers of his day. On one occasion in 1807, he kept wicket for England against a twenty-three-man team of Kent, stumping twelve of them and catching four.

In that very game played John Willes of Kent, who caused much concern by bowling round-arm instead of convention's underarm, good and safe enough for batsmen's vanity since the game's beginnings. In *Sporting Magazine*'s report of the match it was noted: 'The straight-armed bowling introduced by John Willes, Esq. was generally practised, and proved an obstacle to getting runs in comparison to what might have been got by straightforward bowling.' A landmark in cricket's contour chart.

In a short innings the game had gone from two stumps to three, had seen the formation of the *Laws* and the MCC, and the decline of the Hambledon Club. Now a new track was cleared, which would within one score years witness the great revolution in cricket and the appearance of two of the great names in Sussex cricket.

Chapter 6

In the opening years of the nineteenth century, the great rivalry between East and West Sussex had much to do with the traditional, political and fashionable values of the sprawling, divided region. There were some in the east, as now, who regarded the western end of the county as a totally different part of the world. 'West Sussex? It's in Hampshire!' wrote one academic. Cricket was in some part test and banner of the right to be seen and acknowledged as 'real' Sussex. Yet, as Charles Box suggested, the divided county was losing its right to boast great honour and deed on the cricket field.

As East and West did not come up to much, another experiment was tried between North and South; and although fate forbade the match to be brought to a decisive issue, the former 'looked' the stronger side; one man scored nearly twice as many runs from his own bat as the whole of the 'warmer' side. In another similarly constructed affair, the North won by eight wickets. In both cases there were given men on each side, so that the actual native strength must be viewed as conjectural.

While these and a few other vagaries were indulged in by some sections of cricketers in order to obtain county honour, the mimicry of cricket found a time and place for development. Lewes challenged Hastings with an odd lot. On a given day the challengers took their departure together for the field of action from before the Swann Inn, amid the huzzas of the surrounding multitude, in a waggon arched over with green boughs, and drawn by four oxen ornamented with ribbons; one of the party operated as charioteer with white reins fastened to the horns of the animals.

They were preceded by a car of a minor description (a donkey vehicle) and two Egyptian ponies, which exhibited four musicians with their faces elegantly besmeared with common rouge, and variegated with soot, to the no small diversion of a great number of spectators. After the game (in which two men with wooden legs played with great alertness) the party returned in the same manner to the Swann tap, where a dinner was provided for them.

Sussex cricket may have been in fine and amusing fettle, but its hoped high standard had lost thrusting patronage while royalty and nobility worried themselves with foreign fields where more sordid contests were being played out beneath cannons, formed squares and cavalry's thundered mutilation. The dullness of cricketing deeds was reflected in a report in 1811 of a match played at Brighton:

A match between the cricketers of this place and those of Cowfold took place on the 11th of June, when the latter were victors, and six runs to spare. Formerly, when the Prince countenanced them, the Brighton eleven were a match for All England, and the Marylebone Club were more than once beaten by them, and reluctantly compelled to acknowledge the superiority of their skill. But as nothing flourishes in this part of the world, but in the renovating rays of the patronage of the Heir Apparent, our cricketers had no sooner lost that fostering influence which could alone inspirit them to action and give new energies to every effort, than supineness succeeded, and they at last, in the gymnastic sports, dwindled and degenerated into their original insignificance.

A scathing quill scratching sharp truth. Meanwhile, across at Goodwood, oblivious or perhaps justly amused, the Goodwood Cricket Club was dressing overall in white jackets trimmed with blue silk and publishing its commandments for gathering, play and pecuniary business.

Established
RULES
of the
GOODWOOD
CRICKET CLUB
July 5, 1813

Rules, & c.

1.

The Members of the Goodwood Club to meet twice a week in the Park to practise, and a Marquee will be pitched by Mr Gilbert, Landlord of the Duke of Richmond's Arms, Waterbeach, for their sole reception and accommodation.

2.

The days of Meeting are Mondays, and Fridays, at Three o'clock in the Afternoon, the time to be regulated by the Goodwood Clock: and any Member that attends later than Four, will be subject to the fine of Sixpence; a non-attendance of any Member, will be subject to the fine of One Shilling; such fines will be collected by the Steward of the Club, the succeeding day of attendance.

3.

Should the services of those persons be found necessary to play a Match, who consider themselves incapable of bearing their own expenses, they are to be defrayed from the fund of the Club, which is established by the collection of fines.

4.

No fresh Rules are to be adopted for the better regulation of the Club, without being approved by ballot.

5.

No person can be admitted a Member, unless approved by ballot; four black balls excludes him.

6.

When a Match is proposed and accepted by the Club – those Members who volunteer to play, must put down their Names, and should there be more than the complement necessary, the overplus will be discharged by ballot.

7.

The Dress approved to distinguish the Members of the Goodwood Club, is a white flannel jacket, trimmed with blue silk, and white trowsers, which must be worn on all particular occasions; Notice will be given by the President when that will be thought necessary.

8.

Captain Rowe, of Norton, is appointed President, and Mr John Peerman, Vice-President, to the Club, whose duties are to decide disputes, when an excuse is made by any Member for non-attendance, owing to the badness of the weather, or other pretences. – To take the chair at all meetings, and propose Challenges that are offered to the club, thro' the medium of any Member, as none can be accepted without their sanction and approval, and to conduct all arrangements that may concern the Club.

9.

Mr. T. Halstead, Woodcote, is appointed Steward to the Club,

whose duty is to collect fines, and conduct all pecuniary business
that may concern it.

10.

Mr. Gilbert is responsible for bats, balls and stumps, the property
of the club, and he will keep the Stewards account book, and
produce it the days of meeting, that every Member may sign his
name, as an assurance of his being present.

Let it not be thought that cricket squandered its inheritance in
Brighton and, left destitute, attracted nothing but the scorn of passers-
by. Famous names were keen still to turn to and play, especially when
guineas and good ordinary might be offered. Hammond remained at
his crease, and even that great nineteenth-century sportsman, 'Squire'
Osbaldestone, took the southern air, the field and the gold of the
Prince's Gardens.

George Osbaldestone was born in 1787 in London, although he
was almost a Yorkshireman given that his father was from Scarborough
and the Squire himself chose to live in that great county for some years.
He was a famous sporting man and better-remembered by some as
Master of Foxhounds of the most celebrated hunts, including the
Quorn and the Pytchley. The Squire was a stocky man, sturdy
of character and breeding. He played his early cricket at Eton
and Oxford and his first match at Lord's for the MCC against
Middlesex. That was in 1808. Within a few years, though, in a
fit of anger, he scratched his name from the list of the MCC because
of the result of a game. The MCC, perhaps even then displaying
the autocracy that became so much part of its character, ignored a
plea for his reinstatement. Its officers had been utterly offended, and
there's none so unforgiving . . .

It must be assumed that it was the cricket rather than the chase
which attracted the quick-tempered but truly skilful Osbaldestone to
Brighton, and his name is to be found with some certain honour on
the scoresheets of the early nineteenth century. In 1811 he scored 54
for 'Sussex' against Storrington and accounted for six of the village
side, including Hammond. The following year, he played for The
Coast against The Weald, hit 38 runs and dismissed eleven men –
again Hammond fell victim. And in 1815 it was Osbaldestone who
arranged the Sussex game against Epsom, to be played for 1000
guineas at Brighton. It was during this game that the first record
is found of one of the greatest Sussex cricketers of the time, James
Broadbridge, playing representative cricket. He was called 'Jem'. A
note in *Brighton in the Olden Time* tells us:

56

It was a toss-up previous to the match whether he should play or not. His appearance was against him, for he had probably, as was his custom, walked in from Duncton that morning, and did not dress for the occasion. As he stood apart, with his hands in his pockets, and attired in farm labourer's fashion, with his bright red waistcoat, some of the gentlemen eyed him askance and doubted the desirability of having him in their side. But it was eventually decided that he should play.

The match was full of noted players, including Lord Frederick Beauclerk and the splendid MCC member Benjamin Aislabie, who was thought such a swell that in later years he was to be found leading an MCC side in *Tom Brown's Schooldays*. From the scoresheet, Jem Broadbridge apparently did not make a great impression as a batsman. He went in at number eleven: 0 not out in the first innings; bowled Beauclerk for 1 in the second. However, he did account for four of the Epsom batsmen. Within two years Jem Broadbridge was established, and so was his brother William.

In 1817 (some have said 1816) Jem opened the batting for a side which was firmly entitled Sussex, in another encounter with the Epsom team which once again included Mr Aislabie and the amazing Long Robinson, sometimes known as 'Three-fingered Jack'. He was described as a mighty off-driver and cutter using a bat with a specially grooved handle to cope with his torturously maimed hand. It is thought also that Long Robinson (he stood well above six feet in his talloned and long-spiked shoes) was perhaps the first to use pads, though they had no such name in those days. They were made of wood and attracted much attention and, it is said, ridicule. Robinson abandoned his leg guards. When they were introduced a few years later, pads were worn under the 'trowsers', for it was not considered manly to protect even the finest silk and buckled shins, calves and lump-bone knees from their daily bleedings. Broadbridge thought little of such protection.

C. F. Trower, writing sixty years after that Lord's game, suggested that it might be called the Sussex man's first-class début. However, although Trower writes of the game as being in 1816, at the end of July, he perhaps confused it with a game the following year. Nevertheless, what he has to say is pertinent to our story.

In 1816 James, the more celebrated of the two brothers Broadbridge – who were exactly the same weight (12 stone) [others have

57

suggested 16 stone, an altogether more formidable figure for one so tall; burly rather than lanky] – made his first appearance in any match of note; and a pretty good one, too, it was; for he made 57 runs. For several seasons he was accounted the best 'all round' player in England; and no first-class match was perfectly made up without him. He was particularly clever at one hit. When a ball was bowled rather outside his legs, he would swing his bat between the wicket and himself, and make a square leg hit, or a sort of half 'on' drive. He usually stood with his bat well over his shoulder, and, on one occasion, it is said, kept in for a day and a half! He was also very artful as a bowler. He soon 'reckoned up' his opponent, and proceeded to attack his weak points. He had great command of pitch and pace, and some of his more enthusiastic admirers used to say, 'he could do anything with a ball except make it speak'!

Broadbridge was said to be a stern man; purposeful in mind, step and skill. He lived and farmed in Duncton, as did his brother William, and he would walk the twenty-five miles or so from Duncton to practise ball and bat with the 'superior players'. He died in 1843, a bachelor and but forty-seven years of age. Trower remarks that, along with Lillywhite and Knight, Jem Broadbridge 'must be considered to have been the joint originator of the round-hand bowling'. Certainly, a few years later the three are to be found at the eye of the argument and turmoil that swirled about the inevitable change from underarm to round-arm bowling, and which was to lead to seven famous All-England players refusing to play against Sussex.

But, first, more of that 1816 game in London, for it was a historic meeting although it did not, I think, include a Broadbridge, neither Jem nor William. It took place over five days, between 29 July and 2 August, and it was, as far as we know, the first time that a side called Sussex and deemed to be the county had played at Lord's. The Sussex hero Hammond failed to score in either innings, a rare event, and he appears to have had an indifferent day in the field. There is a sadness in the record of that game, for Hammond was towards the end of his playing days; he would then have been perhaps forty-nine years of age and he did not appear the following year, 1817, when Sussex returned to Lord's to take on Epsom once more.

This, we might consider, was the game in which Jem Broadbridge established himself as the leading figure of his day. He opened the batting with Mellersh, made 12 in the first innings and 45 in the second. Brother William did even better: he scored 75 altogether. But the honours (perhaps not quite the right term, as we shall see) of the Sussex side and the day went to old William Lambert, one of the most famous of all cricketers, who scored 107 not out in the first innings and 157 in the second. He was the first cricketer ever to do this; for the first time, two separate hundreds at Lord's. It didn't happen again until 1893, when A. E. Stoddart, playing for Middlesex, scored 195 not out and 124 against Nottinghamshire.

The irony of the event must be explained: in the same year, 1817, Lambert played against Nottingham in the England team. He is said to have 'sold' the match, on which, as was usual, huge sums were riding. He was banned. And so the enormous score of two centuries in one match at Lord's marked also his last appearance on that ground. He played on in minor games until about 1839, but never again at Lord's. A matter of the times. Lambert's last outing to Lord's was a feast of runs. As well as his two centuries, another came from Sussex's Squire Osbaldestone, and altogether both sides scored 1047 runs. It was the first recorded game in which a thousand runs were hit. But would they have been if round-arm bowling had found favour by then?

Cunning and craft, and skimming speed to devious lobs, had all been the bowler's lot since the game began. The haughtiness of the batsman's pedigree dominated game and spirit as if it were a feudal right to beat yeoman bowlers until they cried for mercy and more. In 1775 it was conceded that, even if skill, eye and chance managed to beat the bat, the odds still stretched just as far because the hope of striking down one or two stumps was indeed slim. The third stump was added in that year. But still it was underarm bowling. John Nyren's description of John Harris, considered the finest of bowlers in the late Hambledon days, gives a good account of the most devastating power of the underhand style.

> His attitude when preparing for his run previously to delivering the ball would have made a beautiful study for the sculptor. First of all, he stood erect like a soldier at drill; then, with a graceful curve of the arm, he raised the ball to his forehead, and drawing back his right foot, started off with his left. His mode of delivering the ball was very singular. He would bring it from under the arm with a twist and nearly as high as his arm-pit, and with this action push it, as it were, from him. How it was that the balls acquired the velocity that they did by this mode of delivery I never could comprehend. In bowling, he never stooped in the least in his delivery, but kept himself upright all the time. His balls were very little beholden to the ground when pitched; it was but a touch, and up again; and woe to the man who did not get in

to block them, for they had such a peculiar curl, that they would grind his fingers against the bat: many a time have I seen blood drawn in this way from a batter who was not up to the trick; old Tom Walker was the only exception – I have before classed him among the bloodless animals.

So there we are: fast, fierce and bloodthirsty. A demon at the split knuckles of many a player, but not Tom Walker. Walker, although a batsman, was one of the first to start the new style of bowling, but he was deeply and thoroughly chastised. It was throwing, nagged the authorities – most of whom were batsmen, of course. But come the style did. Indeed, Nyren talks of a man of Sussex being the most noted exponent. He was John Willes, who was more correctly from Suton Vallence in Kent. A. G. Steel's account towards the end of the nineteenth century is as complete as any:

> Mr. Willes, being a most enthusiastic cricketer, and not content with the summer months for his favourite sport, used in winter daily to repair to his barn, and there measure out the proper distance, pitch the stumps, and, with his sister (also an enthusiast) as bowler, enjoy a good practice. Now everyone who has seen ladies attempting to throw a stone or cricket-ball will remember that they invariably have a half-round, half-under sort of delivery, and this Miss Willes, in common with the majority of ladies, seems to have possessed. Her brother, accustomed to play against what in those days was the only known style of bowling, viz., under-arm, was somewhat perplexed and worried with this unknown feminine species of ball, which doubtless he found difficult to tackle. We are not told whether his feelings of shame at being thus defeated, or of a delight at discovering this new style of bowling, predominated, but we are told that shortly afterwards he made his debut as a round-arm bowler, and met with (until he was stopped by the conservatism of the crowd) the greatest success.

Some say that Miss Willes bowled with such style because normal underarm bowling would have been impossible for a young lady in full skirts. Whether Willes was one of the first is not of much matter; certainly he persisted in reviving the skill which had most certainly been practised before. For Willes the end came in 1822 at Lord's. He was no stranger to the ground, having played there as early as 1806 in the first Gentlemen *v* Players match, the same year in which he first tried out round-arm during a game of 23 of Kent against England,

60

at Benenden Heath. Sixteen years later, at Lord's of all places, he expected differences, and none was disappointed.

Willes opened the bowling for Kent. The umpire at his end was Noah Mann, Jnr, who immediately called no ball! Willes had often been rebuked thus; on some days he had been sent from wicket and field. He had at times been banned, so he was used to rejection and official torment. On this day at Lord's, something snapped. Willes is said to have thrown down the ball 'in disgust', left the field, leapt on to his horse and truly ridden out of the first-class game of cricket. He should have waited, for the revolution of which he is perhaps the best-remembered agitator was at hand.

Bowlers had long had argument in favour of surer methods of ridding themselves of stubborn batsmen. The architecture of two slim stumps was unhelpful to most. Even if ball did beat bat, then the gap was wide enough to give the striker yet another chance. The band of batting brothers that tended to rule the game may have seen the sporting injustice in this, but judiciously resisted change until it was inevitable. In 1775 two stumps were replaced by three. Later someone tried four, but this was somewhat excessively radical, and in fact served little purpose.

In the 1770s the notion of bowling with a higher action than simple underarm had never taken great hold. Tom Walker had seen the wisdom of this, for it was a variation many batsmen hated. The differences of angle, swing and pitch touched at the nerves of dominant batters, and Walker was discouraged, perhaps as others were. But the game in Sussex, having gone into some decline towards the end of the century, was by the early 1820s emerging with a higher standard and new ideas. Jem Broadbridge was taken by round-arm bowling and so was the young William Lillywhite, born in West Hampnett, enlisted by Goodwood in 1792 and set fair to become one of the legends of Sussex cricket.

Chapter 7

William Lillywhite and Jem Broadbridge were formidable cricketers. Possibly because the revolution in bowling technique was more correctly an evolution, Lillywhite did not come to attention until he was about thirty. Moreover, the doldrums that drifted across the county at the end of the eighteenth century lingered long enough to see Lillywhite through his teens at a time when there was little opportunity for many to be noticed for their exceptional performances unless they were members of the Brighton circle of batsmen and bowlers. It would seem that first record of William Lillywhite as a player was in 1822, when he played for a team made up of Hampnett, Goodwood and Boxgrove against Midhurst. He played as a batsman, for although now in his thirtieth year Lillywhite was thought a greater striker of balls than of stumps.

It is said that as a youngster Lillywhite badly injured his right arm, which made underarm bowling very difficult, certainly uncomfortable. For good reason, then, he sprang eagerly to pick up and understand the craft of round-arm. His father James was a brickmaker, and William followed his father's trade. In that same year, 1822, Lillywhite moved to Hove and took up with James Broadbridge and, it would seem, the new style of what was for a long time called 'Sussex Bowling'. An oil painting of Lillywhite shows a thick-set, short man with a sharp nose, black broad eyebrows and determined eyes, wearing what Trower called 'his unfailing black broad-brimmed hat, which he never exchanged for any cooler fabric, even in the hottest day'.

This tightly braced figure was such a demon with a ball that, again according to Trower:

63

. . . he could pitch it nearly to a hair's breadth; and, always bowling well within his strength, he was always able to put on a little extra steam whenever he chose, and never tire. Consequently the pace of his ball was the most difficult thing possible to judge, because, with the same apparent velocity in the air, the rate at which it got up would vary in the most extraordinary way. He was very fond of getting his hand 'up' if he thought he could venture it; and in country matches, where umpires did not dare to find fault with so great a man, he would often raise it well above his shoulder. His accuracy of pitch he learned by practice in a barn or shed, where he would bowl away at a stump with a wooden bail at the top, and he never considered it a good ball unless he hit the wooden one, for his great aim was to make his ball 'get up' well, in order to increase the chances of the batsman being caught. In addition to his mechanical precision, which is the first requisite in a bowler, he had the advantage of 'bowling with his head' . . . he not only thought of the exact spot where the ball ought to pitch, but made it pitch there! It was no use to flatter yourself that he would not find out the flaw in you, if you had one. He 'took stock' of his man almost instinctively, found out directly whether he played forward or back, what was the hit he was looking out to make; and woe betide him, if he had a weak point 'in his harness', for 'Lilly's' eye picked it out in a moment, and thick and fast came his shafts upon it. Perhaps the greatest bowling feat performed by him or any other man, when we consider the consummate batsman he was facing, was when he bowled Fuller Pilch [the celebrated Kent batsman of the day] sixty balls without a run, and with the sixty-first got his wicket! Though I always thought and found him very free of conceit, he must have been conscious of his great powers; and one need not be surprised at the seemingly boastful oft-repeated declarations attributed to him 'When I bouls and Fuller bats, then you'll see cricket'; and again, 'I bouls the best ball in England'.

A mighty man of Sussex was William Lillywhite. His habit of putting his hand 'up' was noted by the nineteenth-century cricket writer William Denison, as an action adopted by Jem Broadbridge when batsmen took on his bowling. The better the batting, the nearer Broadbridge came to full overarm action: 'If he finds a man hitting his balls away he will, without hesitation, throw his hand and his arm as it were over his head, in other terms shy at the wickets.' Mr Denison, like many of his generation, was no patron of the new style. The matter came to great head and spectacle in 1827, when the Sussex side was used in a trial of three matches to decide the future of bowling actions.

For Sussex, the five years to that point had been as eventful as the most optimistic prediction from the doldrums of the century's turn could have imagined. The state of the Prince's Ground had long suffered since its regal opening and royal blessing in the last decade of the eighteenth century. In 1823 it was taken over by a gentleman known as James Ireland. Ireland's Gardens, as the area became known, was far more than a cricket ground. It was described by the new owner as 'Pleasure Grounds'. As the name suggested, there was meant to be something for everyone. In the *Brighton Gazette* of 1824 J. Ireland begged respectfully to announce that during the previous winter 'unremitting exertions' had been used by the proprietor, not to mention 'many thousands of pounds', in order to provide families with a grand addition to the town's attractions. The new saloon was 'capable of accommodating dinner parties & c on a large scale, and will also be used as a Breakfast or Promenade Room; and a Pump Room for supplying Medicated Waters, where the Daily and other Papers will be taken in . . . The Gardens are fitted up with every attention to the amusement of Visitors, and comprise among other things a well stocked Aviary.'

Subscriptions were available for the Gardens from as little as four shillings (20p) a month for a single person to £2 2s (£2.10) a year for a family ticket (not including servants). There was a maze with a 'safe and elegant Swing, on Merlin's principle', a bowling green, a racquet court and, of course, the cricket ground – 'bats, balls, rackets, & c will be furnished on the grounds at a moderate charge'. And, as a great incentive, 'On the Cricketing Ground, there is an excellent Billiard Room with a very superior Table', and as a bonus there was 'No extra charge for Lamps in the evening'. Mr Ireland was clearly a businessman and showman of some distinction. It was here that the County Ground under the management of Mr Ireland and others existed until 1848 until the developers claimed the site, and bats, balls, stumps, linseed and all moved to the Brunswick Ground.

It has been suggested that it was this sense of business that encouraged the arrangement of a new series of important fixtures for Sussex, including those against the MCC. The first was fixed for June 1823 at Lord's. It was the first appearance of the formal Sussex side (though not yet the 'First Class County' side) at Lord's and the first game against the MCC. Sussex won by eight wickets. It was revival in fine form. Two Junes later Kent travelled across the border and down to Brighton to play what is accepted as the first county match between the old rivals, although from the line-up of the teams they were distinctly Hawkhurst and Brighton. It was a curious game. Sussex went in first and scored 284. Kent were then all out for 40. In their second innings, Sussex made but 42, and in theirs Kent 43. So Sussex won by 243 runs. The names of Jem Broadbridge (his brother William hit 42), William Lillywhite and George Brown, who scored 77 and took six wickets in the second innings, are well noted in the formal scoresheet.

As well as being a fine cricketer, George Brown was one of the successors to Ireland as manager of the Royal Brighton Cricket Ground, as Ireland's gardens became known. His craft was that of tailor and he lived in the west of the county, at Emsworth. He started playing at Brighton, probably in 1818, with a reputation for great breath and stamina. On one occasion, it is said, Brown was playing in a single-wicket match against a side which included Squire Osbaldestone. One report writes of him in almost Homeric terms:

> After Brown had bowled for a little while, Osbaldestone said, 'You won't keep that pace long, I know.' 'Oh yes!' said Brown, 'I can bowl like that all day, if you like'; and he did bowl in that fashion for four hours and a half without intermission. Off 230 of his balls only 8 runs were made. When he went in, he drove the first ball through a paling, and across a lane that ran outside the ground. He was an uncommonly powerful man, and a regular 'hitter' though not a fine bat. His arm was said to be as large round as an ordinary man's leg, and proportionately muscular. So tremendous was his pace, that he always had two long-stops, and generally all the field behind the wickets . . . At Lord's a man once tried to stop a ball with his coat, but Brown bowled right through it, and killed a dog instantaneously on the other side.

Perhaps. It is certainly true, however, that the Brighton wicket-keeper, William Dench, found it prudent to wear a vest of packed straw to protect his chest from the sometimes unpredictable power of giant Brown.

A fortnight went by, and the two sides met once more, this time at Hawkhurst. Kent won by 16 runs. In August of the same year, 1825, a Sussex side played Hampshire and, although there were imported players on both sides, it is generally accepted that, as with the two Kent matches that year, this was a county *versus* county affair. Sussex won by 177 runs with Jem Broadbridge putting together 155 runs and bowling out eleven Hampshire batsmen. Whether or not these games were really county matches in the sense they would have been after 1839 is open to some debate. Yet, given that there was no formal table of county representation, these must have been the nearest possible to such competitions. It is a harmless pastime to assume them to be so.

During the first three years of the Lillywhite and Broadbridge round-arm bowling partnership, Sussex was considered a most powerful, daunting side for any team, including the All-England elevens of the day. By no means unbeatable, as the records show, the Sussex bowlers nevertheless appeared to mount enormous and sometimes controversial performances, much to the chagrin of defending batsmen. For many years, bowling style had been decided by custom because until the *Laws* were revised in 1816 there was nothing to stop a bowler raising his hand as long as he kept one foot behind the bowling crease and within the return crease. In 1815, during a match at Brighton, one of the bowlers, probably Broadbridge by all accounts, got his hand 'up' above his head, much to the scandal of the cricketing authorities. For the MCC, enough was enough. The revised *Laws* of 1816 were clear:

> The ball must be delivered under-handed, not thrown or jerked, with the hand below the elbow at the time of delivering the ball. If the arm is extended straight from the body, or the back part of the hand be uppermost when the ball is delivered, or the hand horizontally extended, the Umpire shall call 'No-ball'.

Exit John Willes in accordance with the *Laws*. But even the ruling of the MCC was not going to stop Lillywhite or Broadbridge, and it must be considered that other players were also mindful that the new style could on occasions give the bowler, in more ways than one, the upper hand. The added problem was enforcement of the law. Umpiring was a less than professional practice and the 1816 *Laws* demanded much of official as well as bystanding attention. Keeping an eye on foot, elbow and hand was difficult; consequently umpiring decisions were rarely consistent, and determined, intimidating and crusading bowlers were able to exploit the capriciousness and bewilderment of those who stood by to interpret. By the time Lillywhite and Broadbridge appeared in the 1820s, the cast of round, and even overarm, bowling was well set; furthermore, enthusiasm was growing apace, even among some favoured by the MCC. But the decision to acknowledge and then sanction change had yet to be made.

And so it was that three matches were arranged for Sussex to play All-England. It is generally accepted that these events were indeed 'test' matches, to decide the future of the round-arm bowling methods. Perished records perhaps hold the secret of the truth of this supposition, for none survives to prove conclusively the trial by bat and ball. The games took place, yes. That they were controversial is in no doubt; after all, nine of the All-England team refused to play unless Sussex reverted to underarm. But there is no surviving record of the matches having been set as a trial for the Sussex style.

Of particular note was the choice of ground for the first of the three matches: Sheffield. Now, why Yorkshire? The previous year, 1826, a game had been played in Sheffield between England and twenty-two of Sheffield and Leicester. (It had long been common for a strong side to be pitted against twice the number of players.) The England XI had included Jem and William Broadbridge, Lillywhite and Brown. There is an account of a match the previous year when a Yorkshire twenty-two played England, during which Brown bowled twelve men and Broadbridge ten. It might be imagined that some in Yorkshire felt that an account had to be settled with the arrogant southerners who believed cricket their own and northern pastimers simply amusing. And why not? Had not Marsden of Yorkshire hit 227 against Nottingham in 1826?

> Oh! Marsden at cricket is Nature's perfection.
> For hitting the ball in any direction.

For that first game in 1827 the England team included three Yorkshiremen, Marsden, Barber and Dawson. Sussex inevitably had Broadbridge and Lillywhite. In the first innings the two men at one point had England five wickets down with only 2 runs on the board. The mighty Fuller Pilch from Norfolk, who played for Kent and had seen the Sussex pair bowl, hit 38 before Lillywhite clean bowled him and England finished their first hand all out for 81. But it was that sort of match. Sussex replied with 91, England then got 112 with Lillywhite and Broadbridge taking all the wickets, and Sussex won by seven wickets.

The second trial took place at Lord's. Let it not be thought that Sussex only were in the witness box; for the England side included G. T. Knight, who was inclined to the new bowling style and who bowled out Cheslyn, Morley, William Broadbridge and Thwaites. And the MCC decided that the bowling was not only to be watched, but also played. Ward and Kingscote, both eminent members, played for England and it was William Ward's 42 in the first innings and his 20 in the second that allowed the All-England side to give such a good account of themselves against Sussex. But the 'warmer county' (as one writer called Sussex) won by three wickets. Two points of further interest emerged from this Lord's game. William Ward is said to have remarked that, although he was opposed to the bowling style, he found

68

it not in the least bit difficult to play. Second, there is a suggestion that Broadbridge and Lillywhite bowled higher than round-arm, more or less over-arm. Certainly not many were as sanguine as Mr Ward. One commentator was obviously racked with nostalgia at least:

> For the last three years there has not been so great an interest excited with lovers of this manly game as within this month on account of the grand match which has lately been made between 'All England and the County of Sussex', for 100 guineas a side. On the part of England there are one or two men from the neighbourhood of Sheffield, who have displayed great skill, and convinced the cricket world that the South must not, as heretofore, presume to wear the wreath for ever. On the part of Sussex there are some very fine players; but their victories have been undoubtedly owing to a singular novel, and perhaps we may say unfair, manner of bowling, by the over-cast from the arm, instead of the under-hand and graceful method of the Old School. There has been considerable discussion on this point – whether it could be allowed, and whether it shall continue to be practised. The writer of this, an old cricketer, really shakes with fear at its adoption, as it certainly gives birth to the hope of gaining a wicket by chance, by a wild twist, instead of the fine steady length, as shown us in former times.

Perhaps a croaky voice from deckchair's gentle curve, as Mr Arlott might have said. Some of the most stalwart of All-England players were more adamant in their condemnation. So upset were nine of England that they issued an ultimatum:

> We the undersigned do agree that we will not play the third match between All England and Sussex, which is intended to be at Brighton, in July or August, unless the Sussex players bowl fair; that is, abstain from throwing.
> T. Marsden
> W. Ashby
> W. Searle
> J. Saunders
> T. C. Howard
> W. Caldecourt
> F. Pilch
> T. Beagley
> W. Matthews

But the intrepid and fearless nine withdrew their objection, and play they did – probably the last time that Sussex bowling was so blatantly and extravagantly feared. The game took place in Brighton during three days in July 1827. What happened? What did it prove? Let us take the account from the Reverend James Pycroft's book *The Cricket Field*.

> On this occasion it was determined to play all the best batsmen. They played Fuller Pilch, Beagley, Ward, and Budd, with Searle and Saunders, and also Messres Osbaldestone and Henry Kingscote, the latter a fine, clean hitter with great power and long reach, standing about 6ft 2ins in height. [Also the maker of the match.]
>
> Our old friend Richard Cheslyn played in the last two matches. 'We headed England' said he 'by 50 runs; we made 77 to their 27 in the 1st innings, and I stood to win a good round sum'. Down for only 27 runs seemed a triumph to Sussex bowling, and most conclusive of the issue of the match. Others were not so sure of this conclusion – one of them was Mr Budd from whom we also heard the story of this match too. 'I went up to Captain Cheslyn' said Mr Budd 'and said "If you have heavy bets, take my advice, Captain, and hedge, for these men can never beat those. Believe me, this is a game that must turn about." But Cheslyn was too sanguine to be persuaded by me.'
>
> Sussex 120 to win. This did not look so well, said Cheslyn. Still I told our side 'We can do it yet if we all resolve to play a quiet steady game. I only wish they had all done so.' But almost at the first set-off James Broadbridge, about our best bat, threw his bat clean out of his hand at a wide ball, the ball mounted in the air and was caught by Mr Ward at point. There was much dispute afterwards in the case, but the umpire gave it out. This loss was great damage to our side, and we all went down for 95, and England won the game.

William Denison's account is equally worth repeating. He states most definitely that the game was organised to examine the new style of bowling. The England selectors of the day picked eleven batsmen in an effort to show that Lillywhite and Broadbridge were far from invulnerable and could truly, if played properly, be hit to good effect.

> The last trial between 'England and Sussex' is now over, at least the third match; but we augur with a certain degree of confidence that another struggle between the hitting and the new-fashioned 'throwing' will be exhibited. The issue of this

has been in favour of England, after as fine a match as was ever played, and in which as much play of the first-rate character was shown. England's Eleven went in first. Their innings lasted but a short time and carried a face that only strengthened the confident front of their opponents, and baffled the justly formed anticipations of their friends. They fetched only 27 runs, whereupon the betting assumed decided odds in favour of the county. The bowling of Lillywhite and Broadbridge seemed irresistible as heretofore; and it really appeared as if no hitting could be found to oppose it effectually. Their second 'hands' however did the hearts good of all the 'Old School', convincing them that this mode of delivering the ball only wanted once to be shaken off to lose the power of its effect. Saunders, Budd, and Beagley beat it away, and made a capital example of it. The score now altogether amounted to 196; the two hands of Sussex only reached 172, leaving at least 24 in favour of England.

It must not be forgotten that this match was originally made purposely to produce 'hitting' against the bowlers of the questionable mode. It is therefore not to be wondered at that in other points England was weak, her bowling was not equal, her fielding was not near so good, and the whole of the game was not so well played as by Sussex. The turns in the game during the three days were extraordinary; and odds as high as 4 to 1 were betted. Altogether a finer match was never seen. It was supposed that £250 was taken at the doors in sixpences.

On the part of England, Mr Knight adopted the 'liberal system' as it is now called, and with much effect. However, this gentleman is not so extravagant in his manner as Broadbridge; who if he finds a man hitting his balls away, will, without hesitation, throw his arm and his hand as it were over his head, in other terms, shy at the wicket.

G. T. Knight, although from Kent, was a member of the East Sussex side which took on West Sussex at Broadwater Green in September 1827. Lillywhite played for East Sussex and Jem Broadbridge for the West. East Sussex won by 12 runs with, apparently, round-arm bowling being a main feature of the match. By now it was essential that the 'liberal system' have more than wickets and examples to prove its worth. The style was in search of an eloquent champion, and Mr Knight in three letters to *Sporting Magazine* demonstrated a mighty pen, which led eventually to the proposal before the MCC in 1828 to change the *Laws*, so allowing bowlers to raise their arms 'not higher than the shoulder'. In his first letter, Knight teased authority with the wisdom and guile of courtroom silk:

71

It is my intention, early next season, to propose to the Marylebone Club a law, which will afford to bowlers a larger field for the exertion of science than they now enjoy; and as this measure does not seem to be generally known to cricketers, either in its nature, the reasons which have given rise to it, or the benefits anticipated from its adoption, I should be glad to afford an explanation of these points through the medium of your valuable magazine. It may not be generally known that, from the earliest time of cricket, down to the very late period, *no law whatever existed to restrain the bowling.* From time immemorial the under-hand style alone was practised; for the best possible reason, namely, that it was found amply sufficient to meet the batting of those days. About twenty-four years ago, however, the system of batting suddenly underwent an almost total change, and was carried to a degree of perfection never before known. Instead of the cautious defence hitherto practised, with one foot always within the crease, the method then introduced was running in at the ball, hard hitting, and a bold forward play, which altogether changed the nature of that part of the game. The effect of this was that the number of runs increased greatly; matches, from requiring more time, and consequently more expense, soon became much less frequent than they had been before; and thus, from the single circumstance of the batting having got the start of the bowling, cricket, in some measure, began to decline. The superiority of the batting to the bowling, with the bad effects above mentioned, has been for years a theme of universal complaint and has never been checked, except when it has been met by the straight-armed bowling (erroneously called throwing), which it is my wish to restore.

And so the forcing style of batsmen, especially Hammond of Sussex, to go out and meet the bowling, particularly the slow lobbers, was the catalyst of the new method. How appropriate, then, that its proponents were men of Sussex and the most famous trial, if that is what it was in 1827, should have taken place against the Sussex side. And bowling now a science, says Knight. A science! How the pseudo-bards by pavilion's veranda bristled at lip and chop and shuddered.

Soliloquy by an Old Cricketer

Gone are the days, the merry days of youth,
When I with others through the island ranged;
But cricket's altered, and the game, forsooth,
Barring the name is altogether changed.
Full well I prize the oft repeated truth,

'This is the age for science making way';
But why at cricket men should be so ruth
I can't make out. Farewell! it's had its day.

Bless me! How altered since those days of yore
When Bird and Beldham, Budd, and such as they –
Lord Frederick, too, once England's chief and flower –
Astonished all who came to see them play;
When in the field turned out, they looked like men
Fit for great deeds, and by true play were tried.
The ball was bowled, no slingy, round stuff then –
'Tis all up now – the game's transmogrified.

It certainly was not all up then. English cricket was wending its way towards formal county organisation, although the first of the First-Class Counties, as they became known, Sussex, was going through a dismal patch. G. T. Knight had championed the new style of bowling as a means of taking on the more aggressive attitude of modern batsmen. Sussex may have wondered at his claim of dominance for clubbers of ball. Time and again, games crumbled for the southern county. One event at Lord's against England illuminated the difficulty lived with by Sussex for a decade to come. On 7 and 8 July, Sussex, with Lillywhite, both Broadbridges, George Brown and Pierpoint, were beaten by ten wickets. The two sides met again that month, at Brighton; England won by 96 runs. In August, Kent beat Sussex by 33 runs at The Vine. When the return match was played at Brighton, Sussex had the old enemy on the run; they knocked up 118 in the first innings and 102 in the second. Kent could manage no more than a miserable 23 in their first innings. Surely victory was Sussex's. No. The game is recorded as unfinished.

The match at The Vine was notable for the first appearance of Tom Box. He was then about nineteen and opened the batting with Slater, got a single in the first and nothing in the second innings. His name did not appear again on scoresheets for Sussex until 1832, but his name was to become one of the most famous in Victorian Sussex cricket.

Like many an old cricketer, Tom Box was a craftsman. He had been apprenticed to a cabinet-maker, and the patience, deftness and sure and close eye of one whose skill will mark him out stood Tom Box well in the game. For Box was a wicket-keeper above most. A safe pair of hands, they said. In a nineteenth-century engraving, Box

73

is seen standing close by and to the off side of his stumps, loosely trousered, cuffed and with white top-hat set square and low at his brow above large and soft smiling eyes. Trower recorded him as almost the perfect wicket-keeper.

> He for some time kept the Egremont Hotel, at Brighton, and after experiencing, I fear, some vicissitudes of fortune, and pecuniary anxieties, became ground-keeper at Prince's. In his prime he was unsurpassable, even if he was ever equalled, behind the wicket. Wenman, Herbert Jenner, and Lockyer, have, of course, their admirers, and it may be a moot point, which of their styles was most to be commended. There can be, however, no doubt of this, that he rendered Sussex infinite service in filling, well nigh to perfection, a post which, if insufficiently represented, must make the best eleven worthless. Smart, trim, and dapper, almost to a fault, in his dress and manner, with cheery smile, nerve and coolness which nothing could intimidate, a faultless action, and a 'return' as quick as lightning, it was the greatest treat to watch the ease and dash with which he managed that difficult post in a first-class match. He had none of that elaborate posture which modern [1870s] wicket-keepers seem so fond of cultivating – an exaggerated and extravagant action – but there was an inexpressible grace in the ease and quietness with which he would 'take' the most awkward balls, sometimes even from Brown. Highly gifted as he doubtlessly was by nature for the difficult task, he was fortunate in having to 'keep' to two such men as Lillywhite and Broadbridge, for their balls were a medium pace, rose well, and were easy to 'take'. This soon perfected his talent, and gave him the very best opportunity for exhibiting it to advantage. It was a long time, however, before he could do anything with the bat, and it was not until 1837 that he ever got a large score; after that he improved rapidly, and was for many years among the foremost bats in his county, or indeed, in England.

Tom Box was pure Sussex and played for the county for more than thirty years, keeping wicket, it is said, without gloves and pads. Later in life he ran the Brunswick Hotel and had the cricket ground there until it was assigned to the county club in 1863. In 1876 Tom Box, no longer a player, was watching Sussex when he suddenly collapsed and died.

The 1830s were preparatory years for the formation of Sussex as a First-Class County towards the end of the decade. George Brown, who had kept himself busy by bowling faster than any man, fathering eighteen children and running a tailoring business, took over the Royal Brighton Ground in 1831. There were some fine games with big crowds. In June the following year, England beat Sussex by five wickets at Lord's. The next month the two sides played at Brighton, and Sussex took sweet revenge by five wickets with Lillywhite bowling seven of the England side including Harenc and Kynaston in both innings. But, in spite of this win, Sussex were once again travelling a dull and run-dry road with extras showing on some scorecards as the leading run-maker. But people gathered in their thousands still to watch cricket by the sea. It was, as George Brown advertised, a 'Grand Match of Cricket'. The clothes of fairground barker would have fitted Mr Brown as he cajoled and enticed all to witness contests at his ground. Typical was a notice he posted in July 1839 for a game against Kent:

> G. Brown respectfully informs the Public that the above Match, in which are included the names of players of the greatest celebrity in the Kingdom, will come off on his Grounds on Monday next, July 1, 1839, and following day

Sussex	Kent
C. Taylor Esq.	A. Mynn Esq.
G. Langdon Esq.	W. Mynn Esq.
– Lillywhite	– Felix Esq
– Box	T. Selby Esq.
– Hodson	– Whittaker Esq.
– Millyard	Pilch
– Hawkins	Wenman
– Dean	Adams
R. Picknell	Hillier
– Ewen	Dorrington
– Wells	Clifford

> London Umpires, Bailey and Sewell

> Admission to Non-Subscribers 6d. each. No Return Cheques after Four o'Clock.
> A Good Ordinary in the Saloon at 2 o'Clock, at 2s.6d. each

> A Public Ball

> On the above Evening. – Doors open at Nine o'Clock –
> Admission One Shilling

This was the year of Sussex County Cricket Club, and the names on George Brown's poster were fine indeed. Taylor and Langdon were members of the original club committee, as may have been the number eleven, Wells. Mr Langdon was the Reverend Langdon, the club's first secretary. Jem Dean played for years, a chunky all-rounder. Picknell was one of the many Sussex cricketing brothers throughout the years. George Millyard played for a score of years. Along with the Lillywhites, they were there at the beginning of the official club, which boasted a grand pedigree. For when the County Club was formed, as has been told, cricket lineage in Sussex already stretched across two centuries.

Chapter 8

There has been much argument and contention about the origins of first-class county cricket. Who was first? Who was the original side? Norfolk, from whence came great players such as Fuller Pilch, rightfully claim early county status. Kent, proud as its rearing white horse, played as a county in the earliest cricketing times. And what of stern Yorkshire, spreading news of bat, ball, catch and throw from the prosperous city of Sheffield? Of quiet, wooded Hampshire and its Hambledon men? Surrey, and its Royal Grammar School in sixteenth-century Guldeford? Middlesex, where homage was paid to the hallowed layings and rollings of Thomas Lord and the noble patrons tired of coffee house and cellar?

Cricket emerged from the basic idea that man could throw and hit in contest with others, and skills vulnerable to chance would produce champions and style to such a standard as to result in money being set in wager to thrill and delight. String-tied trousered workman would come to play alongside, and for, buckled and silk-legged nobleman. Cricket slipped easily from pastime to contest, so that village played hamlet, and duke vied with earl until pride of origin led to challenges between those naturally divided by hill, wood, river, town and dialect. The broadest border in English society cordoned the rivalries and boasts so that loyalty to county, above all, met the claims and needs of the widest contest. County cricket was born, but, as historian Eric Parker remarked, organisation of enthusiasm, spirit and venture was all:

It was not only the fast bowlers and the big hitters who made name of this or that place famous among cricketers. It was the men who helped with money. It was men like the Duke of Dorset, the Earl of Winchilsea, the Prince of Wales – the patrons of the game, who put up money to be played for in the days when money meant much, being limited to the few, and when betting was popular because it seemed a chance of getting cash. From the very beginning it was plain that money was needed to make the game go. Grounds were needed on which the game could be played, and grounds need money to be kept in order. Players were needed to make sides, and it was not every man who could spare time from work. Meals were needed, bread and beef and beer, and somebody had to pay for them. And so with the rich men paying – and playing the game themselves, too, like the Duke of Dorset and Sir Horace Mann – county after county gradually stood apart.

The first to do so was named the Royal Sussex Cricket Club, its title reflecting more than twenty years of regal patronage. Sussex was quickly followed by Kent, born during the festival of cricket, Canterbury Week, and then came Surrey. Nottingham followed many years later in 1859, Yorkshire three years after that in 1862, Hampshire in 1863, Middlesex and Lancashire in 1864. However, county sides were not simply established over a glass and a whim. The long history of cricket in the county amounted to the Sussex club's period of gestation. The grounds, the organisation and, above all, the inherited enthusiasm of the people were drawn to the spirit that settled into the mould of county cricket. But there came a time when all the years of playing and the sense of time and loyalty had to be structured; this started in Sussex in or about 1836.

Interestingly, the hopes of those who brought about the formal existence of the first First-Class County were never jumbled by a flurry of matches and challenges. Indeed, in the 1830s there had been relatively little county-level cricket, though it had been played further afield than ever before. The usual round of Sussex and England at either Brighton or Lord's and Kent across the eastern border was enlivened by the first official county meeting between Sussex and Yorkshire at Sheffield, in September 1835, and the previous month intriguing games against Nottinghamshire. At Brighton, Nottingham, thanks mainly to the bowling of Barker and Redgate, dismissed Sussex for 94 and 65 and won by two wickets. For the return game, Sussex went north to the Forest Ground to play on 7 and 9 September for fifty guineas a side. William Howitt was there, and paints a glorious

78

picture of carnival, fairground and open-mouthed glee at what took place:

On Sunday morning early, we saw a crowd going up the street, and immediately perceived that, in the centre of it, were the Sussex cricketers, just arrived by the London coach, and going to an inn kept by one of the Nottingham players. They looked exceedingly interesting, being a very fine set of fellows, and with their white hats and with all their trunks, carpet-bags, and cloaks, coming, as we verily believed, to be beaten. Our interest was strongly excited; and on Monday morning we set off to the cricket-ground, which lies about a mile from the town, in the Forest, as it is still called, though not a tree is left upon it – a long, furzy common, crowned at the top by about twenty wind-mills, and descending in a steep slope to a fine level, round which the race-course runs. Within the race-course lies the cricket-ground, which was enclosed at each end with booths; and all up the forest-hill were scattered booths, and tents with flags flying, fires burning, pots boiling, ale-barrels standing, and asses, carts and people bringing still more good things. There were plenty of apple and ginger-beer stalls; and lads going round with nuts and with waggish looks, crying – 'nuts, lads! nuts, lads!' In little hollows the nine-pin, and will-peg men had fixed themselves to occupy loiterers; and, in short, there was all the appearance of a fair.

Standing at the farther side of the cricket-ground, it gave me the most vivid idea possible, of an amphitheatre filled with people. In fact, it was an amphitheatre. Along each side of the ground ran a bank sloping down to it, and it, and the booths, and the tents at the ends were occupied with a dense mass of people, all as silent as the ground beneath them; and all up the hill were groups, and on the race-stand an eager, forward-leaning throng. There were said to be twenty thousand people, all hushed as death, except when some exploit of the players produced a thunder of applause. The playing was beautiful. Mr. Ward, late Member of Parliament for London, a great cricket-player, came from the Isle of Wight to see the game, and declared himself highly delighted. But nothing was so beautiful as the sudden shout, the rush, and breaking up of the crowd, when the last decisive notch was gained. To see the scorers suddenly snatch up their chairs, and run off with them towards the players' tent; to see the bat of Bart Goode, the batsman on whom the fate of the game depended, spinning in the air, where he had sent it in ecstasy of the moment; and the crowd that the instant before was fixed and silent as the world itself, spreading all over the green space where the white figures of the players had till then been so gravely and apparently calmly contending

– spreading with a murmur as of the sea; and over their heads, amid the deafening clamour and confusion, the carrier-pigeon with a ribbon tied to its tail, the signal of loss, beating round and round so as to ascertain its precise position, and then flying off to bear the tidings to Brighton – it was a beautiful sight, and one that the most sedate person must have delighted to see.

The ribboned pigeon must have flown many times to Brighton during those 1830s with sad, rarely joyful tidings, for the Sussex side were not so grand as had been known. Yet indifference of fortune did not stop the roadmen of Sussex cricket's future from fixing the signposts of formal county standing in the downs, deep-cuts and lanes.

There seems to have been no great outside pressure to form an official county side; more likely the impetus came from within. The long rivalry of east and west had something to do with it, and the jealousy of favoured, fashionable and influential town was also relevant. The so-called Sussex team had for years been picked from Brighton and Midhurst. Yet the whole county had strong sides. Cricket was very much alive and full of talent in the old villages and small towns. Records show mighty games and enthusiasm at Lewes, Duncton, Goodwood, Arundel, Bexhill, Hastings, Henfield, Slindon and Storrington, North Chapel, Firle, Eastbourne, Hurstpierpoint, Horsham, Shillinglee, Uckfield and Ifield, Lindfield and Petworth. As communications became easier, so recognition and say were demanded. No longer could the gentlemen and players of the Prince's town be assumed the rightful minders of the county's cricketing reputation. Even in Brighton itself there was faction, debate and side.

George Brown had taken over the commercial running of the Prince of Wales Ground, later Ireland's Gardens, in 1833. The importance of this field is remembered by the fact that all the major matches were played there, including the famous round-arm trials of 1827. In 1834 another ground was set out on what is now Montpellier Crescent. It was known as Lee's Trap Ground, after the lessee. In or around 1835, William Lillywhite became landlord of the Royal Sovereign Inn in Preston Street and took over Lee's Trap, whereupon it became Temple Fields.

Lillywhite was immensely popular and there was a certain rivalry as to which site should be the home of first-class cricket. Another need for structured representation – the inference being that Lillywhite's supporters felt that he and they should be the guardians of Sussex county cricket. The mood between opposing camps can only be guessed, but

80

conflict of any sort is often the catalyst towards consolidation and, it is to be hoped, financial strength.

The need to fund was not lost on George Brown and his supporters. An advertisement was placed in the *Brighton Gazette* on 16 June 1836 which appealed to a sense of Brighton patriotism as well as to the good people's pockets.

Cricket

Fellow Townsmen – the undermentioned gentlemen, being anxious to establish in the Town of Brighton a 'Cricketing fund' to be supported by voluntary subscription under the superintendence of a Committee to be chosen by subscribers, I beg respectfully to solicit your attendance at a Meeting to be held at the Town Hall for that purpose on Friday next June 17th at 11 o'clock in the forenoon.

Your Fellow Townsman,
Your Obedient Servant,
George Brown
Hanover Arms Inn

John Ade Esq., High Constable
H. Everitt Esq.
J. Smith Windham Esq.
Richard Heaviside Esq.
Montague David Scott Esq.
F. Allen Esq.
John O'Reilly Esq.
– Horton Esq.
Captain Freeman
Captain Fitzpatrick
R. Tamplin and Son
W. Catt, Bishopstone
W. Catt, Jun.

The name of Lillywhite was not appended as an undermentioned gentleman. The signatures of Ade, the High Constable, and Tamplin, the brewer, gave seal and impression to the notion that this was the sound and blessed faction for the rightful government of the Sussex game. And a sense of the importance of the meeting might be noted from the fact that it was held not in the snug at Brown's Hanover Arms, but in the Brighton Town Hall. The *Gazette*, with full seriousness of responsibility and recognising aldermanic issue above all matters, noted:

81

We have much pleasure in referring our readers to an advertisement in another part of the paper under the heading of 'Cricket' by which it will be perceived that a meeting is to be held tomorrow at the Town Hall with a view to establishing a Cricketing Fund. We have frequently pointed out the advantages resulting from cricket matches; and we hereby wish success to the project.

The following week, the newspaper noted that the gathering in the Town Hall had met with success and had resolved that 'it would contribute greatly to the benefit of the town and to the amusement of the visitors and inhabitants if a Cricketing Fund for making matches were established – to be called the Sussex Cricketing Fund'. Immediately, the Lord Lieutenant of the county, Lord Egremont, offered financial support, whereupon his lordship was offered the patronage of the venture. No dawdler he, Lord Egremont accepted. On 31 August 1836, a club was formed; funds raised included a generous donation from the King. That money was acknowledged in an announcement in *The Times* and the *Brighton Gazette* the following year, 1837:

We have just had communicated to us another instance of His Majesty's liberality in promoting all establishments for the amusements and benefit of this town and county. It is generally known that a Sussex Cricket Club was, at the close of last season, established for the purpose of raising a fund by subscription, to be expended in playing County Matches, and His Majesty has been graciously pleased to submit through Sir Henry Wheatley the sum of Twenty Pounds towards the undertaking, with a strong expression of His Majesty's desire to encourage the manly exercise of cricket as a game which so peculiarly belongs to this county.

However, the setting up of a county cricket club was still a way off. Cricket sits easily in nature's cycle, and its closed season of rain and frosts dulls urgency and the need for decision, as any village will testify. So perhaps it gives little surprise that it was not until the closing games of 1838 that the final steps were taken to form the club that would become the first of seventeen. The energies for this action were found in one George Langdon.

Langdon was a young man at the time, still in his twentieth year. He was a man of patience, learning and vocation; indeed, he was one of the far from rare breed of cricketing clerics. He took holy orders when he was twenty-four and left what had the makings of a fine career with bat and ball to become a parish parson, eventually moving across the border to be vicar of St Paul's Cray, a village by the main London road to Maidstone. He was a strong left-handed bat and was said to have been an aggressive stroke-maker for Sussex and in the Gentlemen *v* Players matches. Langdon took on the duties of the new club's secretary. W. Scott Stonehewer was treasurer, and William Catt, a member of the committee of the 1836 Cricketing Fund, sub-treasurer. A committee of sixteen was formed. It was a group which reflected the politics of the county's cricketing, with ten at the table representing Brighton and district and six speaking for the interests of the outlying clubs. At its head was the Earl of Winterton, attended by W. Barchard, H. Borrer, G. Campion, H. Everitt, C. Goring, G. Hill, W. Ladbroke, G. L. Langdon, B. Mostyn, E. Sayers, W. Scott Stonehewer, Bright Smith, J. Strange, C. G. Taylor and H. Wells.

It was a club which intended to gather the finances for a game that could exist no longer on the patronage of one person, however noble of birth and pocket, and to unite the talents in the Sussex villages to play as a true county side. In a style similar to late twentieth-century mail canvassing, one of the first letters of the new secretary expressed the following sentiments:

Sir,
The members of the newly-instituted Cricket Club request the honour of proposing you as a member at their next meeting. Should you feel inclined to give them your support, it will greatly promote the interest of cricket in the county; inasmuch as it will form a fund for making matches, and be means of selecting and bringing together able cricketers from every part of the County. An early answer will oblige.

Your humble Servant,
George L. Langdon
(Secretary)

Collingwood House
Brighton

Langdon's energies were little wasted. The heads bent together in the drawing up of plans and ideas, and of course the rules of constitution and management for the new club.

1. There shall be two classes of members, viz. County members and Non-County Members; the former to pay two guineas annual subscription, and the latter one guinea annual subscription.
2. The Club shall engage one or two to bowl, for two or more days in the week, for practice.

3. A match shall be played every Monday in the season, if possible, among Members of the Club.
4. Persons residing on the spot shall be elected as Secretary and Treasurer who, with committee, shall manage the affairs of the Club.
5. All new Members shall be elected by ballot.
6. The Treasurer to have a book, wherein he shall enter the names of all persons subscribing for the support of matches made. These subscriptions to be voluntary, and not restricted to the Members of the Club.
7. All persons subscribing to the amount of one guinea for the support of Matches made (although not Members of the Club) shall be admitted free of expenses to see the play.
8. In all matters to be arranged by the committee three shall be a quorum.

The response to Langdon's membership circular among the gentlemen of the county was an undoubted success and by the late winter of 1839 the first pre-season dinner of the Club was arranged, to which of course the new member was invited:

Sir,
I beg to inform you that you have been unanimously elected a member of the Sussex Cricket Club.
The members of the Club will dine together at the York Hotel on Tuesday the 2nd of April, at six o'clock precisely, on which occasion your attendance is most earnestly requested. An early answer, signifying your intention, will oblige.

Collingwood House
Brighton
1st March 1839

Your humble Servant,
George L. Langdon
(Secretary)

The *Brighton Gazette* reported the dinner in its Thursday edition.

In the absence of The Marquis of Exeter, the chair was filled by Mr W. Scott Stonehewer, and there was a good attendance of members. The dinner went off with much eclat and many excellent speeches were delivered. All present appeared exceedingly gratified at the encouraging prospects of the ensuing season. We hail with pleasure the formation of a club on so respectable a footing for the promotion of this truly English game. It has long been a desideration of the town, for although in the winter season there is no lack of amusements, yet in the summer we have heard it complained that the public amusements were not sufficiently

84

attended to. The support from the nobility and gentry of the county must ensure success. Nearly £150 is at present in the hands of the Committee, and it is hoped by the assistance of subscriptions from the town and county generally, the club will not only be enabled to bring the whole strength of the county against Hampshire, Kent, Marylebone, etc., but that our old opponents of Nottingham may this year have another opportunity of retrieving the lost laurels of the north.

Thus Sussex began the 1839 season as the first First-Class County in England. It was a time for example and rejoicing, but not for winning. So, the first shall be last; Sussex, it is sad to record, played five county matches that year and lost them all.

Chapter 9

Perhaps beaming still with the glow of good crack and tuck at Pegg's Royal York Hotel that evening in April 1839, the sports writer of the *Brighton Guardian* was at his most optimistic when declaring fortune set fair for the coming season of the new club:

> Never was Sussex in better cricketing condition than at the present moment. The Sussex Cricket Club, although in its infancy, bids fair to produce some excellent players. At the head of these is C. Taylor Esq., who is decidedly the best amateur player in England . . .

Certainly the players mentioned in the newspaper's hopes for the season were of splendid standing. They inherited lot and mantle of a century of Sussex cricket and when selection was made for Gentlemen and Players, their names crammed bills and scoresheets of famous games for the first half of the nineteenth century. Many today speak of those who came after – Murdoch, Ranji, Fry, Tate, Gilligan, Langridge, the Parkses, Doggart, Bartlett, Cox young and old, Marlar, Sheppard, Dexter, and on to today's Imran and Parker – yet the earliest players had grace and power that can be inferred from scores and an understanding of fashion and fortune of those years when truly Royal Sussex Cricket, down in the dumps, may not have survived. So who were these few men with fewer equals in their time?

C. G. Taylor was rightfully described as the best amateur in England. Charles Taylor was born in November 1817, not in Sussex but in

Middlesex. He played for Eton and when he went up to Cambridge he gained a reputation for being almost unbeatable at any ball game; the more difficult conditions appeared to amuse the young man. Taylor thought almost anything possible, given a sporting chance. It is said that he once took on a bet that he could not make a pair of trousers for himself. He won handsomely and appeared in his home-made 'bags' striding along King's Parade, the most to-be-seen-in thoroughfare in Cambridge. Another time he declared piano playing an innocent but simple pastime; he wagered that he could learn to play and sing in six weeks. So he did.

Taylor could not have claimed his superb sporting eye as patron of his musical achievement, unless he counted sight reading (although it may have been an advantage for close stitchwork when trouser making), but surely it was his celebrated eyesight that presented him with great speed and agility in ball games. If a ball needed hitting, then C. G. Taylor had little thought but that it could and should be struck, with whatever came to hand. He once accepted a challenge to give up his racket and play singles tennis using a ginger-pop bottle while his opponent made do with the traditional and more conventional gut-strung instrument. Taylor did not win, his opponent, a Mr Broughton, being something of an expert at the game and determined not to look foolish in front of the young crowd gathered to watch the fun. But it was apparently a close-run thing.

Taylor was everything one might imagine the young amateur to be. Thanks to the fortune of Harrington, his maternal grandfather, he was comfortably off, carefree, effortless in almost everything he did, and of course physically gifted. Trower described him as one 'whose every movement was graceful, and who, for several years, was uppermost on everyone's lips! . . . he was the gentleman cricketer all over. His clear, brown, full, bright eye, slim, upright and well-knit figure, are still before us all.'

> His figure and face, for beauty and grace,
> To the best in the county had scorn'd to give place.

Alfred Taylor wrote of him:

> Apart from his incomparable batsmanship, he was one of the most brilliant fieldsmen of his time, and a bowler with a 'devil of a twist', to use Nyren's phrase. Pilch used to declare his balls hopped all over the shop like a flea in a bed . . . It was at Eton

where he first acquired the rudiments of the game, and Cambridge where it was developed to perfection. He assisted Sussex from 1837 until 1854, though he did not play regularly after 1846, being compelled to abandon the game in his twenty-ninth year for the more serious paths of life. Like Fuller Pilch, he was once dismissed by the unusual entry 'Hat knocked on wicket'. It was he who registered the first individual century ever scored on behalf of the Sussex Club, to wit: 100 not out, *v* MCC, Brighton, 1844.

And what of George Picknell, almost forgotten by this day? He was born in the eastern part of the county, in Chalvington, in November 1813, a young man in that first great season of 1839. He was sturdy and strong with the arms of a farmer used to swinging and stroking, tossing and fetching. He had a reputation for being slow and sometimes lumpkin-like in the field, but his strong grip on bat and ball and his loose shoulders gave him strength and swing which he put to good use. He was a very quick bowler, round-arm; but, said Taylor, 'he had a peculiar habit of delivering the ball close to his ear'. He was not the foremost bowler in the country by some chalk, but he was what was later known as a good trundler, accurate and containing and the bogy of many a batsman able to cope with more illustrious figures.

Picknell, like the rest of his family (father and six sons), was a good all-rounder. Many a day saw him wielding his bat with powerful smites throughout an innings during his twenty years for Sussex. His life came to an end in his fiftieth year. As a young man he had suffered sore injury to a leg; the decision was taken to amputate. What went wrong is uncertain, but in the winter of 1863 Picknell died and was buried in the churchyard at Chalvington.

Also in that early group of players was Edwin Napper, like his brothers a left-handed bat and right-arm bowler. And there was Hodson – James Hodson, whose mill in its earlier days was moved across Brighton town by eighty-four oxen. He first played for the club in 1838, and in the first official county match in 1839 against the MCC took eight wickets in the first innings. A. J. Gaston recorded in the nineteenth century that Hodson and Hawkins started playing for Sussex the year after Taylor. Hodson he described as a useful man . . .

> . . . being a good field, especially at short slip, a fair bat, and an excellent bowler. Unfortunately for him, upon the occasion of his first appearance at Lord's, Caldecourt, who was one of the

umpires, was seized with a fit of virtuous indignation, and called him, though he was not really bowling higher than many who were allowed to fire away unchecked. In trying to get his arm down he somewhat injured his bowling, but it was nevertheless of the first class, and wanted nothing but a certain steadiness which none but professional bowlers who are always at work ever attain. His brother colt, Hawkins, was indeed a wonder while his career lasted, and had he been as steady in private life as most of his compeers, he would probably have been for years the finest bat in England. He died before he had nearly reached his zenith, and in him Sussex cricket sustained an irreparable loss, for he was not only strong in defence, but one of the finest, most brilliant hitters ever seen. His action was quite unlike that of anyone else. He took guard within two inches of the wicket, and then, as the bowler was running up to deliver the ball, advanced his right leg up to the crease and brought his left foot more or less in front of the crease, so that he met the ball in playing forward or hitting with the full weight of his body, and his hits were tremendous. He had the habit of going through eleven different actions while preparing to play each ball, pulling up his trousers, pulling on his hat, etc., and never omitted one of them.

There was Millyard, described once as a 'good general player, not very successful with the bat, but an excellent change bowler, and a wonderful field'. Barton was said to be the first gentleman of note that the county had seen for some years. He was swift in the field, especially at cover point, and had a darting throw that was as accurate as it was sharp. Gaston describes him as 'a first-rate bat in point of style, and won more than one match for his county by contributing 30 or 40 runs at a critical moment, though from over anxiety he seldom did himself full justice in a match'.

In all, sixteen men played for the new county side in that first year: James Taylor, C. G. Taylor, G. L. Langdon, E. Napper, C. Hawkins, G. Pescott, G. Daniels, G. Millyard, T. Box, M. Ewen, G. Barton, R. Picknell, F. Wells, J. Dean, A. Mynn and W. Lillywhite. Of course, Lillywhite.

For decades there would always be a Lillywhite in Sussex cricket, from F.W. to James the younger who finished his career in 1882 – nigh on sixty years of county cricket between five of the same family. The bowling of Old Lilly, (F.W. that was William Lillywhite) has been remarked on earlier. In the county's first season, a less than splendid playing year for Sussex, he was, at forty-seven, far from a youngster to be bowling over after over. Yet he took at least thirty-three wickets in the five first-class matches of the season – at least, because the account of eleven of the wickets is vague. Thirty-three was more than twice as many as the next-best Sussex bowler, James Dean (Jem Broadbridge having given up the game). And he was sixth out of sixteen in the batting averages.

Old Lilly had three sons, James, John and Fred. James, the eldest son, was born in 1824 two years after his father moved from Goodwood to the Brighton area. He was a medium-pace bowler and middle-order batsman, but was never considered to be in the same class as his father, although he played for Sussex and for Middlesex. But as a teacher of the game he was said to be outstanding. He coached at the public schools including Westminster and Eton and at Cambridge and Essex. He saw out his days coaching at Cheltenham and promoting what became the Cheltenham Cricket Week with the Gloucestershire County Club.

John Lillywhite, the middle brother, was a born cricketer. Alfred D. Taylor remembers:

> He did nothing but play the game all his lifetime. For over twenty years he did duty for Sussex, and with bat and ball achieved great distinction on the 'tented field'. Considering that he suffered somewhat from defective vision, his numerous successes in the field must be recorded as marvellous – there was no better cover point than John in his day, and certainly no cricketer, whether amateur or professional, who possessed greater knowledge of the game . . . Playing for Sussex against Kent, in 1856, he played a superb innings of 138, and the following year claimed 118 not out against the same county. John Lillywhite – who from his remarkable success with the leather on wet wickets, was better known as the 'mud bowler' – seemed very partial to the Men of Kent, for in 1855 we find him credited with fourteen victims for 97 runs. The same year he was credited with seven Surrey wickets for 28, and in the return fixture claimed six for 18 only.

By modern standards these figures may not appear remarkable. But, in the early days of first-class county cricket, wickets, bowling and batting styles did not encourage the fabulous scores that were to become seemingly commonplace with the arrival of better wickets and the Old Man, W. G. Grace. John Lillywhite, remember, was the son of one of the two against whom England players had refused to play in 1827 because of their round-arm style. It was he who continued the Sussex and Lillywhite connection with the controversial style of attack. By the 1860s John Lillywhite had taken to umpiring and found himself

91

caught up in the throwing dispute that had its origins in the previous century. An account of the matter, and a reminder that at that time round rather than over was still the way of the day, is contained in a history of the MCC:

> During the Surrey *v* England match at The Oval in 1862 Willsher was no-balled six times in succession by John Lillywhite, son of the ancient rebel, for his hand being above his shoulder. This led to an alteration on 10th June 1864, in Law X, respecting the height of the bowler's hand, when, on the proposition of Mr. C. J. B. Marsham, seconded by Mr. Perkins, the following became law: 'The ball must be bowled; if thrown or jerked, the umpire must call no-ball.'

The Hastings historian and Sussex batsman Arthur Haygarth wrote shortly after the decision, which as the wording suggested, was clearly a fudge:

> This new rule would never have passed or found favour, with any having the slightest pretensions to knowledge of the 'noble science', only it was found impossible to obtain umpires (not only at Lord's, but all over the country) who would, could, or 'dared' impartially carry out the law as it existed previously, from 1827 to the end of 1863.

And so the Sussex Lillywhite family had seen the issue, if not to its conclusion, through its development to overarm bowling.

The third son was Fred; and in some ways, although he was never a cricketer of note, his lasting contribution to the game was as great as that of the rest of the family. Fred was the game's statistical chronicler, the Frindal of his day. It was he who produced the grand volumes entitled *Cricket Scores and Biographies*, which, given the ever difficult task of verifying dates, scores and statistics of the period, became invaluable to cricket historians. He also printed scorecards at matches and could be seen in his tent offering every two hours for a few pence the up-to-date detail of the game. And at Lord's Fred Lillywhite is particularly remembered for setting up the first printing press in that ground.

The three brothers, James, John and Fred, had a cousin, James Lillywhite, born three years after the formation of the County Club and set to become one of its most famous players. Born in West Hampnett, the origin of so many a Lillywhite, he first appeared for

Sussex in 1862 and continued, so it is said, to play for twenty years without missing a game. Taylor's opinion is that James Lillywhite 'probably did more, by his individual efforts, to popularise the game in Sussex than any other professional cricketer since the days of his immortal uncle'. He batted and bowled left handed and arm and was described variously as quick or medium. Whatever his speed, he was powerfully accurate. During a game against the MCC at Lord's on 16 and 17 June 1862, James Lillywhite Jnr, as the scorecard described him, took fourteen wickets for 57 runs in 242 balls on what was said to have been a 'very heavy wicket'.

The great honour came for him in the winter of 1876–7 when he took an England eleven on tour to Australia. Eric Parker, in his *History of Cricket*, wrote: 'A team was taken out in the autumn of 1876 by James Lillywhite. Of the matches played, two take their place as the first worthy of the description "Test"; they are the first which were played on level terms.' And so Sussex was not only the original First-Class County, but also provided the first England captain of an England Test side.

The Lord's game against the MCC in which Lillywhite got his fourteen wickets was notable for two other important names in Sussex history: Stubberfield and Wisden. Old Stubber, more correctly Henry Stubberfield of Brighton, once a carpenter and joiner, then a tobacconist, took the other four wickets in that game with his fast round-arm. The second player, Wisden, is but vaguely remembered where cricket is talked as player. But none needs jogging to make reference and deference to that yellow-covered everlasting testament to his name.

Thomas Wisden was a builder who lived and worked from 15 Hampden Place, Brighton; it was there that on 5 September 1826 his son John was born. He became apprenticed to his father, but when Thomas died his son broke his indentures and took up as living-in pot-boy in a large pub. The lessee of the inn, the Hanover Arms, was Tom Box. It might be guessed that Box, a local as well as a national figure, caught the imagination of the young Wisden who, in spite of his almost diminutive size ('scarcely five feet tall' according to Marshall), showed a ready eye for the game. His ability as a bowler was without doubt, even though he was small and weighed little more than seven stone. He quickly learned the art of bowling and the frailties of batsmen by offering himself as fielder in F. W. Lillywhite's cricket ground on the hill which became Montpellier Crescent, mentioned earlier. Would-be batsmen would attend the court of Lillywhite, to be bowled at for fun or serious practice. In those days there were no such luxuries as nets, so lads were employed as long-stops. Wisden picked up his pocket money and knowledge of the game from boundary's edge, a hungry-looking lad, glad as C. F. Trower remembered 'of one's sixpence for his trouble'.

In later years Wisden proved that his knowledge of wicket-taking was matched only by his understanding of that more intricate science, money-making. But that was to come; first his name as a cricketer was to be secured. Alfred Taylor, noticing the influence of Box, recorded:

> Having submitted himself to the advice and guidance of that worthy [Box], his latent abilities and keen enthusiasm did the rest, and he quickly became the finest all-round recognised fast bowler of his day, and certainly the finest all-round cricketer Brighton has yet produced.

A year after he went to live with Box, Wisden, then barely eighteen, made his first appearance for Sussex; by the time he was established in the side, Sussex had once more become a team to be reckoned with. But, in what should have been a grand year of celebration, 1839 for Sussex was less than cork-popping.

The first game was not a count affair, but a three-day match between Brighton and Chalvington. Let no one scoff at this meeting. The Brighton side was once again a goodish county eleven with Lillywhite getting 79 runs and bowling five of Chalvington's batsmen. George Brown was in the Brighton side, so was Tom Box, who took three catches, and Langdon and young H. G. G. Duff who played for Harrow that year. Chalvington was hardly smocked and straw-chewing, either. Fuller Pilch played for them and was said never to have bowled better. Pilch also took 114 runs off the Brighton side which included 'some of the best bowling in England' in the second innings until he was bowled by Lillywhite. The game ran its full three days before a crowd of about a thousand. Brighton got home with just two wickets to spare, thanks to a steady innings from Langdon.

When the first of the official county matches for the season started, the difficulties in the game against Chalvington and the omens set for the future were at hand. The game, against the MCC, was not at Brighton but at Lord's on 10 and 11 June. Sussex suffered a series of disasters. Only William Lillywhite made double figures in the first innings. Hodson, though, took eight MCC wickets in their first innings, but it was in this game that he was continually no-balled by umpire Caldecourt in MCC's second. Sussex lost by seven wickets.

94

In August the team travelled to Fuller Pilch's ground in Malling to play the first game against the old enemy as a fully fledged county side. Lillywhite and Dean bowled well in the two innings, but Kent won by three wickets. As so often in those days, it was a low-scoring game with Sussex getting 86 in the first innings and 101 in the second and Kent 112 and then 77 for seven wickets – a reminder of the esteem in which Pilch's 114 had been held earlier in the season.

The week after the Kent match, Sussex had a return game with Marylebone, this time at George Brown's ground in Brighton. Looking at the scorecard, for there is no match report yet discovered, it was a keenly fought contest. Hodson may have been out of sorts after his no-balling malady in the earlier game, for his name appears only as a batsman and without any mark. Marylebone played three Grimstons, including the Hon. Robert Grimston, who was described along with the Earl of Bessborough at Harrow School as 'famous cricketers, loyal Harrovians, blameless gentlemen' and as one who taught 'manliness and honour'. Unfortunately the Hon. Robert was bowled by Lillywhite for 1 in the first innings and 0 in the second. Again Lillywhite's guile was displayed, to the misery of fine batsmen including Bayley, Everett and Sewell. Alas, Lillywhite's thirteen wickets in the match, by far the best figures of the three days, could not turn the game for Sussex. Indeed, with but 5 runs needed to win, Lillywhite himself appears to have been bowled by Cobbett for a duck, and that was that, once more.

Back to Brighton and George Brown's ground in September for a very damp game against an England eleven. No covered pitches then, and a heavy autumn threatened. Sussex apparently found difficulty keeping their feet and finding their form. Lillywhite got 14 but the next-highest score, 11, was gathered from seven byes and four wides. England went in, this the first day still, and by the evening were 66 for 6. The next morning,Tuesday's heavens opened and ignored all pleas for clemency until Wednesday, just after noon. England finished on 152 and with a sloshy pitch it was more in determination than in hope perhaps that Sussex took to the field and, in fact, almost doubled their first-innings score. They were all out for 119. England won by six wickets. In terms of results it was a miserable first season, but cricketers are used to seven kinds of misery and there is always the next time. This certainly was the mood when the *Brighton Gazette* mulled over the season that late September 1839:

Our cricketing season is at length brought to a close, and must have afforded ample amusement even to the most ardent admirers

95

of the game. Could we record that the career of our county players during the year had been victorious, we should discuss the subject with more pleasure; but unfortunately we have only the recollection of successive defeats before us. This is not attributable, however, to any falling-off on the part of our players, but to the tide of ill-luck which set in against them at the beginning of the season, and has continued uninterruptedly to the end. Hawkins, Millyard and Lillywhite have displayed increased skill, and Mr Langdon has performed wonders. We hope and have reason to believe that the disposition evinced in the early part of the season to promote cricketing in this county is as strong as ever, and that the game will be liberally supported next year as it has been during the present season.

This optimistic and far from down-hearted column set the music for the end-of-season dinner at the Old Ship Hotel on the sea front. It was presided over by the hero of so much good company and pavilion good nature, old Benjamin Aislabie. A list of subscribers was made to offset the cost of next season's battles, and Aislabie, it was said, 'took occasion to say how sanguine were the hopes that Her Gracious Majesty would follow in the steps of her royal uncle, our late, amiable, kind-hearted King, in allowing her name to be inserted at the top of the list'. It is not recorded whether or not Her Gracious Majesty was as amiable and kind-hearted as her royal uncle, or if she was amused by the notion.

Business over, the last supper of the first season settled into reflection while 'many humorous songs were sung, some entertaining stories told, the company separated not long before the rosy-fingered goddess had illumined the celestial regions, very much delighted'. Should the scribe have been more reporter than bard, he might have taken the 'rosy-fingered goddess' at that dawn as an omen, for shepherds may have told him something of red skies in the morning and what they knew of times to come.

Chapter 10

Cricket does not simply go into decline with the drawing of a season's stumps. Enthusiasm for such a game, which by the 1840s was well established, remains among the few until some great event once again selects it as a spectacle for all; for the majority it is nothing more than that, and so the spectator, having watched and perhaps gasped in admiration, by and large passes to the next amusement. Thus it was for Sussex, where cricket was about to go into a long autumn and even a dreadful winter of apathy. The Prince was dead; long live the Queen – which of course she would, but not in Brighton and never with bat and ball in the wardrobe. The spectator was left with a changing Britain, and his heroes fought with valour but decreasing support.

Cricket's heroes outlive the matches they play. There is little reason why it should be different; that is the way of pastime and sport. Heroes and their deeds reflect the times in which they live. Batsman and bowler with long, unbroken years to notch and strike, to punch triumphantly at sweet air as another unfortunate's wicket tumbles, often mirror the level of stability in a county's or nation's fortunes. Two fine bowlers bowl for each other, to the batter's discomfort. Two opening batsmen, in commanding form together, make it hard for the bowler to get on top. And what of nation? There too, stability must be good fortune for sportsmen. Peoples at peace have the time and inclination to relax and tend the hopes and endeavours of county and more. How often war has called away great men from the middle, proved them where no proof was needed, and then forgotten to return them. Sussex cricket lived in relative peace during the

1840s and 1850s. The heroes were bold and recognised. Games were won, though they were few enough.

In 1840 Lillywhite, Box, Dean, Langdon, Taylor and Hawkins played for England or the MCC. Eighteen players turned out for the county, including Fuller Pilch as a given man against the England eleven, though he scored but 45 in his four innings. Lillywhite took more of the wickets and at the annual dinner reflected, according to one report, that he, 'like the dog with his tail in his mouth, had managed to make both ends meet'. Lillywhite had done well for himself and for cricket. He was again top of the bowling averages in 1841, taking twenty-four wickets in the four matches, including nine against the MCC in the August of that year at what was now known as Harvey's Ground, it having passed from the hands of George Brown. The following season was a higher-scoring year for Sussex, with five first-class matches, two with Kent, two with the MCC and another with England. Nearly 1000 runs were scored, which was a good tally considering the pitches and style of the 1840s; big scores by today's standards were rare. For example, Tom Box, the top scorer for Sussex, in ten innings made but 133 runs. The following year, 1843, Sussex batsmen scored a total of 1308 runs from six first-class games and not one player made a fifty. This was no sad Sussex performance – those outside the county did little more, sometimes much less. It was simply the norm of the day.

As may have been expected, Lillywhite was top of the averages with forty-six wickets: eight against the MCC in their first game and nine against them in their second; five and eleven in the two matches against Kent; nine against England and four against Nottinghamshire. It was to be his last full season for the county. The next opened against Kent. Lillywhite took twelve wickets and that was that. He was bowled out of puff. Twelve months later he played for the MCC at Lord's and took ten wickets, four in the first innings and six, all clean bowled, in the second. But, then, those toppled batsmen could expect nothing less in this tourney, for they knew Lillywhite well – the MCC were playing his old county, Sussex. By now, the county's bowling was dominated by James Dean and John Wisden.

It was Wisden who joined in business with Fred Lillywhite in the mid-1850s, perhaps 1856. John Lillywhite had opened a sports store in 1850 and taken into partnership his father and his two brothers, James and Frederick. But Frederick wished to follow his own commercial instincts. He broke away and was to become better-known for his *Cricket Scores and Biographies* and cricket-match reports with the scorecards he printed on the ground. But this was all to come.

The following season, 1844, Wisden and Dean picked up fifty-eight wickets between them in the usual games against England, the MCC and Kent. Scoring not forgotten, both were high enough in the batting averages. And it was in that year that two new names appeared in the Sussex dressing room. One was Sussex through and through, although born in Florence. Herbert Mascall Curteis learned his cricket at Winchester in the late 1830s and had his first game for the county at the age of twenty-three. He lived at Windmill Hill, and was one of the first to play on the newly opened lawn of Windmill Hill Place when it was marked out for twenty-two men in May 1850. He carried a reputation as a fine sportsman and champion of causes, not all of them lost. He became Master of the East Sussex Foxhounds and Rye's Member of Parliament, as was his father before him. His first game was the last of the season, against England. He managed 8 runs and did not bowl, nor was he expected to. He was a genial player who turned out for fourteen years with an influence over the government and committee of Sussex that outshone his influence over the ball. He eventually became the club's president, this during a difficult and sometimes dreadful period.

The second new name was Alfred Mynn. Mynn was really a man of Kent, and opened the batting for them with his brother Walter; but he 'assisted' Sussex, and should be mentioned if only as an excuse to quote from Taylor's description of this man of six feet one inch in his silk stockings:

> Despite his gigantic proportions, he frequently put on weight during the summer months. But then, he was a notable trencherman, and discussed the delectable viands with refreshing avidity. Beer and roast beef for dinner and beer and roast pork for supper (and plenty of it!) is not conducive to diminishing one's girth. During one Canterbury Week – where good cheer is ever prevalent – he weighed exactly 19 stone on the Monday and 19 stone 5 pounds on the following Saturday morning.

Good fun and glorious description; yet the fact of his playing was a reminder that, with the easy way in which one player might turn out for any side, there was little chance of credibility for a truly representative inter-county championship. It was a state of cricketing affairs that was to exist until 1873. Meanwhile, another giant, even larger than the great man of Kent, appeared on the Sussex scorecard in 1847 and played in the same match as Mynn against England. He was Charles Gausden.

C. H. Gausden was a modest number eleven and made 3 runs in the first innings and 6 in the second. As Sussex won by 27 runs, every nine counted. He was in most other respects a very big man indeed: six feet six inches tall and at one time nearly 23 stone. The game was played at Tom Box's ground. This four-day game in September, in spite of Sussex's win, was a sad affair for it was the last of the big matches to be played on The Level. As stumps and bails, balls and bats were rubbed and oiled to hibernate until spring, labourers moved to the sea front and winter work began on the Brunswick Ground. It was ready for play the next season, 1848, and became known also as C. H. Gausden's Ground. In July Sussex baptised its fine wicket by beating Nottingham by an innings and 32 runs. Wisden rather liked the new ground; he took fourteen wickets. A month later he went one better against Kent. He took fifteen wickets, twelve of them bowled, including both Mynns, Alfred and Walter, Fuller Pilch, Martingell and, in the second innings, Felix.

The ground became the headquarters of Sussex cricket until 1872, when the call for profit once again out-bellowed shout for single and two and the Brunswick Ground fell to the developer's hammer and Sussex, thanks to a sympathetic Stanford Estate management and trustees together with some smart footwork by the club's inner management, retreated, perhaps withdrew, to its present site in Eaton Road. But let us return to the 1840s, for the story has more to run.

In 1849 Sussex went off to The Oval to play Surrey for the first time since becoming a First-Class County side. Surrey won by 15 runs, thanks to some extent to 44 not out from Chester in the second innings. The nearest Sussex batsman was Edward Bushby who, also not out, scored 42. Bushby's tale is a sad one. He was thought to be one of the brightest prospects as a batsman – strong wrists, a good eye and a natural flair for stroke-making rather than simple hitting power. His pedigree was impeccable, for he came from Sompting, the village of more than one famous cricketer. But he was a sickly man. The previous year he had been too ill to play at all. He was given a job as gamekeeper by Alfred Smith of Henfield, another of the famous Sussex cricketing villages, and gradually regained his strength enough to play regularly until 1854. He batted at about five or six and was always among the runs. He ended that 1849 season second in the averages with 17. (The top man, George Picknell, had an average of nearly 21 but from fewer innings.) But he was not to play for long. He died during the winter of 1856, just short of his thirty-ninth birthday, and his body was returned to Sompting.

Wisden by this time was very much the businessman and entre-preneur as well as cricketing rebel. With George Parr of Nottingham, Wisden owned a ground at Leamington and was to be found playing away from his southern club. It was in such a match when he played for The North against The South in July 1850 that he took all ten second-innings wickets, clean bowled. The next month the MCC went to Brighton to play Sussex and won by an innings and 40 runs. The score and report note that 'Wisden did not play for his county, being engaged at Leamington, which, it must be said, made a difference in this match, his bowling being much missed'. William Lillywhite was playing for the MCC and took six Sussex wickets. When the two sides met the following June, the Lillywhites' cousin James got two wickets for Sussex; Wisden took seven, Dean four, but they could not stop MCC winning by five wickets.

But in spite of splendid characters and exciting matches it became increasingly difficult to maintain the popularity of the game in the county. Remember what tiresome matter travel would have been for spectator, however enthusiastic he or she might be. It was essential for players and their deeds to be seen across the county and not simply in Brighton.

By the 1850s Sussex were playing on 'home' grounds other than Brighton. They were at Horsham, where in 1855 all the MCC side were caught out in their first innings, and further to the east and along the coast at St Leonards, where in 1857 Sussex, against a depleted MCC side, recorded their only first-class win of the season. The old names were still there. And Southerton was to be the first to take two hundred wickets in a season, which he did in 1870. Dean and Lillywhite were fit as ever; Lillywhite was yet to clean bowl W. G. Grace five times. But for many of the famous of Sussex the 1860s were years of change. Age would not wait.

As an aside, for some, age was unimportant. W. G. Grace was twelve when in 1860 he was selected to play for West Gloucestershire against Clifton. He went in eighth and got 51. Four years later, at just sixteen, he appeared at Hove. It was after playing for South Wales against Surrey, as he remembered some years later:

We came to London to play, and I made my first appearance at Kennington Oval on July 12, 1864. I secured four wickets in the first innings, and made 5 and 38 with the bat. After the Kennington match the captain of the South Wales told my brother that he didn't want me to play in the next match, which was at Brighton. Then, as now, it was always easier to get men to play at

101

seaside resorts than in the provincial towns, and the Hove ground has always been very popular. But my brother Henry would not have me left out of the Brighton match, and insisted that I should play. I did, and went in first wicket down. When I had made 170 in the first innings and not-out 56 in the second, the captain did not repent that I had been included in the team. That was my first notable achievement away from home. The match was against the Gentlemen of Sussex, for whom those fine old cricketers, E. and W. Napper, were playing. Mr. W. Napper has often told me since that he ought to have captured my wicket, because when I had cut him three times to the boundary off successive balls he bowled me another which I also cut (but through Point's hands) to the boundary. Mr. Napper still thinks that Point ought to have taken that chance.

It was during this period that English cricket passed, as Grace himself recalled, through its most critical period.

The game itself was then in a transition stage, and it was quite a revolutionary period so far as its rules were concerned. A good deal of jealousy existed between the All England Eleven and the United Eleven and there was constant bickering between the North and the South. Numerous schisms led to the display of much ill-feeling, and to a considerable extent jeopardised the progress of the rapidly expanding popularity of the game. Combinations and strikes among cricketers were almost painfully frequent.

One of the rebellions was led by Jem Dean and John Wisden of Sussex, supported by John Lillywhite. They were much aggrieved by the high-handed attitude and poor paying policy of the All-England leader, William Clarke, who is reported to have paid his leading professional players as little as £4 a week. And so Dean and Wisden, as noted elsewhere, set up the rival team known as the United England XI.

The dreadful state of English cricket, a phrase that seemed to follow the game and reappear every ten years or so, again failed to dull the enjoyment and development of players establishing themselves at Hove. C. H. Ellis, who had emerged as a remarkable lob bowler, took three wickets in one over at Brighton against Kent in June 1863. It was a high-scoring game with 779 runs coming in the four innings, with Ellis taking nine wickets altogether and scoring 46 runs to boot. The following month, on the Royal Brunswick Ground, Ellis picked up fifteen Surrey wickets, all but two of them clean bowled. And he scored 83 in the only innings in which he needed to bat. Scores in county matches were impressive, especially when just a few years earlier three-figure totals had been rare. After one match against Surrey at The Oval produced more than 800 runs and a Surrey six-wicket victory, one report noted: '804 runs in this match for 34 wickets lowered. Bowling generally very inferior in great county and other matches (with a few exceptions) to what it was a few years back.' It was a malaise that Sussex suffered with difficulty.

Alfred Taylor wrote that 'In the later forties and early fifties interest was practically lost in Sussex cricket, and the Club dwindled into insignificance.' One of the problems reflected the fact that Sussex county cricket did not include the whole of Sussex. Many felt left out. Enthusiasm that might have been put to good use was rarely tapped. One particular man attempted to turn the interest to its best use. He was Bridger Stent, who had been born in Petworth and was just nineteen when the club was formed in 1839. Charles Box wrote that he was 'educated at Winchester School. In 1855 he resided at Brighton, and was a magistrate. He thoroughly understood cricket, and the way in which it ought to be conducted; he would allow neither trifling nor nonsense.' He held sway over meetings and energies until his sudden death in 1870.

Perhaps Bridger Stent's most important task was to rescue the apparently lost county from the brink of disaster. He did so towards the end of the 1857 season when he took on the job of secretary and called an emergency meeting of the club to consider its reorganisation. The fact that Sussex had won but a single match that season may well have had something to do with the sense of urgency that attended that August 1857 meeting. The club was restructured and more attention was given to the so-called outlying districts of the county in the hope that autocracy would appear less obvious in the affairs of Sussex cricketing.

This reorganisation was long overdue. The club was now in an era where it could no longer exist as the toy of a favoured group. It had ceased to be a private team. The cost of putting on matches, of maintaining a ground, of retaining certain staff meant budgets and planning. Also, if enthusiasm among the public was to be rekindled, then Sussex cricket had to be seen to be successful, especially as other sides appeared to have enviable organisation and competence. The vision of success had to be county-wide.

There were also the beginnings of a vision of identity, for it was at about this time that the club badge started to be worn, an indicator of the more formal footing of the reorganised county. Caps, however, were still varied and motley and the first pictures of players wearing the Sussex cap did not appear until 1887, and blazers not until 1900.

The reorganisation was relatively successful and the playing calm of the team was little disturbed. Indeed, only one match was lost the following season and none at all the next. At the same time there was hardly runaway success and no looking back for Sussex, in spite of some of the most glamorous and inspiring players of the day being in the side. The Earl of Sheffield, who had been club president at the time of the changes, was forced to resign to attend to other affairs, including politics. From 1869 to 1879, Herbert Curteis of Windmill Hill sat as president. It was an important and eventful ten years for cricket, and for Sussex in particular.

The year of 1870 was barely under way when, in February, the man who had revitalised and almost single-handedly reformed the club, Bridger Stent, died. One obituary declared that

> For very many years had this late lamented gentleman been ready with his advice, his influence, his energy, and his purse, in furtherance of, and upholding the good old game in his native county, and in acknowledging and encouraging good cricket and good conduct among the County Professionals. Mr. Stent was a thorough English gentleman, an open-hearted admirer of all that was manly, true, and good, and an earnest, genuine lover of the sports and pastimes of his country – of cricket especially.

The season's play seemed in mourning for the man described as the very life and soul of Sussex cricket. There were only four first-class matches for Sussex. They beat and then were beaten by both Surrey and Kent. The next year was the last on the old ground, which had with passing fashions been turned from a delightful cricket ground by the sea into an 'eligible plot'.

One commentator wrote at the end of the season of the mighty deeds seen on the famous ground. The writer's style owed, perhaps, something to the order of biblical prose, yet it was a true record of honourable times past.

> So we have now seen the last of the uniquely situated and famous run-getting old Brunswick, whereon for the past 28 years the accomplished cricketers of Sussex have bowled, batted, and fielded; whereon, in 1864, the present Hon Secs, Mr. G. W. King

and Mr. C. H. Smith, scored 96 runs before the first Gentlemen of Sussex's wicket fell to the Gentlemen of Hampshire; whereon, in 1864, Mr. H. Biron made 214 for the Quidnuncs, Julius Caesar 132 not out for Surrey, and James Lillywhite bowled 101 overs (or 404 balls) in one innings for Sussex; whereon, in 1863, so many as 1062 runs were made in the Surrey v Sussex match wherein John Lillywhite made 91, Charles Ellis 83, Mr. F. Burbidge 101, and Griffith 89 and 142; the ground whereon Charles Payne made 137, James Lillywhite 81, H. Charlwood 65, and John Lillywhite 43 in Sussex's second innings of 413 runs against M.C.C. and G. in 1867; the ground whereon Stubberfield and Charles Payne made 69 runs for a last Sussex wicket in '67, and Jupp and Thomas Humphrey 113 for a first Surrey wicket in '64; the ground whereon Thomas Hearne hit 100 runs in 80 minutes for M.C.C. in '62; the ground whereon Mr. C. Ewbank and Mr. Hyndman made 155 runs before the first Gentlemen of Sussex's wicket fell in '64; the ground whereon Mr. Spencer Leigh made 114 and other great scores, and Killick hit his 182 not out; the ground whereon, in 1865, William Oscroft scored that splendidly played 197 for Notts, and in '69 Mr. C. I. Thornton 156 not out for the Gentlemen of Kent; and above all, the ground whereon Mr. W. G. Grace made 170 in 1864, and 217 in 1871. These, and other great cricket feats achieved by celebrated cricketers on the sea fronted ground, crowded on every memory as, on the 16th of last September, we witnessed young Mr. Jeffrey finish his innings of 116 runs – the last three-figure score hit there; and, as the blue flag of the S.C.C.C. fluttered in the breeze at that last match played by the Club on the old ground, we heartily wished it might flutter through many a successful season to be played by the Club on their new ground.

The new ground was hardly difficult to come by. But there were stipulations and formalities in attendance. The ground had been part of the old Stanford Estate and the club did not have the freehold. But the committee had already eyed a ten-acre plot directly north of the Brunswick Ground and had an informal understanding with one of the Estate trustees, Mrs Bennett Stanford. On 15 July 1871 the club wrote to the agent for the trustees, pointing out among other things that:

It is vitally important to the numerous boys' schools in the town that they should have some ground for cricket and other recreations to which their pupils may resort, and it is also of consequence to the well-being of the town that it should not be

105

deprived of the cricket ground, as the opportunities of recreation are few, and cricket is among the most popular of them.

Under these circumstances, the gentlemen on whose behalf I address you are very anxious to procure a new ground, and are willing to undertake some amount of personal responsibility and risk for the purpose of securing one.

I am instructed, therefore, to inquire whether your clients and the trustees would consent to grant a lease for twenty-one years of the land I shall presently name to you upon the terms sketched out in the following proposal:

1. Ten acres of land, the site and situation of which have already been agreed upon between Mrs. Bennett Stanford's surveyor and ourselves, to be let for £100 a year for twenty-one years.
2. The lessees to be Mr. H. M. Curteis, our President; Mr. Ashby, our Treasurer; and Messrs. Smith and King, our Secretaries.
3. That the lessor expend a sum of about £1000 in the erection of a public-house suitable for the purpose of the Cricket club, and that such house shall be let to the same lessees, on their paying five per cent. on the outlay, at a further rent of £50 per annum.

And so the deed was penned and done and the Sussex County Cricket Club removed to the new ground at Hove, 'between Mr. Rigden's farm and the railway station at Cliftonville', taking with it goods and chattels and, at a cost of £1200, every turf from the Royal Brunswick pitch. Throughout the closed season workmen built a six-foot wall about the ground, and work started on 'a commodious inn, with capacious rooms upstairs, capable of dining 100 persons', which was to cost an estimated £1924. For less than a third of that, a pavilion was going up and a croquet lawn had been laid, together with a running-path and roller-skating rink, the latter roughly where the Gilligan Stand is set. By the opening of the 1872 season, the grass had wintered in and all was set for play. Membership fees were doubled from one to two guineas, admission to matches was one guinea, and it was no longer necessary for a gentleman who played for the county to be a member of the club.

They played six first-class games, including Sussex's first meeting with Gloucestershire, winning three and losing two. The county's bowlers by then were Lillywhite and Southerton. In that season they took 84 of the 113 opposing wickets, although Richard Fillery's 15 wickets should not be cast aside. Moreover, Fillery was the first man to score a century on the new ground, 105 during the Surrey game. But it was Henry Charlwood, one of four cricketing Charlwoods, who led the batting – in that year with an average of 42. Two further names were picked out by the sages of 1872: Jesse Hide, and Henry Phillips the wicket-keeper.

There were two Hides, Jesse and Arthur. They were fishermen and had perhaps learned their patience off the East Sussex coast rather than on the cricket field. Jesse scored more than 4000 runs for Sussex and took 460 wickets. Arthur, not so great a batsman, was distinguished as a bowler and took 459 wickets for the club. Jesse is remembered also for being the first professional coach in Australia.

Phillips, too, was a member of a cricketing family – that is, cricketing by pastime, for the family living came from undertaking. The bewhiskered Henry Phillips was born in 1844 in Hastings, one of five batting and bowling brothers. They were all good cricketers, but Henry and his brother James were the two to play for the county. Henry first appeared during the 1868 season and took over from Ellis as wicket-keeper. He was said to be the finest of his time, which was considerable – a full eighteen seasons. During the last year of the Brunswick Ground, Phillips caught thirteen batsmen and stumped eleven in five games. In the following year, at The Oval, he accounted for eleven players in one game, and in 1873 during the Gloucestershire match Phillips is said to have done without a long-stop, the first wicket-keeper to do so.

That year was an important one for English cricket, and in some ways a dismal one for Sussex. Southerton decided to play for Surrey, which meant most of the bowling was done by Richard Fillery and James Lillywhite. The records show that, of the 1618 overs bowled by Sussex in the 1873 season, 1422 of them came from these two. Fillery's haul included bowling W. G. Grace out for 6 and 1 during one game.

During the late 1860s there were, perhaps, eight main county sides: Sussex, Surrey, Kent, Nottinghamshire, Middlesex, Lancashire, Yorkshire and eventually Gloucestershire. Consequently there was recognition among those clubs that played each other as to which one was the best. Simple arithmetic decided the winner of the season's trials of skill. But cricket legislation was still sometimes vague and so doubt was cast on the value and title of county teams. One example was the lack of guidance that allowed players to appear for almost any county they wished, or which wished them to do so. This anomaly could make county listings and positions something of a nonsense, if vagabond bowlers and batsmen could be brought in at any time to turn tables.

By the 1870s there was general recognition that the time was right to put playing rules on sounder ground and, if necessary, to recognise that the game had become more than enthusiastic challenge. Now counties, players and supporters sought more formal acknowledgement of the season's gains and efforts. They wished also, partly at the instigation of the Surrey County Club, to remove the vagabond anomalies, thereby in some ways setting out what was and what was not a county cricket club. That there was pressure to do this reflected the importance of cricket as a game. After all, had not H. H. Stephenson taken a team as far as Australia in 1862? Was not the game growing season by season in public esteem? As W. G. Grace wrote of the year 1873: 'During the preceding two or three seasons County Cricket had been making rapid strides into popularity, and was now exciting great interest.' It was in 1873 that the rules governing players were tightened up by the MCC so that:

1. No cricketer, whether amateur or professional, shall play for more than one county during the same season.
2. Every cricketer, whether amateur or professional, born in one county, and residing in another, shall be free to choose at the commencement of each season for which of these counties he will play, and shall during the season play for that county only.

It was a help, and once the qualifications of residence had been tightened and added the new regulations stood until 1888, and even then only slight amendment disturbed them.

Part of the 1873 shuffle of rule and requirement included the MCC's attempt to set a contest to prove which was the mightiest county of the season. At a committee meeting of the MCC on 24 January 1873, it was decided:

With a view to promote county cricket, and to bring counties into contact which might not otherwise have an opportunity of competing with each other, and to establish an interesting series of first-class matches on a neutral ground, the committee propose to offer a silver cup for competition . . . The matches will be played in strict accordance with the rules and regulations in force at Lord's Ground . . . The name of the winning county, with date of match, shall be engraved on the cup at the cost of the M.C.C.

The trophy was to be called the County Challenge Cup, and no more than six counties would be invited to take part in the competition. The problem was that many counties did not agree to the regulations and did not like the idea that the MCC would invite a select band of counties. Surrey gained a deal of support for its opinion that players might be tempted to play for 'some inducement beyond the honour of victory, and that the suggested arrangement might be made a precedent for cup matches in other places, and so discourage the existing system of county cricket in London and the provinces'. Consequently, the MCC bowed to these thoughts and withdrew the offer of a cup. Moreover, the whole scheme had become slightly farcical in that four of the six counties had withdrawn and left Sussex to play Kent at Lord's for a cup that did not exist.

This nonsense out of the way, the counties settled into the idea of tabled competition between a select few, made all the more reasonable and acceptable now that the rules for players' qualification had been set out. The eight major counties mentioned earlier dominated this inter-county competition until 1891. If it is accepted that no formal 'league' existed until 1873, then Sussex must stick to its doubtful honour of never having won the Championship. However, in 1875 the county tied with Nottinghamshire, but only on the basis of having been beaten by Hampshire, which was yet to be accepted as a full County Championship side. Therefore, some have argued that Sussex should have received its one and only Championship title. Argument must be in vain. But if the Championship had dated from 1871 it would have been a different matter. In that year Sussex sat at the top of the table with Nottinghamshire second, Middlesex third, Gloucestershire fourth, Yorkshire fifth, Lancashire sixth, Kent seventh and Surrey bottom (although the methods of calculating positions were somewhat doubtful).

For the Championship years until 1891, when there were but eight first-class sides, Sussex had a less than distinguished record:

1873 7th (2 wins: Kent and Surrey)
1874 8th (1 win: Notts)
1875 2nd (some still say 1st)
1876 6th (3 wins: Kent, Lancs and Surrey)
1877 8th (no wins)
1878 8th (1 win: Kent)
1879 6th (1 win: Kent)
1880 8th (no wins)
1881 8th (no wins)
1882 8th (1 win: Surrey)
1883 6th (2 wins: Yorks and Kent)
1884 6th (4 wins: Yorks, Kent, Gloucs [2])
1885 8th (2 wins: Gloucs)

1886 5th (4 wins: Surrey, Lancs, Kent, Gloucs)
1887 6th (2 wins: Kent, Gloucs)
1888 8th (1 win: Lancs)
1889 8th (1 win: Yorks)
1890 8th (1 win: Gloucs)
1891 7th (out of nine; Somerset now in table. 4 wins: Middx, Kent, Yorks, Gloucs)
1892 9th (1 win: Gloucs)
1893 7th (4 wins: Middx, Surrey, Somerset, Gloucs)

It was an apparently lean twenty-year period in the life of the oldest First-Class County. It might be imagined that life in Sussex cricket had stopped. It had not. But to test the undying enthusiasm of the club we must first return to the earlier years.

As ever, there were fine performances with bat and ball, and the committee room rumbled through its tones and hues of argument and effort as in any generation. From 1869 Herbert Curteis of Windmill Hill had sat as president, but in 1879 Sheffield was re-elected. Sheffield's was a remarkable career as president. His enthusiasm for the game and his benefaction became vital to the team. Later, his name was recognised elsewhere when in Australia the Sheffield Shield became the most cherished trophy in inter-state cricket. But it was hardly a benign and comfortable office. Few governing bodies in cricket escape harsh criticism and worse, and Sheffield's time was no exception.

At the start of the 1887 season his lordship let it be known that he had received abusive letters and felt that it was time, once gain, to stand down. The burghers of Brighton were horrified. A petition was hastily produced with two hundred signatures, including some of the most prominent men of the day, and Lord Sheffield stayed on. Taylor remarks: 'At one time the Club was in such difficulties that it would have been dissolved but for Lord Sheffield's timely help. He said: "Spend what money you like, and send the bill to me; I'll pay it," and on another occasion gave them a cheque for £400.' However, time stepped on at a relentless pace, and Sheffield felt he could no longer keep up. On 23 March 1897 his letter of sad resignation was read at the annual and general meeting of the club, held at the Old Ship Assembly Rooms. It was written to the then secretary, Billy Newham, who had first played for the club in 1881 and had been captain in 1889 and again in 1891. There was a certain sorrow in the Earl's letter:

Dear Newham,

110

I shall be extremely obliged if you will kindly express to the members of the Sussex County Cricket Club, at your meeting to-morrow, my deep regret at having to sever my connection with them as president, and my warm gratitude to them for having for so many years elected me to that post. As you are aware, I have long entertained a wish to retire from that position, in order to make way for someone who would give greater attention to the general management of the affairs of the Club; and a more constant attendance at the deliberations of the Committee than I am able to give; and I am confident that the time has come when it is for the best interest of the Club and County cricket that I should carry out my wish. If, as you suggest to me in your letter, it might be proposed that I should be offered the position of one of the Patrons of the Club, I would send you a reply to such proposal as soon as I received it. At the same time I would send you a fuller explanation of my reasons for resigning the presidency and withdrawing from further participation in public cricket than I can possibly in the limited space of this letter. I hope you will assure the meeting that of the reminiscences of a longish life, now advancing towards its eveningtide, I can think of none more happy, more pleasant, or more satisfactory to look back upon than the recollections of the kindness and indulgence of the Sussex County Cricket Club in electing me their President for something more than a quarter of a century.

Some felt that a quarter of a century was a trifle long for any one man, however worthy, to occupy the president's seat. And so once Lord Sheffield had gone the rules were changed and it was decided that no one man should hold the office for two successive years. And so was born a line that read like an extract from *Burke's Peerage* or *Who's Who*, as dukes, earls, viscounts, baronets, knights and gentlemen and even a prince presided over the county's fortunes.

But fortune on the field is not decided, only viewed, from committee room's rattan and wicket. During this whole period between 1857 and the final years of the nineteenth century the game of cricket had evolved towards a form that would be similar to that a century further on. The biggest change was witnessed among the players themselves. For in that brief forty-year period, there was more than simple change of generation. The players who had been witness to the stormy revolution of underarm to round-arm to overarm, who had seen grand patronage and princely legacy, were no more. A new order of heroes now wielded bat and ball.

111

Chapter 11

James Lillywhite took a team out to Australia in 1876. The first 'Test' match may have been something of an occasion in cricketing history; it was certainly something of a surprise for English cricket, and a taste of magnificent things to come during the next hundred years. Australia beat Lillywhite's England side, thanks largely to Bannerman scoring 165 before retiring hurt. It was the first century against England.

But to return to the Sussex coast. In 1880 Sussex played the Australians at Hove. Perhaps the most memorable point of that game was the lob bowling of Walter Humphreys, who had been in the Sussex side for some years but had really been considered much more a batsman. In that 1880 season he came to the fore with the ball and, tossing up his strange lobs, got a hat-trick against the Australians, something he was to repeat in the 1884 season. In 1888, again against the Australians at Hove, Humphreys took nine wickets in two innings and greatly helped the county side to score a famous victory.

None felt the glory of that success more than one P. Lucas. Having failed to get into the Harrow and Cambridge sides, he nevertheless played for Sussex along with his two brothers, C. J. and F. M. Lucas. He scored a fast 66 runs off sound Australian bowling and judged them 'well stroked'.

The Australian captain during that 1880 tour was W. L. Murdoch who, thirteen years later, was to become the first overseas captain of Sussex. Murdoch, from Victoria, was considered the finest Australian batsman of his time. He eventually came to live in England and in

113

1893 appeared for the first time for Sussex at Trent Bridge against Nottinghamshire. From that year he captained the side until 1899, when he shared the job with Ranjitsinhji; and so, for eleven seasons, Sussex was led by an overseas player.

He was said to be a good coaxer of partner. There was in that first season ample chance to show his powers of nursing, and when Sussex went to Old Trafford that year, he 'gentled' George Bean through a long stand, the pair of them putting on 226 runs for the second wicket. Bean was to learn patience with ball as well as with bat. Two years later at Trent Bridge, Nottinghamshire hit the highest total ever against Sussex – 726. George Bean the batsman was sorely tried as bowler and came through a twenty-nine-over spell with six maidens, 71 runs and two wickets, a remarkable piece of bowling.

Murdoch's reign was impressive as a player. He scored more than 6000 runs and once hit 226 against Cambridge University at Hove. In 1882, two years after that first game at Hove, he returned with the Australian side and scored 286 not out. No wonder the Sussex committee was impressed. W. G. Grace described him as the 'best batsman Australia ever produced'. It was fortunate that he became Sussex captain because in 1884, not yet thirty years of age, Murdoch had announced his retirement from cricket. But he was persuaded to continue and returned to England as leader of the 1890 Australian team. He then made his home in England and qualified for Sussex. By scores and tactics Murdoch's record with Sussex is impressive, yet there were some, including Grace, who believed that in England Murdoch never realised his full potential.

During the 1882 Australian tour, at the time of Murdoch's 286 at Hove, a new name appeared in the Sussex averages: C. A. Smith. Runs 213. Wickets 14. C. Aubrey Smith was born in 1863, the son of a Brighton doctor. He learned his games at Charterhouse and played them with distinction at Cambridge. Perhaps everything about C. Aubrey Smith was distinguished, from his tall, chiselled, beak-nosed good looks to his style of life as teacher, sometime broker, sportsman and eventually screen actor, the Hollywood star of epics such as *The Prisoner of Zenda* and *The Life of a Bengal Lancer*. To millions of screen and cricket followers, Smith, later Sir C. Aubrey, was the perfect Englishman, with all the idiosyncrasies that that description implies. To Sussex he was 'Round-the-Corner Smith', and anyone who witnessed his run-up to bowl would understand why. But opposing batsmen certainly never scoffed at his unusual style. In the 1883 Varsity Match at Lord's, his nine wickets earned him

CRICKET.

A GRAND

Match of Cricket

WILL BE PLAYED

On Monday, August 24th, 1818;

SIR JOHN SHELLEY

AND THE GENTLEMEN OF

UCKFIELD and MARESFIELD,

AGAINST THE GENTLEMEN OF

LEWES,

On the Downs, near the Lewes Race Stand.

Wickets to be pitched at a quarter before Nine o'Clock, and the Game to be played out.

Good Accommodation on the Ground

By the Public's Obedient Servant,

Lamb Inn, Lewes.   W. ROGERS.

Lewes: Printed by J. Baxter,—who has just published a New Edition of Lambert's Cricketer's Guide.

FOR

TEN GUINEAS.

A SINGLE WICKET MATCH OF

CRICKET,

WILL BE PLAYED AT MARESFIELD,

ON WEDNESDAY THE 28th. INSTANT,

BETWEEN TWO GENTLEMEN OF LEWES & TWO OF MARESFIELD.

Wickets to be pitched at 11 o'Clock, good accommodation on the Ground,

By the Public's Obedient Servant,

Maresfield, 16th August, 1816.   T. ALCHIN.

BAXTER, PRINTER, LEWES.

The Dripping Pan at Lewes in 1833 from a sepia wash drawing, probably by T Henwood

*George Leopold Langdon,
the first Secretary in 1839*

Original Subscribers Ticket for the opening season

The Scorer, William Davies of Sussex by T. Henwood, 1842

Cricket at Brighton in 1844

CRICKET.

A MATCH OF

CRICKET

WILL BE PLAYED AT

SOMPTING,

On Tuesday next, July 2nd,

Between Eleven Gentlemen of the

SOMPTING CLUB,

And Eleven Gentlemen of the

Worthing Club.

Wickets to be pitched at 10 o'clock.

Every accommodation will be provided on the Ground, by the
Public's obedient Servant,

T. BUSHBY.

Sompting, June 27th, 1844.

Cook, Printer, Worthing.

*1844 and it seems only
gentlemen played*

ROYAL CRICKET GROUNDS, BRIGHTON.

GRAND MATCH.
SUSSEX, with A. Mynn, Esq. given, v. ALL ENGLAND.
For the Benefit of the Veteran Brown.

FIRST DAY, Monday Aug. 17th. Royal Cricket Ground.

1846

State of Game---2 o'clock.

ALL ENGLAND.

Adams, run out	14	....	
Clark, st by Box	11	....	
Martingale, c by Hammond	..12	....	
Pilch	 6	......	
--- Felix, Esq.	 7	......	
Ponsonby, Esq.	..............''	..	
Dorrington,	....	..	
Hillyer,	....	..	
Guy,	....	..	
Parr,	....	..	
Sewell,	....	..	

Wide Balls .. Byes, 2 .... 2 Wide Balls,. Byes, ...
No Balls...... No Balls

52

SUSSEX.	
First Innings.	Second Innings.
C. G. Taylor, Esq.	
E. Napier, Esq.	
A. Mynn, Esq.	
Box, ...	
Bushby, ...	
Hammond, ...	
Sopp, ...	
Dean, ...	
G. Picknell, ...	
Wisden	

Wide Balls ..Byes ...... Wide Balls .. Byes ......
No Balls,............ No Balls,

At the close of each days' play they will be printed on Sattin;
also on Letters, with a handsome View of the Ground.
An Amateur Performance at the Theatre Royal, Brighton,
this present Evening and To-morrow, for the
Benefit of Mr. BROWN.---Tickets to be had at the Gate.

GRAND MATCH.
SUSSEX, with A. Mynn, Esq. given, v. ALL ENGLAND.
For the Benefit of the Veteran Brown.

FIRST DAY, Monday Aug. 17th. Royal Cricket Ground.

State of Game---5 o'clock.

ALL ENGLAND.

Adams, run out	14	....	
Clark, st by Box	......; 11	....	
Martingale, c by Hammond	..12	....	
Pilch c by Mynn	 6	....	
--- Felix, Esq.	26	....	
Guy,	13	....	
Ponsonby, Esq.	....	..	
Dorrington,	....	..	
Hillyer,	....	..	
Parr,	....	..	
Sewell,	....	..	

Wide Balls .. Byes, 3 .... 3 Wide Balls,. Byes, ...
No Balls...... No Balls

85

SUSSEX.	
First Innings.	Second Innings.
C. G. Taylor, Esq.	
E. Napier, Esq.	
Curtis, Esq.	
Box, ...	
Bushby, ...	
Hammond, ...	
Sopp, ...	
Dean, ...	
G. Picknell, ...	
Wisden	

Wide Balls ..Byes ...... Wide Balls ..Byes ..
No Balls,............ No Balls.. ....

At the close of each days' play they will be printed on Sattin;
also on Letters, with a handsome View of the Ground.
An Amateur Performance at the Theatre Royal, Brighton,
this present Evening and To-morrow, for the further
Benefit of Mr. BROWN.--Tickets to be had at the Gate.

1846. One of the first illustrated scorecards.
August 17 between Sussex and All England

A Cricket Match at Brighton. This game never took place. It was a painting sometime after 1850 meant to show all the famous cricketers of the day.

Charles Payne in the 1860s wearing perhaps one of the early helmets. He later became a Sussex umpire

'Harry' Phillips born and lived in Hastings all his life and considered one of the finest wicket keepers of his day. The first to do away with long stops

*Herbert Mascall Curteis of Windmill Hill and
President of Sussex CCC between 1869 and 1878*

*Richard Fillery scored the first century
on the present Hove ground in 1874*

*Arthur (left) and Jesse Hide. Arthur was the first Sussex bowler
to take 100 wickets in a season*

HR Butt took over as wicket keeper from Harry Phillips. First played in 1890 and caught 927 and stumped 274 batsmen. Became an umpire in 1912.

Billy Newham. For 63 years, from his debut in 1881 until his death in 1944, Billy Newham served Sussex as player, captain, secretary and then as assistant secretary

FW Tate

high praise and the ball was mounted to honour a splendid piece of bowling.

In 1887 he was appointed captain of Sussex, and he held the job for two seasons. It was not a splendid period in the county's history. The side won but two games, one against Kent and the other against Gloucestershire. When a side has a recent record of little success, it is fascinating to find handsome encouragement written charitably and optimistically. Thus:

> Apart from the important county matches, Sussex did very well indeed, beating the M.C.C. and Ground at Lord's, twice defeating Hampshire, and playing a remarkable drawn game at Brighton with Cambridge University. Altogether, therefore, the friends of the county have no reason to despair of the future. Beyond all question the feature of the season was the batting of Quaife, who made an immense step in advance, and fairly took his place among the prominent professionals of the day . . . The bowling of the team was not formidable, but considering the excellence of the Brighton wicket, Mr. Smith and Arthur Hide did very well. Mr. Smith, indeed, threw himself thoroughly into the county matches, and was a most energetic, painstaking captain.

Sussex finished sixth out of the eight county sides.

The next season was even worse. Sussex won but one first-class county game and, as the official record noted, 'that when Lancashire had patriotically let off Briggs and Sugg to play for England against the Australians at The Oval'. The report went on:

> We should think, nevertheless, that, amateurs and professionals alike, the Sussex men found a great deal of pleasure in fighting the battles of their county under so keen and energetic a captain as Mr. C.A. Smith. It was clear that on several occasions the team were over-matched, but more than once a really fine finish was brought about, and the losers deserved almost as much credit as the victors . . . Quaife scarcely came along as might have been expected . . . the committee worked hard to maintain the high character of the county ground.

Sussex finished bottom of the table. The following season, 1889, was the county's fiftieth birthday. Billy Newham had replaced C. Aubrey Smith as captain, Ashby was treasurer still, and Sheffield the

115

President. It should have been a time of celebration, but the mood of the club was hardly able to raise the puff to blow out a mourning candle, never mind fifty in praise of play and history. There was talk of bringing in players from other counties to lift spirit and standard before Sussex awoke one morning to find their reputation drifting anonymously on what was a certain and ebbing tide. Let the writer of *Wisden* tell the impartial story of that season one hundred years ago.

The Sussex eleven had a thoroughly unsatisfactory and dispiriting season, worse indeed in its record and in its incidents than was the summer of 1888. In that year, although only one of the twelve first-class county matches ended in victory, Sussex played a brilliant game against the Australians, and, with Mr. Aubrey Smith for captain, a series of matches which were a long way from being discreditable. The successes were few and the defeats many, but on several occasions the team played up and made a lot of runs. During the past summer, however, the side lost their form, and in match after match played a spiritless, hopeless sort of game, never once making in a county match an innings of 300 runs, and often enough having big scores hit against them. Mr. W. Newham, who in succession to Mr. George Goldsmith and Mr. Aubrey Smith, fulfilled the double duties of secretary to the club and captain of the eleven in the field, worked very hard, and came out with the respectable average of something over 24 runs per innings for the season, which was but little below his figures for the previous year. For the rest Jesse Hide and Major, each largely aided by one big innings, did moderately well, but, except for his innings against Gloucestershire, Humphreys was seldom seen to such advantage as before, and though Bean was able to play, he did not shape like the hardy cricketer he was. [In 1886, George Bean became the first Sussex cricketer to score 1000 runs in a season.] The great batting disappointment of the side was Quaife, who in first-class county engagements, played twenty-four innings with an average of 12 runs each. He was always making double figures, but his top score for his county was 27 – a melancholy result for a batsman with his experience and method, and especially so in view of what he did for the Players at The Oval. The five bowlers who did the bulk of the work were all very costly, as the figures will show. They, like the batsmen, seemed generally to have made up their minds Sussex must lose. There were several wicket-keepers tried during the season, the veteran Phillips being the best of them. [In 1887 Phillips was considered 'past it'.] Mr. W. H. Dudney on one or two occasions kept wicket very well, but Mayes, a Yorkshire-born professional, was very erratic and uncertain. He

116

several times brought off brilliant catches, but he did not shape like a stumper, and he was by no means trustworthy when the ball beat the batsman, or indeed when it was thrown up to him in the field.

The almost complete failure of the Sussex eleven was the more remarkable as of the first four county matches played one ended in victory, another was drawn by pluck and determination, and the two defeats were at the hands of admittedly stronger sides, Nottinghamshire and Lancashire. From that point, however – June 26 – the southern team only played two good matches. Nottinghamshire thrashed them at Brighton; Kent scored a big innings against them and won anyhow at Gravesend; Surrey beat them by three wickets after a capital fight at Brighton, and then, to make up for this comparatively close game, won in a single innings with 84 runs to spare at The Oval. Then followed three single innings' defeats by Gloucestershire, Lancashire, and Kent respectively, the season finishing up with the return against Yorkshire, which the northern eleven won by 68 runs. We believe that Ellis, the Yorkshire wicket-keeper, who was tried some time ago, is now qualifying for Sussex, but a great deal more than this must be done if the team are to keep their place in the cricket world. That place has now been at the bottom of the first-class counties for two seasons, and, unless some recruits are found, home grown or imported, even this position will soon become untenable. The men who do most of the work for Sussex are not likely to improve, but are, on the other hand, getting past their best. Mr Newham's batting ability is handicapped by the cares and anxieties of his position as captain; Humphreys, one of the most individual of cricketers, is, as a player, an old man; the brothers Hide, though they do work steadily and conscientiously, can never hope to do much better than they have done, and for the rest the amateurs are either too much engaged in business or too lukewarm in the cause to be of real service, and the professionals, except Quaife and Bean, are players of distinctly inferior ability.

We have thought it well to state clearly and uncompromisingly the unfortunate position of Sussex, and we should say that the best remedy is to import some young professionals from Nottinghamshire or Yorkshire. We do not think that anything will excuse one county club endeavouring to take away from another men who are actually employed and wanted in their own county. Further than that, before importation is resorted to long and earnest efforts should be made to find native players. Sussex have tried for years, and in the nett result have failed. The courses now open are either to adopt importations as a settled policy or to be content to gradually sink to the position of their neighbour

117

Hampshire. The present writer has on several occasions, while thoroughly opposing anything like the offering of unfair induce- ments to a professional to leave a club that is employing his talent, spoken in favour of taking full and legitimate advantage of the residential law. It is notorious that in Nottinghamshire and in Yorkshire there are scores of cricketers who will in all probability never be wanted for their own counties, but who would certainly strengthen less powerful elevens. The strict birth qualification is a beautiful thing in theory, but in practice it goes for very little. County cricket to-day owes an enormous share of its importance to the wise adoption of the residential law by Surrey, Lancashire and others, and those who will look at the facts fairly and squarely and free their minds from sentiment and prejudice must admit that residents are quite as loyal and quite as contented as the majority of those men who were born in the counties for which they play. We by no means wish to see English professionals become mere mercenaries, as American base-ball players confessedly are, but we do not believe there is any danger of such a condition of things coming about so long as the present restrictions are in force and committees exercise their powers with judgement and good feeling. But, as we have said, the alternatives present to the Sussex committee to-day are, that either they must slide down hill and drop out of important cricket – they the possessors of perhaps the finest bit of playing turf in the country – or else find the money and summon up the energy to recruit their eleven fairly and openly from the good but unemployed material ready to their hands in the villages of the great cricketing counties of the north.

Thus was the state and feeling of Sussex cricket on its fiftieth birthday, 1889. The following year was worse. There was talk of having first-class status withdrawn. Some counties were infinitely finer sides than Sussex, but were yet considered minor counties, and this was thought far from fair. For three seasons, 1888–90, Sussex sprawled at the bottom of the county table. Telling team and those who watched of heritage and honour, of times and glories past, was little but ghostly pastime. In 1891 there was brief rally, Kent and Gloucestershire beaten, Middlesex, then Yorkshire, too. Team spirit was higher than might be imagined from the results, although the scores do not at all times reflect keenness of contest. In the match against Cambridge University, for example, 1402 exciting runs were scored, at the time an aggregate record in English cricket.

A closer look at that season will show that the most successful wicket-taker for Sussex was F. W. Tate. Fred Tate was not yet the famous player he would become.

118

Some of his performances indeed, notably those against Oxford University and Kent at Brighton, were extraordinary. On slow wickets he showed himself quite a first-rate bowler, and there is no reason why, with increased perseverance and a better command of his pitch, he should not become proportionately good when the grounds are fast.

That 1891 season, in 14 matches, he took sixty wickets for an average of not much more than 17 runs. Popular memory of Fred Tate is twofold: he was the father of one of England's greatest cricketers, Maurice Tate, and he dropped a catch that was said to have cost England a Test match against Australia. Tate first played for the county in 1887, in just one game in which he scored 1 and 26, bowled twelve overs for 26 runs and did not get a wicket. The following season he came second in the county's averages with twenty-five wickets in a full season of 12 matches. The confidence in him expressed at the end of the 1891 season was to be fully honoured.

Tate's early batting suggested that he would never head the averages, yet he was a very useful tail-ender. Over the years he played 312 innings and scored nearly 3000 runs with a highest score of 84. And that is all that need be said of Tate as a batter. He bowled at medium pace and with considerable success. In 1888 he took five wickets for 1 run against Kent at Tonbridge in just four overs (in that period an over was four balls). In 1891 at Hove he took nine Hampshire wickets for 24, and during the same year on the same ground he took seven Oxford University wickets for 7 runs, bowling five-ball overs. His most brilliant seasons were 1900 and 1902. In each of those years he took more than a hundred first-class county wickets – 114 and 153 – although, if non-first-class fixtures were included, a hundred wickets in a season was something Tate achieved five times.

It was in that last season, 1902, that Tate made his only appearance in the England side. The game, at Old Trafford, was going England's way. At the end of the first innings, Australia was just 27 runs ahead. The England bowlers took command of the Australian second innings and victory was thought to be well on the cards, until, that is, the captain Archie MacLaren decided to pull Tate from his normal position as a slip-fielder and station him way out on the leg boundary. Darling, the Australian captain, thumped the ball high and in his direction. Tate got his hands to it, but couldn't hold on. The innings continued, and Tate took wickets. England batted and with nine men out were within 4 runs of victory when the last man was out. It was Tate. Oh misery! Defeat always seeks reason. Tate's dropped catch was already reason

119

enough, and he took the entire blame in cricketing memory for a finish that had been agonisingly close to an England victory. But he had a son.

In 1891 the woe and dudgeon of Tate and MacLaren were of the future. Sussex was looking to a revival of fortune; the season had been reasonably successful and the next year was full of hope. Sadly its end-of-term report had little to celebrate: 'Unfortunately Sussex did not in the season of 1892 maintain the gratifying improvement that had been shown in the previous year, and the county has again to be placed at the bottom of the list.'

The season of 1893 was better, and is remembered for the change in captaincy. Newham, who had first played for the county in 1881, gave way to Murdoch, by now qualified to play for Sussex. Relieved of the lead, Newham appeared more relaxed, although his duties with the club continued elsewhere. He was with the club for sixty-three of his eighty-four years, scored 14,554 runs, and when he handed over to the Australian Newham had still to make his top score, 201 not out against Somerset at Hove three years later.

It would probably be hard to find a more devoted servant of any club in the history books of cricket than Newham. He became an adopted son of the county when he went to Ardingly College, which was where he blossomed as a good cricketer before arriving at the county ground in 1881. Although Newham achieved enormous success, it was by hard application of his skills rather than by simply exploiting any flair that was in him. In some ways his stocky 12½-stone figure reflected a stern grittiness that showed through when the batting order needed him to close up and defend. He was a natural defender (indeed, playing left back for Corinthians), not a bad trait for one who had to be captain and secretary for a sometimes beleaguered side.

The 1881 season did not bring him instant applause – only 76 runs from eight innings. But by the following year he was at the top and he hovered there for a decade to come. It was generally agreed that, when it was time to hand over the enormous responsibility of being captain at a particularly difficult time, Newham did so with the understanding and, to some extent, the stoicism of the schoolmaster and good sport that he was.

Murdoch undoubtedly lifted the seaside team. His own batting that first year was impressive enough, nearly a thousand runs in sixteen games and an average of more than 35. Bean, Brann, Wilson and, of course, Newham followed his leadership, all making centuries, or very nearly. Even C. Aubrey Smith, now a thespian of the more traditional description, put in eight appearances and nearly three hundred runs.

120

As a batting side, Sussex were becoming an impressive lot. But oh for a bowler to help the lobs of Humphreys. He took 122 wickets in first-class county matches, but that was more than all the other eight Sussex bowlers could muster between them.

Humphreys arrived in Sussex from Hampshire a few weeks after he was born in the late autumn of 1849. His story is remarkable if for no other reason than that he achieved his fame by bowling lobs, underarm – if nothing else, a reminder that in spite of the revolutionary antics of 1827 there was nothing written in cricketing law that said underarm could not be used, as long as it was fair and with sensible warning. 'Cobbler' Humphreys (a name stuck to him when he made shoes in Upper North Street in Brighton) became a leading light of the famous Brighton Brunswick Club, which is where he developed with both bat and ball so that for many seasons he topped the two tables of averages. He did not try his underarm lobs for many years in the first-class game, and in spite of his promise and ability as a club cricketer found it difficult to change to county standard; consequently, for many years he could not hold on to a place in the Sussex side.

It was in 1880 when he took 5 for 74 against Surrey, and that was the signal for his inclusion in the side against the Australians and his famous 5 for 32 including a hat-trick. Nine years later Sussex beat the Australians by 58 runs, not least thanks to Humphreys' nine wickets. The next season, 1890, he picked up eight wickets in an innings on five occasions, and when in 1893 Humphreys took 148 wickets he became the first Sussex bowler to top a hundred wickets in a season.

Why was Humphreys – not a fast, but a lob bowler – so successful? Murdoch's intelligent captaincy may have had a good deal to do with the bowler's record, which was his best season until that year. Murdoch put him on against every new batsman, but only for short spells so that the strikers would never quite have time to settle down. Credit should perhaps be given also to the wicket-keeper Butt, who took many a catch and flipped many a stumping off the cunning Humphreys. For wicket-keepers, Humphrey's unusual style must have been an acquired taste.

H. R. Butt, who started to play for the county in 1890, was celebrated in Sussex as the worthy successor to Henry Phillips. In a sometimes spectacular career in which he often scored many runs, Butt's agility and anticipation snared 1201 victims, 274 of them stumped. At the end of that hopeful season 1893 it was noted, 'Butt kept wicket in much better form than he has ever displayed since he first came into the Sussex eleven; and his success was the more remarkable as during part of the season he was handicapped by an injured hand.'

121

In 1894 Sussex were fortunate in being cushioned from the hard bottom of the table by Gloucestershire. The season started with distressing reflection on sad times past. Then followed eight defeats in the first nine matches; the other drawn. They then played Nottinghamshire, a side they had not beaten in twenty seasons. Sussex won. It was an especially splendid affair as it was Jesse Hide's benefit match. It had also an unusual point of note, for Arthur Shaw, who had played for Nottinghamshire in the 1874 match against Sussex and who, until the previous year, had retired from county cricket into the employ of Lord Sheffield, now found himself playing for Sussex against his old side. He had not been persuaded from retirement by Sheffield, who was well known to be against 'imported' players. Some careful talking to by members of the committee and by the captain, Murdoch, together with soul-searching from Shaw, who had been engaged by the county as coach, convinced him to turn out for his adopted county.

Shaw, even at the age of fifty-two, was much needed in the bowling side, with only Fred Parris showing the form he displayed in that season when he took fifteen wickets against Gloucestershire with his floating spinners. Shaw reminded anyone who may have needed his memory jogged that his arm and eye were as true as ever. Against his old side that year he took seven wickets for just 50 runs at Hove, and another seven at Nottingham.

But the year 1894 was afterwards noted as the season that another new player, C. B. Fry, arrived in the second half of the summer to play for Sussex. He was the Oxford captain and already with a reputation as an all-round athlete, a triple blue who had once held the world long-jump record. One report welcomed his appearance, noted his keenness and determination and then commented: 'Though perhaps not a batsman of very high class, his indomitable pluck several times rendered him invaluable . . .' Class is not always in the eye of the beholder. Charles Burgess Fry, who became captain in 1904, scored 20,656 runs at an average of 56.43. On twelve occasions he scored more than 200 runs in an innings. In 1901 he scored eleven hundreds and in 1904 ten hundreds. Once again Sussex was on the move, and there was more to come.

It did so the next season, 1895, in the form of Kumar Shri Ranjitsinhji. K. S. Ranjitsinhji's life and deeds have been described in many places, most readably perhaps by Alan Ross in his *Ranji, Prince of Cricketers*. But in the context of Sussex in the 1890s a few points about the man, and not simply the cricketer, are worth noting and may indeed inspire those who have not already done so to read the full tale of this extraordinary man. For example, where did he come from? Why did he play for Sussex and not, say, Surrey or Middlesex?

Ranji was born in September 1872 in Sarodar, which lies in the western Indian province of Kathiwar, which itself is in that great bulge of Gujarat bubbling into the top corner of the Arabian Sea to the north of Bombay. Sarodar was as far removed from the sea end of Hove as might be imagined. Browns, fawns, smudged ochres and dust-settled landscape spawned no leather-hoofed cut wickets or neatly lined crease. Instead there was to be found the heat and swirl of intrigue and malice that was the inheritance of India, its rulers and their concubines. Plot and internecine strife were the hallmarks of palace ambition. Wives schemed that their sons should rule above other favourites of the palace.

Jam Vibhaji ruled in Jamnagar and, while unusual benevolence was visited on his peoples, cruel torment and horrid manipulation lurked in the passages, galleries and punkahed rooms as he searched for a successor to the throne. His Rajput queens gave him no heir and he took up with a Sindi woman of doubtful morals and very unroyal pedigree. From this association a son, Kalobha, is said to have been born and it was he who was declared the crown prince. But the intrigues and jealousies could not wait for Jam Vibhaji's death, and he discovered a plot to poison him. Kalobha was banished.

It was then that the ruler turned to Sarodar and the seven-year-old son of Jiwantsinhji. The boy would one day be ruler. The new heir apparent was Ranjitsinhji and, in terrible danger from that moment, he was officially adopted at Jamnagar and then in great secrecy taken back to Sarodar with instructions that he be protected and not allowed back to Jamnagar for fear his life be taken.

But such was the determination of the palace women, and perhaps the weakness of Jam Vibhaji, that later another boy was born and declared by the Sindi mother, a sister of the original fancy of the ruler, as heir to the throne of Nawanagar. The unsteady Vibhaji was forced to ask the Bombay government to declare null and void the standing of Ranjitsinhji. The government of Bombay refused. But, presumably reluctantly, the ruler turned to Lord Ripon, the viceroy, who overturned the decision and Ranjitsinhji was disinherited. Jam Vibhaji died in 1894.

Eventually, but not immediately thanks to more intrigue and the fact that he had not reached his majority, the young man of doubtful lineage became ruler, Jam of Nawanagar. By this time the century had turned, but it had not mellowed or eased the nature of the new ruler. He was an unprepossessing character, certainly by one account of the time set out in Mr Ross's biography:

> He was an unattractive figure. He had every advantage – an English tutor, education at the Rajkumar College, constant coaching at cricket, tennis, polo, pigsticking, hockey, shooting. Yet he never learned to play any game properly. Nor did he ever show the least interest in sport. I well remember my disgust when I saw the loutish bastard of a low-born concubine seated on the throne . . .

He died in 1906, after only three years on his doubtfully inherited throne, without issue. And so Ranjitsinhji, who had often returned to India to find himself disturbed by the sad affairs of state and the people he was one day to rule, at last became the Jam Sahib of Nawanagar.

It is perhaps worth remembering this background of Ranji's. It is removed from the popular impression of a young prince, naturally gifted and blessed with privilege and few cares and an easy path to enviable popularity. It may, in some part, explain why he sometimes appeared distracted and often at odds with those critics who later would mutter that he was hardly committed one hundred per cent to the cause of the game and his adopted county. So how did Ranji come to Sussex, as would also his talented nephew Duleepsinhji?

Ranjitsinhji, or Smith as his friends often called him at Cambridge, had been a talented undergraduate at the university. He had gone up in 1889 but it was not until 1892 that he played regularly for Trinity and then the following season, after a not particularly spectacular appearance in the Seniors' match, turned out for the University. It was in this game that he and C. B. Fry first met, though on opposing sides of course. Surrey had heard of and seen Ranji at Cambridge and there had been suggestions from the county that he might play for them.

But he chose Sussex. Why? Perhaps he liked the idea of playing for a side in which he would shine, rather than for Surrey or maybe Middlesex which had their established figures. Perhaps also he took to the thought of playing with Fry, a man he admired as a sportsman, not simply as a cricketer. And there was Brighton itself – a free-and-easy town, full of fun and with social contrasts that could easily have made him mindful of his life elsewhere; all this in such an avowed regency atmosphere may well have appealed to the young man. So Ranjitsinhji moved to Brighton to prove his qualification of residence. Soon, the combination of Fry the opener with Ranji lower down, but seemingly ever together, became one of the joys of Sussex and English cricket.

Ranji and Fry were to be together for some of the most scintillating and golden years of Sussex cricket. That first season Sussex had perhaps the strongest batting side of its fifty-six-year history. Ranjitsinhji started in fine style with 77 not out and 150 against the MCC at Lord's, always a satisfactory way in which to start a county career. However, Sussex in general had a difficult start to that famous season. They travelled to Nottinghamshire, who promptly took 726 runs off some pretty indifferent Sussex bowling. An innings defeat. But all was far from lost that year. They won five of their eighteen games, beating Gloucestershire, Middlesex, Hampshire and, twice, Kent who for a change were bottom of the table that year. The following season, Sussex were back at the bottom.

The 1896 season should have been a good one. The county's batting line was impressive, on occasion the best in England. The reason for the dismal position was one which was repeated season after season. Sussex could bat, but could not bowl. As *Wisden* remarked in the report of the season: 'Given one or two first-class bowlers, Sussex would probably prove as hard to beat as any county team in England.'

But still no progress was made in spite of the almost mystical batting of Ranji, the style of Fry and the proving of the Horsham player Ernest Killick. The Indian prince scored seven first-class hundreds that season, including two against Yorkshire, plus 171 against Oxford University. He ended the season with 1070 first-class runs. Killick was originally a bowler, but it was Shaw who, watching the young left-hander in the nets, encouraged his batting. For anyone, never mind a twenty-one-year-old, Killick's 191 against Somerset at Taunton that year was by all accounts pure joy.

The year 1896 is also remembered as illustrating the colonial attitudes of the MCC towards Ranji, and also as the year in which the method of selecting England sides changed. Until then there had been no one team of selectors. Instead of the England side being picked by a committee of the MCC, the county on whose ground the match was to be played was allowed to pick the team. The Test series of three games in that year was against the Australians. The first was at Lord's, the second at Old Trafford and the third at The Oval. That meant that the MCC chose the first team, Lancashire the second and Surrey the third. There seemed much agreement in cricketing circles that Ranjitsinhji should play. But popular support did not extend to the opinions of the then President of the MCC, Lord Harris, who had until 1890 been Governor of Bombay, and 'knew all about these people'. Lord Harris regarded Ranji as a bird of passage, and he was not chosen for the Lord's Test. There was much grumbling by public and

125

the scribes, but to little avail. It had been spoken. Lancashire had few difficulties in selecting him, although Ranji asked that the Australian side should be approached to see if they had any objections to him. There was not one.

It was a remarkable Test, with W. G. Grace losing the toss and having to bowl on a heat-baked wicket. Australia were all out for 412. England batted; Ranji made 62 and Lilley 65, but the side had to follow on. Another collapse looked likely until Ranji took charge of the Australian bowling and hit 154 not out. The next-highest England score was 42 from A. E. Stoddart. Grace had opened the batting and scored 2 and 11, Abel had made 26 and 13, and Lilley, the England wicket-keeper, 65 not out and 19. The Australians needed only 125 and, in spite of some nail-biting and superb bowling by Tom Richardson, they won, so gaining revenge for their six-wicket defeat at Lord's three weeks earlier. Ranji, though, was established. Yet there had been some who had supported Lord Harris's attitude, and certainly past Sussex presidents, including Lord Sheffield, had been reluctant to go outside even the county for players, never mind having them in the England side on such a flimsy residence basis.

In 1897 the Earl of Sheffield handed over the presidency to the Duke of Norfolk, thus beginning a long formal relationship between Arundel and the club. And, as if to celebrate, Sussex ended sixth, in the top half of the table. The cry for a successful bowler was heard as far away as Yorkshire. Cyril Bland was a twenty-five-year-old from Lincolnshire who had started his cricketing career in and around Skegness but had developed in Yorkshire club cricket under J. T. Brown, the famous batsman. He appeared also to have played some games in Hertfordshire and so, in all senses of the term that would have been so disliked by the retiring president, Bland was an import. He played for only four regular years for Sussex and in that time took 552 wickets. As *Wisden* noted:

> . . . considering he had never gone through the strain of a long season on hard wickets, with contests often extending over three full days, his success in the Sussex eleven was, to our thinking, one of the chief features of the season of 1897. In the county engagements he took 95 wickets, and though he was several times expensive, it must be borne in mind that he had to bowl very frequently on the Brighton ground, notoriously one of the fastest and easiest in the country.

Now armed with a bowler, batsmen flourished with purpose, especially

George Brann. Brann was a locally grown cricketer who first played for Sussex in 1883. His was a dashing career which produced 25 centuries for the county, two of them in the 1892 match against Kent at Hove. Ten years later, on the same ground against the same county, Brann and C. L. A. Smith (the 'other' Smith) scored 229 for the eighth wicket, a record still. The 1897 season was his best. He scored 1589 runs with an average of a decimal below 40, and it was said that year that 'There is scarcely a more popular cricketer who has ever played for Sussex'. So 1898 should have been a season full of great expectations. But, as Billy Bunter would have known, like postal orders, expectations are sometimes a long time in their realisation.

The season opened without the county's star batsman. Ranji had left at the end of the previous summer for Australia, but not before giving every member of the side a gold medal with enamelled blue Sussex crest on one side and the player's name and 'From KSR' on the other. He then spent the summer of 1898 in India. He was, after all, a prince and had need to take his royal duties as seriously as Sussex took his cricket. The team slipped again to the lower half of the table, but still above Hampshire, Somerset and Leicestershire.

Ranji may have been far away, but there were compensations, particularly the batting of C. B. Fry. In 31 innings he scored 1604 runs and ended the season with an average of 59. For excellent measure, Fry joined W. G. Grace, Ranjitsinhji, Brann, Stoddart, Storer, Tyldesley and MacLaren in that select brotherhood of seven batsmen who had scored a century in each innings of a single match. Irony crept into one comment on this batting phenomenon: 'On all kinds of wickets Fry as a batsman was head and shoulders above anyone else in the team and the fact that he was so rarely on the winning side only served to emphasise the remarkable character of his play.' The season's apparently least-noticed event was the encouraging trial given to the 'other' Smith, C. L. A., who was captain of the Brighton College side. In 1906, with C. B. Fry, he captained Sussex as he did for the whole of the 1909 season.

In 1899 Ranji was back, and to some extent so were Sussex's fortunes. The year produced a glut of runs for Sussex and more than 3000 for Ranji, the first time a batsman had scored 3000 first-class runs in a season. His County Championship total was 2285, an average of 76.16, with Fry second in the county table with 1579 runs. Brann had an average of 32 and Joe Vine, who was often in later years felt to have been overshadowed by the two main attractions, nearly 28.

The sad tale of 1899 was the falling away of Murdoch during the season. The Australian had scored more than 6000 runs for Sussex, but he had lost his form of old and, after just seven county games, handed over the dressing room to Ranjitsinhji for the remainder of the season. By this time Murdoch, a lawyer by calling, had settled down in England. But he died in Melbourne after a stroke while watching Australia play the South Africans. His body was returned to England and buried at Kensal Rise in London.

The prince had his own ideas about captaincy and tactics, and there was deep rumbling and muttering about his frequent bowling changes, much to the confusion of the opposing batters and, sometimes, of his own bowlers. Yet, it was a good season: twenty-two county games, seven won, five lost. Again Sussex hunted for bowlers to support Bland and Tate, who took 190 wickets between them. Killick picked up 50 and Ranji 31. The son of Humphreys carried his father's style well, but lobs rarely worried batsmen that season and there was talk of importing yet another Yorkshire discard, especially as a demon named Wilf Rhodes seemed set for some time at Sheffield. The first season of the twentieth century demonstrated this weakness very effectively.

So great were the powers of Fry and Ranji that every game started with Sussex set to wear the notcher's pencil to the stub. They each scored nine centuries, Fry for the second time making a hundred in both innings of a match – that against Surrey at Brighton. In 1900 Sussex lost only two of their twenty-four county matches. The less than bright news was that they won only four, against Worcestershire, Somerset, Leicestershire and Hampshire. Sussex made enormous scores; but, with few Sussex bowlers to dread, opponents did the same. Bland and Tate plugged away, and they were helped by a new arrival, Albert Relf.

A. E. Relf played in twenty-five matches that summer and took twenty-one wickets, perhaps nowhere near as many as Tate, Bland and Vine, but not bad for a first season. Relf was born in the eastern part of the county in the tiny village of Brightling, one of three brothers who were to mark well their places in Sussex scorecards. He was twenty-six when he arrived at Hove and was seen as a batsman, having buffed the craft in Norfolk. That first season he scored 891, which was more than anyone other than Ranji, Fry and Killick, the last getting his thousand runs in a season with 117 to spare. Relf established himself as a true Sussex all-rounder, though in later years he was seen as a steady medium-pace right-arm bowler who could bat. In 1909 he took 5 for 85 against the Australians at Lord's. In all, Albert Relf took more than 1500 wickets for Sussex and scored more than 18,000 runs, truly a genuine all-rounder. His ending was sad: in 1937 he shot himself.

The youngest of the three Relfs, Ernest, played no more than twenty times for the county, but nine of those games included his two brothers – a family affair of happy times. There are those who say that the middle brother, R. R. Relf, was the best batsman of the three, although he scored fewer runs than Albert. Robert Relf was born in 1883 and during his long first-class playing career hit more than 13,000 runs and also took 283 wickets, once, in 1910, taking 8 for 79 against Essex at Hove. Six times he made a thousand runs in a season. He ended his cricketing career as a coach to promising youngsters, including P .B. H. May.

And so the summer of 1900 ended for Sussex what the *Wisden* reporter described as a 'curious season'. There was a sense of 'if only' about the county. The century had opened in fine form, Ranji, C. B. Fry and E. H. Killick all in superb fettle. Bowlers toiled and county watched and wished as England settled into the warm, lazy hopes of the years to come in the twentieth century.

Chapter 12

The season of 1901 was a handsome one for Sussex. Enormously high scoring meant another series of draws, twelve of the twenty-four Championship games. Yet it was far from an uneventful summer and not always to the credit of Sussex. Yorkshire, for example, bowled them out for 52 at Bradford thanks to the devastating form of Hirst and Rhodes. But there was little sign of gloom. Humour was in good form and rarely left the dressing room, just in case it was needed to prop sagging spirits damaged by the likes of Rhodes.

On one such occasion Sussex were going through a very disagreeable patch at Taunton, Somerset having put together too many hundreds. The Sussex team met and it was declared, privately, that the following day, a Saturday, Ranjitsinhji would bat all day, make three hundred, and never allow the ball to touch his pads for fear of an unsympathetic lbw. Ranji matched humour with class. He went in the next day and at the close of play was 285 not out; it was said by C. B. Fry that the ball got through to his pads but two or three times.

But it was Fry's, not Ranji's season, and he showed that he had every intention it was to be so during the Hampshire game at Portsmouth. That was in the middle of August and Fry, in spite of injury earlier in the season, had already taken 127 off Nottingham, 244 from Leicestershire, double-hundreds from both Oxford and Cambridge in one week, 116 off Middlesex and 119 not out off Somerset's bowling in the Taunton match. And so, in August, Sussex went to Portsmouth. The wicket, they said, was made for bowlers. Fry scored 106. The next two games were during Hove week. They called it the sweetest of batting wickets, when conditions allowed. He

131

made 209 and 149. The next Monday, Sussex were at The Oval and Fry scored 105, then travelled down to Brighton and hit 140 against Kent. He then went to Lord's to play in C. I. Thornton's England XI against Yorkshire, and scored 105. Six consecutive hundreds gathered with considerable style, often on far from batting wickets. While the achievement was a delight to small and big boys alike, content with its style, cheek and execution, one report was far more analytical in its view of Fry's non-stop hundreds:

> Of the skill and patience displayed in obtaining his remarkable number of big innings it is impossible to speak too highly, for C. B. Fry, with all his greatness, makes nearly all his runs on the on-side. He rarely cuts, he scores scarcely at all in the slips, and he often puts together a big innings without making an appreciable number of off-drives. In on-driving, in placing the ball in front of square leg, and in putting the ball away to leg, however, he has rarely been excelled, while it need scarcely be added that he possesses the invaluable qualities of judgement and self-restraint in an exceptional degree. His present position among the batsmen of the day affords a wonderful illustration of what a man can accomplish by intelligence and application, for during the four years he was at Oxford there was nothing about his play to suggest that he would take really high rank, and two years afterwards he had still his reputation to make as an England cricketer.

There were many who agreed that Fry was a superb batsman who, thanks to playing with Ranjitsinhji, emerged as one of brilliance. The partnership appeared perfectly timed. Fry was proud inheritor of the late Victorian ethic, and for him life was raw-boned and played with straight bat. It was Fry's privilege, by birth, to stand as almost a caricature of manliness and position, as if by unquestioned understanding it was nigh on a duty to smite the efforts of those who would seek his wicket. The utterly professional amateur. Perhaps, then, thoroughly English. And here was the contrast between the two great men. Ranji was possessed of a quiet grace, suppleness of mind, humour and almost mystical power that stroked, flicked, glided, even whispered the straightest ball, the curviest of swings, the most tantalising break, mesmerically to the furthest reach of fielder and boundary's safety. As Cardus describes, 'this visitation of dusky, supple legerdemain happened; a man was seen playing cricket as nobody born in England could possibly have played it'. Ted Wainwright of Yorkshire said, 'Ranji, he never made a Christian stroke in his life,' to which

132

Cardus replied, 'Why should he have done? The style is the man, and Ranji belonged to the land of Hazlitt's Indian jugglers, where beauty is subtle and not plain and unambiguous.'

And so Fry watched. The silk-buttoned wrists of Indian genius at one end, the determined and martinet figure of Englishmanness at the other, watching, analysing, adapting, learning. As H. S. Altham remarked to Fry: 'It is an open secret, which he himself would be the first to admit, that it was his association with the Indian Prince that raised Charles Fry from a good into a great player.' Fry ended the season scoring 2413 runs in County Championship matches and with an average of 80.43. It was an altogether happier season, and Sussex celebrated in fourth position in the table. The next season was even brighter in terms of results, but somewhat overcast in the way of morale.

That Sussex should have reached second position in 1902 was remarkable, because the record books show at first glance no enormous improvement. Furthermore, Ranji, still captain, appeared in fewer than half the twenty-four Championship matches and his non-appearance caused muttering and grumbling among some members. There were rumours of differences of opinion among the players, between Ranji and the professionals, and he withdrew from the team although keeping the captaincy. The time taken for the rumours to mature was such that differences were rarely aired with any clarity in public. Consequently there freely roamed tales of restlessness, and of dressing room and committee gallery tinged with disloyalty alien to the would-be image of manliness and honour.

When he appeared, the crowd loved the young prince. He went to Hastings and scored 234 not out against Surrey, took 230 off the Essex bowlers and another 135 from Surrey at The Oval. Ranji ended the Championship season with an average of 66.61, but he failed to make the thousand runs which many of his supporters felt was his right. Ranjitsinhji was out of sorts. But the side was good enough to play well together without one man's genius and Fry, Relf, Vine and Killick batted strongly and ruthlesslessly against some fine bowling.

It was a dank summer, perhaps clouded over by the death of the Queen, but certainly to the amusement of bowlers throughout the Championship. And Tate, still plugging and off-breaking away with little support, was ever consistent: 153 wickets in twenty games with an average of 14.28 was rather special. Worthy, too, considering the number of overs he had to bowl, was the left-arm slow pace of George Cox.

Cox had joined Sussex in 1895, and bowling still in 1921 against

133

Somerset took five wickets in six maiden overs. In 1926 when, at the age of fifty-two, he was thinking about standing down for good, he took seventeen wickets at Horsham against Warwickshire. In that 1902 season his bowling average was 21.77. In his whole first-class career Cox took 1810 wickets for an average of 22.80 a wicket, a remarkably consistent record. For good measure he scored more than 14,000 runs for Sussex.

By 1904 Fry had taken over the Sussex captaincy. It was a good side, although change bowling was hard to come by and even the ever-reliable Tate was having difficulty in getting into the eleven. In spite of Fry telling all who would listen that Sussex were a better team than some thought, they slipped from second to sixth place in the Championship. The next year was marginally better, although by all accounts it began with a certain lack of confidence, for Ranjitsinhji was not playing; he was back in India. The season opened badly, perhaps reflecting nervousness, bringing defeat about their ears in the first three important matches, against MCC, Surrey and then Middlesex. The county season then perked up and they finished winning thirteen out of twenty-eight games and losing but four. Much of the batting success was due to the opening partnerships between Fry and Vine. That season Vine made 1647 runs in the twenty-eight Championship games.

Perhaps there were times when Vine felt that the salvers of glory were laden only for Fry and Ranjitsinhji. Portraits of Fry and Ranji are found wherever Sussex – indeed, any – cricket is acknowledged. Yet Vine too was a giant of long days. He played first in 1896 when he was twenty-one and was picked for his extraordinary fielding, which was said to save more runs than many batsmen score. It was a remarkably consistent career for any cricketer. He played his first 421 games without a break, then missed one and played another 82 straight off. His run-making, although sometimes stodgy for the spectator, was equally consistent. It was said that Vine had originally been an attractive batsman with a locker full of shots. Fry apparently transformed him into a kedge anchor who would maintain his professional end while the swashbucklers fenced and foiled their way through the averages.

Certainly Vine was as steady as the role envisaged for him. In the long term it paid for county and player. He scored 24,130 runs, many more than either Ranji or Fry, and took 621 wickets. It was Vine who, in 1901, was the first Sussex player to score a thousand runs and take a hundred wickets in a season. Indeed, he made a thousand runs in a season fourteen times and scored 32 centuries. On six occasions he shared with C. B. Fry an opening stand of more than 200 including 238 for the first wicket in 1902, when Sussex made 705 for 8 declared against Surrey at Hastings. It was also at the Central Ground in Hastings that A. E. R. Gilligan remembered Vine, towards the end of his career, making a completely un-stodgy 202 against Northamptonshire. In his memoirs, *Sussex Cricket*, Gilligan wrote:

> He hit wonderfully well, and the stroke which brought him his double-century was a magnificent upper-cut, which sent the ball almost full pitch to the pavilion enclosure. It fell just inside the playing area, and by coincidence landed first bounce on Mrs. Vine's leg. Far from being distressed, she was most enthusiastic at her husband's 200, and took not the slightest notice of the blow, which must have given her a nasty bruise. I remember, too, that when Joe was out, I congratulated him on his innings, and said how much I enjoyed his hitting.
>
> 'I wouldn't have dared do that when Mr. C. B. Fry was playing,' he answered. 'I once hit three fours in the same over, and Mr. Fry came up to me and told me plainly that it was my job to stay there, and leave that sort of cricket to him.'

Mr Fry did not have a chance to get on with 'that sort of cricket' in the 1906 season. In the second match of the year he tore an Achilles tendon, and that was that for 1906 and C. B. Fry. Sussex sorely missed him, especially when it is remembered that in the past three seasons he alone had scored nearly 6700 runs in Championship games.

The season of 1906 was, however, something of a celebration for John Elicius Benedict Bernard Placid Quirk Carrington Dwyer. He was more easily known to his friends as E. B. Dwyer, but with such a splendid string of Christian names he inevitably had a somewhat exotic background. J. E. B. B. P. Q. C. Dwyer was a great-grandson of Michael Dwyer, a Wicklow chieftain who was described as one of the boldest leaders of the 1798 insurrection and who was eventually captured and transported to Australia. It was there, in Sydney, that E. B. Dwyer was born in 1876. He was a tall, dark and handsome fellow with a ready humour, who bowled with a high right-arm action that produced lift and not a little turn. He was encouraged to come to England by Pelham Warner and persuaded by C. B. Fry to play for Sussex. In 1906 his registration was approved and he immediately proved his worth with 9 for 35 against Derbyshire and 9 for 44 against Middlesex. Fry, his mentor, could only watch from the pavilion while he nursed his disagreeable tendon.

135

A further difficulty for the county's batting was the lack of Ranji. He had hoped to return to Hove, but as the end-of-season report noted:

> Compensation for Fry's enforced retirement might have been found if Ranjitsinhji had fulfilled a half promise to return to England during the summer, but he did not come, and Sussex had to get through the season as best they could without the help of either of their two great batsmen. Small wonder under the circumstances that the general result was unsatisfactory.

Inevitably, the gloom spread to the supporters of Sussex. Few came to watch and there was apparent ill-feeling about the way in which the club was being run, almost as if the management were out of touch, yesteryear's generation. Newham, the dedicated servant, stood down as secretary at the end of the season and acted as assistant to the new steward, Colonel E. A. Bruce. The hope was to pull together what interest there was in all parts of the county, once more a reminder that Sussex cricket was not simply Brighton and a few select clubs. The stand-in captain, C. L. A. Smith, had what was accepted as a 'thankless task', and he may not have been too upset when he was asked to hand back the dressing room to Fry the next season. It was noticed in sometimes stern tones that Fry was not always 'available'.

The side had won six times during 1906 and in 1907 there was but one more victory to celebrate. The next year Ranjitsinhji returned, having attended to his affairs in India. Indeed, he was now His Highness Jam Sahib of Nawanagar. To most in Sussex he was Ranji still, though not always the slim, mystically brilliant batsman they remembered. He played in ten matches and scored 716 runs. A celebrated and welcome return. Sadly, though, it was Fry's last season. He left the county to play for Hampshire, with, as the Sussex season report euphemistically observed, 'which county all his interests are now associated'.

In 1909, with Ranji having returned to India, Smith became captain once more. It was a very popular appointment among team and members. He was known as a modest man with an ability to bring people together when they most needed to be. He had shown enormous promise at Brighton College as both batsman and bowler, but emerged as a useful rather than exceptional batter. His innings often proved painful experiences for him, taking some time to get going, almost as if he did not believe he was good enough to be doing the skilful things he did; perhaps this lack of confidence

136

reflected his benign character, which most agreed was much needed by the side, used to a more unbending and opinionated type of leadership.

Even without Fry and Ranjitsinhji, Sussex settled into a harmonious season. They won seven of their games and lost only three, and finished fourth in the Championship. It was a rigorous programme of twenty-six matches, and one comment was that the occasional full day of rain was a blessing on the team's stamina and temper. Robert Relf took on the mantle of leading batsman with relish. His 272 not out against Worcestershire at Eastbourne was by all accounts chanceless and masterly. Closely in support were Vine and Heygate, playing in every game and each scoring more than a thousand runs that season.

With Robert Relf hitting magnificently, his brother Albert took care of the opposing batsmen, taking 92 Championship wickets at an average of 18.81. If he had a weakness, it was said that he bowled too well. His line and length were so perfect, and therefore to some extent quite predictable, and batsmen sorted out a technique for themselves and simply defended until a fresh bowler appeared, although Relf's figures suggest that some lacked either technique or patience, or both.

The next season Sussex slipped to seventh position, but this had more to do with the system of awarding places than with true worth. There had been much thought given to the way in which Championship points were calculated. It was possible for a team to play fewer matches than another and finish higher in the table, rather like a batsman ending with a good average from very few innings. In 1908 and the following year there was serious support for the new idea of deciding the Championship placings by calculating points as a percentage of wins against games played. For Sussex, the keenness of county positions was of little practical interest. Not until the late 1920s and early 1930s did they ever look as if they might contend for the greatest honour of all. They were far from alone in this fix and in the year 1910, with a new captain, H. P. Chaplin, they seemed not the least fussed.

Like Smith, Chaplin was a very modest man and was told at the end of the first season that, while such modesty was commendable in the nature of man, it did little for the batting performances of Sussex. He was thought to bat too low down for his skills, and the seven times he was not out seemed to support this view. Yet Chaplin missed a thousand runs by just 50, hit a fine 172 not out against Hampshire – a captain's innings indeed just when his team needed it – and finished

137

the Championship season third in the averages behind Heygate and Robert Relf. Not far behind, in terms of runs scored, was E. H. Killick, by then in his seventeenth year with Sussex. The averages for that year contained the name of a lad born just a few months before Killick, the youngster's hero, had appeared for the first time with the county. The new name in the list was P. G. H. Fender, perhaps the most attractive cricketer Sussex ever lost.

Most people would rightly associate Fender with Surrey. But his first four seasons of Championship cricket were spent with Sussex. His maternal grandparents, the Herberts, lived in Brighton, where his grandfather played for the Brunswick Club and had coached Humphreys to perfect his lob-bowling technique. The Fender home was in south-west London, but young Percy George spent long months on holiday with his grandparents, and it was this rather tenuous quali- fication of local residence that allowed him to join Sussex during his last term at St Paul's School in London. In Richard Streeton's superb biography of Fender, he records the connection with Killick which must have been made during the summer holidays at Hove: 'One of my schoolboy idols was E. H. Killick, a tiny left-hander whose late cutting always sticks in my mind. I remember going through a phase of trying to cut everything and this, perhaps, made me bat left-handed whenever possible.'

Fender's career with Sussex was far from sensational, yet clearly temperament and skill, together with his early aptitude for annoying authority and those who assumed it, were to be witnessed in those Sussex years. One tale, relating to the 1912 match against the Australians at Hove, suggests also something of the more relaxed, sometimes wandering temperament of Ranji. Fender and Ranji were batting and the local paper, the *Sussex Daily News*, was overjoyed by Fender's 'powerful and resolute style'. But, as Streeton pointed out:

> What the newspaper could not be expected to disclose, how- ever, was the remarkable private challenge that Ranjitsinhji set himself during that stand. He casually suggested to Fender between overs that it might be 'interesting' to nominate in advance the strokes he intended to play. 'I'll send the first ball down to Kellaway's left hand at long leg and the third ball to his right – he's always slow to get back; we'll run 2 each time.' Sure enough the famous leg glances brought this about with Ranjitsinhji reminding Fender, as they crossed, to run 2. In another over it was late cuts to Bardsley at deep third man which brought 2 runs to the fieldsman's left and

then 2 more to his right. There were some drives through the covers too, and it did not matter what sort of ball was bowled, Ranjitsinhji never failed to achieve what he warned Fender to expect.

As for the first year for Sussex, Fender played but two matches, scored 19 runs and along the way picked up a wicket. For Sussex, drenched with rain that year and wallowing in certain financial difficulties, the season was trying though not a disaster. Yet wet weather and, to a lesser extent, lack of success meant small crowds, and members were asked to put in the county coffers a shilling each, to help the club through a difficult time. The season ended with a respectable record of wins, draws and losses, which is worth noting, if only for one unusual entry:

County Championship Matches
Played 26 – Won 10, Lost 9, Drawn 6, Limited to two days
owing to King Edward's Funeral – 1

Matters of skill and support did not improve the following year, and Sussex was again being described as a 'second-rate side'. The next season, 1912, even with the Jam Sahib of Nawanagar playing in nine games and Vine and Robert Relf each scoring more than a thousand runs, was far from a reasonable improvement on 1911, a 'wretched' year as one writer put it. Sussex finished tenth. The season saw also the gradual retirement of H. R. Butt after twenty-two years as wicket-keeper. His successor was George Street.

Sussex, like Kent, has invariably produced outstanding wicket-keepers. Street, who kept until 1923, was thought to be 'as good if not better than any other wicket-keeper in England during the early 1920s'. In 1923 he caught 69 and stumped 26, a record still for Sussex. He could bat on occasions and once scored 109 against Essex in 1921. His end was tragic. He lived in Warnham and was riding home on his motor cycle on 24 April 1924 when he swerved to avoid a lorry at Portslade and crashed into a wall. A sad end to what had been a safely gathered and reliable career that had promised so much in 1912 and, in spite of the interruption of the Great War, had delivered.

In that last season of Butt's another man appeared for the first time in the playing side, a familiar name but unfamiliar initials to be written into the Sussex scorebook in 1912.

Also bowled: M.W. Tate 14–3–28–1

139

The appearance of Maurice Tate's name was a reminder of the misery of Fred when ten years earlier he had muffed that Test-match catch. Afterwards, consoled by the bowler Len Braund, Fred Tate is said to have promised, 'I've a little kid at home there who'll make up for it to me.' And how he did.

In cricket, the old order changes but slowly. There is always someone coming on while others fade. So it was at this time with Sussex. Tate in 1913 was top of the averages, yet it was a false position because he bowled in few Championship games – five – while Albert Relf toiled through forty-eight matches and took 116 wickets. He also scored 1560 runs that season – a good season's work for a player approaching forty. What was more, Robert Relf, Vine and Chaplin also made more than a thousand each, evidence that the old order was not yet ready to go.

For the younger generation, Fender hit his first thousand in a season, 1631, and even picked up 22 wickets. Yet there were moments in that season when the young Percy George had difficulty in keeping his place. He did everything worth doing in the first half of the year, a fact which won him a place in the Gentlemen *v* Players at Lord's and The Oval. But gradually he fell to one side and during the last twelve games scored no more than 67 runs. Another new name, H. L. Wilson, who was to be the team's first post-war captain, joined Sussex and scored 1341 Championship runs including a hard, driving century against Gloucestershire.

It was a mixed season, one when Sussex were either very good or very indifferent, and they ended up seventh in the Championship. And so Sussex cricket flickered with uncertainty and, with an equally faltering Europe, waited for the coming season of 1914.

The county played twenty-eight games that year, won ten, lost six and finished sixth in the Championship table. When the season started, few guessed that it would be the last until 1919. There was a casualty of a minor and peaceful nature half-way through the year when Robert Relf, who had played thirteen matches and scored 829 runs, suffered appendicitis and was out of cricket for the rest of the season. There may have been but few of the spectacular innings of years gone by, but five batsmen made a thousand runs each – A. E. Relf, V. C. W. Jupp, the captain H. P. Chaplin, Vine and Bowley – and H. L. Wilson missed a thousand by three.

And so the season was to close, appropriately, with the match against the old rivals Kent during Canterbury Week – sadly, just as German troops began their invasion of Belgium to the tune of

Bethmann-Hollweg's hollow complaint that Britain was going to war 'just for a scrap of paper'. Far away in Canterbury, another 'scrap of paper' was being printed at the Kent County Ground by J. A. Jennings Ltd – the scorecard of famous names and their deeds that Sussex yeomen would take to their wretched trenches in dreams of bat and ball.

Chapter 13

The Great War marked the end of another era in English society. In an earlier conflict Kipling had wondered at flannelled fools at the wicket: 'Each man born in the Island entered at youth to the game – As it were almost cricket, not to be mastered in haste.' And as this new roll of misery began Sassoon watched in horror:

> I see them in foul dug-outs, gnawed by rats,
> And in ruined trenches, lashed with rain,
> Dreaming of things they did with balls and bats,
> And mocked by hopeless longing to regain
> Bank-holidays, and picture shows, and spats,
> And going to the office in the train.

For cricket had become manifestly so much a part of the English make-up that for Sassoon, and his fusiliers, mental retreat from loathsome warfare conjured dreams of chestnut-edged field and long, always sunny, afternoons, long-hops and sixes, tea at a quarter to five and never a dropped catch that mattered. Indeed, cricket was still a game for schoolboys played by men. It retained pride in its manliness. Things remained cricket, or not cricket. The officers were amateurs who could still buy a commission in their regiment and the right of fair trial for their county, while the professionals were called up and told to play and how to play the game, be it of war or of bat and ball.

The officers and men would have been pleased to learn that while they were away affairs of the club were being handled with prudence

143

befitting the responsibility of a club's officers whose country is at war. The 1917 Annual General Meeting reported that expenditure was being kept to a minimum and despite the sum of £82 10*s* (£82.50) spent in repainting the roof of the new skating rink the balance of the year 1916 was £58 7*s* 11*d* (£58.39). All was in order; the Flower Show Match was safe from the sound of gunfire. And so at the outbreak of war, the game was so filled with its old and perhaps hard-earned values and sentiments that it was thought 'almost unseemly' to play cricket.

Cricket, like any good regiment, looked to its general headquarters for example. The Army moved into Lord's, and staff and members made 18,000 hay nets for horses at the Woolwich Garrison. Cricket's decorum, blessed with an honour guard of colonels in secretaryship, was found in the MCC, and sides were sent to play the public schools, while the ground at Lord's was used only for service matches. The counties took their lead, and at Sussex there was a great attempt to keep forces cricket going. It was part of the war effort, like knitting comforts for the troops, but also it was a recognition that life would proceed as normally as possible and that there was little point in dressing in weeds and mournful down-turned mouth in respect of the tragedy that was playing across the English Channel.

Then some went to that war. Oddie, the club secretary for one year when the 1914 season ended, was killed in action. Yet irony had its moment. Ranji, too, fell horribly wounded during the war years, but not as might have been. Immediately hostilities were declared, Ranji offered his services and those of his people, including the Nawanagar State Imperial Lancers. The Indian princes took the war effort very seriously and made enormous promises of financial and material support. Many of them, however, once the effort was under way, saw little prospect of remaining close to the conflict. After all, for them it was an alien form of warfare, and they sought a chance to return home. Ranji found new purpose in the war. He loved the comradeship that it engendered, but regretted that he was handicapped by his health and, more hurtfully, by the fact that few would take him seriously. His possessions, including his cars, he felt were appreciated more than he. The Jam Sahib became ADC to Field-Marshal Sir John French.

In spite of his enthusiasm, Ranji's war was far from dramatic. He had long suffered from asthma, and France and its cold did him down. In 1915 he was in England on sick leave. During his time away from France, he took a shooting party to Yorkshire. One of the guns alongside him was considerably unsafe and managed to hit the prince rather than the bird. Although badly hurt, Ranji is

144

said to have continued shooting, but eventually had to be taken to hospital. He lost his right eye and for ever after wore a glass one. He would undoubtedly have preferred even a 'blighty wound' rather than so nasty an injury for no real purpose at all, especially with the main shooting match taking place just a ferry ride and hardly a day's staff-car motoring from his moor.

Down in Sussex others were preparing for war, but with less style. George Street the wicket-keeper, Curly Roberts who took 340 wickets for the county, and Maurice Tate enlisted in the 2nd/6th Sussex Cyclists' Battalion. For the nineteen-year-old Tate the war was not difficult, though he would have wished never to have been sent from cream flannels to khaki just as he was flexing his skills at batsmen's expense. Yet Tate's was not a dreadful time. When the battalion was sent to India, Tate transferred to become a signaller in the Gunners. Instead of Ranji's homeland he went to France.

Tate played on during the war and by the time he was demobbed in January he was eager to get back with Sussex. He was no longer a lad of nineteen, but a young man, stronger and perhaps wiser. But the county was slow in welcoming him. He nearly went to play for Middlesex, and would have done if Eastbourne had not asked him to play for them. The committee at Hove then had a minor panic, because they heard that Bowley and Jupp and probably Robert Relf would not be ready to play at the new season's start. Tate was offered terms and was safely in, much to his relief, later to Sussex's and, much later, to future Sussex sides.

It cannot have been easy for any county to slip back into the routine of first-class Championship matches as if nothing had happened. The men who were in their prime when the war began were now a good few years older. Some, perhaps, had lost their edge. Others, like Tate, who was a youngster at the end of 1914 and did not even know that he was a pace bowler, had lost four seasons of seriously competitive cricket. Valence Jupp had come into the side only in 1909 as a professional, George Street had not taken over from Butt as wicket-keeper until 1912, and Ted Bowley, who was to go on to score more than 25,000 runs and take nearly 700 wickets, played for the first time in the same year.

The committee's stewardship at Sussex, tested during the war years as the ground kept going with service games and other non-first-class fixtures, was even further stretched as the 1919 season got under way with its series of two-day matches; three days was considered too ambitious. Indeed, when the three-day game appeared in 1920, Sussex were criticised by many as taking on more than they could reasonably

145

handle. However, the committee and in particular the new secretary, Major W. G. M. Sarel, and the captain, H. L. 'Bertie' Wilson, were rather determined people.

Sarel was not an office-bound wallah. Post-war cricket needed men of energy who would apply themselves to basic tasks. To a small extent the situation was similar to that in the 1830s which had led to the formation of Sussex. It was all very well agreeing that people would like to play cricket, and of course there was a wealth of experience and a formal structure for them to do so; but it had still to be properly organised at county level. The county had ticked over, more on a standby basis than anything else, with painting and repairs going on as normal. But in 1919 Sarel, the committee and the captain had to provide simple answers to difficult questions. What were the finances? Who would play? How many games would be played? Who would watch – and, therefore, where would some of the money come from? At the start of the war, Sussex had 1900 paying members. How many would be returning to Hove, Eastbourne, Hastings and Horsham? Where were the new members to be found? Who was going to find them?

For Sarel, who was also occupied as a batsman of some distinction, the committee and Wilson, the immediate problem, however, was to provide attractive cricket with so few younger men quickly available to put together a sound run-scoring and wicket-taking side. Inevitably, they had to turn to the older players for a lead. And how splendidly they responded. Joe Vine and George Cox were now well into their forties. Vine, no longer overshadowed by C. B. Fry, but who, remember, had been born at the start of the 1875 season, batted with a style rarely before seen from him. He had first played in 1896 and was yet to make his highest score of 202 against Northamptonshire at Hastings. The post-war crowds, and Vine, would have to wait another year for that great event. As for Cox, he had first appeared for the county in 1895. But no has-been he. In 1920, when he was forty-seven, he was to take seven Derbyshire wickets for 8 runs in sixteen overs at Hastings. And there was still the 1926 session at Horsham to come, when he took seventeen wickets against Warwickshire.

So, the 1919 season opened with a reliance on old players and new enthusiasm, and a few new faces including Gibson, Jenner, Miller and Harold Gilligan, whose brother A. E. R. Gilligan was playing at Surrey, though not for long. In spite of the reliability of veterans and newcoming keenness, Sussex, not for the first time, lacked balance, certainly in the opening games of the season. Peacetime cricket struggled through its return to the county circuit. Like some individual

146

and private warrior tribe, it regrouped but slowly. The Relfs and Jupp did not come back until half-way through the season and Ted Bowley not until the next; nor did Street, and three wicket-keepers were tried that year, the two Williams and Miller.

The first game was on 21 May against Somerset at Taunton. It was a curious affair, for it ended with Len Braund (the bowler when Fred Tate missed 'that' catch) invoking the two-minute law against the last Sussex batsman, R. B. Heygate. The poor fellow so penalised was in rheumatic pain and was still in the pavilion. Sympathetic though the umpire may have been towards the sad striker's twinges, the law's the law, the game was over, the scores equal and a tie was recorded. Seemingly, that oddity of a result set the pattern for Sussex for the rest of the season. It was generally decided that Sussex were the poorest side in the table; yet when the Australian XI played them Sussex had their visitors' backs to the wall and stonewalling to hang on for a draw.

Fortune eventually managed a weak smile, and a perky grin appeared on the face of the besieged dressing room. A lot had to do with the return of Seventh Cavalry, disguised as the Relfs and Vallance Jupp. The balance adjusted, scores mounted and wickets were taken. And in August victory. Yorkshire, who were to take the Championship that year, fell to a battery of Sussex bat and ball. But there was no great revival and charge for honours. Instead Sussex finished eleventh, with the old firm of Vine, Jupp and Albert Relf at the top of the county's batting averages and Cox, Albert Relf and Roberts atop the bowling. The next year was better. Ted Bowley was back, so was Street, and K. H. Higgs and A. E. R. Gilligan joined the club.

Arthur Gilligan made his first appearance in Sussex club cricket when he was twelve. Bognor were a man short, and Gilligan in 'white knickers' went out to bat with the seaside club needing 31 to win. He got the 1 and his very senior partner, George Bell, the 30. Gilligan went on to Dulwich College where he was a very fast bowler for schoolboy cricket and where, in 1914, he took 78 wickets and scored more than 500 runs. Surrey were very impressed and that year gave him a place in the second eleven, a quite legitimate registration because he was born in Denmark Hill in south London, and Dulwich but two hills away from The Oval. Instead of going straight up to Cambridge, he joined the Lancashire Fusiliers and by 1915 was in France.

In the first year after the war he was in the Cambridge side and played three times for Surrey. However, having watched Sussex as a lad and through one of his brothers, Harold, Gilligan's inclination

147

was towards that county. Furthermore, there was a strong family connection with the county apart from Bognor. His grandmother had been born in Burwash and some of her family, complete with Sussex accent, lived between Chichester and Pagham at North Mundham. By the end of the 1919 season he had decided, like his brother Harold, to play for Sussex – unlike their brother F. W. Gilligan, who was playing for and in 1920 captained Oxford, and who went to play north of the Thames for Essex. The ever-industrious secretary, Major Sarel, wrote to him, Surrey and the MCC, and A. E. R. Gilligan was registered and ready to play the following season after the University Match; 1920 was altogether a better year for cricket by the sea.

There was much criticism of the fact that the county took on thirty Championship games that year – more than any other side. Over-ambitious, it was said. Yet they won eighteen of them, lost eight and ended up in sixth position in spite of having a very difficult time of things during the middle season, although there was an amusing event to brighten the closest of defeats. Sussex had suffered at the hands of Nottinghamshire, and so confident were the latter of winning, which was reasonable since they wanted but 29 to win with all their second wickets intact, that many of their team had changed. Wilson, never a remarkable bowler for Sussex, opened with Ted Bowley at the other end. Much to everyone's surprise, Wilson began to have a golden day and took four wickets. There were only two Nottinghamshire batsmen left on the ground; the others had gone home. Richmond, the number eleven, was called to the wicket in such a hurry and fix that he had no time to change properly and arrived at the crease wearing a pink shirt. Embarrassing perhaps, but Nottinghamshire won.

Finishing sixth was far from disgraceful, and four of the side – Wilson the captain, Tate, Jupp and Bowley – each made more than a thousand runs that season and George Cox plundered 106 wickets. It was a season of contrasts once more. Three-day matches were back, and with the longer programme this in theory amounted to a full month's extra cricket. Quite a demand for any side, especially as the recovery from the enforced lay-off was taking some sorting out.

It was a season of two memorable occasions, both involving Maurice Tate. He had gone to live with his grandfather at Wivelsfield and had found a winter job hauling a horse and cart and logging. It was good for him. The lanky lad, filled out by the war years, was maturing into a strong young man, very different from the nicknamed 'Stalky' of 1914. Tate, it must be remembered, was not yet the quicker bowler, fast-medium perhaps, for which he is mainly celebrated. He was an off-spinner who got runs as well as wickets.

148

His batting was considered more important than his bowling at this stage, even though he took more than fifty Championship wickets in that year.

The first point of interest that season was Tate being asked to open the bowling with Arthur Gilligan against Kent at Tunbridge Wells. The omens of this partnership were perhaps not realised, especially as Tate's quick one was occasional rather than the norm. Then, at Hove, during the game against Oxford University, Tate shone as an all-rounder. The sides, if the scores are anything to go by, were almost perfectly matched. Sussex scored 221 and 216, Oxford 231 and 214. For the first time Tate hit a hundred runs and, bowling at about medium pace, took ten wickets in one game. Nevertheless, at the end of that year it was the old firm of Vine, Bowley and Jupp with R. A. Young who topped the batting and Cox, Jupp, Roberts and A. E. Relf the bowling.

The following year, 1921, saw the arrival of W. L. 'Titch' Cornford in the side, although he was yet to keep wicket. Young took over from Street during that season purely because he was the better batsman rather than the better wicket-keeper, a point of contention for all those who advocated the principle of playing the best wicket-keeper whatever his talents with a bat. Tate appeared third in the county's bowling averages, but the man who sat second, Jupp, took 93 wickets and topped the batting with 2000 runs.

The season ended with Sussex in ninth place and a change in the hierarchy. W. L. Knowles became secretary, a job he was to hold for twenty-one years, and Bertie Wilson gave over the captaincy to Arthur Gilligan. It was in 1922 that the Gilligan-Tate partnership began to shine with a brilliance in bowling terms that would capture the imagination as Ranji and Fry had done in batting. It seems, also, that it was Gilligan who realised the full potential of Tate as a quick bowler.

It was often said that when Tate bowled his standard off-breaks it was difficult to tell from a distance his action from that of his famous father. The change is said to have come about during one day in the middle of the 1922 season, Gilligan's first as captain. The Sussex side had started the year in fine style, winning five of the first six matches. The new captain was more than disappointed with the batting, and so, one afternoon in July, Gilligan called them all to the nets for practice. In his memoirs, *Sussex Cricket*, he tells how he 'discovered' Tate's hidden talent, a talent thus far suppressed by Tate's belief that he was a slow bowler.

149

I took my turn at the wickets, and Maurice was one of the bowlers at my net. He ran up and delivered the ball, and before I knew what had happened something flashed off the pitch, and there was a terrible noise behind me.

A kind gentleman, standing behind the nets, politely asked me if I would like my stump back. I accepted it with my pride, like my wicket, terribly shattered.

Up came Maurice again with a smile all over his face, and down came a slow delivery, which I hit as hard as I could into the deep field. Two minutes later, Maurice bowled me another lightning delivery, and once again the very kind gentleman handed me back my stump from behind the net, without passing any comment. The next ball from Maurice did not knock one stump out of the ground; it sent two instead, straight through the back of the net.

Gilligan knew that Sussex were on to a good thing. After all, he had three splintered stumps and a hole in the net to prove it. The next day, Sussex went to Tunbridge Wells. The Kent batsmen endorsed Gilligan's enthusiasm, although without much of their own. Tate took 8 for 32.

There are some who say that Gilligan did not 'discover' the fast-medium Tate. Certainly Tate did not bowl the way he did that day in the nets by fluke. He wrote once that he produced a similar fast-off-the-pitch delivery to dismiss Phil Mead in the Hampshire game that same year. What seems very possible is that Tate found that he could bowl this way and tried it on Gilligan in the nets, and that Gilligan did something about it.

Whatever its origins, Tate's new style, though still off eight brisk paces, meant that two years later, 1924, he was playing for England. The change in Tate's fortunes was amazing. From 1922 until 1936 he was at the top of the bowling averages except in 1933 and 1935 when he was second to James Langridge. In 1923, his first year as a quicker bowler, he took 219 wickets at an average of just 13 runs a wicket. When Gilligan was appointed captain of England, he took Tate with him on the 1924–5 winter tour of Australia and he picked up 38 wickets, which was more than any bowler of either side had ever done and ever did again until 1953 and Alec Bedser's 39 wickets.

And Tate should not be forgotten as a batsman. In a remarkably consistent spell of eight seasons, between 1922 and 1929, he completed the double, a hundred wickets and a thousand runs in each season. His career total of 17,086 runs gave him an average of 24.27, and his 2211 wickets 17.41 each. For sheer statistics, the two games in 1925

150

against Glamorgan take the breath away: a total of 27 wickets for an average of 5.07 a wicket.

The ten years from 1920 until the end of Arthur Gilligan's captaincy in 1930 saw the blooding of some of the most famous names in Sussex and England cricket. Gilligan himself was a mixture of amateur brilliance and professional thoroughness which inevitably brought about criticism. He was also the victim of cruel injury.

In a Test match against the South Africans in 1924, Gilligan had Tate at the other end in the England side. Tate's first ball in his first Test produced a wicket. The pair of them went through the opposition in under an hour, and the South Africans were all out for 30. It seemed almost possible that Sussex would at last be able to bowl out sides for modest totals.

If it had not been for Gilligan's misfortune during the Gentlemen v Players at The Oval, who knows what would have been possible that Championship year? Gilligan was batting and was hit over the heart by a quickish ball from the Worcestershire medium-pace man Pearson. Tate, who of course was playing on the other side, was in the slips and immediately ran to help his county captain. There was already a bruise appearing over the heart, and Tate often said that he thought Gilligan should have retired for the rest of the match. He did not, of course; he got out next ball, caught by Jack Hobbs in the covers. He felt groggy, rested, then came in next innings and hit 112. In the good stories, that would have been that. But owing to that injury Gilligan was never again able to bowl with his old fire. England and Sussex lost the full powers of a great player, and Tate the partner that every bowler needs at the other end. That was all in 1924. Sussex finished tenth.

It was also the year that Duleep arrived. Just as his polysyllabic uncle had always been Ranji to the Sussex crowd, so Prince Kumar Shri Duleepsinhji was nicknamed Smith with affection. He did not play for Sussex that year, but it was the time that an arrangement was made for his marriage to his uncle's former county. According to Arthur Gilligan, on Whit Saturday Sussex were playing Middlesex at Lord's and batting rather indifferently. The talk on the dressing-room balcony had turned to the need for a good number three. Cue His Highness the Maharaja of Nawanagar.

He arrived in the dressing room quite unannounced but very welcome and invited Gilligan and his brother, Harold, to Jamnagar House, the unlikely name of Ranji's home in Staines. It was a lunch party with the great and famous scattered about the table and afterwards about the gardens, putting-green and bowls-lawn. With all the discreetness of court intrigue, Ranji invited Gilligan to his study for a private conversation. Gilligan remembered:

'It is very kind of you to come here today,' he said, 'for I very much wish to discuss with you the chance of my nephew, K. S. Duleepsinhji, playing county cricket. He has acquitted himself quite creditably at Cheltenham, and he is a very fair bat. He is qualified to play, if he wishes, for three counties – Hampshire, Middlesex and my own county, Sussex. Naturally I wish him to play for Sussex, but I told the boy that I would leave it entirely to him to choose, and that I would not prejudice him in any way in his decision. I am glad to tell you that he gave his answer very quickly and decisively, and said he would like to play for Sussex.

'Splendid,' I replied, remembering our talk on the pavilion balcony the previous day at Lord's.

'Well, now, the question is,' said the Jam Sahib, 'would you like him as a player for the county, and if so, will you, Gilligan, ask the Sussex Committee whether he may qualify for us?'

I gave a quick answer to His Highness, and said: 'I will answer for the Committee: your nephew may qualify immediately.'

His Highness very kindly agreed that Duleep should qualify by residence at once, and made arrangements for him to live at Eastbourne with a personal friend of his, Dr. W. G. Heasman.

So are marriages made in Staines. Duleep had been well taught at Cheltenham, where cricket was taken seriously. He had the advantage also of being coached by Albert Relf and when he went up to Cambridge, the new 'Smith' had few problems getting into the 1925 side. His first appearance for Sussex was in 1926, during the university's long vacation. He went up to Leicester and scored 97. The team travelled back to Hove and Duleep scored a century. Not long after that runs became hard to find, a lean spell which produced a stern telegram from his ever-watchful uncle. It must have done the trick, for he then went to Scarborough and hit 71 in the Gentlemen v Players.

But Duleep probably never realised his full potential as a batsman. He suffered terrible ill-health and at one point was so poorly that his devoted uncle Ranji feared for his nephew's life. Duleep's was a short cricketing career, but one which produced 15,485 runs, including fifty centuries, thirty-four of them for Sussex, and an average of almost 50. And, like his uncle before him, Duleep captained his adopted country; that was in 1931 and 1932 after the retirement of Arthur Gilligan. In Gilligan's last year as captain, 1930, the first match of the season was at

Hove against Northamptonshire. Sussex scored 521 for 7. Tate hit 111 and took nine wickets in the match. But the game – or, rather, one day of it – belonged to Duleep. He scored 333, still the highest individual score for a Sussex player.

To return to 1924, the year of the arranged marriage between K. S. Duleepsinhji and Sussex County Cricket Club, is to find another new and to-be-famous name in Sussex cricketing history – J. H. Parks, the first of four extraordinarily gifted players in that family: himself, his brother, H. W., his son, the Sussex and England wicket-keeper J. M. Parks, and now Bobby Parks, his grandson. He was twenty-one when he first played in 1924, and Arthur Gilligan thought him an important addition to the side, which considering Parks' record was something of an understatement. In fact Gilligan was less than flattering when he described J.H. as 'rather on the stodgy side as a batsman . . . he watches the ball well, but is rather apt to get his hands too much down towards the ground'.

It was hardly a bad technique considering what he did with it. Although he was rarely in the top three of the county's batting averages and only half his career in the leading bowling figures, his gifts with both bat and ball were rarely doubted. He made nearly 20,000 runs, took 795 wickets and scored a thousand runs in a season twelve times. Most will remember the season towards the end of his playing career in 1937 as his greatest. For the county he scored 2578 runs during that year, a record still for Sussex. When his 1937 international matches are included, Parks' total is another record: three thousand runs and a hundred wickets in one year.

The other two new names in that 1924 side were James Langridge and G. S. Grimston. Langridge was just eighteen when he joined Sussex, a left-handed bat and left-arm bowler. He was frail and quiet and like his younger brother, John, who was to play four years later, good-natured, almost unassuming. James Langridge became recognised from about 1928 onwards as a true all-rounder. Between 1927 and 1952 he scored a thousand runs in each season and took more than fourteen hundred wickets in his career. His time with Sussex saw many changes of style and fortune for the county, spanning nearly thirty playing years that were crowned in 1950 when he became captain, the first professional to do so.

Grimston was anything but a professional in the sense that he was the typical amateur of the game. The previous season, Grimston had been considered something of a bowler at Winchester, where he headed the averages. He joined the Army and played for Sussex when he could, though never enough to make many runs or take the sort

153

of wickets he did for the Army. His fullest contribution to the county was after the Second World War, when in 1950, as Lieutenant-Colonel Grimston, he took over as secretary to the club.

The Langridges and Grimstons of the cricketing world, the promising professional and the good-natured amateur, somehow personified the Sussex of 1924. In June of that year they were at the top of the Championship table, but simply did not have what was needed to stay there. Gilligan and Tate were so good that they were away playing representative cricket for some of the time, which was difficult for a side that had so long searched for such a partnership, and, of course, this was the year of Gilligan's accident during the Gentlemen v Players. Vallance Jupp, who had decided to take on the captaincy-cum-secretaryship of Northamptonshire, had been sorely missed for two seasons in spite of the efforts and free scoring of Tate, Bowley and Wilson.

Twenty-four batsmen turned out for Sussex that season, most of them amateurs. Nearly as many had turned arm over for county. And so a side which could, certainly during the first half of the season, boast the most piercing attack in the land could not find the combination to get anywhere near the Championship. Instead, they ended tenth in the table. And matters were to get worse.

The following year they slid to thirteenth, even though many were in fine form. Tate, such was his celebration as a sporting character, had started the season at Harrods department store in Knightsbridge, demonstrating his bowling technique. It must have done him a power of good, should he have needed such extra power, because within a couple of weeks he took fifteen Glamorgan wickets for 58 runs at Hove (egged on from the other end by Bert Wensley, who got 103 wickets that year), got another thousand runs and 208 wickets, 110 of them bowled – the most wickets he ever got in a season. And, seemingly inevitably, there was George Cox, now into his fifties, plugging away with ball and bat; nearly 800 runs and more than fifty wickets that year.

Gilligan, slower now than before and playing fewer games, was understandably a loss as a performer and as leader. It was his brother Harold, who had joined the club at the end of the war, who stood in as captain. Harold Gilligan became captain in his own right in 1930 and led an England touring side. But he was never in the same league as his brother Arthur. He started playing in 1919 and scored nearly 8000 runs in his career, more than 3000 of them during 1923 (1127), 1927 (1010) and 1929 (1087). The following year, another of those Sussex brothers joined the team.

154

For many years after 1926 there were few times when the name Parks failed to appear in the top three bowling or batting places. H. W. Parks started playing in that 1926 season which also saw the first appearance of Duleepsinjhi after the University games, the return of Gilligan to the higher reaches of the bowling and batting figures, and a famous and hard draw against the Australian tourists. This Parks, three years younger than his brother, was a batsman of considerable strength and determination, as his 200 not out against Essex, at Chelmsford and not on the easier Hove wicket, showed. He put together nearly 22,000 runs, including 42 centuries, before he retired in 1948, still at the forefront of Sussex batting and just a year before his nephew, Jim Parks, played his first game for the county. Harry Parks could not have joined at a more interesting time. Sussex were hardly in prime condition, and this had nothing to do with that other malaise of the year, the General Strike.

Arthur Gilligan was away as a Test selector, and Tate, of course, was playing for England and missed ten Sussex games. However, the two of them made an enormous contribution to Sussex struggling to tenth position. Early in the season Sussex went up to London and beat Surrey at The Oval, the first time Surrey had been beaten there since 1920. Gilligan made 62 and 100 not out, and Tate took seven wickets for just 90 runs. But it might be remembered that with the long stretches of bowling Tate had also to open the batting for the county with Bowley, and that season more or less ended top of the averages having scored 1347 runs as well as taking 147 wickets. More or less at the top, because Duleep appeared for the first time after the university year had ended and scored nearly 700 runs, to be at the head of the table, his position assured by arithmetic rather than by consistent performance. His first innings was against Leicestershire, and he ended just three short of a century, almost a dream début and a taste of the two centuries that were to follow off the Hampshire and Middlesex bowling that season.

Then there was George Cox, still playing more than thirty years after his first appearance for the county. This was the year that Cox took seventeen wickets in the match against Warwickshire. Small wonder, even at the age of fifty-two, that he should finish second in the Sussex bowling averages.

At the end of that season, Gilligan took the MCC side on tour to India. The strenuous series was the first England tour of India since 1902–3; and apart from Tate's 1160 runs and 116 wickets, a record for any player on tour, it produced one of the more amusing incidents in tour cricket, not always to be found in the sub-continent. According

155

to Tate, the magnificently bearded Maharaja of Patiala came in to bat and snicked Tate into the slips before scoring. There was a long silence. Nobody was prepared to appeal. Tate looked hard at the umpire. So did the Maharaja. And that was that. He carried on. Later, Tate was asked why, when the regal batsman was obviously out, he had not appealed. Said Tate, 'Don't be a fool. We've got to go and stay with the chap later on in the tour. Do you think I want to be poisoned?'

The tour put Tate in form for the opening of the 1927 season. When the side went to Portsmouth in May, Bowley and Tate opened the batting and put on fifty in 25 minutes. Within ten minutes of that, Tate had scored fifty of his own. He hit a century in 68 minutes, was out in the next and the partnership had made 144 runs. With form like that, it was a wonder that Sussex did not blossom with the spring weather. They again finished tenth, but they were on the mend after years of ending the season in the murkier depths of the Championship table. They were also ending a small era in their history. Famous names were about to disappear from the Sussex scorecards.

Chapter 14

There are moments in cricket when it is easy to imagine that nothing in the world has changed since first impressions. To those who would mutter furiously about sponsorship and money-making, let them think back to the late Victorians and the blatant advertising and endorsement, good and great. Average-mongering and money-making have always been there. To those who would, with the surest reason, bemoan the loss of that tranquil oasis, the Central Ground at Hastings, let them remember Brunswick and Ireland's Gardens. And standards? Not quite the same, with coloured clothes and motifs worn and sported by players. Let those who grieve look back to the last century: England players in spotted shirts then.

Change has come in concrete forms and in terms of tempo, in one-days and tours, in so many ways and differences since, say, the twenties and thirties when manliness and clean-cut heroes were claimed for the game – quite bogus claims perhaps, but nevertheless images put up to portray the atmosphere of cricket that could be recognised whether it was in huge pavilioned headquarters, county cushioned-seated terraces or Sussex villages where sons of sons of sons still bat and bowl out this game in a curious time-warp.

For it is the atmosphere of yesteryear that is often captured, especially among the spectators. Is there not a special feeling of timelessness and expectation on the first day of every season as those who have watched year after year stroll once more into the ground? The small boys armed with scorecard and handbook, smudging felt-tips and autograph book. The less agile with sandwich bag and flask, seeking out favoured seats atop pavilion or by third man's patrol,

157

watching eagerly to see old friends without names, just familiar faces, reassured that winter's grip has slipped and another year been spared. It has long been so. Bricklayer and carpenter have left new marks, but there is an unchanging shape to a cricket ground; it has a face of its own that no amount of mortared make-up can disguise. Sixty years and a few on, and a new season opens with all the hope, expectation and scrubbed, painted and still-peeling atmosphere of the twenties or thirties, the forties, the fifties, the sixties. So it was in the mid-1920s when the steadiness of an older generation called time and once more another order made itself felt.

Tom Burchell, sober and three-piece-suited, brim-down trilby and stiff white round studded collar, prepared his ground at Hove with all the care of the respected craftsman the head groundsman was expected to be. No better a craft then, just different ways and stations. No tracksuits and trainers. No ride-on samurai chariot to roll and cut. The wicket packed hard as the horse, carefully shod in big leather galoshes, hauled the heavy roller up and down, up and down. Always somewhere a hobbledehoy to pull and tug when the mare went lame, was pensioned; and another to run with telegraphs for the senior men and to carry the page slate when one, perhaps hidden in the crowd, was wanted to telephone or come quickly.

There was the small main pavilion with its centre clock, from beneath which the amateurs emerged to take the field, and to the south the balconied but far less grand block in which the professionals dressed and kept their distance. Until the pavilion was extended to the north in 1928, the ladies were sheltered – 'enclosed', they were told – well away from their menfolk. Laetitia Stapleton in her book *A Sussex Cricket Odyssey* writes about the mid-twenties and what to do with the ladies:

> The only shelter provided for the female sex was a rather rickety stand, known affectionately as the 'hen coop'; this now stands – just – on the eastern side of the ground . . . The 'cowshed' at the southern end had a high wooden front, painted white, against which the ball would hurtle with a satisfying thud to register yet another four.

As a postscript: beware, then, those who would call the hen coop the cowshed. The cowshed was at the southern end until the Arthur Gilligan Stand was built. Across by the pub, beyond the single-bench boundary, spectators in caps and braces would sleep off lunch, while in the pavilion trilbied, homberged and club-tied gentlemen smoked their pipes and occasional cigars. The ladies, in hats and gloves, still knew their place in the Enclosure, and their cricket beyond it. And why not? Their enthusiasm was beyond question, and it was encouraged in the relaxed atmosphere at Hove, where players and staff were enormously approachable. As Mrs Stapleton describes her girlhood:

> Almost the whole of the Easter holidays was spent watching the county players in the nets and when they disappeared for rest and refreshment trying, however feebly, to emulate their achievements. Looking back on those days I can see how fortunate we young people were in having Mr. W. L. Knowles as the Sussex Secretary. Our tickets did not give us permission to practise in the nets and it was entirely due to his turning a blind eye to our activities that we enjoyed so many happy hours on the County Ground, the highlights of our day being when Tate, Bowley or Jim Parks – or one of the other players – would send down a few balls to us or give a bit of advice. Mr. Knowles and his assistant, dear old Billy Newham, both of whom played for Sussex, smiled benignly on our efforts and, provided we did not get in anyone's way, were content to let us pursue our heart's desire.

The 1928 extending of the men's pavilion may have more fashionably corralled the ladies, at hand's rather than arm's length, but it also drew closer the amateurs and professionals. The amateurs had always lived in the pavilion in overstuffed comfort, *The Times* and portrait-hung walls. The rebuilding meant that the professionals could move into the new structure and by walking through the interconnecting corridor be led out, until 1950 by an amateur of course, from the same exit. It was against this background that Sussex's fortune started its slow change, like some three-masted barquentine, sluggishly at first, but sure in tack and direction.

At the end of the 1927 season, a year in which the county finally cleared their mortgage on the ground, George Cox, it seems, had decided to retire from first-class cricket. A total of 1810 wickets and 14,353 runs is memorial enough for a man who began his playing career before the majority of the team were born. He had known men who had watched Sussex cricket since it was first formed into a county side, and he was as revered as any who had played in it. He played on and went in 1928. Innocent ball, fashioned and stitched by docile and patient hand, in his hands became ruthless judge of skill and foe. The rub of fingers on ground, long hard look at batsman, the back of the hand rubbed across the mouth, the left arm raised high and the ball even higher, seeming, tamely even, to waft and then – and then 7 for 8 runs against Derbyshire, 17 for 106 of Warwickshire, and against Somerset 6 overs, 6 maidens, 0 runs, 5 wickets. Cox was a master.

The guv'nor, the senior professional of the twenties, was regimental sergeant-major to his skipper's colonel. It was he who kept the other paid players in line (the amateurs were officers and apparently knew how to behave). Cox was RSM extraordinary. Said Gilligan, his colonel: 'As senior professional he set a very high standard to the other professionals, instilling into them the best traditions of an English gentleman.'

With Cox gone, the county's pace-stick was handed to the solemn-faced Ted Bowley. Gilligan, still captain, liked his 'quiet, gentlemanly, modest and charming ways'. The members liked his 280 not out against Gloucester the following year, 1929, his 13 for 153 against Derbyshire the same year, the 8 for 62 against Northamptonshire, his first-wicket partnership with John Langridge of 490 runs in 350 minutes against Middlesex at Hove in 1933, his last season, and altogether his 25,439 first-class runs and 670 wickets.

He believed that if a bowler sent the ball down, then as batsman his job was to hit it, the harder the better and particularly off the back foot. In the years that he played from 1912, Bowley often found himself having to shoulder responsibility for building the Sussex innings when other batting was unreliable. He carried burdens just as thoroughly as he punished bowlers, took wickets and made impossible slip catches look simple. Cox had left the Sussex professionals in good hands.

The year that Cox went, 1928, John Langridge joined his brother Jim in the team. Jim Langridge, himself but four years in the side, was beginning to shine as an all-rounder, ending that season in the top three of both batting and bowling averages. Sussex went from seventh place in 1928 to fifth in 1929 and gained sharp recognition as one of the best sides in the Championship. It was a year of high scores, typical of 1920s cricket. During that decade it was commonplace to hit three or four hundred an innings. In 1929 Sussex scored more than four hundred on no less than six occasions and twice fell just a handful short of five hundred.

But the most glorious feast was to be found at Hastings. The game was against Kent over three baking August days. Sussex batted first and at lunch were 201 for 4. Duleepsinhji had batted for only 100 minutes but had scored 115. The innings finished with Sussex on 428. Kent replied with 398, and the battle for runs was on. Sussex then made 381 for 8, with Duleep making 246 not out, just the fifth batsman ever to score a century and a double-century in the same. game. In all, 1451 runs in three days and Tate taking 13 wickets for 194 runs.

For Arthur Gilligan it was a satisfying season for the side, but hardly a personal success. Because of illness he played in only ten games, with his brother Harold leading the side in the other matches, and finished the summer at the bottom of the batting averages and not much higher in the bowling. It must have been difficult for him. At the end of 1928 Gilligan had realised his ambition, and it was one that was reflected in the number of runs scored during the relatively few years of his captaincy.

Gilligan frowned when batsmen scanned the averages for their personal triumphs. He found it a distasteful pastime. He believed also that when batsmen started playing for an average. then the batting suffered and so did the game. Yet reflected in those averages of batsmen between the time he took over the leadership in 1922 and the end of the 1929 season, and perhaps beyond, were the fruits of his careful ambition and husbandry.

He promoted the search for youngsters and in particular the efforts of the captain of the nursery side, Alan Saunders, who travelled throughout East and West Sussex searching for new talent and encouraging up-and-coming players. By the successful early 1930s, all the professionals with the exception of the two old hands Bowley and Tate were the products of this policy of home-growing and bringing on young talent. Gilligan's playing talents aside, Sussex owed him and people like Alan Saunders and the ever-travelling, ever-talent-searching secretary Lance Knowles a great deal during that period, a fact just occasionally forgotten and hidden behind overwhelming totals and wicket maidens.

Certainly Arthur Gilligan's sides had been recognised as some of the most attractive cricketers of the time. Sussex were considered to be the finest fielding side in the Championship and arguably the most celebrated mix of all-rounders. Gilligan's own view of his men, the professionals in particular, may be found in his autobiography, *Sussex Cricket*.

Albert Relf:

> . . . was a magnificent all-rounder, and one of the finest triers of them all . . . One tip he gave me at the end of my first over still remains in my mind: 'Get your head over the ball, when you make your stroke, and let your head guide your shot.'

Bob Relf:

. . . was one of the very few Sussex batsmen to hit a ball clean over the 'cow-shed', the small pavilion enclosure at the south end of the Hove ground.

Joe Vine:

. . . loved fielding on the boundary, and despite his advancing years he showed plenty of speed and always delighted the crowd with that wonderful under-arm jerk of his, when he returned the ball to the bowler or wicket-keeper.

George Cox:

. . . was one of the very best fighters I have ever known, and I always gloried in having him on my side, whenever there was a possibility of a tight finish. His advice was always sound, and he helped me more than I can adequately describe. Some of my side christened him 'the old war-horse', and for his years he was an absolute marvel. When we were having a good old leather-hunt, and our bowling had been knocked to every part of the field, I used to look round in desperation to know whom to put on.

Suddenly I would catch George's eye, and with that broad smile covering his sunny old face, covered in perspiration, he would come up to me and say: 'What about me having another turn?'

'All right, George, and God bless you,' was my reply time and time again.

Maurice Tate:

. . . is the Sussex Peter Pan, and his boyish enthusiasm continues unabated after several years of wonderful hard work with the ball . . . I find it extremely difficult to remember his sending down many loose balls. So much so, that it was always an extremely difficult task, as his skipper, to take him off. He was tireless, and could bowl for long stretches, without losing any of his fire and precision.

'Tich' Cornford, one of the smallest men then playing first-class cricket:

Maurice is running up to bowl; down goes Cornford on his haunches, and on days when the sun is not shining, and the light leaves much to be desired, it needs every little bit of one's vision to see, whether the small figure is still there, or whether the earth has swallowed the ball-like dwarf to its bosom. But no; as the batsman plays at the ball and misses, there are the safe pair of hands taking it cleanly and without any fuss, and if the batsman raises his foot those bails are off in a flash.

Bert Wensley:

> . . . is one of those bowlers who can bowl for an interminable period, and he is a born trier. No matter how badly things are going against our team, Bert never gives up trying, and he will 'stick' it to the bitter end.

Jim Parks:

> I always likened him to a cat on the field, for he would pounce on hard drives, and return the ball to the wicket-keeper with a lightning delivery.

A reminder that this was to be so for many years, was Gilligan's praise for his men.

> I can think of no better description of our Sussex professionals than that which the 1932 President of the Club, Sir William Campion, late Governor of Western Australia, gave to them at the dinner held at Brighton in honour of the Sussex team's great performance in occupying second place in the County Championship. Sir William, in a splendid speech, paid tributes to K. S. Duleepsinhji and his team, and then turning to Ted Bowley and the remainder of the professionals, who with their wives and sweethearts were seated at the centre table, said: 'Sussex have every reason to be extremely proud of our professionals, who have set a grand example; but also we value very highly the way in which they play the game like gentlemen.'

Arthur Gilligan must surely be rated as one of the finest cricketers to have played for Sussex and England. For too short a period he inspired those about him with a sense of all that he thought was decent about the game. Had he not suffered that terrible injury, his

163

remarkable career would probably have been even more impressive and perhaps Sussex fortunes that much greater. But, then, he carried no malice towards bad luck and maybe, for one particular reason, was understandably thankful for the cricketing life he did have, a life that could easily have ended one day in 1915 while serving at the Front with the Lancashire Fusiliers. A German sniper took a shot at the anonymous Gilligan. It missed, but it was close enough to splinter a brick into the eye of the young cricketer. Fifteen years later, while shaving Gilligan discovered a quarter-inch sliver of that same brick. It had finally worked its way to the front of his eye and to his realisation that in that other queer game he, too, had had his share of near-miss and good fortune.

And so Gilligan's reign ended and Harold, A. H. H. Gilligan took over. Inevitably, his career is remembered less often than his county brother's. Certainly, as noted elsewhere, it was less spectacular and, although he captained the MCC's 1929–30 touring side to New Zealand and stood in at Sussex on many occasions, he was appointed for only one year as the county's leader. It was far from an unsuccessful year. Sussex had gone from fifth place in 1929 to seventh in Harold Gilligan's season, a year in which Ranji, His Highness Jam Sahib of Nawanagar, was elected president and celebrated his preferment with a donation of £1000 to the county, a much-needed and welcome offering.

Ranji had not disappeared to India from England. He spent much time watching cricket and especially the fortunes, sometimes mixed and controversial, of his nephew Duleepsinhji, whom Ranji was supporting financially. During the 1929 season, the year before Ranji's presidency, Duleep had scored 2500 runs including two double-centuries for Sussex. Such was his form that he was picked at last to play for England. He went up to Edgbaston to play against the South Africans, but was far from successful. He got 12 in the first innings and 1 in the second. O'Connor of Essex, his replacement in the Lord's test, which was captained by the third Gilligan, F. W., did even worse and it was generally believed that Duleep would be brought back. He was not. The selectors recalled Woolley, who did rather well, which supported the selectors' decision although there were suggestions that Duleep was the victim of the politics that sometimes lurks beneath the doings of international cricket.

One hypothesis of the time was that the South African government had objected to his inclusion. Certainly H. G. Deane, the then South African captain, was concerned enough to write to Duleep telling him that the team had no objections to his presence in the England side. Whatever the truth of all this, it was interesting that in spite of his

164

extraordinary form that year Duleep was not picked for the Gentlemen *v* Players match. Alan Ross in his biography of Ranji noted: 'The suspicion grew that had Duleep played a big innings for the Gentlemen it would have been difficult to resist public insistence for his reinstatement.' In 1931 Duleep became captain of Sussex.

The 1931 season was an exciting time for Sussex and an important one for county cricket in general. There had, for some time, been many doubts about the way in which the Championship was decided. The table was determined by the percentage of possible points any one side achieved, even though they had played more games. For example, a side could win all games, and even beat the champions, but still lose on percentage calculations. As a result, that year the new points system was introduced: 15 for a win, 5 for a first-innings lead and 3 to the other side, and 4 points each if the game was rained off if there was no result seen, in the first innings.

In Sussex, Duleep took over the leadership and John Langridge became Bowley's opening partner. John Langridge has been described as the finest opening batsman never to have played for England. His record as a batsman and slip-fielder can only make curious reading for anyone wishing to ignore him for the ultimate selection. He was eighteen when he first played for the county and scored more centuries, 76, than any other Sussex player, including Fry and Ranji. On eight occasions he scored more than two hundred runs and in more than 900 innings hit 34,152 runs. In 1949 he scored twelve centuries.

As a slip-fielder Langridge had few peers. He held 779 catches for Sussex, 133 of them off his brother's bowling. In his last season, 1955, twenty-seven years after he first appeared for the county, John Langridge took 69 catches in the season, a figure only five other players anywhere had bettered. In that first season as an opening batsman he was steady and feeling his way behind the free hitting of his captain, Duleep, who topped the Sussex batting averages in front of Bowley and Harry Parks.

It was a season full of change. In spite of a splendid win over Lancashire at summer's opening, the first half of the season saw Sussex sliding into the doldrums of earlier years. But Duleep's style and grace, which have been compared only to his uncle's, led the cavalry gavotte towards the top. Duleep hit nine Championship centuries and ended the year with 1859 runs to his name – far more than the three other Sussex thousand-makers, Bowley, Harry Parks and Tommy Cook. Cook and Bowley played well together, as those who had seen their 200 Horsham partnership against Warwickshire four years earlier would testify.

165

Cook's best season was to come. In 1934 he scored more than 2000 runs including 220 against Worcestershire, perhaps his favourite county because he also took 214 off their bowling at Eastbourne in 1933. But in that first year of Duleep's leadership, 1931, Cook had to be content with fourth place in the averages, a mark of the Sussex batting power which, with Tate, James Langridge and Wensley getting a hundred wickets, carried the county to fourth place, the highest they had finished since 1909, the year after John Langridge was born and before Bowley or Tate had ever played for Sussex. The bowlers were at the front of the Sussex challenge for the Championship, and it was Tate's international misfortune that became the county's good luck.

That year, 1931, was the first time that New Zealand had played Test cricket in England. Tate was not chosen for the first game at Lord's, the only time that he had been dropped from the side since 1924. Perhaps because the New Zealanders surprised everyone at Lord's by winning, Tate was brought back into the side and quickly took four wickets for just 37 runs. But this was not enough for him to keep his place, especially as Harold Larwood was in fine form and available. Because he was more easily available for Sussex, the county capitalised on England's loss, which is probably why he was able to take 111 wickets that season and New Zealand was to get another, but different, taste of the Sussex bowler.

Tate was no longer considered the great all-rounder of a few seasons earlier, but when the New Zealand side went to Hove towards the end of the tour Tate opened the batting, something he rarely did by then. He hit 142. The game was eventually drawn, but it was a fine close to the season with Tate, James Langridge and Wensley first, second and third in the bowling and Duleep, Bowley and Harry Parks the batting.

There was more and better to come in the way of three new players that year, including Jim Cornford (who was no relation to the wicket-keeper Titch Cornford), the new Cox: George Cox Jnr. and R. S. G. Scott, who within two years would be the county's captain. Fourth position that year was better than for a long time, and it was but the beginning of a joyful period for batsman, bowler and those who watched Sussex cricket. But a cloud was to hang gloomily over the Sussex pavilion before the following season was out.

The official note of the 1932 season remarks:

Duleepsinhji again captained in 1932 to finish in runner-up position in the Championship with only one defeat and that by the champion county Yorkshire in the last match of the season, although

166

the deficit of points was beyond our reach should we have beaten them. Duleep's health prevented him from playing in the last five matches and this, together with an extremely wet summer, were factors that did not help. In his absence R. S. G. Scott took over the leadership. Duleep, Harry Parks and Jim Langridge took the batting honours whilst Tate, taking over a hundred wickets as usual, Jim Langridge, who just failed to complete 'the double', and Scott headed the bowling. 'Tich' Cornford kept wicket with his usual enthusiasm. A new name appearing this year was A. Melville who was to lead the side in the near future.

Within those precise notes of the season are contained the hopes and disappointments of the county and its people, but in particular of Maurice Tate and Duleepsinhji. The year had opened with great and justifiable hope for Sussex. Quite possibly thanks to Arthur Gilligan, they were the finest fielding side in England. Tate had finished the previous season with more than a hundred wickets; Wensley had taken 121 and was in fine form with bat as his 80 in 40 minutes against Kent had proved; James Langridge had got a hundred wickets, as he had in 1930 and was again to do in 1933; Cook had got a thousand runs; and Duleep, batting as graciously and richly as ever, was proving to be an intelligent and inspiring leader.

The captain had talked long about the chances of success and determined that, in spite of the individual talent, it was a side that won Championships, not simply stars. His aim was to fashion the team into an unbeatable unit, each playing his part and each realising that he had an important part to play. The team swept into the season with great enthusiasm. The result at the end of the summer was impressive with Bowley, Harry and Jim Parks, James Langridge, Tate and Cook getting their thousand runs and the three reliables, Tate, Langridge and Wensley, their hundred wickets. Tate, however, was a troubled man.

Tate's ambition that year was to play in the single Test against the Indians and be chosen for the winter tour of Australia. He was not selected against India, and when he appeared in the Gentlemen v Players he had a miserable game. Nor was he chosen for the first Test trial of the year, although he was asked to play after one of the Players, M. J. C. Allom, who played for Cambridge and Surrey, dropped out. Tate took 7 for 99 in the match. Nevertheless, he did not get into the next Test trial, nor did he get on the preliminary list for Australia. If he was as disappointed as one would imagine, in spite of his outgoing personality he tried not to show it. He took

13 wickets against Middlesex at Hove and began scoring runs again. But the strain did tell on his playing and his private life. However, that was all to come after the season was over.

Sussex had set off in fine style for the head of the Championship table, with Duleep leading from the front with big blazing June scores including centuries against Worcestershire, Surrey and Lancashire and 'near-misses' against Gloucestershire and the champions, Yorkshire. By the end of July it seemed that Sussex might at last have a first-class chance of winning the Championship. Then fate started to nibble at the edges of the county's success. The side included a worried Tate and a clearly unwell Duleep when it played a concentrated series of games away from home. Glamorgan, Gloucestershire and Somerset were soundly beaten. But the price was devastating.

Duleep had become progressively worse in himself, and it naturally showed in his batting which on paper looked little better than an inconsistent tail-ender. There was an added pressure for him. Throughout Duleep's career his famous uncle had kept watch on his progress, usually with great pride, for he deeply loved his nephew. But there were sometimes firm telegrams of advice when things were going less than smoothly. Duleep's enormous regard for Ranji reacted to this pressure with absolute respect and in an obvious manner. This time, his loss of form was due entirely to ill health, and doctors told him that he should stop playing and take a much-needed rest. Ranji was not in England and could not realise that Duleep was a sick man. Alan Ross, in his biography of Ranji, gives a perceptive insight into the relationship between uncle and nephew; it was more that of father and son.

> Ranji, learning only of Duleep's comparative loss of form and ignorant of the gravity of his illness, telegraphed him from Aix-les-Bains not to pay any attention but to see the season through. More than once before, when Duleep had struck a bad patch, Ranji had flippantly wired him to give up the game and concentrate on tennis, preferably against women.
>
> It was a fatal misjudgement on Ranji's part, and one that he came to regret bitterly. His deep love for Duleep was never in doubt but he sometimes chided him in that insensitive fashion parents show for their children. As a result of Ranji's injunction Duleep disregarded his doctor's orders. Ranji's cable, in fact, had been concerned and encouraging, but it also contained the phrase 'think more of the interest of the side than of your reputation'. The cable ended: 'I put your fielding much above most people's batting. Therefore go on. Love and Success.'

168

And so Duleep went into that winning game against Somerset at Taunton with a determination to succeed. He scored a magnificent 90. But before his innings had ended he was totally drained and bleeding internally. All the efforts of doctors in England and Switzerland could not help him. For the prince among cricketers, it was the end of his career.

For Sussex, not yet realising the full implication of Duleep's illness, his absence was compounded by injuries to Wensley and Bowley and minor ailments to many more in the side. When they arrived at Hove for the game of the season against Yorkshire, the Championship leaders, the Sussex side must have wondered at their chances and ill fortune. The team's gloom dulled their performance: Sussex struggled to make 166 and then 150. A very richly batting and bowling Yorkshire, unscathed by Tate's 6 for 89 in their first innings, scored 258 and then 225 for just three wickets. The Championship race was over. But misery had not yet done with Maurice Tate.

Tate had heard that he would be selected for the Australian tour after all. But he was called to Lord's and, according to him, told that the authorities felt he was not giving one hundred per cent and that he was very lucky indeed to be included in the side. Remembering Gilligan's opinion and those who forever watched him, it is difficult to believe that Tate could be seriously accused of not giving one hundred per cent. Nor does his end-of-season average of 160 wickets at under 16 runs a wicket suggest a man giving less than his all. True, Tate was now thirty-seven years old and at times must have felt the strain of daily cricket, but he kept himself enormously fit and was driven by thoughts of taking wickets, especially Australian ones.

He had his own worries. He had been unwell, and his wife was expecting their baby and was far from full of boundless energy herself. The pressure got to Tate. He had thrown himself into his bowling for his England place and for the sake of Sussex. The strain might be imagined. He telephoned Lord's and said he could not go on tour. His wife secretly telephoned Findlay, then the MCC Secretary, and asked him to ignore her husband's request to be stood down. After a great deal of thumb-sucking and consideration, Tate was told to report to Marseilles and catch a boat for Australia. He went but, as the story tells, was all but ignored. His wife went through her own agonies, including the trauma of having newspapermen staking out their home and even trying to break in.

That tour, with its demonstration of leg theory, was famous, or infamous, for well-recorded reasons and included the Adelaide Test, 'a match that will go down in history as the most unpleasant ever

169

played', according to *Wisden*. To Tate, an enormously popular figure in Australia, it was a totally alien form of the game. He returned with the rest of the team in May 1933, seemingly none the worse for the experience, ironically probably well rested and keen to see his son, Michael, and get on with helping Sussex.

Duleep had by now handed over the captaincy, although he hoped that a long rest (he talked of five years or so) would mean that he could play again. He never did. It was an enormously depressing start to the 1933 season. The sadness of Duleep's departure was made worse by the news from India that, during the early hours of the morning of 2 April, Ranji had died.

Later there was to be a series of controversies about the circumstances of his death, that it had been forecast to the exact day by an Indian mystic and, worse, that it was the result of the strain of political disagreement with the British representative, a charge for which there is no conclusive evidence. It would seem more likely that Ranji's health simply failed him, yet it was somehow unremarkable that such a man, the Maharaja Jam Sahib of Nawanagar, with his origins in intrigue and scheming, should die within a hall of echoing speculation. To Sussex, he was Ranji, and it was sad enough that a great cricketer was no more.

The season at Hove began with the new captain, R. S. G. Scott, who had batted well during the mixed summer of 1932, full of hope, although he could not know that in spite of the victories on the field that year he, too, would finish the season with grief. The summer of 1933 was certainly one of long hot days and wickets full of runs. Scott started his leadership with something of a flourish by scoring a century in his first game as captain; even better, it was against Northamptonshire under the captaincy of the former Sussex all-rounder, Vallance Jupp. Jupp was then forty-three, but hardly over the hill. The previous year, for the ninth time in his career he had scored more than a thousand runs and taken a hundred wickets, including all ten in one innings against Kent. Scott took seven sixes off him in that opening game of 1933.

Maybe it was the weather, perhaps the different style of leadership, possibly a sense of caution now that Duleep was gone; but, whatever the reason, some of the Sussex side's attractive punishing cricket had escaped them by mid-summer. They were accused of being slow and stodgy. Certainly the scoring rate slowed, although Cook seemed little bothered by it and ended the year at the top of the county batting averages for the first time in his career with not many short of two thousand runs, including that 214 against Worcestershire at

Eastbourne. The mightiest hitting of the summer was seen in one day at Hove against Middlesex. Bowley and John Langridge put on 490 runs in ten minutes short of six hours' play – hardly stodgy, crowd-yawning cricket.

Whatever the grounds for the earlier criticism, and whatever its result on the county's final position, Sussex finished second, only four points behind Yorkshire, even though they beat the northern side twice that year. The one major influence that could have made a difference to the outcome had nothing to do with the run rate of the earlier weeks of the season. Sussex, seemingly as ever, were always stretching their bowlers. Duleep had said when he captained the side in 1932 that they needed an extra bowler, and Gilligan often thought the same; Fry and, even earlier, Murdoch had understood the need for not simply good county bowlers, but one, perhaps two, in reserve, with that little extra.

True, in 1933 Tate, Jim Langridge and Jim Cornford bowled well, sometimes brilliantly. There was little short of wonder at Tate's nine wickets for just 50 runs in the Somerset game at the season's opening. But for the first time in his pace-bowling career Tate did not take a hundred wickets that season. And, more significantly, towards the end of August he was injured and played no more that summer. Tate was just one short of his hundred. There were six matches still to play, but Sussex had lost their bowling edge. They also lost Bowley, who, after scoring more than 25,000 runs and taking nearly 700 wickets since joining in 1912, at the age of forty-three decided to go to Winchester as coach.

Sir Home Gordon's comments on Bowley perhaps put the Sussex professional in a light some have forgotten:

> When Arthur Gilligan was re-making the Sussex side in the middle twenties the team was absolutely dependent on Bowley as a bat. If he did not come off the whole eleven would be out for under a hundred. Never, perhaps, has the responsibility for the run-getting of a county team been thus thrust on one man.
>
> Therefore it is all the more commendable that he never played pawky . . . in those years he felt the responsibility acutely, but he never shirked it or grumbled. All along he was scrutinising younger players and eager to improve them. Whenever I said to Ted that So-and-So was acquiring some bad habit, he would reply: 'I'll tell him about it and have him to a net to put him right.' That was characteristic of one of the most unselfish cricketers who ever walked . . . Great as has been his cricket, most attractive to spectators as well as invaluable to Sussex – will some juniors

171

note the combination – I do not want now to dwell on his fine batting, his insidiously tossed-up slow bowling (always delivered a yard behind the crease so that never once in all his life has he been no-balled) or his admirable fielding in the slips. I wish to emphasise the fine character of the man, his notable team spirit, and his quiet watchful vigilance over the youngsters. Not even John Tunnicliffe himself proved a better 'senior pro' in a county side.

Praise indeed, and easily and recognisably deserved.

Bowley's departure left a gap, but there were other problems for the county. One of them was financial. It had cost more than £10,300 to run the club during 1933. Subscriptions from Sussex's 3212 members had brought in £4,000. Only £3750 had come from match receipts. From the size of the crowds it was clear that most of the public were interested in watching the county only when there were deciding matches in the Championship table. Extra money had helped to swell the subscriptions and gate takings to around £9600, but this left a deficit of nearly £700. It was a worrying time for the committee, Bevan the treasurer, and the secretary Lance Knowles.

One difficulty, looking at the team, was that more of the players were being paid. Usually, ten of the team were professionals and received match fees. It was, for a struggling club, one of the soundest reasons to retain the amateur status of cricketers. Of the £10,300 running costs for 1933, £5605 had gone on wages for professionals and umpires, whereas the expenses for the amateurs had amounted to little more than a hundred pounds. The gatemen alone had been paid £264 that season.

The £697 loss would have been worse if it had not been for Sussex's £300 from the profits on the MCC Australian tour and £20 14s 10d (£20.74) made by 'Cushions', that wonderful character who wandered the ground hiring out padding for the less firm of seat. But there was a further loss to the club, one of sadness and of more practical implication.

One of the vice-presidents, T. G. Scott, died towards the end of the season. He was the father of Scott the captain, who had made such enormous strides as a batsman and leader. But he now decided that he could not continue, and left to look after the family business. After the almost-champion seasons of 1932 and 1933, Sussex was eager to get on with 1934 and so it was easier for them to cope with drawbacks. The committee, quite pleased with itself, had even approved the design of the 'new' club tie which was based, of course,

172

on the colours of the Royal Sussex Regiment, and it was 'cordially authorised by the Commanding Officers of all the Battalions'.

Enthusiasm for the coming summer was cordially authorised by the new president, the Earl of Athlone, and when play was called in 1934 many believed Sussex were heading for the Championship. Bowley may have gone, and Duleep was obviously missed, but there was every sign that Tate was back in form. The Langridges and the Parkses were just as eager; Cook, who had missed two thousand runs in 1933 by just 17, was keen to carry on where he had left off and use his 'excellent footwork' against whatever bowling came his way, or nearby for that matter; and the South African Alan Melville had shown that he was potentially a batsman of the highest class. And it was to the twenty-four-year-old Melville that Sussex turned for leadership, the fourth overseas player to captain the side in forty years.

In his time as captain, it was said that there was no better batsman in the side than Alan Melville. In the four years he played for Sussex, Melville scored nearly five thousand runs including twelve centuries. In terms of fine batsmen and famous Sussex captains, this was not really an outstanding record and certainly most would remember him for his captaincy of South Africa in that run feast of 1947. In 1934 he scored nearly 1500 runs and led the county to second place. Perhaps they could have been champions but for two important factors – injuries and nerves.

As ever, Sussex lacked a match-winning attack, which even with John Langridge and Tommy Cook each scoring more than two thousand runs and four others reaching a thousand – the Parkses, James Langridge and the captain – meant that the other side were scoring instead of being contained. But the list of injuries must have been Melville's biggest handicap. At one point, six of the leading players were out of cricket, including Jim Parks with a broken middle finger that took its time to heal. Even the happy-natured Wensley, the morale booster of any dressing room, found himself stricken and laid low with 'internal' troubles, although he did find time between pains and cramps to catch out the first five batsmen in the game against Oxford. Melville, too, was out some of the time, and Tate led the side, the first professional to do so, but was not appointed captain (that fell to James Langridge sixteen years later).

The second hangup for the side came when they looked like winning the title. With ten matches to go it was clear that Sussex were the best county in the Championship. But the batsmen were struck down with an enormous dose of lack of confidence, and Melville's lack of experience showed. He could not galvanise the team into returning to the attacking cricket that had made them so attractive to watch and devilishly difficult to beat. This aggressiveness was perfected by Jim Parks, with both bat and ball. He was thought to be the most improved cricketer on the circuit, and as Sir Home Gordon remarked:

> Such an advance in a man who had played county cricket regularly for years was difficult to parallel. His flighting of the ball was as clever as the way in which he boldly stood up to the most formidable attack, such as that of Larwood at Horsham, or H. D. Read at Colchester, playing as though these were slow bowlers.

But the batsmen lost their nerve, and of those last ten games, only one was won. As the articulate baronet observed: 'Until these fine fellows realise that they cannot win fifteen points by pawkily playing for safety and being content with a mere five, they will never get the Championship.' Nor did they. Nor were their troubles over by next season.

Tate took five wickets for 9 runs against Gloucestershire in 1935. He was chosen to play for England against the South Africans and ended the season with 97 Championship wickets. James Langridge nearly got his hundred wickets, and he did get a thousand runs. His brother John scored more than two thousand, 1800 of them in the Championship. Cook made a thousand; so did Jim Parks, and he took 108 wickets. His brother Harry got a thousand, and so did Melville. It should have been, on paper at least, the year they had been waiting for. It was not. The club slipped from second to seventh in the Championship and was so badly off financially, more than £1000 in debt, that there was a strong hint that wages would be cut.

Of all the players, only Harry Parks and George Cox managed to stay fit for the whole season. James Langridge took too long to get started that year, and even the irrepressible Cook 'displayed increasing inability to play any sort of fast bowling, every long innings that he made being bereft of it'. There were hints, too, that Tate, who had a good season and was rightly praised for it, was considered to be heading towards his career's end, and needed more careful use, perhaps even fewer games. It was subtlest taste of sad things to come.

That season, the Royal Albion Hotel advertised itself as a cure-all for woes and misery: 'The hotel where you shed your cares, and let others do the thinking for you; where, after a day in the bracing,

174

sun-washed air, you dine with enterprising zest, and later sleep the sleep of the just.' Perhaps the committee should have negotiated a loan and put up the whole team at the Albion the following season. There were cares aplenty to be shed during the summer of 1936.

Melville left to return to South Africa and A. J. Holmes took over. Holmes had first played in the same year as Gilligan took on the captaincy, but the 'irreparable calamity' of Melville's departure was difficult for Holmes to cope with. The weather was appalling, which did not help the players and positively hindered the finances of the club. The committee reported a loss of nearly £2000, 'due largely to inclement weather and to the fact that the team did not reproduce its best form'. The 3518 members were asked to give generously, and some of them did; but this was hardly enough. The crisis was real enough, and the secretary and his assistant both volunteered to accept for three years a £50-a-year cut in salary, which at that time was £550 for Lance Knowles and £260 6s 10d (260.35) for the assistant. The players themselves, perhaps recognising their part in the club's financial downfall, agreed to take a five per cent cut in wages.

The saddest part of the club's misfortune was the sound of a knife being sharpened, albeit quietly, behind the professionals' dressing room. Tate was under deep scrutiny. Maurice was no longer the mighty striker of the ball and the cunning bowler, in spite of his 7 for 19 runs against Hampshire at Hastings that year. Sir Home Gordon reported at the season's close:

> Tate for long had been predominant, setting a magnificent stand-ard which incited the rest to do their utmost, spurred on by his skill. Now he can only show flashes of his former formidable con-sistency and the moderation of some supporting him has become more evident.

Tate, like others have done since, may have annoyed some with his plainly written newspaper column, but his Championship bowling figures were hardly to be discarded. He bowled more overs than anyone in the Sussex side and took 73 Championship wickets. No one took a hundred that season, and only Harry and Jim Parks and James Langridge scored more than a thousand Championship runs. The Royal Albion Hotel was still encouraging the weary to rest with it. Its cable address was 'Brilliancy Brighton', and it had a new claim: 'Only an hour to Sunshine'.

Dismally, there was little brilliancy at Eaton Road, precious few hours of sunshine and little else for members to bask in during 1936.

Between 1932 and 1934 Sussex had been runners-up in the table, and in 1935 they were seventh. They ended the summer of 1936 fourteenth.

It was Coronation Year in 1937, and the crowning glories at Hove belonged to two families, the Parkses and the Langridges, although there was the encouraging sight of two newcomers full of southern-county promise, H. T. Bartlett and S. C. Griffith. It was a season of sad moment for Tate and thoroughly enchanting batting for the crowds. A season of firsts.

For the first time, seven Sussex batsmen made a thousand runs in the same season – both Parkses, the Langridges, Cook, George Cox, Jnr, and the gallant captain, Flight Lieutenant Holmes, the first thousand he had scored since 1923, the year after he joined the club. Jim Parks was the first to score more than three thousand runs and take a hundred wickets in the same season.

For the first time, two brothers made two thousand runs in the same season – James and John Langridge, although the former scored only 1765 of his in Championship games.

For the first time, three batsmen – Jim Parks and the Langridges – each scored two thousand runs for the same county in the same season. In all, Sussex played thirty-two Championship matches that year, won thirteen and lost seven, and climbed back to fifth position in the table. With such batting, some hoped for higher things. With such bowling, such hopes were bound to be smashed to smithereens.

There was also a slight problem of tiredness among the players, hardly a phenomenon of the 1980s. Sir Home Gordon's end-of-season comments praised the batting, castigated the bowling and lamented over the state of some players.

> Sussex did so well because the batting was admirable, the fielding excellent – at Maidstone it seemed superlative – and the side was led with consummate judgement by A. J. Holmes. Subsequently the team failed because it possessed the weakest bowling except that of Northamptonshire and because some of the regular members exhibited exaggerated fatigue. It is absurd to assert that Englishmen in their early prime cannot play cricket for four months, necessarily passing much of the time resting in the pavilion, without being fagged out. Men engaged in hard manual labour all the year round, or golf professionals, would laugh at such nonsense.

The saddest note, and perhaps the most cruelly put, was kept for Tate:

> The premature ageing of the county's greatest cricketer was

176

obvious. The popular play-boy has now become a mere trader on his past reputation of having been the best English bowler since the War, and is still the idol of the faithful non-critical. He can still bowl a length, but his fire has gone, his batting has become problematical, whilst his gravest weakness is his slowness in the field.

The committee's report mentioned that Tate had been given the 'sum of £250' and 'their best wishes for every success in the future'. There were many who thought he had been treated rather shabbily. Certainly, at forty-two, Tate was past his best and there were rumours and few counter-rumours that all was unwell between the senior professional and the committee. He had been kept out of the side since the end of June and most believed that was to be his end. Then, in August, Tate was called to the committee room at Hove and told that the selection committee would recommend to the club that Tate should not be given a contract for the following season. Furthermore, they said, it was not envisaged that he would be needed for the rest of the 1937 season.

Four days later the selection committee was in a fix. They needed Tate to open the bowling at Hastings against Kent. Sussex batted first, had 400-odd on the board and in went Tate. He was there for not much more than an hour and hit 73 I-told-you-so runs that had the crowd as happy as could be. And he bowled. Not perhaps as he once had, but he found six wickets in that match against Kent, and Sussex won by ten. And so for the rest of the season Tate played, and even took the last wicket of the summer in the Surrey game at Hove. But it was all up. 'It was the way they did it,' was what he said. And perhaps it was.

So Sussex, needing one for its hundred years, went into the 1938 season without a Tate. There had been a Fred or a Maurice Tate at Sussex for more or less fifty of those 99 seasons. Some thought it a sad end to a handsome age. So it was. But more, and as time went by even more, remembered the hundreds of wickets season after season and the buckets of runs, seemingly forever coming; and the good memories stuck. Holmes was still there as captain, although because of injury his place was sometimes taken by R. G. Stainton. Yet in spite of times stretched out with strain Holmes made nearly a thousand runs that season.

But the members turned out to see the batting of the Langridges, the Parkses and the young left-hander Hugh Bartlett, who that year made well over a thousand Championship runs in twenty-four innings

177

at an average of 51. Bartlett, 'who makes far more use of his wrists than have the majority of great smiters', had a particularly glorious innings at Leeds that year, when in just under an hour and quarter he scored a 'perfectly stroked' 94 including seven sixes off the daunting Hedley Verity. Bartlett had a good mighty hitting season, including thirty-six sixes and a century in 57 minutes against the Australians, a more remarkable score when it is remembered that at the end of the first fifteen minutes of that innings Bartlett had made but four runs. Passers-by in Eastbourne and Hove were known to come into the grounds just to see Bartlett bat.

It was a great year for the crowds, perhaps inspired by Hutton's 364 against the Australians that year at The Oval during the game when England made 903 for 7 declared, and the fastest double-hundred that year, Stan McCabe's 223 against England at Nottingham. Bartlett may have become something of a folk-hero, but the side's batting backbone was John Langridge, gradually showing why he was later considered the best opening bat who never played for England. He scored 2302 Championship runs including two double-centuries, and on eleven occasions was in a century partnership, including one of 295 with Jim Parks against Leicestershire, another with Harry Parks of 281 against Glamorgan, and a third double-century with Cox against Northamptonshire.

Sadly, but almost predictably, it was the bowlers' union that held the county back that year. The three Jims – Cornford, Parks and Langridge – bowled their hearts out, but with only eleven wins it was clear that once again Sussex could not bowl other sides out. Nor could they catch them out. For a side that was known throughout the country for its fielding, there were some amazing lapses; they actually put down twenty catches during the Eastbourne week alone. From fifth in 1937 they dropped to eighth in the 1938 table.

Jim Parks' benefit year came in 1939. The idea of gathering money for long-serving players dated from the nineteenth century, when Henry Charlwood, one of the four Charlwoods of Horsham who played for the county, was granted a benefit in 1883. Some gathered great purses in recognition of their popular play, and Henry Phillips, the county's Victorian wicket-keeper, received £900 in 1886. The same sum came in 1900 to Butt, Phillips' successor. Fred Tate got £1051 the following year, yet Joe Vine received no more than £137 in 1913.

Between the wars, most players, with the exceptions of R. R. Relf and H. E. Roberts, each ended their benefit seasons with more than a thousand pounds. Maurice Tate, hardly surprisingly, was the highest

178

The Brothers Relf

George Cox Snr. First played in 1895 and scored 14,353 runs and took 1,810 wickets. A member of the side which scored 705 for 8 declared against Surrey at Hastings in 1902.

KS Ranjitsinhji one of the greatest batsmen of all time. The first batsman to score more than 3,000 runs in a season. Three times he scored more than 1,000 runs in a month. He once played three games in one day at Cambridge and scored a century in each of them.

Joe Vine in 1901 became the first Sussex player to score 1,000 runs and take 100 wickets in a season. He scored 32 centuries and made 1,000 runs in a season 14 times

Member's Ticket for 1906. Purple with gold lettering.

George Benjamin Street took over from HR Butt in 1912 as wicket keeper. Perhaps the best wicket keeper in England during the immediate post Great War period he was killed in a motor cycle accident in 1924

Watching cricket at Hove in 1913

The storm clouds over Hove in 1914 and recruits to the Royal Sussex Regiment parade on the county ground in September of that year

Bert Wensley played for Sussex between 1922 and 1936 and was one of the few players to hit a century going in at number ten – 120 v Derbyshire at Horsham

The Sussex County Cricket Team
That beat Surrey at Horsham 1928

The 1928 side shortly before beating Surrey at Horsham. Top: AF Wensley, JH Parks, HW Parks, R Hollingdale. Bttm: Jas Langridge, AHH Gillingan, MW Tate, AER Gilligan, EH Bowley, W Cornford.

Lance Knowles with AER Gilligan. Knowles, born in 1871, became Sussex Secretary in 1922 and resigned through ill-health in 1942

C Aubrey Smith takes strike with the horror actor Boris Karloff keeping wicket

*HW Parks scored more than a thousand runs in a season fourteen times
and in 1931 hit 200 not out against Essex at Chelmsford. With his brother, JH Parks,
created a fifth wicket Sussex record of 297 (against Hants in 1937)*

beneficiary of the crowd's goodwill when in 1930, the year he took six Australian wickets for 82 at Hove, he made as much as £1900. Sussex was generous in its recognition of popularity. Accordingly, Jim Parks should have been richer by as many hundreds of pounds in 1939. The decade had been one of relative success. With the exception of that curious 1936 season, the club had a good record, the membership stood at about 3500, it was its hundredth birthday and Jim Parks was dazzling testimony to what could be, and had been, done with bat and ball. Yet Parks received as little as £734.

Undoubtedly the county had a difficult season. Cornford, Hammond and Wood hardly took the wickets they might have done, and only Jack Nye improved, as Arthur Gilligan had forecast that he would, and got his hundred wickets in the season. Holmes had to leave the team and Bartlett took over a side that once again was renowned for its batting rather than its bowling. John Langridge got two thousand runs and his brother James, both Parkses, Cox and Bartlett a thousand each. And with 'Tich' Cornford away Billy Griffith became wicket-keeper of some distinction, prompting the speculation that here indeed was a future England cap.

But with the approaching war came the gloom that so easily settled over many county grounds. The West Indies cut short their tour, 'owing to the international crisis', which also cut the funds that Parks would have had for his benefit. He had been promised the proceeds from the Hove match against Yorkshire, and certainly the crowd turned out to support him. They may have been disappointed, for Sussex lost. But they did see Cox hit 198 and Len Hutton and Norman Yardley stroke, punch and glance centuries each. But most distinguished was Hedley Verity: seven wickets for just 9 runs. Sussex tottered back to their dressing rooms with as few as 33 runs. Parks collected £75 and the season was at an end. Sussex sat in tenth position and, for the moment at least, the lights went out in the Hove pavilion.

179

Chapter 15

On 23 July 1942, Andy Ducat of Surrey died at the wicket. Sir Pelham Warner, in his history of Lord's, recorded that sad death:

> The match between the Sussex Home Guard and Surrey Home Guard was abandoned because of the tragic death at the wicket of Andrew Ducat. He had made 29 when he played a ball to mid-on. The ball was returned to the bowler, who had started to deliver the next ball when Ducat collapsed at the wicket and was found to be dead when carried to the pavilion. Such an event had never happened at Lord's before, and the sudden tragic passing of this very popular Surrey cricketer and famous footballer, apparently full of health and vigour, was a severe shock to those present.

It was indeed. There is something in the telling that conjures the attitude and atmosphere of the wartime years. If it reads like a bulletin of the old *Empire News*, then that was the style of Plum Warner and his times. It is a reminder that in spite of the difficulties presented by what Warner called 'The Second German War' cricket played a straight bat through the crisis. As Warner reflected: 'If Goebbels had been able to broadcast that the war had stopped cricket at Lord's it would have been valuable propaganda for the Germans.' More simply, from Warner's point of view, while cricket continued, then the British peoples, wherever they were in the world, knew that all was not lost and that no stiff upper lip had quivered for one moment. Warner later wrote to Bill Edrich:

It was a bit close the other night. Several high explosives near by, a few incendiaries on the ground and an oil bomb at deepish mid-on, if you were bowling from the Nursery end. After a little clearing up we shall be all right to start again soon.

Once war was declared, every effort was made to keep the game in a far more organised way than had happened during the 'First German War'. In Sussex the cowshed remained intact, though like the maid's night off, this time in broad, but wartime, daylight, there were some near-misses. But there was a similar Warner-like determination to keep things going, not to draw stumps on a way of life and a hundred years of first-class county cricket.

From the beginning, there was an assumption that England would win the war. Not for one moment did anyone believe that Hitler would succeed and possibly, just possibly, there would be no cricket under the same laws, the same emblems and the same social and organisational Christian committees of pre-war England. The committee room represented something that may in future times be lampooned; but it was the rear-guard of more than county cricket in Sussex. It signalled a belief that war was simply an interruption of a value held dear, not its downfall. It expected its casualties, especially among amateurs who were, by social definition, likely to be officers and therefore from the experience of the First War expected to lead from the front and suffer the first fusillade. It was an attitude based on strength of character, not on weakness of chin.

As Britain went to war in 1939, the Sussex honours board of management past and present under A. Miller Hallett, the president, illustrated the determination that Churchill called for and which cricket by then had deemed its right to represent. Past presidents included Lord Leconfield, Viscount Hailsham, Viscount Gage, the Earls Castle-Stewart, Winterton and Athlone, and the Duke of Norfolk. The active vice-presidents were the Marquess of Willingdon, Lord Rankeillour, Sir Home Gordon, Sir Alfred Sargeant, Arthur Gilligan, C. B. Fry, G. S. Godfree, Lieutenant-Colonel Gwynne, W. E. F. Cheesman, O. E. d'Avigdor Goldsmid, W. W. Grantham and T. Baden-Powell.

Lance Knowles, seemingly tireless, was secretary still, Godfree chairman and Bevan treasurer. For them, 1939 was a hundred years not out and they recognised the incentives to carry on regardless. First, there was great opportunity to play, for some of the famous names in the game were still in the area and others, including a large Australian contingent, had arrived, thanks to the war. Moreover, the fellowship of Sussex realised that unless interest was maintained, then the young players needed when conflict was done would not be there. Many remembered the slow start and scramble for players in 1919.

The energy was generated at Hove largely by Sir Home Gordon, A. K. Wilson, the slow bowler who later became chairman of the club, the secretary Lance Knowles, and Billy Newham, who had captained Sussex in the previous century, had played against Australia during the 1887–8 tour and whose 344-run partnership with Ranjitsinhji against Essex in 1902 had become a seventh-wicket record. Newham was approaching eighty when wartime cricket got under way. The start stuttered, as might have been expected during the uncertainties of the times. Club and service teams went to Hove to play and in 1941 there was a two-day match against Cambridge University and three against the strong Royal Air Force sides, as well as the Brighton and Hove Cricket Association. Just as the Home Guard teams had been strong with players, enough to play at Lord's, so it was at Hove. And irony, of course, cocked her nose at previous sadness when Captain Maurice Tate, no longer sitting out the game in his car and reluctant to talk to his old friends, found himself playing for Sussex once more.

In 1942 there was cricket at Hove on Wednesdays and Saturdays, with the county side playing five full matches. A Sussex league of Royal Navy, Army and Royal Air Force sides, with the Civil Service and the Auxiliary Fire Service teams added, was able to put together some good-class matches. And cricket, the great leveller, made little of Squadron Leader This, Corporal That or Lieutenant-Commander The Other. Thus, in mufti, elevens with men such as Compton, the Bedsers, Gover, Allen, Sellars and Cranston appeared at Hove and, for a few hours, the war might have been another world.

By 1943 there were nearly sixty games played at Hove, and during one at Horsham against the RAF, Keith Miller, who was in England with the Royal Australian Air Force, played for Sussex. He played again for the 'county' and was almost adopted for the future. The Australian contingent, many of whom were living in the commandeered Metropole Hotel in Brighton, was strong enough to produce a representative side against a Sussex eleven, boosted by Tom Reddick, Peter Sunnucks, Eric Bedser and Trevor Bailey. In one match against the Australians, Keith Carmody made a century before going back to flying duties, being shot down and finding himself alive but a prisoner of war. The good news was that he was released in time to return to England to play in the so-called Victory Test of 1945.

But it should not be thought that all the cricketing activity was at such a heady level. If the interest were to be maintained, and the nursery of those who would once again take bat and ball in a few years to come encouraged, then more needed to be done. One vehicle for this ambition was the Sussex Cricket Association.

Towards the end of the 1938 season, the Southbourne Cricket Club at Eastbourne put forward the notion that a cricket association be formed. Southbourne sent circulars to other clubs, but nothing much happened other than general discussions, and when the war broke out at the end of the 1939 season the idea was shelved, although not abandoned. In 1942 Southbourne once again made a serious attempt to get the concept adopted so that all would be set once the war was ended. In the wartime spirit of Combined Operations, the Sussex committee, through Lance Knowles the club secretary, suggested that Southbourne should get together with the Brighton and Hove District Association. W. N. Hardy of Southbourne met with S. H. Baker of Brighton and Hove and G. Kent of Lewes Priory Cricket Club and established the concept of the Sussex Cricket Association with six district associations.

Sussex appointed their chairman, G. S. Godfree, to co-ordinate the matter and fifty clubs went to a meeting at the Hove ground in the July of 1943. Godfree expressed a view that the club not only encourage the idea, but be anxious to see 'cricket established on a sound basis in readiness for immediate operation after the war'. The *Eastbourne Courier* reported that on behalf of the club W. N. Riley had declared:

> From the highest club to the lowest, each member shall have a chance to play for the County team. Heretofore we have lost a number of good cricketers because we have not had an organisation similar to the one proposed to enable us to keep track of young players.

And so, through necessity and the encouragement of people willing to work for an idea, the basis of bringing on young Sussex cricketers was established. A successful wartime baby. Meanwhile, while Tom Burchell and Beach kept the wicket cut, watered and rolled ready, the committee flew the Sussex flag over the pavilion and in search of funds launched a wartime appeal for members to part with half as much again as their previous year's subscription. Those who did were sent a cardboard pass to Hove valid 'for the duration of the war'.

Every man jack of the Sussex side was serving somewhere. As if to continue their lifelong school, student and playing partnership, Griffith and Bartlett both joined up and went into the Glider Pilot

184

Regiment, winging together into Arnhem. Major Griffith and Captain Bartlett proved on another field a difficult pair to get out. In Hove, the Sussex Home Guard became a fixture of the county ground, moving into part of the pavilion, and could be regularly seen training there.

Dad's Army or not, during the opening rounds of the conflict the Germans must have taken exception to the Sussex CCC war effort (either that or they were seeking Gunner Spike Milligan who was stationed further along the coast at Bexhill on Sea), for on one particular occasion during a game between a Sussex eleven and the Brighton clubs to raise money for the Spitfire Fund, the official enemy bombed this southern outpost of resistance. Shortly before lunch there was an air-raid warning, which the two sides ignored. After lunch there was another warning followed by two explosions in Brighton. Then two German aircraft flew over the ground. The cricketers, who included Spen Carma, Pilot Officer and later Squadron Leader Arthur Gilligan, Maurice Tate and John Langridge, played on, which clearly infuriated the Luftwaffe, for one of the planes banked and turned for the attack on these flannelled English fools. This time they scattered and the German plane dropped two bombs. One landed on the sports club, the other in the south-eastern corner of the ground. Neither exploded. It was that sort of war for Sussex.

One day early in 1945 the lights were turned up a little in the pavilion, and Sussex gathered together and took stock. W. N. Riley, who was then committee member and President of the Sussex Cricket Association, again promised that when the war was over it would not be the same as last time. Sussex were going to need all the young cricketers they could find to rebuild the team and hopes for the peaceful years. He was mindful also of the greater feeling that Sussex county cricket was more and more about the privileged amateurs and their friends plus the hardened professionals.

It was an oft-expressed feeling, and one which reflected the attitudes of the century until the Second World War. Moreover, its sentiment and resentment had existed for a hundred years or more. Had there not been rivalries in the early nineteenth century as to which part of the county should represent all? Had there not been deep feeling in the 1850s, which in part led to reorganisation in 1857 and the promises that Sussex County Cricket Club should be for everyone, across East and West Sussex, and that the hearts of the generation beat in even the smallest of villages? Was not the cricket heritage of Sussex found in Slidon, the Dickers, Duncton, Brightling, Storrington, Henfield, Oakendene Green, Hastings and Ninfield, and was it not in tiny Catsfield that Arthur Gilligan himself had talked of the finest sporting

185

spirit, the heart of the game? Was this not why Sussex cared about the memory of George Brown, Noah Mann riding his twenty miles to practise every Tuesday, and then back? Hammond, Little Dench, Jem Broadbridge, the Lillywhites and Wisden?

Some of the county's stewards were having to accept that if Sussex were to play again with confidence in the future, then the search for players had to be county-wide. After all, after a hundred years there was little evidence to suggest that the old system of patronage and too little talent-spotting worked with great success. Riley was eager to call on the Association and its managers to reassure the world that Sussex CCC was for everyone, and was not the closed circle that many believed it to be. In an article written in 1945, Riley noted:

> This Association will provide a wide net of fine mesh through which no young cricketer will be allowed to escape. We want real cricket democracy in the County so that every young Cricketer will know that if he has the requisite ability he will have the opportunity of representing his County.
>
> There have been notable exceptions: the Jam Sahib of Nawanagar (more affectionately remembered as Ranji), his nephew K. S. Duleepsinhji and more recently Major S. C. Griffith and Capt. H. T. Bartlett (both in an Airborne Division) and there may be others in the future, but generally speaking Sussex men play for Sussex County.

An echo of one of the longest-serving presidents, the nineteenth-century Lord Sheffield, who must have grieved when the county appointed Murdoch – an overseas player for the first time, and as captain, too.

Times had moved, the war in Europe was drawing to a close, and other figures had already slipped away from Hove. Lance Knowles, the secretary, had fallen ill and died in December 1943. Even the seemingly everlasting Billy Newham had died in 1944, the direct link with the greater past now gone. A. J. Holmes, no longer captain, had retired from first-class cricket. So had Jim Parks, by now almost Jim Parks, Snr, for his son was soon to carry on the name that had excited so many thousands of Sussex watchers.

Once again this century, a bloody conflict had interrupted the careers of cricketers. There were some, Bartlett among them, who perhaps wondered what might have been if they had continued play in six or seven years of Championship games instead of the occasional match lodged between learning new skills dictated by alarm, routine, trauma and the alien logic of war. But even in 1945, the war now over, the effort was to press on.

County matches were fixed for 19 May against the Royal Australian Air Force, two in June against neighbouring Hampshire, one at Chichester with the West Indies, who had withdrawn across the Atlantic at the onset of war, followed by Northamptonshire at Hastings. But most of the games were with the Australian Air Force. The important task of that summer was to get cricket firmly on its county feet and the crowds and their money back into the county grounds. 'Increased Membership Is Essential' pleaded the advertisements of the day.

Once again, through the limited county and Association games, there was a chance to see the attractive names and future heroes. A twelve-a-side match between the Association and the Australians included Ken Suttle, still four years away from his county playing days and cruelly lbw for 5, and in the Australian side Hassett and Cheetham. At the end of the season at Hailsham, the South of England included John and James Langridge and Harry Parks batting alongside Southbourne's W. N. Hardy against a side aptly named from another age – The British Empire – with Arthur Fagg opening the batting with C. J. Andrews who was out for a duck, bowled by Hardy and caught by John Langridge, and C. Knott, F. Appleyard and A. R. Gover not even getting a knock. There, too, were Bognor, with their president, Squadron Leader A. E. R. Gilligan, not far from Arundel where he used to pedal, kit balanced on handlebars, as a twelve-year-old for an afternoon's game.

By 1946 the strands were together and Sussex County Cricket Club was once again formally fighting for the Championship. Members, still paying only one guinea a year as they had since 1930, turned out in spite of the horrid weather, perhaps hoping for sunshine and bright fortune for their side. It was not to be the most dazzling start to a new era.

Sussex finished last in the 1946 Championship table. In spite of the departure of Holmes and Parks, there was a sturdy gathering of the old order when that season opened. All the 'Jims' were in place – Wood, Cornford, Langridge and Hammond. So, too, was the other Langridge, the Oakes brothers, Charlie and Jack, George Cox, Harry Parks and Jack Nye and, of course, the ever-genial features and nature of Billy Griffith, now secretary and captain. His was an onerous task. The batting, as ever, was impressive. The bowling was unsound.

When, that summer, the Indian tourists set about the Sussex attack, there was little that even Griffith's good humour and coaxing could do. Indian tourists: 533 for 3 declared, V. M. Merchant 205,

187

V. Mankad 105, the Nawab of Pataudi 110 not out and L. Amarnath 106. Sussex first innings: 253. It was a devastating morale-shatterer for any county side. And this in spite of George Cox carrying on where he had left off and hitting 234 not out in the second innings.

The season had opened with all the good intention and hope that may be visited on a side so eager to show the way to the top. Indeed, Worcestershire had fallen to Jim Langridge's nine wickets for 94 runs in the first game of the year. But then almost nothing. Only four wins out of twenty-nine games. Sussex had not had such a terrible season for exactly fifty years. Nevertheless, five Sussex batsmen scored more than a thousand runs that year. But only James Langridge seemed to be able to bowl, and even he managed only 89 wickets, which was nevertheless almost twice as many as any other bowler. Not even the batsmen could avoid the county's most dreadful defeat by Glamorgan at Horsham. In one innings, Sussex were all out for 35.

It was a season to forget, especially for Griffith who must have found the task of combining captaincy and county secretary a hopeless ambition. If he had been in his usual seat, Billy Newham could have warned him. The last time it had been attempted was by him when he became captain and secretary in 1889. That year Sussex came last in the table; though, to be fair, they were already there when the season opened. For the 1947 season Griffith remained secretary and wicket-keeper, but handed over the leadership to his close friend Hugh Bartlett.

The year 1947 may have called for an entire rain-forest to supply the reams that were written about the runs plundered by English batsmen, including D. C. S. Compton's eighteen centuries. And for Sussex and its supporters there were brighter days in prospect, yet also the makings of sad controversy which few could have enjoyed.

Bartlett's captaincy was almost inevitable for one who had had such a story-book career. At Dulwich he was an outstanding left-hander and captain. In his first year at Cambridge he played for the University, and when he joined Sussex he scored a century off the Cambridge bowling in his first match. Even when the conflict with Germany interrupted his career, the *Boy's Own* tale continued. Bartlett had what used to be called 'a good war', was decorated and returned to Hove ready to carry on as before.

Some say his batting was never quite so sharp, so devastatingly abandoned after his return; men do change, and perhaps there was a retained tenseness in his style, especially when he was loaded that year with the added concerns of captain and the memory of the 1946 season that Sussex wished to forget. Yet there are jumbles of statistics

188

to say he was impressive enough; there were bowlers, too, who would sooner not have had to wait while the ball was found in the crowd and beyond, including that straight-faced Yorkshireman E. T. Robinson. Bartlett hit him for three consecutive sixes in 1947 – and, just to rub in the indignity, again at Bradford.

There were quite a few bowlers with long faces that year, especially those who faced Compton and Edrich. When Middlesex arrived at Hove for the first of their two games that season, Compton not only scored one of his eighteen centuries, he took four Sussex wickets. When the return game was played at Lord's, he picked up another century.

The high scoring continued at Hove that year, with more than a thousand runs coming in the game against the South Africans, led by Alan Melville who had captained Sussex in better times to second and seventh positions. He scored a century in South Africa's 555 for 6 declared, somehow inevitably the highest total of their tour. But Sussex were not to be trampled this time. George Cox and Harry Parks each scored hundreds and with altogether well over 1200 runs coming in the game it was drawn. The side won nine games that year and finished joint ninth with Glamorgan, and again the top of the county's batting had a pre-war look about it: the Langridges, George Cox, Jnr, and Harry Parks. Jim Cornford was top wicket-taker with the firm of Cox, Carey and Nye following up behind.

It was a good year to be in county cricket, especially for new faces inspired by run-makers and hot summer days. An ideal start for two young men at Hove – D. S. Sheppard and A. S. M. Oakman. However, the following year Sussex was once more sorely testing the loyalty of its camp-followers.

Harry Parks retired in 1948, and it was a shame that this player of enormous heart could not have gone out with the club flying all standards instead of as limp-winded martlets sheltering against the gale of poor bowling, missed chances and general sadness that left them in sixteenth out of seventeenth in the Championship. He first played in 1926 and had put together more than 21,000 runs for the county, often in tight games when a broken partnership might have heralded defeat. On eighty-seven occasions Harry Parks had shared hundred partnerships, perhaps few more telling than with George Cox, Jnr, after the war, 213 for the third wicket at Worcester in 1946 when every game counted, and again with Cox in 1947 when the two put on 219 for the fourth wicket against Glamorgan at Hove. He would be much missed by the crowds, but he was by now slower than before and the chance of a coaching job made it easier for everyone

189

when he was 'not re-engaged'. Yet if there had been one year more it would have been good to have seen him steering his young nephew Jim Parks through his first season with the club. Instead, he finished fourth in the averages, just getting his thousand Championship runs, and without scoring a century that year. He had a good benefit year – £1930, which was considerably more than the £734 his brother had picked up shortly before the war. Nevertheless, a sad year to go out.

What went wrong? It was a question the club's president, Sir Home Gordon, had to answer in his usual blunt manner: 'the weakest bowling in the Championship, combined with uncertainty both in run-getting and catching'. The answer to the problem, according to Griffith, the secretary, was to bring on the youngsters and find new bowlers.

The young players were indeed waiting in the wings, and some had even come on stage. Oakman looked promising but had gone off to do his National Service. D. V. Smith had finished top of the second eleven batting, with D. S. Sheppard, tucking 157 not out against Kent seconds into his records, a whisper behind; G. H. G. Doggart had joined his brother in the side that year and was marked as something of a stroke-player. Naturally enough, the lead was taken by the senior professional, James Langridge, described in the 1933 *Wisden* as the 'best all-rounder on the side', and in 1948 still wearing that crown.

Poor Bartlett came in for heavy criticism, especially from the one man loath to deliver it, Sir Home Gordon. 'Hugh Bartlett, indefatigable in leadership, conscientiously directed his side and deserved grateful thanks.' Then came the sting: 'But deliberately he would not give certain regular members of the team regular places in the order of going in.' Bartlett was still there as captain the next year, and Sussex rose from sixteenth to thirteenth place. But the grumblings continued and there was little sign of the bowling strength that everyone knew was needed.

The steady and sometimes frenetic efforts of the fast-medium pace of Cornford and the left-armer Wood were not enough, even when supported by James Langridge and Charles Oakes. None of them managed to get a hundred wickets, although Cornford, who had a remarkable spell including 9 for 53 against Northamptonshire, missed by only three. But the real evaluation of the magical one hundred scorers was the amount by which this target was exceeded, and in times past when there had been bowling strengths the excess had been as large as the actual totals the Sussex bowlers were now picking up.

The batting once more sparkled, and in two particular areas. First, John Langridge missed three thousand runs that season by

190

just 150. Only C. B. Fry, Ranjitsinhji and Old Jim Parks had ever achieved it. But on his way he hit twelve centuries, something no Sussex player had ever managed. And those hundreds included 154 against New Zealand and 234 not out against Derbyshire. All this with a strained back towards the end of the season which meant he missed a possible five more innings. Not bad for a man approaching forty, but not good enough for the England selectors, who gave the impression that Langridge was a little too old for England.

Langridge's style and enthusiasm were catching the talent of others. David Sheppard and Hubert Doggart, both part-timers while about their books and supervisions at Cambridge, were full of promise. Sheppard played only twenty-one innings but scored nearly a thousand runs and began his first-class career of centuries with a double – 204 against some very good Glamorgan bowling. Doggart, though further down the averages, was already being spoken of as a future tourist. And what about those players of the future that Home Gordon and Billy Griffith had pleaded for? Griffith himself, still secretary, still keeping wicket, was coaching Rupert Webb as an understudy, and Patsy Hendren, who ran the club's nursery, was bringing on the new Parks and Oakman.

The future was starting to look good, for the material was there, but the difficulties that had grumbled away now found full throat and 1950 did not turn out to be the delightful prospect some had imagined, especially when Bartlett and Griffith resigned.

Chapter 16

The day of 17 March 1950 has been called the 'Great Walk Out'. It was the day that the Duke of Norfolk picked up his hat and gloves and walked out of one of the sadder annual general meetings in the county's history. The Duke was the club's president, and he made it clear that he expected the committee to follow his example. It was an occasion that, to some, appeared to cancel out all the hard work that had gone into illustrating that the days of reactionary committee rule had gone, and that Sussex was now a forward-thinking and approachable county and not a glass-cased and stuffed replica of the MCC at its most oligarchical. Such a view was harsh. It was unreasonable. Yet, it existed. And for some, coming innocently enough to the opening of the 1950 season, there was evidence enough to support this uncharitable opinion.

Even casual followers of the county may have wondered when they read the rousing words of Arthur Gilligan in that year's Handbook and then, a few pages later, the curious piece that suggested that something was a little rotten in the state of Hove. An unsuspecting Gilligan wrote:

> Right down the years from round about 1700, when the infant Cricket was cradled in our Sussex sheepfolds, season has followed season, Slindon and Northchapel, Goodwood and Firle, Henfield and Southwick, Brighton and Hastings, the great cricketers they produced, and the legion of famous clubs and players who have succeeded them, falling in to make up the grand cavalcade of Sussex cricket and the traditions which have become our present heritage. What a trust it is they have committed to us; how proud we should be to maintain it!

There might have been cause to ponder A. E. R. Gilligan's words which, though nothing to do with the events of that spring, reflected the feelings that most expressed for the club but which seemed, for the moment at least, to be lost in distant abstract wondering about the trust put in the leaders of the county game and the pride with which they maintained it. A few pages later, the reason for any misgivings could have been found, under the heading 'Joint Captaincy of Sussex':

> Closely following the announcement that H. T. Bartlett, captain of Sussex for the last three seasons, had resigned, the Sussex County Cricket Club Committee appointed G. H. G. Doggart and R. G. Hunt to share the leadership for 1950.
>
> It was expected that Hunt, an all-rounder, would lead the side until Doggart finished the term at Cambridge, where he is cricket captain.
>
> Then came another surprise: S. C. Griffith, Sussex and England wicket-keeper, resigning his position as secretary of the County Cricket Club. Announcing his decision, Griffith stated that, after considerable thought, he had accepted a staff appointment with a London newspaper, as he felt that his future was in journalism.
>
> (Since the above announcements were made there have been certain developments, and at the time of going to press the question of the captaincy appeared to be in abeyance.)

What was all this? How could a county, at the start of the season, be appointing not one, but two new captains, and then none at all? To lose one captain was misfortune; to lose two surely carelessness? And why had Bartlett resigned? There was talk of the club being unhappy with his command, yet had not the committee reported: 'Great credit is given to the captain, H. T. Bartlett, for the way in which he handled, and, indeed, produced the best from, an always moderate attack'? Hardly resigning stuff. Yet inevitably the story had its origins in the poor performance of the side and the way in which Bartlett had handled it. The public criticism by Sir Home Gordon was evidence enough of that.

The newspaper writers had, with some reason, speculated over the position of Bartlett and his leadership and by the time of the AGM there were two camps, one of them suspecting that Bartlett was being badly treated by the committee and ready to support him to the end. Laetitia Stapleton, who was at that meeting, recorded her view of events in *A Sussex Cricket Odyssey*, and remembers a noisy group

194

at the back, most of whom it was supposed were not even members, constantly interrupting the Duke of Norfolk.

'I do not wish to ask more than once to be allowed to finish my remarks,' he said coldly. He then went on to say that the captaincy was a matter for the Committee and that, as Bartlett did not have the confidence one would have hoped for, R. G. Hunt and G. H. G. Doggart had been appointed joint captains for 1950. Upon this announcement there were cries of 'No!' and 'Shame!' Amidst the uproar the Duke managed to explain that after discussions and letters between himself and Bartlett the latter had sent his letter of resignation. At this point Fr. George Long jumped to his feet and asked if we might see the letters. His request was refused, the Duke saying that it was not for him to read out Mr. Bartlett's letters and he had no intention of doing so. The Duke of Norfolk could be very firm indeed when occasion demanded, but others refused to let the business rest. Mr. A. C. C. David, a preparatory school master said, 'We must have some elucidation. The Committee's decision is disastrous.' Fr. Long, too, stuck to his guns and was supported by the 20-year-old David Sheppard, who was sitting next to him. Fr. Long wanted to know why the Club's report had praised Mr. Bartlett for the way he handled a moderate team to the best possible advantage and yet the captain had resigned without members knowing the full facts . . . By this time there was general disorder . . . Mr. David made himself heard sufficiently to issue his challenge. 'It grieves me as a very old member of the Club to do this. I shall move a vote of no confidence unless I have an answer,' he said.

'Then it had better come to a head,' replied the Duke . . . When the counting was over there was a shocked and bewildered conclave on the platform, then the Duke announced, 'The motion has been carried, and as President of the Sussex County Cricket Club I tender my resignation. The Committee will no doubt do the same.'

And that is what happened – not then, but at a later meeting.

Sir Home Gordon described the event as 'the worst day we have had in Sussex Cricket for nearly two hundred years'. The Duke called for 'everyone to keep their heads for the next few weeks'. Bartlett was upset by the events and even indicated that he would reconsider his position but that it was not up to him. It would be for the committee, perhaps pressed by the members, to ask him to do so. Meanwhile, as David Sheppard pointed out, it was hardly right that the professionals would be reporting to the ground for their first training sessions the

195

following week without a captain. The management of the club was further confused by the resignation of the committee and the county was put in the 'hands of the following vice-presidents: Group Captain A. J. Holmes, A. E. R. Gilligan, W. N. Riley, Sir A. Saunders, J. K. Mathews and E.G. Maltby'.

More than a thousand members crowded into the Hove Town Hall on 17 April under the chairmanship of Sir Alan Saunders. The atmosphere was quite different. The compromise had been reached and James Langridge, a singular man of Sussex, was elected captain and the Duke of Norfolk was asked to resume the role of president, which he did and continued to do for many years to come. Billy Griffith, who was due to go on 30 April, agreed to carry on until a successor was appointed. So, to all appearances, the crisis had gone its way. As Sir Alan Saunders was quoted as saying: 'Sussex have shown that they can go to war and can make peace, too.'

And so, with all but a few happy that the matter was over and with a lesson learned, Sussex opened the 1950 season, somewhat shaken but stirred into action for the coming summer under the first professional to be appointed captain for a season. Tate had stood in for absent skippers before the war, but had never been formally appointed. Griffith departed, and into the secretary's office strode the imposing personality of Lieutenant-Colonel George Grimston, an impressive bowler in the Winchester XI, for the Army and, on the odd occasion, for the county in the late 1920s.

New brooms wisely used are often kept at first for tidying up rather than scrubbing out yards, and the team needed careful handling during those opening months. Certainly, by all accounts the side was very happy under Jim Langridge. They needed to be, for harmony in the dressing and committee rooms did not produce the turn-about on the field that many had hoped for, though few could reasonably have expected.

The first match of the season ended in a rainy draw against Cambridge. Sheppard, playing for the University, made 130 of their 359 for 5 declared and another undergraduate, P. B. H. May, 85. At Taunton there was high scoring and Sussex won, largely thanks to George Cox's 165 not out, Charles Oakes' 5 for 35 and Jack Oakes' 5 for 68. That was in May. At the end of the month, having lost to Worcestershire, Yorkshire (when Wardle took nine Sussex wickets for 70 runs in the match) and Warwickshire, the side went to Gillingham and beat Kent by ten wickets. It was a match distinguished by Doug Wright's 6 for 131 and a sign of many big innings to come from Jim Parks the younger. He scored 159 not out, his highest innings of the season.

196

At the end of the summer, with Sussex but thirteenth in the table, the tally of wickets once again told a miserable tale. The batting was brighter with Cox and John Langridge both getting two thousand runs and Jim Langridge, Charles Oakes, his brother Jack and Don Smith each more than a thousand. Of the twenty-eight Championship matches only five were won and eleven lost. There were losses of a sadder nature to come. A. J. Holmes, who had captained the side so resolutely during the four years before the war, died. So, too, in February 1951, did Tom Burchell, the groundsman for fifty years and unofficial sage to many a player and member. There were those who said that had not Butt been such a fine wicket-keeper at the start of the century, then Burchell might well have kept wicket rather than ground for Sussex.

By the 1951 season, the newer names were more established. Jim Parks, who was doing his bit for King and country in the Royal Air Force, turned out for seven matches including the one at Tunbridge Wells when he hit 188 in a 294 third-wicket partnership with James Langridge. At the end of the season Parks, just nineteen, was awarded his county cap along with Alan Oakman. Sheppard was still at Cambridge, but once down played in eleven matches and scored a thousand runs. He was talked of as a future Sussex and England captain. Junior to Sheppard at Cambridge was Robin Marlar, who for the first time was seen at Hove that year. The year Marlar was born, 1931, George Cox, Jnr, had first appeared for Sussex, and in 1951 he was granted a benefit which, somehow typical of a Cox, set a record – £6000.

By the time the season was done, Sussex were tenth and, in spite of a sad incident involving Jack Oakes which led to his resignation, the club was settling into a style for which they had strived for so long. However, having to some extent got over the problems in the dressing rooms, the management were now having problems with the books.

The finances of county cricket, seemingly ever poised for disaster, had always troubled Sussex. When there might have been opportunity for investment in the pre-war period, it was not taken and one result was a club always just one step ahead of penury. The first warning of poverty to come appeared in 1950 when the committee reported a loss of nearly £3000. A big element in the badly balancing books was that fewer people were watching cricket. A combination of less than summer weather and a side struggling to keep off the Championship table's bottom was keeping all but the most loyal supporters away.

George Grimston launched yet another drive for more members.

Life membership was £50, full membership four guineas and county membership three guineas. As well as the normal benefits of getting into the ground and pavilion, full members were allowed to practise in the nets with professional bowlers. It cost the club £20,000 a year to keep going. Members' subscriptions brought in about £8300 and gate money about £7000. The cry from the secretary's office was for everyone to sign up a new member. But economies could not be kept waiting. Patsy Hendren had been coaching the side for two seasons. He was called in and told that Sussex could no longer afford him. The training ground for new players, the second eleven, was pulled out of the Minor Counties competition.

Meanwhile the team, well aware of the county's financial difficulties, was getting on with overcoming those on the field. The weakness of the general side may be judged by the way that it improved dramatically in the late summer, and for a reason that was truly academic.

The 1952 Championship season opened with a tie against Warwickshire. It was the first tied game for Sussex since playing Somerset in 1919. Sussex then went to The Oval and were beaten convincingly by ten wickets, in spite of a good 138 from Jim Parks. Then Northamptonshire beat the county; so did Hampshire; so did Middlesex. There was a brief celebration in June when Sussex beat Somerset. Not only was it something of a success for Oakman, who bowled his first hat-trick and toiled away for 45 minutes without conceding a run, it was also the first game Sussex had won since the July of the previous year. Next, Warwickshire beat them, and Leicestershire, and Glamorgan, and Worcestershire, and Gloucestershire, and Northamptonshire and Surrey – and then it was the end of the university term.

Sussex went to Hastings with Sheppard to open with John Langridge against Kent. They put on 216 for the first wicket. After a tail-end panic, sighs of relief. It was the first time in fourteen years that Sussex had beaten Kent at Hastings. Then to Portsmouth and a ten-wicket victory for Sussex; Middlesex went down at Hove, partly thanks to thirty-eight-year-old Jim Wood's 7 for 31 and 5 for 52 by a very young Ian Thomson in his first year. Wood, bowling ever-reliable if often unspectacular left-arm pace, was what most might call a good old county player. That season he was rather special: he took a hundred wickets, something no Sussex bowler had done since Jack Nye had taken 110 in 1939.

The last three Championship games of the year were clear wins, with Marlar, in only his second year and still at Cambridge, taking 7 for 82 against Glamorgan, 6 for 52 against Lancashire and 5 for 20 against Derbyshire. An enormous batting and bowling feast for

198

Colonel Grimston's new members, and the first time in more than fifty years that Sussex had gone through August without being beaten. Yet they actually slipped from tenth to thirteenth.

It was not an entirely disappointing year for the captain James Langridge: he had, once again, made a thousand runs. But it was his last full season. Now forty-six, he had first played for the county in 1924. It was time to go. But not far, because he was to take over the reinstated job as coach. And not quite yet. Sussex had a game with the Australians in 1953, and Langridge decided that would be his swansong. After nigh on 32,000 runs and, although he did not bowl his slow left-arm that 1952 season, more than 1500 wickets in all types of cricket (something only five other players had done), it was a good time to move over.

The same applied to Jim Cornford, who had at last got his thousand wickets. Though ready to move on, Cornford still inspired and impressed with new, hard ball, and few aspiring bowlers could afford to turn the other way and ignore his effortless run-up as a simple exercise in harmony and effort, perhaps well proved by the fact that he was never no-balled in his first-class career. He left with energy and style for a coaching job in what was then Southern Rhodesia. And his captain, having promised to stay on, showed that he, too, was not to be there as passenger. As a reminder that Langridge was far from finished, he opened the 1953 season with a century off Somerset at Taunton.

That first Championship game of the summer heralded one of the more remarkable changes in Sussex fortunes. It was also the brief reign of David Sheppard, just twenty-four years old, as captain. His rise had been straight from a schoolboy's annual. In three of the very short Cambridge seasons Sheppard had scored 3545 runs including fourteen centuries, four more than anyone else had hit. From his first appearance at Sussex, the knowing, and the others, too, for that matter, had recognised a rare talent, an almost classical amateur. Some knew also that they would have Sheppard for only a brief period, as he had been called to take holy orders. The summer of 1953 became one which showed clearly what might be done with leadership and inspiration, especially when the talent and materials were at hand.

The Sussex line of amateurs and professionals that year was impressive enough for most sides. Sheppard, Cox, Suttle, Parks and John Langridge all got a thousand runs, Sheppard hit two thousand. Batting only a few games were Jas Langridge, Smith and Doggart, and there was a single but impressive performance from the young Denis Foreman from Cape Town. The bowlers were less spectacular, but wisely bowled and coaxed they produced results. Thomson and James each took a hundred wickets. Marlar, bowling far fewer overs, took 56, Wood 79 and Oakman 63 including five during two marathon spells of thirty-one and forty-one unbroken overs at Lord's. Between them they produced the sort of figures that crowds love to stack in their memory.

There were big scores: 404 for 7 declared against Essex; 402 for 6 declared against Somerset; Sheppard's 186 not out against Leicestershire; Jim Parks and Ken Suttle in a fifth-wicket stand of 230 against Derbyshire; Jim Parks' eleven sixes and David Sheppard's nine; Robin Marlar's seven Gloucestershire wickets for just 42 runs; and twice Ted James took 6 for 19, once against Gloucestershire and then against Hampshire. By the end of the season Sheppard had led them from thirteenth to second place behind Surrey in the Championship. No wonder newspapers wrote about a revival of interest in Sussex. Not since the thirties under Duleep, Scott and Melville had Sussex cricket looked so hearty. But could it last?

In 1954 Sheppard had given up the captaincy to Doggart, and rain had done its best to stop play. It was a wretched summer. Sussex slipped down to ninth position. Yet they started with one improved element of chance in their favour. Doggart knew how to win the toss. He won it nineteen out of thirty-two times that season, which was an improvement on Sheppard who had called correctly on only four occasions during his captaincy and had won but eight tosses. On such luck rests the outcome of three days, especially in days of rain and uncovered wickets. Sussex went four Championship games, including one with Northamptonshire and a very fast young Frank Tyson, before winning any points. The committee must have looked with envy at genuine speed, for again Sussex did not have a very quick bowler. Yet it was an inability to get on with the success from the previous season that had much to do with their slide down the table.

Thomson was economical, accurate and a bowler of impressive stamina and showed signs of being more than the defensive bat he imagined himself. Six batsmen, including David Sheppard who played when he could, made more than a thousand runs and, although the old firm of George Cox and John Langridge hardly had the command of yesteryear, it was difficult to think that they both planned to retire the following season. One who did go that year was Charlie Oakes.

Oakes' father had been the groundsman at Horsham, and 'Joker' Charlie Oakes, which said everything about his temperament, was born there towards the end of the 1912 season when Chaplin

200

was captain, Ranji topped the batting, and the father of Charlie's dressing-room companion, George Cox, was atop the bowling. He joined the county's ground staff in 1930 and appeared in first-class cricket in 1935. That was the way of some professionals: the steady grind of net bowling and hope until one day a county cap. For Charlie Oakes, that came in 1937. The war did to him what it did to many – stole valuable playing years from his career; but in 1946 he perked up as a player and probably looked better than ever. Many remembered for a long time his 133 and 8 for 152 against Surrey that year. In 1947 he was considered the best of the Sussex all-rounders and scored 1500 runs and took 54 wickets to prove it. By 1954 he had been injured and was tired. In what must have been something of an anti-climax to his career, Oakes played only one game that year, his benefit match against Yorkshire at Hove which helped to raise more than £4000 that year for him. At the end of the season he said goodbye and went back to Horsham, thinking to become groundsman like his father before him and then to coach at Stowe.

If the season was not what it might have been for Oakes, then Sussex were glad to see the back of it and the weather which, as a Sussex groundsman later remarked, had made the season one of the mildest winters on record. No sooner had the scoreboard been shut tight than the workmen moved in, because with the new confidence came building work over the winter. By the spring of 1955 Hove could seat 8000 spectators and the plan was for 15,000 to watch without 'discomfort or overcrowding'. The pavilion itself got a new look with its own Long Room between the committee and dressing rooms and a bar to go with it so that members could order their drinks without spilling a drop of cricket. The members' bar had been converted into the players' dining room, and the whole building now had seating for 1400 members.

The 1955 season meant another change. There was a new captain, the third Cambridge man in a row. And like Doggart, who had returned to teaching at Winchester, and Sheppard, Marlar had captained Cambridge. Unlike them, he had beaten Oxford. It was the sort of joke and ribbing that flowed through the veins of Sussex cricket in the mid-fifties – a much more light-hearted place than it had been for some time. Marlar was an easy choice as captain, even though his first-class experience was limited, even more so than that of his very young predecessors.

In theory, he had a great basket of talent that year from which to pick eleven men. Sussex had thirty-one amateurs registered including Sheppard, the Doggarts, Marlar himself and a couple of useful players if need be, such as D. C. Dickinson who had been in Marlar's

Cambridge XI. But the strength was in the twenty-five professional staff. The stalwarts were obvious: Cox, Langridge, James, Thomson, Oakman, Smith, Wood and Parks. Yet Jim Wood, George Cox and John Langridge were retiring, and new talent had to be found from James Langridge's nursery. Graham Cooper was showing all the signs of being a good off-spinner, Gerald Cogger and Don Bates were fancied as quick bowlers, Les Lenham was described as 'a Sussex opening batsman of the future, and a classy one at that', and Denis Foreman was the quickest learner in the stable. So the 1955 season opened with Marlar determined to recover from the slide, and with hopes of bags of sunshine to assist ambition. The sun came out, and Sussex finished fourth.

Day after day of sunshine provided a glorious backdrop to cavalcades of strokes, turns, googlies and wickets, while in stuffy box, scorers sharpened and resharpened to settle new heroes with fresh figures and asterisks. Marlar, Thomson and James each took a hundred wickets. Should Oakman's off-spin have been used more often? Did Marlar bowl too often, too little? No young captain escapes, even when in favour. But he did give Don Smith, batsman, a chance as bowler, which others had not, and the club was thankful enough for that: medium-pace left-arm at Tunbridge Wells, M. C. Cowdrey 48, Smith 5 for 35. Marlar unchanged in Kent's second hand and six wickets over 5 hours and 23 minutes. A record, they said. D. C. S. Compton 150, Marlar 4 for 50. Parks 175 against Cambridge, Goonesena 3 for 68, Parks 118 and Sheppard 104 against the South Africans. Marlar 7 for 67 against Gloucester, four of them in nine balls without a run scored. Then 6 for 73 and 9 for 46 against Lancashire, Parks 205 against Somerset.

It was a thrilling season. Marlar, James and Thomson each more than a hundred wickets. Oakman perhaps under-bowled, but he got his maiden century. Parks, his own man but still son and nephew, got his two thousand runs, and a place on the tour of Pakistan. It was a season for cricketing poetry when moment scans and those who watch know they have seen rare occasion. Alan Ross was at Tunbridge Wells on an earlier day, before the double-century and the two thousand runs and more. He describes a younger Parks, but one who would do much more:

J.M. Parks at Tunbridge Wells

Parks takes ten off two successive balls from Wright,
A cut to the rhododendrons and a hook for six.

202

And memory begins suddenly to play its tricks:
I see his father batting, as, if here, he might.

Now Tunbridge Wells, 1951; the hair far lighter,
The body boyish, flesh strung across thin bone,
And arms sinewy as the wrists are thrown
At the spinning ball, the stance much straighter.

Now it is June full of heaped petals
The day steamy, tropical; rain glistens
On the pavilion, shining on corrugated metal.
The closeness has an air that listens.

Then it was Eastbourne, 1935; a date
Phrased like a vintage, sea-fret on the windscreen.
And Parks, rubicund and squat, busily sedate,
Pushing Verity square, moving his score to nineteen.

Images of Then, so neatly parcelled and tied
By ribbons of war – but now through a chance
Resemblance re-opened; a son's stance
At the wicket opens the closed years wide.

And it is no good resisting the interior
Assessment, the fusion of memory and hope
That comes flooding to impose on inferior
Attainment – yesterday, today, twisted like a rope.

Park drives Wright under dripping trees,
The images compare and a father waves away
Applause, pale sea like a rug over the knees,
Covering him, the son burying his day

With charmed strokes. And abstractedly watching,
Drowning, I struggle to shake off the Past
Whose arms clasp like a mother, catching
Up with me, summer at half-mast.

The silent inquisitors subside. The crowd,
Curiously unreal in this regency spa, clap,
A confectionery line under bushes heavily bowed
In the damp. Then Parks pierces Wright's leg-trap.

And we come through, back to the present.
Sussex 300 for 2. Moss roses on the hill.
A dry taste in the mouth, but the moment
Sufficient, being what we are, ourselves still.

Modern lines that would have versed long-limbed waggoner when stumps were two and breeches split and smudged from skimming under-arm. Marlar, Parks, gentlemen and players were all in their glory, and Langridge and Cox were gone. Since the nineteenth century there had been a Cox. Since the twenties, a Langridge. There would be another, but not yet. First there had to be 1956, and the prospects were gloomier than the memory of the year just gone. Marlar, captain once more, pondered that, with Langridge gone, who was there to take those slip catches that win games? From whence would come the close catchers, trained to stand, concentrate and hold on with all the agility of a circus performer? And where would the spirit rise? 'More than half the battle is in the mind; if we can win the battle there, we shall also win it on the field of play.' To do so Sussex needed still a great and consistent bowler. There was no replacement yet for Jas Langridge, though none doubted Thomson's skill. But the warning buoys were marked and set.

The first problem of 1956 was the weather. As 1955 had been glorious, 1956 was miserable, and sad for a more traditional reason, for at the start of the season Maurice Tate died, on 18 May. He had been coaching at Tonbridge until the previous year and had recently also taken over the Greyhound public house at Wadhurst in Kent. For a man with such magical history and who had given so much to cricket, it seemed almost unfair that Tate had been far from comfortably off when he died. But he had friends, including it is said John Arlott, who came to his widow's financial assistance. Strange, also, that many of the young tigers Sussex were about to rely on had never seen the great bowler, and certainly none was old enough to have seen him in his prime.

The young professionals did not do well on the wet wickets that year. Oakman and Smith set themselves as an opening pair and Parks once again looked on course for two thousand runs, although he never made it. It was a hard season and the county ended ninth in the table. As Jack Arlidge of the *Evening Argus* wrote: 'Season 1956 will not linger too affectionately in the memories of many players, teams or spectators.' The following summer Sussex remained joint ninth, but the ever-watching Arlidge was a little more enthusiastic: 'Season 1957 may not have been a particularly successful one for Sussex, but sound foundations were laid for future years by the steady development of several young players.'

Three of the new names in Sussex that year caught curiosity, for one was a Langridge – Richard, a tall all-rounder and the son of Jas. 'A modest enough beginning' was one comment. Another, who watched the young Langridge in his first match against the West

204

Indies, found time between the marvel of Gary Sobers and Collie Smith putting on 92 in 36 minutes to note that Richard Langridge, just eighteen, 'showed much promise for the future'. The other two newcomers had pedigrees of a different style: Ted Dexter and the young Nawab of Pataudi. Dexter, already mature and self-assured, played three games and made 66 runs in all; the Nawab of Pataudi, slight, quiet, princely, talented and, as Dexter remarked, 'able to make monkeys of all bowling', three runs more.

Dexter arrived in Sussex by chance through Robin Marlar. He had gone up to Cambridge in 1955 and by 1956, his first cricket season there, he was spending time wondering about his modern language examinations and golf. For at that stage Dexter had no great ambitions as a cricketer, and having had an undistinguished start to university rugby football he was inclined to devote his spare time to golf. He was cajoled by his brother into turning out for the freshmen's nets and trials; he made 55 and 65 and played in the opening games against the counties. He was fortunate also in being at Cambridge when Cyril Coote was the groundsman at Fenner's. Coote, a former Minor Counties player, would devote hours to giving sound advice and net practice. He had done the same for Marlar, Sheppard and Doggart.

The following season Dexter was convinced that he would play cricket after all, and this coincided with hitting his first hundred against a First-Class County – Sussex. Marlar was captain at the time, and Dexter was approached once discreet enquiry learned he was not committed to a Championship county. He agreed to play later that year, but a diversion at the end of a Cambridge cricket tour of Copenhagen ('I was fascinated by an adorable girl') delayed his appearance at Hove.

Meanwhile, in Sussex, at the top of the averages, sat Smith and Parks, the latter in all games collecting two thousand runs once more, and the man who would in later years be one of Dexter's most consistent partners. Ken Suttle, too, had easily scored his thousand that year, including a splendid 165 against Kent at Hastings and another century at Worcester during the same match in which Parks got a century in each innings. Thomson had picked up another hundred wickets and an average of under 20. There was some good cricket to watch, yet once again Sussex were going through a crisis with membership. To their aid came one of the characters of Sussex, remembered not for mighty hitting or cunning bowling, but simply for his personality and energy: Poona White.

F. G. White was chairman of the club's membership and publicity committees. He recognised that times had changed in English society and that a county club could not rely on the crowds they had enjoyed in earlier years. Ever since the Second World War interest had fallen to such an extent that only about half the numbers who had regularly attended in the forties were spending time watching cricket at Hove, Hastings and Eastbourne in the middle 1950s. Retired people were far more likely to seek second jobs to supplement their pensions. There were restrictions on travel, including limited petrol after the 1956 Suez Crisis, and even Saturday, the nation's day off, was more and more devoted to industrious pastimes rather than watching cricket. 'When I sits I stares and when I stares I sits' may have been simple and sound Sussex logic, but a side with a reputation for never quite making it, and sometimes getting nowhere near at all, had a hard time attracting the rehearsal of such logic in paying seats at Hove. Poona White's committee discovered that gates were decreasing 'at an average recession of between 10 per cent and 15 per cent per annum'.

Apart from the lack of enthusiasm of the crowds, there was a distinct lack of enthusiasm in the finance committee. Post-war costs had risen by about two hundred per cent. Income was hardly keeping pace, and if it had not been for the fund-raising efforts of the Sussex County Cricket Welfare Association, the club would have been in greater difficulties. The team was providing all the entertainment on the field, but there was great reluctance to watch them and, as White reported in 1958:

> Widespread would be the tribulation, indeed the bewilderment, if ever this great enterprise should be confronted by the necessity of having to close down through lack of public support. However, this possibility persists as long as members' subscriptions fail to redress the balance between expenditure and income. Sussex must and will prevail.

Minimum membership was still very cheap, no more than one guinea a year. Poona White's ambition was to encourage every member to bring in a new one. His enthusiasm was infectious, and many members did as he bid. It was the sort of effort that gathered few headlines in those months, a full one hundred years after another crisis had brought about the reorganisation of Sussex County Cricket Club. But his enthusiasm and those who supported him were reminder once again that there remained more to county cricket than eleven men ready to play another eleven.

Come the 1958 season there was little fun and enthusiasm for player and crowd. The heavens, unimpressed by the county's membership drive, opened at will. It was not a cricketing summer, and Sussex slithered from tenth to thirteenth in the table. There were personal successes, as there always are. Ian Thomson once again claimed more than a hundred wickets including 7 for 54 against Northamptonshire. Suttle, Parks and Oakman tussled for batting honours in that order, and each of them made more than a thousand runs.

The most interesting event of the year was the replacement of Rupert Webb by Jim Parks as wicket-keeper. Not everyone approved of the change. There was a great deal of sympathy for Webb, who had been brought on by Billy Griffith exactly ten years earlier. But there were doubts about his ability to take the spinners and, strangely enough, about standing back. Parks, who according to Ted Dexter could do anything with a ball, was described as having 'an electrifying effect on the bowlers when he took over the wicket-keeping'. Another dazzling performance on the field, but without gloves, was given by 'Tiger' Pataudi. He was one of the most attractive cover fielders on the county circuit and a stroke-player of enormous potential.

There was certain Sussex interest also in events away from Hove, north of the Thames, where Dexter was having a glorious final year at Cambridge. He was now captaining the University and he hit a century against Sussex. In his first year he scored 833 runs, his second produced 1209 and selection for the Gentlemen v Players, when he bowled many surprises and took 5 for 8 in the first innings. In his final year he scored 1256 for Cambridge and took 36 wickets. By 1959, Dexter's first full season for the county, there were many who looked forward to a change in fortune and yet another Cambridge man's part in it.

Where the previous season had gurgled and spluttered beneath waxing rainstorms and waning fortunes, 1959 was a summer of remembered bright mornings, sun-warmed backs and evening shadows. The very stuff of cricket's wistful notions. If the crowds had hoped for an amateur as hero, they were given a professional, too. Jim Parks hit more than two thousand Championship runs including 157 against Glamorgan at Hove, the highest score for a Sussex batsman that year. Marlar was full of praise:

Soon, I feel sure, Jim Parks will come to realise what a giant he has become as a cricketer, and with this realisation he will be able to make the field bow to his will when he is in full flow, even in moments of stress. When that time arrives he will deserve

207

to be ranked with the all-time greats along with the Sheppards, Mays and Cowdreys of this world.

His captain's hand on his shoulder indeed. All this and wicket-keeper extraordinary as well. This was his first full season and he caught eighty-five batsmen and stumped six. The catches gave him a Sussex record, the nearest to it being George Street in 1923 and John Langridge in 1955, both with 69. Catching, stumping and hitting were nearly all to be done by a wicket-keeper. The members nodded approvingly, even those who had rightly and loyally defended Webb's tenure. Nor was the crowd disappointed with Dexter's year: 1511 runs in the Championship with six centuries. Suttle, Smith, Lenham and Oakman each scored their thousand runs that year and, seemingly as ordered, Thomson took another 120 wickets.

None of the bowlers even approached this level of cricket, which may well have had something to do with the catches that went down that year. It was generally a poor attack once more, and with the wickets giving chance any superb spinner would have been worth his weight in wickets. That spinner could have been Marlar, then in his last year as captain and urged by some to bowl slower and more to the bedevilment of batsmen. Once again there was talk in the committee room of looking to a new generation to find the needed talent. Certainly some felt there was skill, art and enthusiasm in the nursery, where Jas Langridge as county coach was preparing to hand over to George Cox, now returned from Winchester where he had nurtured the Nawab of Pataudi, and seeking future Parkses, Langridges and, perhaps, even a Cox play-alike. Denis Foreman was there still, and Tony Buss and his brother Michael.

The year had not been a great success, in spite of the signs of summer and the flow of runs. Sussex moved even further down the table, to fifteenth. But perhaps where there is fifteenth, or even sixteenth or seventeenth, there is hope. The saddest moment of the year came well after roller and all were locked fast and the county was waiting for Christmas. One Saturday morning in December it was announced that Duleep was dead. A. A. Thomson's obituary summed up, perhaps, the feelings of all cricket lovers:

He was born to the purple, nephew of the greatest. Cricket was in his blood, his bones and his sinewy wrists. On the field he was an elegant artist; as a man, he was what every boy might wish his favourite cricketer to be: modest and unaffectedly charming. . . . In the five years that remained between his first and second

208

retirements he bestowed on cricket some of the riches that make up its permanent heritage. For Sussex he averaged 2000 runs a season and every run of the 10,000-odd credited to him was made with style and elegance. To Sussex he brought renewed strength, bold leadership and batting of extreme attractiveness. People not especially interested in cricket would come to watch him play, paying him the personal tribute given in the same period only to Walter Hammond . . . But there is in the ranks of Sussex today a young man who has played for the county only in his school days from Winchester, but has already shown, in the artistry of his batting, the vivid keenness of his fielding and the spirit of his sportsmanship, qualities far beyond what are called 'promising'. He is the Nawab of Pataudi. The line of princes is not broken.

'Tiger' Pataudi's moment was yet to come. For the moment it was Dexter's, and 1960 the beginning of a new age of cricket.

Chapter 17

In the late 1950s cricket's lords, masters and reeves watched dismally as the estate which had its origins beyond the days of Guldeford went into decline. It was as if some benign but insistent barony had lost its personality and wit, its grandness and its influence to command the allegiance and attendance of its subjects. Not for the first time, people were staying away from the grounds. In more than a hundred years of county cricket there had been other times of fashion and following in which cricket had suffered. Royal, ducal and noble patronage and not a little interest in exchanging purses and wagers had assured exchequers and fashionable interest in the earliest years. Later, the thrills and the characters had drawn many to watch while others entertained. But there had been many times when interest kept itself elsewhere, to be revived only at some new personality's arrival, deeds and triumphs.

However, this time the decline was more telling. For, although there was positive indication that fewer people went to cricket matches, there was no conclusive evidence that there was less interest in the game. If the interest was there, but people were not attending, then potentially cricket had a bigger problem than ever before. But if the game still fanned enthusiasm for occasion and county loyalty, what kept people from the grounds in such numbers? Many engaged in the game's administration confused low gates with lack of interest; this was but partly true, and the failure to recognise this reflected the amateur status given to the stewardship of cricket.

In the 1940s, with the post-war revival of county cricket, gate receipts and membership figures showed that nearly two million people a season were turning up to watch the Championship games. By

211

the late fifties and early sixties, fewer than one million people were going to the grounds. Some of this dramatic drop could be attributed to lack of interest in the game. At the same time, cricket's supporters were still keen to read the match reports and goings-on in the county circuit. Much of the interest may have remained, but many of those who supported a county did so from a distance and the convenience of their newspapers and journals. In other words, the undoubted interest was demonstrated by proxy. Behind this phenomenon was cricket's failure to be compulsively attractive in a changing society. There was an obvious shift, almost a revolution, in the type and style of British pastimes. The utility mentality that had lingered after 1945 was evaporating. People were becoming less set in their ways and expectations.

By the late fifties Britain had entered the jet-travel age, overseas holidays were no longer exclusively for the reasonably well off, and fashion had, in the years since 1947, swirled from the A-line, through the empress lines, to the freedom of new, brighter, cheaper, synthetic styles and cuts. Pop music had become a sub-culture of do-it-yourself glamour, from skiffle's washboard and tea-chest bass music to plug-in amplified three-chord guitar chart-busters. By the end of the decade the discipline of National Service was no more and television had raised sights and trends to levels of unprecedented acceleration. The New Elizabethans had emerged from post-war monochrome to a Technicolor society on the edge of the social revolution of the sixties that was about to rewrite all the laws of British middle-class values.

The year 1960 was the trip-wire for a decade of change everywhere, not only in Britain. John F. Kennedy was elected President and seigneur of a new Camelot with its inspiration for young people on both sides of the Atlantic. In February, Harold Macmillan made his 'wind of change' speech in South Africa. In the following month came the Sharpeville massacre. The echoes of both events spread as far as Lord's. A colour television transmission between London and Paris led to discussion of new plans for international coverage of major sporting events. Colour viewing, the ultimate in armchair spectatorship – though not early enough to see Cowdrey and Pullar put on 290 for the first wicket against South Africa at The Oval that year. Crime rates were the highest ever, Donald Campbell crashed *Bluebird* on the Bonneville Salt Flats, *Lady Chatterley's Lover* was declared not obscene, and the catchiest tune at number one in the hit parade was 'Fings Ain't Wot They Used T'be'. They were not. The new fast-food society no longer had the time, or the patience, to sit down to a full, three-course Championship match.

Cricket's first response to the changing social character of the nation was to dissolve the one constant in the game since its inception. In September 1962 the last Gentlemen *v* Players game was played and amateur status was abolished. It was an inevitable response to a changing age and not a calculated attempt to bring new energy and zest into a game which was in need of something that would revive curiosity and attendance at three-day games. It had few disadvantages, although some of the more thoughtful professionals could see the advantage of retaining the inclination to seek Varsity amateurs as captains. An amateur leader was not necessarily beholden to committee and management as was a professional, employed as tradesman and craftsman to the county. The amateur could also be dictator to the team. Many professionals recognised the difficulty of becoming captain and then having to lay down the law to men who the season before had been grumbling mates. But the amateur had to go, as one of the first major changes of those opening years of the decade.

The next development was a reflection of events that had been forecast in the Macmillan speech. In May 1961, South Africa left the Commonwealth and consequently lost membership of the Imperial Cricket Conference. The ICC subsequently refused South Africa's return to its folds. (David Sheppard had declared that as long as South Africa persisted with its policy of apartheid he could not play against them.) Those early years of the decade saw also the revision of registration rules, which were to be felt by all but Yorkshire, and which introduced the wandering players. Roger Prideaux of Kent, then of Northamptonshire and then of Sussex was a product of this thinking. So were overseas players, whose registration periods were lowered from three to two years.

The catalyst for the biggest change of all came in 1962 with the formation of the Cavaliers, the first sight for many of quick cricket. The atmosphere, as the name Cavaliers suggested, was entertaining, perhaps even swashbuckling cricket, and it is obviously appropriate that Dexter's name was so closely linked with its success. Crowds were happy to spend an afternoon watching cricketers playing a fast game that would produce an exciting finish and a result.

By 1963 the enthusiasm for a single day's play had been taken up by Gillette. Industry had for some time recognised that the American system of commercial sponsorship was a relatively unexplored form of advertising. It could be enormously profitable, especially if associated with an art form or sport free of suspicion and controversial incident.

213

Cricket, with its whiter than cream reputation, was a worthy subject for sponsorship and relatively cheap. In the first season, 1963, Gillette's offering to the counties was £6500, a modest amount but the first commercial sponsorship of county cricket.

This, then, was the scene set before Sussex in 1960 with its new captain, Ted Dexter. The county had finished fifteenth in the 1959 table and needed an enormous boost to raise their game and position if attendances were not to fall even further in the climate of indifference and social diversion. Dexter supplied the leadership for that revival. E. R. Dexter, as usual, had a theory for success. It worked. The first thing he wanted was an improvement in the standard of fielding, especially in the slips. Like all good generals, Dexter delegated. Alan Oakman was given the job of improving the chances of Sussex holding on to the results of enthusiasm and skill shown by the side's quicker bowlers.

Well before the season's start, Oakman gathered the safest hands and pushed them through hour after hour of slip practice. And before every game the practice continued. As Dexter himself observed, 'the results spoke for themselves when Oakman, Cooper, Buss, Bell and even the captain held good catches in those positions, not to mention other recruits, who managed to sense the enthusiasm and who caught catches almost despite themselves'.

Dexter had to make do with the old shelf of bowlers, who although sound, and with the exception of Thomson, were far from spectacular. Thomson was injured, which made matters more difficult, although not impossible. Bates and Buss were good enough for the job, but Bates needed a new approach and before each game he spent considerable time warming up in the nets. The result was a reduction in the number of wayward balls and 107 wickets from 862 overs. The previous season Bates, who had joined Sussex as early as 1950, had 348 overs and took but 31 Championship wickets. Bell, who had not bowled much the previous season, was under pressure to keep his place. Dexter needed a good spinner. Bell responded and took 50 wickets. As ever, Ian Thomson, bowling in any conditions, triumphed with yet another hundred wickets. 'He bowled like a lion,' said his captain.

Of the batsmen, five each scored a thousand and more, with Ken Suttle playing straighter and sterner than ever, being just 170 short of two thousand Championship runs. He was, as on so many occasions, a minor hero, which made his eventual dismissal from the county all the more sad.

There were thirty-two County Championship matches that year and

214

Dexter, who was playing also against the South Africans, captained the side twenty times in 1960 with Marlar and Sheppard each leading the side on four occasions and Doggart and Smith three. Sussex finished fourth and were, for many, the most exciting side to watch in the whole Championship. For the paying customers there were glorious displays of batting and bowling. The win over Surrey by an innings and 39 runs was memorable for Dexter's 155, Parks' 135, Buss's 5 for 55 and Tony Lock's 1 for 113, the green wicket and the fact that this was Sussex's first win at Hove against Surrey since 1947. And with Smith leading the side the eight-wicket win at Hastings against Kent, with Suttle getting 112 not out and Thomson taking 5 for 20, was another highlight.

There were also disappointments. A week at Eastbourne and going down to Worcestershire by 90 runs with Kenyon scoring a glorious 109 and Gifford taking four Sussex wickets for 55, which arrested the heartbeat of the county's batting and allowed Worcestershire to beat Sussex twice in one season for the first time since 1911, which considering that Worcestershire finished thirteenth in 1960 was a bit thick. There was frustration, too, among the members, the players and the accountants, when the South African tour match was abandoned without a ball bowled, the first game at Hove since 1903 to be completely washed out. For the captain, 1960 was an enormous success, yet sadly he rarely managed to recapture that same mood and enthusiasm for Sussex.

Dexter himself understood, a few years later, that the early part of that 1960 season had been rather special. And ironically, the pressures on cricket to maintain that very special atmosphere helped to dull it for Dexter. By his own admission he was 'an infinitely more exciting cricketer to watch in the early part of 1960' than he ever was afterwards. For him, the continuous daily grind of county cricket meant that the best could not be forever wrung from tired players caught in the round of travelling, hours in field (or, if they were lucky, at the crease), and bowling hundred upon hundred of overs each season. But this was what the members and casual watchers wanted, and with reason. They certainly wanted Sussex to fall no further than fourth come 1961. But fall they did.

Certainly the county started the new season in style both on and off the field. A reflection of hard work by the County Welfare Association was the reconstruction of the pavilion at Hove. Three rows of seats were added to the front of the Ladies' Stand and the bar in the Members' Pavilion moved back to give more space for the drinkers and watchers. The changing rooms were rebuilt on

215

three floors with a glass-enclosed 'viewing gallery' for the players, while downstairs more wall space meant that the result of digging to discover cricketing pictures and prints in the past years could be seen by many more members and guests.

There was a new look, too, for the list of players, with six of them appearing for the first time: Mike Buss, Thomson, Gunn, Ledden, Waters and a new bowler, J. A. Snow. When Mike Buss joined his brother Tony in the side, they became the twenty-eighth pair of brothers to play for Sussex. The family connections were firm when another Langridge, Richard, was awarded his cap, as so, too, were Ron Bell and Graham Cooper, who fell ill with a hole in his lung.

The season started with a series of drawn games, which set a trend for the summer: thirty-two games played, eleven won, eleven drawn, ten lost. Sussex ended eighth in the table. Disappointment was natural when it was seen how well Sussex played. Six batsmen scored more than a thousand Championship runs, including Richard Langridge who made 1569, and Oakman, Lenham and Suttle, each of whom made nearly two thousand. Of the bowlers, Thomson, for the ninth year in succession, took more than a hundred wickets in the season.

But from all the fine arithmetic at the end of the year it was noticeable that Sussex was one of the slowest-scoring counties in the Championship. Dexter hardly helped by example. Although he did very well in Tests, he had a quite indifferent season for Sussex. He went to Pakistan that winter. It must have done him good. He made 205 at Dacca, his highest score in first-class cricket, and came back to England for the 1962 season fairly fizzing off bat and wicket. He played in thirty-one innings, hit 1243 runs and took 60 wickets, including twice getting a hundred runs and taking ten wickets in the same match, both times in away games, Tunbridge Wells and The Oval. Sussex suffered from Dexter's good form. Because of Tests, the Sussex captain missed eight home games, which hardly made the side's task easier. Bates took more than a hundred wickets and, for the tenth season in succession, so did Thomson. Sheppard made brief appearances and in only eleven innings scored 722.

The batting story of that season was the 2057 runs of Ken Suttle, by then one of the most consistent left-handers in England and rather unusual in Sussex, for he was the last player in the county to score two thousand runs in a season. Also that season he made his highest score, 204 not out at Tunbridge Wells. Suttle's career was a good example of the outstanding county player overlooked for finer things. For,

216

although he went on tour to the West Indies in the winter of 1953–4, he never played in the Tests. Yet in a Sussex career that ran from 1949 until 1971 he scored around 30,000 runs, including a thousand runs in a season seventeen times, and took 260 wickets, and certainly in those earlier years was considered one of the best outfielders in the country. As for consistent performance, Suttle still holds the record for the most consecutive County Championship appearances – 423 matches without a break between 1954 and 1969. (Binks of Yorkshire is second with 412 between 1955 and 1969.)

The talk of deeds and disappointment, including differences between players and committee, had to an extent been overshadowed by the expectation that the amateur status in county cricket was to be abolished. Later that year, the Advisory County Cricket Committee voted to recommend to the MCC that the distinction between amateur and professional be dropped. It was not the vast majority on the committee who held the opinion that it should happen, but nevertheless it was a majority of sorts and so it went. Certainly it removed anomalies that dated from the day in 1806 when the Gentlemen *v* Players came about.

The amateur in some ways was the shamateur. Money came from advertising, signed newspaper and magazine articles and endorsements, and was so lucrative that 'a form of legalised deceit was being practised' according to the Sussex view on the committee's deliberation. And, to indicate the county's full endorsement, it noted in its report, 'By paying him for playing, the committee have cut out one juicy, ever-ripe target of criticism, and one aspect likely to bring the game into disrepute.'

Sport in general was shaking the cobwebs from its attitude to amateurs and the way in which payment was made, but in cricket the overwhelming influence on the decision for the abolition of amateur status must have been the social change in society. It was not so much that Britain was becoming a classless society, as some suggested. It had more to do with the emergence of the new middle class together with the feeling that the social separation of amateur and professional was too blatant an anachronism. As it was, professional cricketers were often treated by committee and governors as performing dogs, to be discarded to the glue factory once tricks and energy were exhausted. The time had come for the bespatted mill owner–clogged loom worker relationship to change. It did not entirely, but the removal of the by then outdated practice of cricketers dressing apart was a step and, more important an indicator that the wind of change was blowing also through cricket.

217

And so, in 1963, Sussex cricketers, no longer amateurs and professionals, took to the field to seek the Championship and the new and
sponsored trophy from Gillette. Dexter was captain still and there
was a new chairman, Arthur Gilligan. Gilligan, who had taken over
the captaincy forty years earlier with the task of building Sussex into
a strong all-round side, had not lolled in committee armchair awaiting
his turn at centre table. From the very start of the Sussex Cricket
Association he had encouraged the Southbourne concept and the four
main members of the group that tried during the war years to get it
going, Billy Walker, Hardy, Kent and Baker. As the Association's
president, Gilligan had been the working figurehead, campaigning
for its use as a talent-basket of young players. The forties were
the testing times, but full, as Gilligan noted in 1963, of talent that
had come good. The scorebooks gave testimony to that. In 1945 the
Association played the Australians at Hove. A youngster named
K. Suttle opened the batting against a side which included Hassett
and Pepper.

The need and the difficulty for Sussex to breed from its own
nursery had been recognised and championed by Gilligan since the
1920s. He understood also the need for new ideas, but ones which
would be easily and comfortably balanced alongside old ways. For,
while there were many at this time eager to drag cricket into this
whirlwind decade, Gilligan and others knew perfectly that once the
tempest of the 1960s had subsided, then cricket, which would inevitably bend in places to the social change, would have to rely on the
strength of the good things in its innate conservative foundations. It
was a simple and classic philosophy of preserving the old in order to
persevere with the new. If the revolution were not adapted to with
great caution, then cricket might find itself discarded like last year's
mini-skirt. Sussex adapted to the new era with some style and success,
thanks largely to a combination of tradition and thoughtful leadership.

In the Championship the side were in fine form. In 1962 they had
finished twelfth. During the new season, there were matches when
their followers held their breath for days on end. Between 28 May
and 4 June they were at the top of the table, then Yorkshire went
top, then Sussex, then they shared the lead with Yorkshire, then took
it once for three days in July, then shared with Yorkshire, then held it,
then shared again with Yorkshire who went on to win while Sussex
slipped, but only to fourth position, which is where they ended the
season. Why could they not hold on? Other teams were going well, is
the first and obvious answer, and Dexter and Parks were away playing
Test cricket. But Dexter pointed out at the time that that 'was not the

218

whole answer to our failing to hit the jackpot'. He continued:

> We still lack a little something in the spin division though Alan
> Oakman and Ronnie Bell nearly produced the goods for us this
> year. The other lack is a reserve force of any quality. Young
> cricketers on the groundstaff hardly seem to get enough good class
> competition to bridge the gap into the first side and there is better
> material coming to the County side from outside sources. Where-
> as Yorkshire can find new players of the class and experience in
> league cricket of Boycott, Hampshire and Nicholson we have only
> John Snow to show for some years of groundstaff training and
> club activity outside the county ground . . . already George Cox
> is doing untiring work with the younger generation but he needs
> the best material available if he is to bring a successful new look
> to the Sussex side in 1970.

Dexter was looking ahead, realising that the changes would bring
about added, not fewer, pressures. And that year, 1963, Sussex triumphed in the first of those changes. On 7 September the county
became the first winners of the Gillette Trophy. To get there they
beat Kent in the first round by 72 runs at Tunbridge Wells, Yorkshire at Hove by 22 runs, Northamptonshire away by 105 runs in the
semi-finals, and then in the final at Lord's they beat Worcestershire
by just 14 runs. Sussex batted first in every game, including the final
when only Richard Langridge with 34 and Jim Parks with 57 made
many runs. Sussex were all out for 168. Worcestershire went in and
through rain and gloom nearly made it, but were all out for 154 just
before seven o'clock, with John Snow taking three wickets for 13 runs.
At last Sussex had won something.

Not everyone was pleased with the way in which Sussex had triumphed. The county was accused of playing negative cricket, and there
were even those who watched at Hove who felt that the idea of bright
and breezy one-day knock-out had been foiled by defensive tactics by
their own side. The simple truth was that Dexter, again with one of his
theories, had out-thought the other county captains. The idea was to
set a defensive field and defy the opposition to break through. Many
of them were setting conventional fields, as if they were playing on
the first day of a three-day match. At the end of Sussex's innings at
Tunbridge Wells, for example, Kent were still bowling with two slips
and a gulley. Sussex scored 314 for 7 off the sixty-five overs. They then
fielded, putting everyone back, which may have given away singles but
saved boundaries. The Kent committee grumbled that Sussex were not

playing fairly and properly. Dexter was playing to win. And to prove it was no fluke of hypothesis, Sussex went out the next year and did it again, and won. For the players the wins were great tonics in a side that was more or less used to the idea that it had never won anything in its history.

Furthermore, the problems of one-day cricket mixing with the county game were not apparent. Most of the players regarded it as fun. For the majority of the side, the pressure of the new styles of cricket did not appear until the Sunday League was established. That often meant a lot of travelling away for one day and then back again for the county programme. Then counties and their sides started totting up the pounds shillings and pence of the one-day game, and this proved an added pressure, though not one that many would have discarded willingly. When they won the 1963 Gillette Trophy, Sussex got a cheque for £1889. When they retained it in 1964, the prize money had risen to £2167 17s 6d (£2167.88) which came from the Gillette donation and television fees plus five shares from gate receipts.

Successful as they were, Sussex were still suffering from falling gates in 1964. In 1963, a damp season, there had been the weather to keep the less than hardy away. But 1964 was good cricket weather yet fewer than 36,000 people watched Sussex that year compared with more than 42,000 the previous season. It was something of a problem for the new secretary, Colonel P. C. Williams, who had taken over from George Grimston. But gates were just one of his and the committee's crosses for the coming year.

The season of 1965 was yet another that Sussex would have chosen to forget. They dropped to next but bottom of the Championship. They were knocked out of the Gillette by Middlesex. The captain had a car accident that kept him out of cricket from June onwards. Dexter, before his accident, Parks and Snow were lost to Tests, there were five different captains, the Hove ground was in a mess – it was in 'a disgraceful state from June to the end of the season', said Gilligan – and a new groundsman, Len Creese, was appointed. Little wonder that team spirit was not at its highest. Hardly good cricketing conditions.

There were some batting and bowling successes, although for the first time in thirteen seasons Ian Thomson did not get his hundred wickets, which was a pity because he was retiring to join the family garage business. But John Snow and Tony Buss got theirs, although only 89 of Snow's came in Championship games. Ken Suttle easily scored a Championship thousand, including a century before lunch at Eastbourne against Gloucestershire. But Sussex's reputation was on the floor, and the chairman, Arthur Gilligan, was

220

the very man to spell out the problems, which he did in stern tones.

> I want to see a much better standard of fielding, particularly by some of the younger players. I have never tolerated slack fielding. It was nice to record both Snow and Buss's hundred wickets, but I want to see a little quicker 'walk back' before starting their runs, and this will also improve the rate of overs per hour, which should be near as possible to twenty in the hour – by no means an impossible target. I would also like to see bowlers' run-up cut down to a maximum of 18 yards, and no more.

This last point was from a captain who knew how to bowl and had watched Maurice Tate run not much more than the length of his shadow to zip off the pitch and devastate good batting sides.

John Snow, for one, while accepting the Gilligan wisdom, was inclined to believe that the majority of the committee members had no idea of the stresses on their players and therefore were rarely good judges of performance. It was an opinion of the committee's fragility that was to lead the bowler on many occasions to words and differences with the club's management, a reflection of his personality as well as of the stock of the stewards. Yet a few years later Doug Wilshin, the chairman of the committee, was to wonder aloud to Snow that, if his views were sound, perhaps it was a good idea for Snow to be appointed captain. The notion came to nothing.

By 1965 Snow had developed from stock to front-line bowler, quicker, more sideways-on. Consequently more was expected of him. This would have been all very well in a well-balanced side, but lack of planning and opportunity, perhaps even of understanding of the game, meant, for example, that Sussex did not have the spinners they needed. On one occasion when Snow made his feelings known rather publicly to the captain, Pataudi, he ended up in front of the committee to explain his explosive behaviour. He took the chance to tell the committee that they needed spinners if they wanted success, and few words on the field. He was reprimanded. Later Snow was accused also of not trying, and the charge, while in part valid, demonstrated the problem before club and players of Snow's like. His claim that the Sussex side of the sixties was unbalanced was not his alone. Because he was the new star, much was expected of him, even on the 'wrong' wickets. As Snow wrote in his book *Cricket Rebel*:

> There is a limit to what one man can do, whatever his job. That

221

limit is reduced when overwork takes toll of a person physically as well as mentally. It was often soul destroying. On wet wickets or slow ones, I was expected to charge up and down and let it go when I knew I had no earthly chance of getting anything out of the wicket.

The other problem was the understanding of those in charge. Snow, again as an example, might perhaps decide to bowl off a shorter run and seam the ball as a way of getting wickets from slower pitches. This would immediately be interpreted as 'not trying'. No one would accuse Gilligan of being ignorant of the ways of bowlers, but often those with firm voice had unfirm learning on which to base their opinions. Whatever the rights and wrongs of complaints in 1965, Gilligan's pep-talk had some effect, but 1966 hardly began with blistering pace and enthusiasm.

The new season meant a new captain. Dexter had gone, and the Nawab of Pataudi took over. Pataudi's appointment was inevitable, and to some extent a hangover from the recent days of Varsity captains. Yet no one doubted his ability as a cricketer, certainly not George Cox who had coached him at Winchester. After Winchester Pataudi went up to Oxford where he hit a century in his first Varsity match and captained the University for the next two years. While still at Oxford he was selected for the Indian side to tour the West Indies, and became vice-captain to Nari Contractor in 1962. Contractor was injured, and so Pataudi led the side in the last three Tests, thus becoming the youngest man to captain a Test side and the only undergraduate to do so. He was captain again when India played Mike Smith's England side in 1964 and scored 203 not out in the Fourth Test and then went on to lead India to victory over Australia at the Brabourne Stadium in Bombay.

In 1961 Pataudi was involved in a car accident in Brighton and seriously damaged and partially lost the sight of one eye. Consequently, he adopted a more open stance, which should have restricted some of his off-side play but, because of his uncluttered agility, did not. It was this same fleetness that gave him his enviable reputation as a dazzling fielder. In all, Sussex did well with the last of their Indian princes as leader, though the figures were pushed to reflect this.

At the start of the summer, Somerset sliced Sussex from the Gillette competition and, to rub it in, beat them in both Championship games by ten wickets and then six. But Sussex did beat the West Indies. The county won the toss, put the tourists in and bowled them out for 123. Sussex then got 185 including 64 from the young Peter Graves, and

222

in again went the West Indies. They were all out for 67, their lowest score in England since 1928. Sussex won by nine wickets. Parks took seven catches and John Snow finished with eleven wickets for 47 runs. It was one of the brighter intervals in the year, although the conditions were dim and dank.

So they were in the next game at Hove when Nottinghamshire went down by eight wickets with Tony Buss taking 8 for 23 including a spell of three wickets for no runs in four balls. The pitch was modestly described as 'a real beast'. The county then went to Leeds and beat Yorkshire by 22 runs, their fourth win of the month (they had beaten Essex) and the third victory inside two days. There was, understandably, a great deal of grumbling about the state of the wickets at Hove. The ground was being openly described as unfit for first-class cricket, and Len Creese was painstakingly re-laying the square with turf from the outfield.

If the pitch was getting a much-needed new look, so was the team. Denis Foreman was at last awarded his county cap, having captained the second eleven so caringly. Another in the junior side was making his name: Tony Greig took 55 wickets and was the second-highest batsman in the team. The important change was the realised ambition of Jim Parks to be captain.

India were to tour England in 1967, and the Nawab of Pataudi was to lead his country. In came Parks with instructions and reputation. He was one of the hardest and most attacking batsmen in cricket, and Spen Cama, the chairman of the cricket committee, acknowledged this and the way in which he hoped this aggression would translate on to the field.

> We all know Jim is one of the most attacking batsmen in the game, and I particularly want to see him bring that aggressive and purposeful spirit into his Captaincy. He has a great opportunity to take all justifiable risks, because the Cricket Committee have for two years declared that to be our policy. It certainly has not always been implemented, but let us hope that some of the negative, defensive, dull and dreary cricket which has been played by so many Counties and which has lost the game so many spectators in recent years, will become only a nightmare of the past.

Spen Cama, one of the most respected members ever of the county committee, was speaking the minds of many. Basically he understood that the follower of cricket sought not a revolution, by which cricket might be damaged, but a simple game of 'batsmen at all times looking

223

for runs and the bowlers always trying to get the other side out'. Parks appeared the ideal man for the task and opportunity. Yet he was, by his own reckoning, at a disadvantage.

Parks was at the pinnacle. It was 1967. He now had the Captain's Room and the skipper's salary of £1200 a year. But he had lost Ian Thomson, Dexter, Pataudi, and was saddled with his instructions and instincts to play attacking cricket and rebuild the side. The first season was not too bad. Everything went more or less according to plan except that the team went from tenth to thirteenth position. But Parks carried out the committee's instructions and they were well pleased. Sussex scored more runs per hundred balls than any other county and were second in the numbers of overs bowled in each hour.

The committee members were tolerant, too, of the slide in position. John Snow had been of little use from about the middle of June because of injury and Test matches. They were happy that a brighter cricket policy would pay off and they reported: 'it is our hope in the next few years to build up a new young side under the experienced guidance of Jim Parks that would take Sussex to the Championship'. The rising star of the new young side they looked for was Tony Greig. He scored a thousand runs and more in the Championship and took more than sixty wickets. But it started to go wrong, both on and off the field, and particularly for Parks himself.

He was enjoying it at first, but then the pressure of batting, keeping wicket and being captain started to get to him. He came to the conclusion that the ideal skipper was a batsman who went in at number five and with time to relax and reflect on the way the game ran. By 1968, matters came to a head. The year had started disappointingly when in February negotiations to sign the South African Barry Richards were apparently agreed, only for Sussex to find out that another county had made a bigger offer and Richards backed out. Gradually the rot set in, and Sussex, in spite of being close runners-up to Warwickshire in the Gillette Trophy, ended the season winning but two of their twenty-eight Championship matches and finishing at the bottom of the table, something they had not done since 1946.

Morale was dreadful, and appeared so by the middle of the year. The team were accused of not trying and appeared to react by losing spirit. Parks, with all the other problems of captaincy, was being drained by the effort of keeping the side together. His play started to suffer and in July he cried enough, and handed over to Mike Griffiths. It was a sad end to his season and a disappointment, too, for his father, Jim Parks, Snr, who had first won his Sussex cap in 1926 and had now decided to stand down as the team's coach.

224

In more practical terms, the 1968 season ended with gloom in the counting house. The finance committee described the season as a disaster. They even lost money on their share of receipts from the Gillette competition. Membership was up, to 6967, but so was the cost of running the club, which now showed a deficit of more than £8000 on the year and an accumulated deficit of £21,168. Once again came dire warning: 'Unless the wasting away of our assets (though these are considerable) is arrested, the continuance of County Cricket at Hove could be jeopardised.' Eeyore would have understood perfectly the mood of the county side as it approached 1969. No wonder the committee issued an ultimatum to the team:

> Let each player, from those of Test Match class to the most junior apprentice, know that the County will demand that he gives every ounce of his endeavour at all times in the interest of the team, and that if he is not prepared to give 100 per cent support to his captain – Mike Griffith – then he would do better to seek his fortune elsewhere.

It seems to have worked.

Chapter 18

The big event for Sussex in 1969 was their climb from bottom to seventh position in the Championship table. For cricket in general, it was the year of the introduction of the John Player Sunday League. Sussex finished bottom. In the Gillette Trophy they got as far as the semi-final and were then bowled out by Derbyshire for the lowest ever total in the competition – 49. In the Championship averages, only Parks scored a thousand runs, although Suttle was just ten short. There was another disappointment for Suttle's eager followers. After 423 consecutive appearances for Sussex, he was dropped. That was in the Surrey game at The Oval. Later he came back into the side, and indeed made a strong 127 against Middlesex at Hove. But for some in the committee room the days of Suttle were numbered.

However, he was there the following year, 1970. And in the last match of the season, against Middlesex, he put on 200 with the newly capped Geoff Greenidge for the third wicket. It was the Barbadian's fifth century of the season, at twenty-two the youngest Sussex player ever to score five centuries in a summer, and brought him to third behind Mike Buss and Jim Parks in the county's batting averages. Sussex finished ninth in the Championship and nowhere in the Sunday League, but lost only to Lancashire in the Gillette final. Tony Greig won a Test place; Ian Thomson moved back to Sussex and was being asked to play in limited-over games; a future captain, John Barclay, made his début; Les Lenham was appointed county coach; and the Indian spinner Uday Joshi was registered. In all, a busy and not entirely disappointing season on the field. There was but little sign of the slippery events heading Sussex's way. But in the committee room there were mis-givings and, according to some, considerable muddle which had more to do with a breakdown in communications than with anything else.

At the start of the 1970 season there had been media reports of mismanagement. For a whole decade, the zephyr of commercial development had swirled about cricket's head. The conundrum was simple: how should Sussex County Cricket Club be put on such a sound financial base as to ensure its livelihood in the seventies and eighties? The answer was problematical. Sussex needed to establish a commercial management that would exploit the growing need for sponsorship and investment. But the truth was that Sussex cricket in the 1960s and early 1970s had no desire to become part of the trend towards a thoroughly commercialised sport. And there were, and are, many supporters of the notion that cricket in the county represented far more than a Technicolor pantomime, whatever the short-term gains of such a show for the Sussex coffers. Nevertheless, if the traditional values that had pleased since the early 1800s were to survive, then the resources that were available had to be better-managed and manipulation of sponsorship had to be achieved by the club and not by the sponsors.

Development of the southern part of the ground had started with the club getting much of its way with the developers, except in the name of the block. 'Ashdown,' said the ground development committee report, 'although admirable, savours more of Canterbury and the Hop County rather than Hove and Sussex.' The name had been picked by the developers from a £50 competition above 1500 other entries which had included Blobbers, Umpire State Building and, cricket's answer to Dunrovin, Madenova. But this was by the way to the serious charge of many at the start of 1970.

The accusations of maladministration were founded on the spirit among some of the players, reports of high-handedness among some officials, and the inescapable fact that Sussex were losing money and members. Finances in 1970 were made worse because of the cancella-tion of the South African tour. Normally Sussex would have received thousands of pounds from the Test and County Cricket Board and television fees as their cut of the tour profits. No tour, no money. There were even representations to the government that the politi-cal nature of the matter should mean that government would have to compensate county cricket for the loss. Overall it was, in 1970, costing Sussex £63,000 a year to run the club.

The questions about management probably turned some away

228

from membership, which that year showed a drop of about 17 per cent, although some of that figure could be attributed to natural wastage. Arthur Gilligan, in his annual report as club chairman, said that every member should be trying to bring in another. He seemed to accept a high annual loss, but felt that it could be contained and estimated that a thousand new members a year would mean that subscriptions would be worth about £22,000. This was ambitious but, then, Gilligan had never been anything else.

The accusations and mutterings continued and at the end of the season the club called a Special General Meeting which agreed to ask the auditors to investigate thoroughly the club's finances. There was no hard evidence of bad management, but with the tendency of a committee to stand sometimes aloof from its members, or equally a membership content to take no active interest in the club's running, the real maladministration was the lack of communication.

Griffith, the captain, was appointed assistant to the new secretary, A. A. Dumbrell, and started giving a weekly news conference in an attempt to explain what was going on and generally to publicise the good side of Sussex. It was the age-old problem of many in the county's outer districts believing that Sussex CCC was run by a select few, mainly from Brighton and partly from Arundel and Eastbourne. Had not this been the case in the nineteenth century? It was going to take more than a weekly meet-the-press to resolve the matter and, more importantly, capitalise on the wealth of enthusiasm and potential membership beyond the main towns.

The following season the accountants were in much better mood. After six years of big 'calamitous losses', 1971 showed a profit of nearly £800 and some nifty penwork in the ledgers. Compensation for the cancelled South Africa tour was worth more than £2000 and should really have been entered in the previous year's books. There was an increase in the subscriptions, but the cost of membership had increased also. In recognition of the need to be professional or hire professionals, the club appointed a firm of fund-raisers to launch a Ground Centenary Appeal. The next season would be a celebration of a hundred years of cricket on the Eaton Road wicket. The mood of celebration reached a high point at season's end. The Arthur Gilligan Stand was finished in October and the former captain opened it himself on 27 November. But if there was a satisfied smile on the faces in the committee room it was not always reflected in the dressing room.

There had been some good results and very special displays of batting and bowling. Roger Prideaux and Uday Joshi were awarded their caps, and Prideaux, Greig, Mike Buss and Greenidge each made

229

more than a thousand Championship runs, with Parks missing by just 41. Greig took 11 for 81 against Kent, Snow 11 for 108 against Essex, and Ken Suttle scored a hundred in each innings against Cambridge and another against Nottinghamshire. But this was to be the end of his first-class Sussex career. In the dressing room there were those who felt that his dismissal was handled in a somewhat unnecessarily feudal manner.

Suttle had first played for Sussex in 1949 and won his cap in 1952. In each of seventeen seasons he had scored a thousand runs. In all, nearly 30,000 runs, 260 wickets, 376 catches and Man of the Match in three Gillette Trophy matches. An impressive record – a senior professional to be treated with consideration and respect, especially towards the end of his career. Certainly by 1971 there were signs of considerable wear, though the three centuries suggested that he was far from being a has-been.

One morning the team was being picked and Suttle was left out, an indication that a contract would not be offered for the 1972 season. One who was reluctantly involved in that decision remembers that Suttle arrived on the ground expecting to play, only to be told by the chairman of the cricket committee, Eddie Harrison, that he would not be needed – again. As one player remarked: 'There are ways of doing these things.' An echo of Maurice Tate's reaction more than thirty years earlier. Essex had been keen to have Suttle even if Sussex did not want him. The complication was that in 1972 the county planned a joint testimonial for Suttle and Parks. It was difficult to see how this could be with one of them north of the Thames, the other south. And so Suttle was kept in Sussex for 1972, but he never again played for the first team.

The season ended with Sussex eleventh in the Championship and an enormous amount of work to do before the next season. The big diary events of 1972 were the visit of the Australians and the new Benson & Hedges competition. The saddest occasion was the end of Jim Parks' playing career for Sussex and the manner in which it ended. In the Benson & Hedges, Sussex got as far as Yorkshire and the quarter-final, and then wallowed around fifteenth in the John Player League. In the Championship life was just as depressing – sixteenth. When the Australians arrived at Hove, Sussex had won but a single game that season when they beat Kent by ten wickets at Hastings, largely thanks to the wicket and Greig's 94 runs and 11 for 46 in the match.

The Australian side looked good on paper: Stackpole and Edwards opening, followed by the two Chappells, then Walters, Sheahan,

Rodney Marsh, Watson, Inverarity, Hammond and Mallett, though no Dennis Lillee. Australia made 294 and Sussex 296, thanks to a good start by the steady partnership of Graves and Greenidge. Australia then declared at 262 for 2. Sussex needed 261 to win and got them for five wickets. It was the first time that Sussex had beaten an Australian touring team since 1888. That occasion had indirectly led to Australia's captain, Murdoch, joining Sussex a few years later and leading the side. There was no such approach in 1972, however, although the job was going.

There was still a difficult spirit both within the side and beyond the dressing room, and Mike Griffith was not enjoying his almost thankless task. It was clear also that Jim Parks and Sussex were on a collision course. This was largely due to Parks' belief that he should continue as wicket-keeper, certainly for another season, and gradually rather than instantaneously hand over to someone else. Again, there seemed some difficulty in applying the sensitive laws of diplomacy to personnel problems. There had been a Parks at Sussex for fifty years (and there was yet another wicket-keeping Parks in the pipeline, although he was barely a teenager). Parks had intended to retire at the end of 1972 and was already working for Whitbreads. But he was fit, scoring runs still and happy enough behind the stumps. His commercial boss told him that it was fine by him if Parks had another year's cricket. Friends on the committee mentioned to Parks that he was to be offered, not a contract, but match money to play as a batsman if he were fit. Eventually he was offered a contract, but only batting, not wicket-keeping.

Parks' father had spotted Alan Mansell as a potential wicket-keeper, and Jim Parks argued that he should be 'senior' wicket-keeper, stand alongside Mansell in the slips and encourage him. The argument went on through the dark months until after Christmas, when Parks withdrew his resignation. This more or less brought the issue to a head. Parks was on firm ground because he had been approached by the Somerset captain, Roy Kerslake. In February 1973, Parks appeared before a majority of the committee led by Eddie Harrison. The committee stuck to its guns; Parks stuck to his. He went to Somerset for two years. And so ended one of the great Sussex family partnerships, until he returned, successfully, as marketing manager – still smiling and proudly wearing his capped player's tie, 'the colours of which were approved by the commanding officers of the battalions'.

In 1973 the new commanding officer of the Sussex battalion was Tony Greig. With little option, Greig looked to the youngsters to put their skills and energies to the county's best use, and energy was in greater demand than ever. Although Sussex had for decades been known as one of the finest fielding sides, the establishment of one-day cricket meant everyone in the fielding side had to be an expert. All had to run, to gather, to throw.

The junior ranks of the team had grown up with one-day while practising the skills of full three-day matches. Young men such as John Spencer and Jerry Morley, bowling and batting, won their caps. Mark Faber came into the side with reputation as a sharp striker of the ball, and Roger Marshall, with his left arm over the wicket, had a valuable asset – temperament. John Denman, though injured, was thought to be a good all-rounder, while Barclay was considered by Greig to be a thinker. In the furthest distance, Gehan Mendis and Paul Parker were being brought along as young cricketers and representing that year the English Schools against the visiting Indians, and this at old-fashioned long-innings cricket; the sort of cricket that was deciding the oldest of the competitions.

The Championship had partly faded from public view, so great was the attention given to the fast-food game. In the table, Sussex hardly budged: sixteenth to fifteenth. But once more they reached Lord's and the final of the Gillette. This time they lost to Gloucestershire and a side which included Sadiq, Zaheer, Procter and Roger Knight, who ironically was to teach at Eastbourne College and register for Sussex, topping the batting aggregate in his first season.

By now the one-day game was perfectly established, even at international level with the Prudential Assurance matches. The John Player League was particularly popular. When it is remembered that attendance at three-day cricket had fallen from some two million in the 1940s to not much more than 900,000 in the 1960s, it is easy to see why some accepted, albeit reluctantly, that one-day was the way forward. In 1973 a total of 750,000 spectators paid to watch John Player matches alone, and this in a very wet season with more days lost to rain than ever before. A further two million watched it on television. Cricket was no longer a changing game – it had changed, and the Packer phenomenon was but an extension of it.

In that same year, Sussex felt the first breath of a more devastating change than any Packer may have dreamed of. The wisps of revolution wafted through the Annual General Meeting when Frances Manning's proposal, that 'male' be struck from the rule governing those able to stand for the committee, was voted on. Her proposal went down; but the notion did not perish. In 1974 she returned; defeat once again. But the signs were in Frances Manning's favour. Women were admitted to the Men's Pavilion, though few actually wished to take up the offer.

There were many within the club, and a few in committee and council, who saw the advantages of the idea, although others wondered about such important matters as 'facilities' for women. When Miss Manning returned to the AGM in 1975 with her motion, it was carried by a huge majority. Typically, Arthur Gilligan was one of the first to offer his congratulations. The then secretary, Lieutenant-Commander I. M. Stoop, was less enthusiastic, but as a former navy man his inhibitions about women in the Sussex wardroom were based on instinctive traditions much older than the county's.

That same year Sussex came bottom of the Championship table. Commander and committee were gracious enough to blame nobody but the players.

In 1974 Greig had continued with the forced policy of encouraging the youngest players. With Prideaux retired from county cricket there was a hole at number three, and Faber and Barclay were both given the chance to prove themselves. But it was Peter Graves who took command of the run-scoring, much to the surprise of his critics: an attractive thousand runs. Only Graves and Greenidge batted consistently well. There were some brave faces put on the analyses for that year, but most realised that times were difficult at all levels. Even the ever-confident Greig had lost the vice-captaincy of the England side, although the selectors were sound enough to send him on the tour of Australia. But John Snow was dropped, and there was grievous speculation that his international career was at an end. It was trite cricketing gossip, as those who watched the following year would understand.

At the end of the season Mike Griffith decided to give up first-class cricket. Of those who had particularly followed his career, most would have wished him greater success and a more enjoyable time as captain. Under his leadership Sussex had risen from bottom to seventh in the Championship in one season, and then slid to sixteenth in three. It was not the happiest time to captain.

Once the season was through, the England side went south to the event which by itself gave the game the most noticeable change since the introduction of pads. In New Zealand that winter, Ewan Chatfield was hit by a ball from Peter Lever. If it had not been for prompt first-aid, Chatfield might have been done for. The incident coincided with the demonstration of good, hostile bowling by Lillee and Thomson. Within two years, helmets had become the rig of the day for batsmen.

The 1975 season opened with Sussex in cricketing difficulties and even worse financial straits. Expenses had risen by 20 per cent and income had fallen by 19 per cent. The net result was a loss of more than £20,000. Gate receipts were down, especially at Eastbourne and Hastings where bad weather had once again demonstrated its indifference to the fine line of income over expenditure. If it had not been for the generosity of sponsors, the books would have looked even more lop-sided.

Once more the sometimes overlooked problems of providing facilities for match and follower were considerable. The introduction of Sunday cricket meant a more carnival atmosphere, a place for families, which was what most had hoped for. But it also meant that, for example, children were running where they wished in the ground, including through the Members' Stand and the practice wickets. So both these areas had to be fenced in, and Lyndale Development promised to pay for the stand fencing. Sunday cricket meant also that an extra wicket was often needed, in addition to the Saturday one. That had to be covered, which cost money. Abbey Life Assurance paid for the new covers. Another company, Sussex Mutual Building Society, readily found the money when it was decided that the old Harmsworth scoreboard was creaking to a halt and the mechanism and fascia needed replacing.

Sussex had good friends, reminiscent of the days of the great and noble patrons. What a pity they could not have won something that year. Instead, in 1975 the county hit the rock of Championship's bottom, were tenth in the John Player League, and came up with most forgettable performances in the Gillette and Benson & Hedges competitions. As might have been expected, poor performance was noted in the membership book. The subscriptions had been raised by 50 per cent in the central areas of the county, from £8 to £12, and by 75p in the outer areas. The combination of poor play and higher subscriptions meant that the number of members fell from 5497 to 5024, although total membership income rose by 25 per cent to £28,789. But, whether or not 1975 was overall value for money, there was little doubt that Sussex supporters enjoyed the entertainment from the captain.

It was truly Tony Greig's year. He scored more than 1400 runs in first-class cricket and topped the Sussex averages in the one-day games. His five centuries that year included 226 against Warwickshire at Hastings and an unbeaten 129 against the Australians at Hove in what was a very high-scoring drawn game providing the Australians with much batting practice, with McCosker getting a century in each innings. Greig was eventually given the England captain's job for the last three Tests. The bowling belonged to Snow, who had been recalled to the Test side, but he had fine support from John Spencer who also scored more than five hundred runs, significantly being not out in more than a third of his innings.

The averages were gradually finding names known only to the closest follower of the side. There were the youngsters that Gilligan, the committee and Greig had talked about for some time: Waller, Phillipson, Mendis and, in the second eleven, K. Wessels, P. Parker and A. C. S. Pigott. But by the end of the 1975 season other faces were departing. Greenidge had decided to retire and return to the West Indies, and Alan Mansell, of whom so much had been expected as a wicket-keeper instead of the disappointed Parks, was considered to have not quite made the grade. So Arnold Long of Surrey was specially registered to take over, the first time in Sussex history that it had had to go outside the county for a wicket-keeper.

The jump from last in the 1975 table to tenth in 1976 and almost winners of the John Player League reflected the attractive cricket to be found in Sussex. Visible excitement and improvements were seen on the field of play. However, the perhaps more important change in the club was, to most, quite invisible. The Sussex side had ended the disastrous 1975 season in a cricketing mire, but this was nothing compared with the administrative mess of the club.

Throughout its history, Sussex had been in and out of management chaos. This had much to do with the very agreeable notion of the right sort of people muddling through. Sussex County Cricket Club must at times have been run along the lines of a boys' very minor prep school: never quite up with what was needed. It was a style which had its attractions. But by the mid-1970s cricket could no longer hold out for times remembered. The ruthless code of commercial administration had to be applied. Tony Crole-Rees, elected chairman in April 1975 and Stanley Allen, the new secretary in 1976, recognised this and set out to do something about it, for a club that was by then costing £135,000 a year to run.

These were times when cricket was beginning to witness the Packer revolution in Australia, the effects of which were to be felt in England and, through Tony Greig, in Sussex. Cricket was in sad difficulty and the player's lot was not always a happy one. But it should not be thought that Mr Packer's motives were a love of the game or even its immediate commercial potential. Packer, it should be remembered, owned Channel Nine television and his crusade was not for the game but for the right to televise. Australians had a trinity of heroes in Chappell, Lillee and Thomson. The Packer concept was as old as Rome, and he gathered about him gladiators to do justice to his

235

curious philosophy of sport and his obvious belief in power and money-broking.

The way in which players were treated was still open to criticism, although in financial terms they were better off. There had been some confusion as to the way in which cricketers were played by counties, many not realising why contracts ran only from April to September, thus giving the impression that a cricketer was cruelly discarded during the winter months. The shorter contracts had to do with the government's imposition of Selective Employment Tax. This meant that the club avoided paying tax if it did not employ a player for a full twelve months, even though he was paid a full year's salary. It meant also that a cricketer who could not find a winter job, say coaching, could as a last resort collect unemployment benefit, which he could not have done under the old system. Hardly safe employment, but not nearly so callous as some imagined.

Since 1968 in England, players' interests had been looked after by the Cricketers' Association, a responsible body respected by both the counties and the players. In Australia there was a different attitude, perhaps because there was not such a long tradition of professional cricketers. The Australian Cricket Board set up a cricket committee at the end of the 1976 season and this meant respectable money for players. But it was not in time to counter the Packer instinct and legal challenge, which resulted in something which owed more to American baseball than it did to a game watched from the Gilligan Stand. It was Christopher Martin-Jenkins who coined the phrase 'pyjama cricket' for the gaudy game played beneath floodlights.

As an aside, Kerry Packer's name should not always be mud. Apart from the catalyst effect on salaries and conditions, Packer was responsible for a little-known success involving Sussex players. Packer's son James was being taught at a prep school in New South Wales by the former Sussex bowler and batsman John Spencer. Packer, Snr, thought that young James was fair dinkum with bat and ball and that more youngsters should have the chance of organised coaching. Over Christmas 1976 a coaching course for children aged nine to thirteen was put together and 5000 children were invited to trials. Six of the eight coaches in that experiment were: Spencer, Paul Phillipson, Chris Waller, Alan Mansell, Jerry Morley and John Barclay. It cost Packer £140,000 to run the scheme.

But such was the feeling against anything Packer that there was criticism that anyone should go to Australia for any reason at all, including the coaching of youngsters. The bubblings from Australia had few benevolent tones to English ears. Certainly the rumblings of

236

the southern volcano may have sounded ominous to stewards such as Crole-Rees and Allen when they gingerly attempted to put their house in order without appearing to be knocking down the walls that had held it together since 1839. Few, then, could have known how these same executives and Sussex would be dragged into the Packer argument and beyond in the new era of the commercialisation of cricket.

Allen's appointment had not been universally popular, not because of the individual but because of his role as 'chief executive'. The secretary was no longer a genial figure in the officers' mess. There was now an almost never-ending diet of one-day, three-day and Sunday cricket. Now there was a constant round of paper-shifting, continual travelling, including Sundays, registration problems with players, including those from overseas, and the steady problem of finding and keeping cricket's gold-dust, the sponsors. Each and every aspect of the workload seemed to produce its own mini-industry of more salesmen, office management, the Test and County Cricket Board and its attendant administration, and the enormously sensitive need to balance old values with new concepts. Gone was the yesteryear comfort of having a retired military type in the secretary's office. Stanley Allen represented the cold light of modern cricket, and for many members it was a shame that things had come to this pass.

That same light appeared on John Snow's clothing during that 1976 season, and many a whisker was twitched and many a top set rattled. It was an advertising sign of things to come. Snow had worn an insignia during a televised game. He had also behaved rather unreasonably towards Umpire Pepper, for which he later, possibly when prompted, apologised. The TCCB wanted Snow disciplined, even suspended from a John Player game. Sussex said no. By the end of the season the TCCB, its authority questioned by Sussex, was demanding satisfaction. The whole matter dragged on, and Snow was eventually suspended from the first three one-day matches to take place in the following season. Geoff Arnold of Surrey, who was to join Sussex, had also been found 'guilty' of wearing insignia. The TCCB obviously realised they had an epidemic on their hands, although how this had been spotted against a televised background of advertising hoardings and twirling bat names was difficult to imagine. The Sussex committee eventually gave Snow a telling-off, and the TCCB, needing to assert its authority, reprimanded Sussex. Eventually, of course, one logo per player was allowed. It had all been rather unnecessary.

On 5 December 1976, Arthur Gilligan died. An unwritten task for the new leadership at Hove might have been to preserve the ethics and style of his generation without ignoring the reality of the modern game.

Sussex needed new players, and strength in the younger ones. The problems of getting players from outside were obvious, especially if they were to have tour commitments for their own countries and, if they were not, were they good enough for Sussex with all the difficulties they undoubtedly caused? There was even talk of Colin Cowdrey, about to retire from Kent, joining Sussex. Jeff Thomson and Garry Gilmour were wanted, but did not want Hove. New names, some famous and others soon to be, had joined the dressing room. Arnold Long and Roger Knight were capped; Imran Khan, unhappy at Worcestershire, was signed up. He was the first overseas player to change counties and there was talk of Stanley Allen setting up a soccer-style transfer system. But it did not end there.

The TCCB, hardly Sussex's greatest fan after the Snow affair, rejected Imran's registration in May 1977. In the *Daily Telegraph* Sussex and Imran Khan were accused of having 'cheapened club-loyalty, diluted county identity and created a money-market with all the attendant unpleasantness'. The matter went to the Cricket Council where the appeal against the TCCB was upheld and Imran was allowed to play in county matches later that year.

But that was by no means the end of 1977 for Sussex. During the early part of the season there had been rumours of talks between Greig and the Australian venture, with the Sussex captain portrayed as some sort of recruiting officer. John Snow, gradually coming towards the end of his more conventional international career, had signed with Greig, and Knott and Underwood were to play for the Rest of the World side in Australia and New Zealand during the coming winter. The Sussex captain held a press conference at Hove, and soon everyone knew that Greig and Greg Chappell were leading the breakaway on Mr Packer's behalf. In May, Greig inevitably lost the England captaincy. At Hove there were mixed feelings, many of them sad, and Stanley Allen was not applauded by all for sticking by Greig's leadership of the county. Kerry Packer arrived at the county ground, although the mood of his being there was somewhat furtive rather than triumphant.

Though Brearley had taken over the England team, Greig was in the side still and this meant Peter Graves leading Sussex, under difficult circumstances. Greig, who had publicly criticised the Old Trafford wicket, inadvertently led Sussex into another confrontation with the TCCB. He had rightly cleared a press article with the club secretary, but Lancashire and the TCCB took issue and Greig and Sussex were once again upbraided and fined £500 by the Board. Greig and Allen paid up. Eventually that year Packer men were banned from both Test cricket and county cricket. The latter decision was overruled

238

in the High Court that November as an unreasonable restraint on trade, and Sussex had to pay more than £9000 as their share of the costs awarded to the Packer organisation.

Greig was reappointed captain of Sussex, George Cox stood down from the cricket sub-committee and a much saddened Billy Griffith from the main committee. It was a dismal year in the history of the game and Sussex's part in it. Greig eventually gave up the Sussex leadership, and half-way through the 1978 summer, Arnold Long took over the captaincy. The sensitivity of the matter and the desire of those in Sussex authority to have done with it might be judged by the fact that in the 1978 Sussex CCC Handbook there was no reference to the turbulent months of 1977 in the official review of that far from happy season.

The county had ended 1977 eighth in the Championship, but with perhaps outstanding questions over loyalties, ethics and personalities; 1978 was altogether more relaxed and successful, although the side dropped one place in what was now the Schweppes County Championship. Greig and Snow left with the well-deserved thanks of the county 'for their services with the hope that they will prosper in their future careers'. Mike Buss also left, without any of the fuss and heartburn elsewhere, after a steady and quite distinguished career as one of the most reliable home-grown all-rounders Sussex had had in post-war years.

If Sussex were used to lows, they were certainly not dragged down by them. Imran scored more than a thousand Championship runs and took 49 wickets; so did Geoff Arnold, who had swung his way into the side from Surrey. Javed Miandad batted in only twelve innings but managed to hit 127 in one of them and finished the season top of the averages, although because he was played in the game against Leicestershire before his registration had been completed Sussex lost their points from the match. In June, Sussex were beaten twice by Somerset. In the first game at Hove by four wickets, in the second at Bath by an innings and 38 runs.

On 2 September, Sussex took revenge. The side went to Lord's for the Gillette final as the underdogs. General opinion had it that Tony Greig was more likely to be elected as next president of the MCC than Sussex was to win the Gillette Trophy. This was a Somerset side with Rose, Richards, Botham, Roebuck, Marks and Garner. Somerset made 207, Botham getting 80 and Richards 44. The fall of the Sussex wickets tells the drama: 1 for 93 (things were looking good), 2 for 106 (not so good), 3 for 106 (not at all good), 4 for 110 (send back the champagne), and then Parker and Phillipson played as if their scripts had been written by the authors of *Boy's Own Paper*; 5 for 207 and Phillipson went. It ended in the fifty-third over, Storey not out 0, Parker not out 62 and Man of the Match. It was just the tonic Sussex needed to end the season and head for 1979 with much more confidence and not a little dignity.

At the end of the 1970s Sussex had one of the most attractive batting lists in the country: Wessels, Parker, Imran, Barclay and Mendis coming along, as his 118 against Nottinghamshire suggested. By the finish of the 1979 season both Wessels and Parker had scored Championship thousands. Wessels had made nearly two thousand including six centuries, and Parker, along with Geoff Arnold, had won his first-eleven cap. Little wonder that Parker, who won also the Commercial Union Under-23 Batsman of the Year Award, was regarded as a future Test batsman. Those same people who held that opinion of him might have wondered why he was never given the early chances offered by the Test selectors to so many others with much less talent.

Sussex bowlers looked in form also, with Imran, Geoff Arnold, Giles Cheatle and John Barclay providing the sort of consistency Sussex had looked for, though without the sort of devastating performances that win Championships. Sussex won none of the trophies that year, but finished fourth in the Championship, and with three new players, Allan Green, Garth Le Roux and Colin Wells, promised themselves a bright new decade, which was more than the accountants could do.

By now Sussex had a new secretary, or chief executive as modern management would have him. R. G. Stevens arrived to a familiar ballad of straitened financial circumstances. It was a time to remind everyone that income was restricted. Cricket runs for but twenty-one weeks a year, but the costs of running it go on for fifty-two. Once more the hunt for long-term sponsorship was on. There was a dark reminder that, although Sussex's greatest asset was its players and their performance, the most constant asset was the ground itself and one county had already found it necessary to sell theirs.

The players did their best to attract Brownie points and spectators. The cricket was bright, and success was never far away. Sussex once again finished fourth in the Championship with Wessels, Colin Wells, Parker and Mendis each scoring a thousand runs and more. The side ended in the middle of the John Player, and got as far as the quarter-finals of the Benson & Hedges and the semi-finals of the Gillette. It had been a good run in this last competition. Sussex had won it three times, been finalists in three others years and semi-finalists in four.

240

By 1981 Arnold Long had decided to retire, and the automatic choice for his successor was John Barclay, who was to lead the side to one of its most successful seasons. But he did not have with him Tony Buss. After twenty-five years as both player and coach, Tony Buss left Hove. His had been a career of that essential element in county cricket, the good, steady servant of the game. Buss had joined the club in 1958 as a professional, was capped in 1963, the year the amateur status was abolished, and played through into the new era of one-day cricket and commercial competition. Between 1958 and 1974 he scored 4250 runs and took more than 900 wickets with his right-arm fast-medium action. He was no Tate or Gilligan but, then few were. He was, however, the sort of player around which good sides are built and who manage to have their moments just as their sides need them, like the hat-trick in the John Player game against Warwickshire at Hastings in 1974.

The season of 1981 should have been the start of the Sussex revival everyone had waited so long for. Stewart Storey had become chief coach, and he and Barclay gathered the Sussex side in April and took them to Avisford Park by Arundel for a pre-season look at themselves. The list of players that year must have added up to one of the most balanced sides seen in the county. The decades-old cry for two attacking and penetrating bowlers had been answered. Imran Khan and Garth Le Roux made an enviable opening attack, especially when Greig the younger, Ian, was there to support and the guile and experience of Geoff Arnold were around to pick up the odd forty wickets that season. Furthermore, there was the luxury of two good spinners in Chris Waller and the captain, John Barclay. On top of this there was more to come with the development of Colin Wells, his brother Alan, and Adrian Jones, who took five Sri Lankan wickets in his first first-class match. There was a deal of concern for another who had proved handy with bat and ball – Tony Pigott, who had a most unpleasant start to the spring by having an operation on his spine.

The batting was equally impressive, particularly as it continued through what had been a very long tail. Seven of the side hit Championship centuries that year. To round off the side, Ian Gould, in his first year with the team, was the best wicket-keeper in the country, three times taking six catches in a match and finishing the season atop the wicket-keepers' league. In John Barclay the committee had the perfect answer to their prayer of positive leadership – a man out to win even if it meant the risk of losing. To him, draws were boring. The one-day series did not bring great rewards but, for those who watched in anticipation of the elusive Championship pennant flying at Hove, 1981 was one of the most exciting years ever. Sussex lost by just two points to Nottinghamshire, and but for a strange decision about the light in the match at Trent Bridge would probably have won at long last. But it was not to be.

And not-to-be costs money and support. By the end of the 1981 season the cost as well as the satisfaction of playing success could easily be counted. The prize money in the four major competitions was considerable. The Schweppes County Championship was worth £13,000 to the winner, £6500 to the runner-up, £3250 for third place and £1650 for fourth. In addition there was £150 for a win and £5 for every bonus point. In the Benson and Hedges Cup, the winner received £9500, the runner-up £4000, losing semi-finalists £2200 each, losing quarter-finalists £1100 each and £385 each for zone winners. The John Player League was costing the company about £35,000 in prize money, and the NatWest was worth £11,000 to the winner, £5500 to the runner-up, £3300 for each of the losing semi-finalists and £1650 for each of the losing quarter-finalists. Apart from the prizes to be collected, the biggest cheques were likely to come through gate money. This meant that a successful and well-supported team could find one-day cricket the most pleasing to spectator and bank manager alike.

But success and support had to go hand in hand. Consequently a bad performance by Sussex in the one-day events of 1981 was reflected in the gate receipts, especially when compared with other clubs. For example, in that season Essex, the John Player League winners, received more than £33,000 through the gates, Somerset, the runners-up, £67,835 and Sussex, who were fifth, only £18,674. In spite of the successful season, few people were watching the county on the home grounds and once again the club had to attempt to attract more members, the constant in cricketing finances. But, if people were not arriving in large numbers to see an attractive and successful side, how were they to be enticed into one of the cheapest forms of entertainment, particularly three-day games? Perhaps the doings of 1981 would be reflected in larger crowds in the following season. Cricket is a curious fellow, and his followers and fortune fickle.

The new season should at least have attracted the curious and seen the return of those who had been a little disheartened in seasons past. The administrators sat and watched the bank and seat balances, but times remained hard. Yet Sussex was not deserted by paying friends nor by playing skills. Sponsorship remained a key in keeping in motion the improvements needed for the club, and the fine line between outlay and return was toed. The then vice-chairman of the committee

Charlie Oakes making Gray's bowling look easy at Lord's in 1950

FC White the founder of the Welfare Association in 1950 who died after a road accident in 1955

Hubert Doggart at Hastings, 1954. In his first first class innings, GHG Doggart scored 215 not out for Cambridge against Lancashire. Became captain in 1950 of Sussex but it was revoked at the infamous AGM

George Cox getting rid of Surrey bowling in 1953

It went thataway! Harvey was just as surprised as everyone else when this went for four.
L-R AAK Lawrence, DV Smith, RT Webb, RN Harvey and DS Sheppard at Hove
against the 1956 Australian side

Cricket at Worthing. The Manor sports ground. Picture by Walter Gardiner

David Sheppard far from the sea end, here in 1956 in a street game in his London parish of Islington. The wicket keeper is unknown

Robin Marlar in 1955 became another in the celebrated line of Cambridge cricketers to play for and captain Sussex. Here is Marlar the would-be politician. In 1959 he tried to overturn the 22,000 Labour majority in Bolsover, a Labour seat made famous by the present MP Dennis Skinner

The Central Ground at Hastings, an oasis surrounded by some of England's less remarkable architecture. The ground, one of the favourites of WG Grace and many other famous cricketers, is to be developed and built on and the county's 150th birthday year will be the last season in which cricket will be played on one of the most celebrated wickets in the country. Here Sussex are playing Kent in 1959

The Nawab of Pataudi here with Rupert Webb. Tiger Pataudi was the third in the line of Indian princes to play for Sussex. 'He could make a monkey out of any bowling' said Ted Dexter

Lest any forget. The memorial tablet erected by the MCC in 1962 to Frederick Lillywhite 'the father of round arm bowling'

In honour of FREDERICK WILLIAM LILLYWHITE 1792–1854. a great Sussex and England cricketer. the father of round arm bowling. who, as his monument in Highgate Cemetery records. achieved a world wide reputation teaching both by precept and example. a sport in which the blessings of youthful strength and spirits may be most innocently enjoyed. to the exercise of the mind the discipline of the temper and the general improvement of man. This tablet was erected by the Marylebone Cricket Club in 1962.

1964 and Sussex win the Gillette Cup once more. Dexter worked out how to play the new-style game before any other captain did. Here with Man of the Match Ian Thomson who took four of Warwickshire's wickets in the final at Lord's. Picture: S & G Press Aency Ltd

Tony 'Lester' Pigott and a picture of 100 per cent effort. Picture: Stephen Line

Looking good! Javed Miandad and Geoff Arnold scent victory in the 1978 Gillette Cup Final. Picture: S & G Press Agency L

Imran Khan in full flow. Picture: S & G Press Agency Ltd

Lord's September 1986 and the great prize: Lancashire captain Clive Lloyd goes for a duck, lbw to Dermot Reeve. Up goes wicket keeper captain Ian Gould with slips Colin Wells and Tony Pigott. Gould's memorable comment after being asked how the team might celebrate their NatWest victory, 'Watch out Soho!' Picture: Sussex Business Times

Andy Babington one of the new band of enthusiasts at Sussex who believes clearly that the only good batsman is one on his way back to the dressing room. Photo: Stephen Line

Paul Parker, gladiator, captain and instinctively, a leader by example

was Maurice Leadley, the deputy chairman of the Alliance Building Society, one of the leading companies of about fifty sponsoring Sussex. That season he summed up the two-way street of sponsorship, upon which Sussex and every other county depended for survival.

> The art of effective sponsorship is to match the financial needs of one organisation with the promotional needs of another . . . it is important for both organisations to define very clearly what results they expect from a particular sponsorship before any commitment is agreed.

This straightforward attitude was not always understood, because cricket's administrators did not comprehend the science of marketing. In most cases, even by the early 1980s, they were not professionals. They were feeling their way, perhaps not even certain what it was they could sell to would-be sponsors. The arrangement, as Sussex illustrated with one scheme with the Alliance, certainly went beyond advertising boards, tents and benevolent handouts 'for the good of the game'.

Sussex needed a new cover. The Alliance supplied it with its own name on. That was the advertising taken care of. The next stage was to give all Alliance investors free tickets three times a year to see a Championship match. To get the tickets the investors had to go to an Alliance office, which gave the building society a chance to 'sell' its latest schemes to customers coming in off the street, and the ticket itself was a reminder of the building society. Everyone was happy. But the team still had to perform well enough to make people want to go to the games in the first place. It was a big task for the coach and the captain.

John Barclay played through the 1982 season with a torn knee tendon, and there was no Imran once June and the Pakistan tour began. The enthusiasm and teamwork that he had emphasised at the start of the previous season remained. The side dropped to eighth place in the Championship, but for the first time won the John Player League and got to the semi-final of the Benson & Hedges. It was an exciting side to watch, the senior men going well although Parker had some doubts and disappointments, and the younger players, especially Green and Aian Wells, looking perfectly moulded Sussex cricketers. But still the seats were empty more times than they should have been.

Competitions and fund-raising efforts by the Supporters Club helped greatly. The Ton-Up Club competition alone had by then given the club £15,000. But to run Sussex by the eighties needed the sort of money normally associated with a small industrial organisation. The cry went out, yet again, for more members, ironically in the year that one of the club's greatest membership drivers, Poona White, died at the age of eighty-three.

The 1983 season began with the sore news that Imran and Tony Pigott both had stress fractures. Imran's was to keep him out for most of the season, although he was full of energy in August against Warwickshire when in four overs he took six wickets for 6 runs. It was the sort of performance that was hard to replace. The omens were no better for the whole side when in a pre-season practice excursion to Spain most of the side went down with stomach complaints. In the middle of June, Ian Greig was injured and out for most of the season, Garth Le Roux had a serious groin strain and was not one hundred per cent fit.

There are not many teams that could survive losing the main thrust of their strike bowling for most of the summer. Sussex was no exception, and the pressure spread to the batsmen. The arrival of Dermot Reeve, nicknamed 'Enid' because of his extraordinary story-telling powers, helped to revive fortunes, but at the end of the season Sussex had fallen to eleventh in the Championship and fourth in the John Player. It was a depressing time for many, but as in all pavilions there was a stronger sense of optimism than of pessimism.

The next year saw the reorganisation of the administrative system, yet again. The chief executive disappeared and the old post of secretary was revived in the form of Richard Renold. Renold, too, looked to modern methods of keeping the county solvent, and noted: 'Society is changing and the successful are becoming both more professional but also more money conscious. The cricket traditionalist with an eye on cricket history and its record may not like what is happening but cannot halt these trends.' It was a sober comment and perhaps a warning. Yet it did not dull the sense of fun that Barclay managed to keep afloat in the side even if there were some sadder times ahead.

The gloomy part was that Sussex went on to finish seventh, fourteenth and then bottom again in the coming three seasons. There were troubles, too, among those who played the game. Mendis went, apparently disgruntled. He came back in his first season with Lancashire and got a duck. Ian Greig was 'let go', which saddened many of his Sussex followers, but not Surrey. Storey, the coach, who only a few seasons before had been described as indispensable, was being blamed for much of the bad feeling in the dressing room. Later, he, too, went.

But Sussex have a 150-year history of problems and upheaval, and

244

they manage to bounce back when all is thought lost. In 1986 there was the glorious win over Lancashire in the NatWest final at Lord's. 'Look out, Soho,' said a short, fat stumper. But, even there, there was a small sad note. Instead of leading the side, the 'Trout' watched from the BBC commentary box. Cruel finger injury had kept Barclay away for so long, and he finally retired from Sussex. When he went it was the departure of a thoroughly likeable Sussex captain but, from the club's point of view, also one of the best cricketing brains in the country. Ian Gould took on the captaincy, but for only one season, 1987. Bottom in the Championship, a reminder that in spite of all the one-day attractions the three-day game, which people rarely find time or inclination to watch, remains omnipotent.

As Sussex approached its great anniversary, it gained a new secretary – Nigel Bett, whose instincts were marketing and management and whose chairman, Maurice Leadley, professionally understood the realities of business tempered by the traditions of the friendly society, not so very different to the benevolence sensed from the sea end. And just along the corridor Jim Parks moved in, back at Hove, this time not forever gathering safely down the leg side but with the equally difficult task of gathering the county sponsors. Two hundred years after the Prince of Wales had pressed his influence and purse on cricket in a small fishing town, patronage in other form meant survival for a game whose origins and excitements were far removed from this championship table and that, from this average and another as played by the team led by Paul Parker, the forty-third Sussex captain since 1839.

Parker's task had been presented to earlier captains: to rebuild a side from younger players. Le Roux had sadly said goodbye; Jones had been capped, then gone to Somerset; and Reeve, hero with Parker of the NatWest final, had departed to Warwickshire, although ironically he was to return as twelfth man to watch and change damp gloves, bearing ragged sweaters and dull bats while Sussex beat eleven of the Midlands at Hove.

Away, too, was Imran Khan, once great inspiration, now tetchy and anxious in a side feeling its way, having given glorious pleasure, sadly leaving little; a complex majesty, perhaps sometimes genius. Fastest in England, it was once said. Noblest all-rounder. Since 1963 few heroes have lived in dressing rooms; gods are seen only through half-closed eyes from deckchair's gentle curve.

Chapter 19

Paul Parker was born in Bulawayo in 1956. George Cox, John Langridge and Jim Wood had just retired and Maurice Tate had died. During that summer, while Parker's nappy was being changed and he was learning to crawl, Jim Parks was scoring 1825 Championship runs and a few besides. Jack Arlidge of the *Evening Argus* noted of 1956:

> All too often the weather was grim and cheerless . . . Sussex met with only modest success, despite a splendid start . . . The apprenticeship of young cricketers can be unrewarding over a period, and I know these aspiring Sussex players will be hoping for more helpful wickets.

Thirty-two years on, with Parks watching by, Parker might have read the same on his first season as captain. Often grim and cheerless weather, a splendid start and then disappointment, a young side eager to learn and follow. The task from 1988 was to rebuild; always Sussex had to rebuild. Yet the material was good. Sound names that had promised as schoolboys had been nursed, had delivered. The Wellses – when one misfired the other ran smoothly; Green – when not injured, reassuringly full of runs; Lenham – a famous father's son, superb in his own right; Pigott – ferocious action, fast, and better than ever with bat; Babington and Bunting – learning and quick, full of enthusiasm; Moores and Speight – two pairs of safe hands and full of future; Clarke – encouraged to spin and spin he did, and full of runs one delightful day at

Eastbourne; then Gould – short, fat stumper once, now short slimmer batsman and chirpy still; and Parker.

It would have been difficult for Sussex to find a more suitable captain for the daunting summer of 1988. Always there, a word for this player and the next, pacing his bowlers, leading by example, fielding with dazzling skill as if early apprenticed tumbler, holding together with century after century, encouraging, coaxing a gangling side into a team of reckoning for the future. Fortune indeed for Sussex that their captain was ignored by England selectors that summer. And so from bottom, the climb back once more began. Into 1989, still in search of a Championship pennant.

But just suppose, suppose, that the Lillywhites, Wisden, Jem Broadbridge, George Brown, Fry, Ranji, Vine, Tate, a Cox, a Gilligan, a Parks, one Langridge, a Sheppard, Marlar, Dexter and all could be brought to be. Should Sussex by conjuror's guile bring names past and present to form a team from all those gold-leaved on honours board, and take the Championship from sixteen counties? After 150 years, maybe it would be wrong to win. Better, perhaps, to dream. Yet there is hope of one chance, the first sweet-scented cut, a new season, a wicket that plays their way, the thump of four against boundary board, the one that lifts just in time, the catch that is held, the hope of chance and victory.

For that is Sussex cricket. No matter the bare pennant's pole; stalk instead Hove pavilion's pictured walls. There is satisfied history of cricket. Stand at the first sap of summer, already warm with a noble past, and like Edmund Blunden's labourer leaning on stackyard's low wall remember those that have gone and with them their great deeds, and watch while the new men play and strike, and bowl and catch. For it has all gone before, as that labourer knew:

> Till the meadow is quick with the masters who were
> And he hears his own shouts when he first trotted there;
> Long ago; all gone home now; but here they come all!
> Surely these are the same, who now bring bat and ball?

EPILOGUE
Three Captains Dream

One hundred and fifty years and never called Champion County. The one-day games may brim with excitement and prestige, but what could be better than the oldest pennant of them all? Yet throughout the history of Sussex some of the finest players to have delighted crowd and statistician have worn red, white and blue or the more modern martlets. Records have been humbled before the craft and guile of Sussex batsman, bowler and all. Many's the time those who know have nodded, applauded, the most attractive side in the counties of first-class cricket. There have been close-fought seasons when just that little luck, that little extra effort, that chance of the weather, the wicket, the toss, would have made all the difference. Runners-up seven times. No disgrace.

If it were possible that a Sussex captain could choose his ideal team to win the Championship, who would open, bowl first, keep wicket? The perfect Sussex side is just a schoolboy pastime, for conditions have changed since Ranji and Fry thrilled all who gathered to see mighty scores. Tate and Gilligan on covered wickets? But three Sussex captains have, in this celebration year, picked the sides they believe they would lead to the title: David Sheppard, who in his one year so nearly did win; Ted Dexter, who inspired by fashioning his theory into practice; and Paul Parker, charged with building a young, often inexperienced team into mature, tenacious and match-winning cricketers without losing enthusiasm when games seem to drift away.

David Sheppard's side reflects faith in past performance and unquestionable skills.

1 C. B. Fry
2 D. S. Sheppard
3 K. S. Ranjitsinhji
4 E. R. Dexter
5 K. S. Duleepsinhji
6 Javed Miandad
7 James Langridge
8 Imran Khan
9 J. M. Parks
10 M. W. Tate
11 J. A. Snow

It is a side which bats down to number ten. It is a team with five recognised bowlers and in Parks a true wicket-keeper and batsman, rather than a wicket-keeper who could bat a bit. It is a team also which relies heavily on four overseas players and four who played more than fifty years ago. Sheppard himself takes on the role of Joe Vine to C.B. Fry, but it is doubtful whether he would succumb to the Fry personality as did Vine. The combination of Tate, so quick off the pitch, of Snow, a more modern concept of new-ball bowling, and Imran, who towards the end of his Sussex career was described as the quickest bowler in England cricket, would be enough to unsettle most top orders. Then there is Dexter, medium paced and capable of thinking out batsmen, and James Langridge, who scored more runs for Sussex than anyone other than Parks, Suttle and John Langridge and bowled at sides from whom he had but recently plundered runs.

The theme of Sheppard's side, though, is yesteryear and remembered players.

Ted Dexter's team also relies on many players long gone, though not so many and not so far off.

1   John Langridge
2   C. B. Fry
3   K. S. Ranjitsinhji
4   E. H. Bowley
5   James Langridge
6   M. W. Tate
7   E. R. Dexter
8   J. M. Parks
9   Imran Khan
10 R. G. Marlar
11 J. A. Snow
12 K. Suttle

Again ten batsmen and another as twelfth man, and one who bowls also. The batting would have been devastating, certainly reflecting the old saying that when Fry failed to score a hundred then Ranji would, yet this might be said about any of the combinations in Dexter's side. He believes it very difficult to pick a side without having seen them play, yet the utter wealth of figures and averages claims places for pre-war players. Batsmen pick themselves in Dexter's side, with the exception of Bowley, who nearly lost his place in Dexter's mind to David Sheppard. He believes that Sheppard should be captain of any side in which he plays, and would be happy to follow him anywhere. John Langridge gets in for his superb record as a batsman and his uncanny ability as a slip-fielder: he held 779 catches for Sussex. His brother James is there as a batsman and for his left-arm bowling. The second spinner is Marlar, who towards the end of his career was convinced that bowling more slowly would bring more wickets.

The bowlers, to Dexter's mind, are harder to pick. Snow and Tate opening, but Imran who can swing the ball would be better once it was worn. Dexter's great regret is to leave out Thomson, especially on wet wickets with his ability to wear a patch bare until the wicket started to dry. Again the wicket-keeping is with Parks, whom Dexter believes was a genius with a ball and who scored more than 29,000 runs for Sussex between 1949 and 1972. His twelfth man is Ken Suttle who, as the second-highest run-maker in Sussex history, could come in as a left-hand bat and slow bowler.

And so to the modern captain. Paul Parker is very reluctant to pick players he has never seen. Furthermore, he represents a newer generation and three of his side are still playing cricket, and a fourth would be but for injury.

1   K. C. Wessell
2   G. D. Mendis
3   P. W. G. Parker
4   James Langridge
5   Javed Miandad
6   E. R. Dexter
7   J. M. Parks
8   Imran Khan
9   M. W. Tate
10 J. R. T. Barclay
11 J. A. Snow
12 I. Thomson

The opening partnership is based on the need for a sound start. Wessell and Mendis would suit each other in style, technique and temperament. Parker as captain and number three would be able to juggle the batting of Langridge, Javed and Tate to suit the start given by the openers. Tate is the token acknowledgement of an older Sussex and is there because, however sceptical one is about unseen heroes, Tate's figures and reputation demand his place in any side. Langridge is there to bat – he made almost 29,000 runs in his career – and to bowl his left-arm spin. He took more than 1400 wickets. Barclay is second spinner and batsman, a hint that in more relaxed seasons Barclay played better than perhaps he did as captain. Parker, another of Sussex's thinking captains, believes in the need for two spinners, and if they can bat, then so much the better. His front-line bowling comes from Tate and Snow, with Imran in support, especially with the older and swinging ball, and Dexter, too, perhaps expected to repeat his 1962 season when he twice scored a hundred and took ten wickets in the same match. Thomson as twelfth man gives Parker the option of consistent seam bowling on the right wickets. Again Parks is the automatic choice as wicket-keeper and his inclusion is a reminder that his 1182 dismissals have been bettered by only four post-war players.

Picking a Championship-winning side is full of fun and fraught with assumption about conditions, wickets, personality and the argument of modern game versus old. In these sides there are no places for heroes who, when they played, gave such pleasure that none could believe that others would ever play with greater skill and cunning. No place for Henry Phillips, fearless, amusing and a wicket-keeper of rare gift. None for a Lillywhite, even James. Could there be nothing for Wisden, or Dean, or Jem Broadbridge? And where is the style and leadership of A. E. R. Gilligan? No George Cox, either one. Nor Joe Vine, ever solid. Relfs? All but forgotten. George Street, perhaps the safest of all. Pataudi, who could make a monkey of the finest bowling.

Hundreds have played, but few may be chosen, and the closeness on so many occasions of Sussex to the most important of titles suggests that not too many generations have to be spanned to find the perfect combination. Just one more bowler. Just one fit, consistent, specialist opener. How many captains must have pleaded for luck and circumstance to provide that thoroughly desirable but so often elusive combination to last the season through? One day, perhaps.

BY THE SUSSEX WAY

One of the delights of cricket fanciers is the fascinating fountain of information from which may be sipped asides, by-the-way remarks, and facts and figures that will offer comfort during winter evening or its disagreeable cousins, Rain and Bad Light Stopped Play. For this reason, I include here a chapter of ready and, it is to be hoped, entertaining reference.

Early Records of Cricketing Villages and Towns

That cricket was played in Sussex as early as the seventeenth century is without doubt. Furthermore, it was an organised game rather than a pastime, thus in part justifying Arthur Gilligan's notion that the county was indeed the cradle of cricket. These early games were often played between the most unlikely sides. In 1782 the Married Men played the Bachelors at Egdean Common. In 1788 the High Sheriff and 10 Javelin Men played Lewes. In 1793 the Married Women of Bury Common played the Spinsters of the Parish. And what of the game between The Blue Ladies and The Pink on Lavant Level in 1821? And why would a Lewes butcher take on two tailors in 1825? Or the following year in Ireland's Gardens, Brighton, Ten Gentlemen Educated at Public Schools *v* Eleven from Private Seminaries? What follows is not a complete list of when hamlets, villages and towns first played the game, but it is intended as an indication of the way in which cricket was part of Sussex life, before the forming of the County Cricket Club in 1839.

1677	Dicker
1717	Dungton Gate
1719	Sandfield (From Marchant's Diary)
1721	Henfield (From Marchant's Diary)
	Stenning v Sandfield
	Isfield
	Cowfield v Sandfield
1722	Broadwater Green
	Newick
1725	Firle (Sir William Gage)
	Goodwood (Duke of Richmond)
1727	Hurst
1728	Coxheath
	Lewes
1730	Mickleham Downs
	Dripping Pan, Lewes
1731	Chichester
1738	Eastbourne v Battle
1739	East Hoathly
1741	Slindon
1745	Sussex v Surrey
1747	Women of Charlton and Singleton v Those of West Dean and Chalgrove
1750	Burwash
	Mayfield
1754	Midhurst
	Petworth
	Rye
	Brighton
	East Sussex
1755	Framfield
	Ringmer
1756	Chiddingly
	Lindfield
	Maresfield
1757	Halland
1758	Laughton
	Rottingdean
	Waldron
	Chailey
	Hamsey
	Wadhurst

Brede
Ripe *v* Arlington at Dicker Fair
Hailsham
Herstmonceux
Wartling
Chalvington
1764 Arundel Club *v* East Sussex on Henfield Common
1767 Sussex *v* Hampshire on Broadhalfpenny Down
1768 Harting
Rogate
Woodmancote
Horsham
1771 Patching
Northiam
Peasemarsh
Barcombe
1772 Seddlescombe *v* Battle
1773 Crawley
Findon
East Grinstead
1775 Hurst Green
Rudgwick
Slinfold
Ninfield
Hooe
Horsebridge
Robertsbridge (Eleven Brothers *v* Eleven of Battle)
1778 Hadlow Down
Seaford
1779 North Chapel
1783 Brightling
Netherfield
1785 Petworth
Ditchling
Brighton (Prince of Wales played cricket)
1787 Shoreham
1788 Alfriston
Bourne
Falmer
1790 Guestling
Hastings
Bexhill

1791	Forest Row
	Turners Hill
1793	Preston
	Withdean
	Patcham
	Pangdean
	Piecomb
	Standean
	Tarring
	Sompting
1795	Broadoak
	Moulsley Hurst
	Ockley
1798	Pulborough
	Lancing
	Hellingly
1799	Westfield
	Catsfield (Quaif of Catsfield *v* Martin of Battle)
1800	Bedingham (Sir T. Carr's Javelin Throwers *v* Others)
	Storrington Green (Storrington & Pulborough *v* The County of Sussex)
	Ninfield Stocks (Ninfield, Hooe, Catsfield & Bexhill *v* The Horsebridge Club)
1801	Rodmell
1802	Chiltingdon
	Beeding
1803	Slaugham
1807	Alciston
	Emsworth
1808	Highdem Hill
1812	Angmering
1813	Highdown Hill (Psalm Singers of Angmering, Ferring and Goring *v* Those Parishes)
1815	Bexhill Down
	Udimore (*v* Whiteman Family)
	Bishopstone
1816	Cooksbridge
	Houndean Bottom
	Jolesfield Common
	Sidley (Played in August, a single-wicket match by candlelight. The first floodlit game?)
	Bulverhithe

Dallington
1817 Mountfield
Watlington
1818 Rotherfield
Duncton (but cricket played there before this date)
1822 Warbleton
Heathfield
1823 Vinehall
Salehurst
Hurst Green
Pett
Tarring
1824 Silham
Lodsworth

Sussex Grounds

1791 Prince's Ground opened, when Thomas Reid Kemp authorised cricket on his land. In 1820 Kemp sold it to a Brighton draper, James Ireland. It became known as Ireland's Gardens. Then sold to Pierpoint and Lee, so sometimes known as Pierpoint's or Lee's Ground. The cricketer George Brown took over lease of Hanover Arms, the gardens and its cricket ground in the 1830s. He was succeeded at the Hanover Arms by Tom Box the wicket-keeper (who employed the young Wisden as a pot-boy) and the ground was sometimes known as Box's Ground. It closed in 1847.

1834 The Montpellier Ground (now Montpellier Crescent) opened and was variously known as Lillywhite's Ground, Temple Fields and Lee's Trap. It closed in 1844.

1848 Brunswick Ground (between what is now Third and Fourth Avenue) opened. It closed in 1871 when the land was needed for housing. The turf was removed to the present Easton Road ground which opened the following year, 1872.

Sussex sides have played on seven other grounds in the county. The dates below are first recorded matches but this does not mean that county cricket was played thereafter on a regular basis.

1853 Horsham
1857 St Leonards
1860 Lewes

257

1865   Hastings
1867   Eastbourne
1906   Chichester
1935   Worthing

Not Many People Know That

1737   John Betts killed at Newick by running against another man in crossing ye wicket. Buried 31 May (Chailey Parish Burial Register).
1773   First record of hit wicket, Hambledon *v* England at Sevenoaks.
1774   Lbw introduced.
1775   Stumps increased from two to three.
1806   Sawdust introduced.
1817   Playing for Sussex at Epsom, William Lambert scored the first recorded century in each innings.
1823   Scorecards first printed in Brighton.
1825   First recorded Kent *v* Sussex (at Brighton).
1827   First match in which wides were recorded instead of being included as byes (Sussex *v* Kent at Brighton).
1828   Law introduced permitting round-arm bowling.
1836   First time name of bowler included in scorebook when batsman out to catch, lbw or hit wicket (Sussex *v* MCC). Up to this point, for example, only the catcher's name would have appeared.
1838   First match cards printed (Gentlemen *v* Players at Brighton).
1842   W. F. Lillywhite was the first player to have a benefit match.
1847   Last match played on Box's Ground, Brighton (Sussex *v* England).
1864   Follow-on introduced (80 runs behind).
1869   Maiden overs first recorded in bowler's figures.
1872   First match at Eaton Road County Ground, 16 June, against Gloucestershire.
1873   Henry Phillips, the Sussex wicket-keeper, was the first to do without a long stop.
1887   Walter Quaife was the first Sussex player to score more than 1000 runs in a season.

Sussex Regalia

1861   Badges first worn about this time.
1887   Caps introduced.
1900   Sussex blazers first appeared in photographs.
1922–3 The first Sussex sweater, a red, white and blue V-stripe.
        First tie, red, white and blue stripe.
1933   New sweater, the present six martlets. New tie, gold and
        light blue stripe on dark blue background as worn in 1989.
1934   Second pale blue stripe added to other side of gold stripe,
        to be worn only by capped players.
1959   Club tie with badge.

Brothers Who Have Played for Sussex

Bean	George	1886–1898
	Joseph	1895–1903
Bourdillon	Thomas Edmund	1919
	Victor Edmund	1919
Broadbridge	C	1838
	James	1815–1840
	Robert	1823
	William	1817–1830
Buss	Anthony	1958–1974
	Michael Alan	1961–1978
Charlwood	Charles Robert	1869
	Frederick	1869
	Henry Rupert James	1865–1882
Cotterill	George Edward	1869–1874
	Joseph Montagu	1870–1888
Curteis	Herbert Mascall	1846–1860
	Robert	1873–1878
Dean	James (jnr)	1862–1866
	David	1871
Doggart	Arthur Peter	1947–1951
	George Hubert Graham	1948–1961
Gilligan	Alfred Harold Herbert	1914–1931
	Arthur Edward Robert	1920–1932
Greig	Anthony William	1966–1978
	Ian Alexander	1980–1985

259

Heygate	Harold	1903–1919
	Reginald Beaumont	1902–1911
Hide	Arthur Bollard	1882–1890
	Jesse Bollard	1876–1893
Hoadley	Simon Peter	1978–1979
	Stephen John	1975–1976
Holloway	Bernard Henry	1911–1914
	Norman James	1911–1915
Humphreys	George Thomas	1869–1886
	Walter Alexander	1871–1896
Killick	Anthony	1866
	Harry	1866–1875
Langridge	James	1924–1953
	John George	1928–1955
Lillywhite	James (snr)	1850
	John	1850–1869
Lucas	Charles James	1853–1882
	Frederick Murray	1880–1887
	Morton Peto	1877–1890
Mawle	A	1896
	Henry Edward	1896
Napper	Edwin	1839–1863
	William	1842–1872
Oakes	Charles	1935–1954
	John Ypres	1937–1951
Parks	Henry William	1926–1948
	James Horace	1924–1939
Payne	Alfred	1880–1886
	William	1877–1883
Payne	Charles	1857–1870
	Joseph Spencer	1861
	Richard	1853–1866
Phillips	Henry	1868–1891
	James	1871–1886
Picknell	George	1835–1854
	Robert	1837–1845
Quaife	Walter	1884–1891
	William George	1891
Reed	Albert Adams	1867–1873
	Walter Bartlett	1860
Relf	Albert Edward	1900–1921
	Ernest Herbert	1912–1914

	Robert Richard	1905–1924
Scott	Harold Eldon	1937
	Kenneth Bertram	1937
Simms	Harry Lester	1905–1914
	Royston Knox	1912
Smith	Arthur	1874–1880
	Charles Hamlin	1861–1874
Tudor	Claude Lechmere St John	1910–1911
	Roland Grimston	1912–1919
Wells	Alan Peter	1981–1989
	Colin Mark	1979–1989
Whitfield	Francis Barry	1878
	Herbert	1878–1885
Williams	Leoline	1919–1930
	Peter Victor	1919
Young	John Villiers	1908
	Richard Alfred	1905–1925

Sussex Cricketers Who Have Played for England in Official Tests

Arnold, G. G.
Bean, G.
Bowley, E. H.
Butt, H. R.
Calthorpe, Hon. F. S. G.
Charlwood, H.
Cornford, W.
Dexter, E. R.
Doggart, G. H. G.
Duleepsinhji. K. S.
Fender, P. G. H.
Fry, C. B.
Gilligan, A. E. R.
Gilligan, A. H. H.
Greig, A. W.
Greig, I. A.
Griffith, S. C.
Hartley, J. C.
Jupp, V. W. C.
Langridge, Jas
Lillywhite, James (jnr)
Murdoch, W. L.

Newham, W.
Oakman, A. S. M.
Parker, P. W. G.
Parks, J. H.
Parks, J. M.
Pigott, A. C. S.
Prideaux, R. M.
Quaife, W. G.
Ranjitsinhji, K. S.
Relf, A. E.
Shaw, A.
Sheppard. Rt Rev. D. S.
Smith, Sir C. A.
Smith, D. V.
Snow, J. A.
Southerton, J.
Street, G. B.
Tate, F. W.
Tate, M. W.
Thomson, N. I.
Vine. J.
Young, R. A.

Sussex CCC Presidents

1838	Viscount Pevensey
1869	H. M. Curteis
1879	Earl of Sheffield (3rd)
1897	Duke of Norfolk (15th)
1903	Lord Leconfield (3rd)
1904	Earl of Sheffield (3rd)
1905	Duke of Richmond and Gordon
1907	C. J. Lucas
1908	Earl Winterton (6th)
1909	Colonel W. H. Campion
1910	Duke of Devonshire
1911	Lord Willingdon
1912	James Buchanan
1913	A. du Cros
1914	Viscount Hythe
1915	Duke of Norfolk (15th)
1917	Lord Leconfield (3rd)
1920	Earl of Chichester
1922	Earl Winterton (6th)
1924	H. F. de Paravacini
1925	Sir A. Ashburnham-Clement Bt
1926	Earl Castle Stewart
1927	Viscount Gage
1928	Major R. L. Thornton
1929	Marquess of Abergavenny
1930	HH Jam Sahib of Nawanagar
1931	Viscount Hailsham
1932	Sir William Campion
1933	Duke of Norfolk (16th)
1934	Earl of Athlone
1935	Rev. E. D. L. Harvey
1936	A. W. F. Somerset
1937	A. M. Miller Hallett
1947	G. S. Godfree
1948	Sir Home Gordon, Bt
1949	Duke of Norfolk (16th)
1974	A. E. R. Gilligan
1976	S. G. Griffith
1977	H. T. Bartlett
1980	S. Carma

1983   A. M. Caffyn
1988   Marquess of Abergavenny

Sussex CCC Secretaries

1839   G. L. Langdon
1843   Henry Everett
1848   G. W. King
1857   Bridger Stent
1869   C. H. Smith
1870   C. H. Smith and G .W. King
1879   G. W. King
1881   G. Goldsmith
1889   W. Newham
1909   Colonel E. A. Bruce
1913   F. Oddie
1916   G. S. Godfree
1919   Major W. G. M. Sarel
1922   W. L. Knowles
1943   Sir Home Gordon Bt
1946   S. C. Griffith
1950   Lieutenant-Colonel G. S. Grimston
1964   P. C. Williams
1970   A. A. Dumbrell
1974   I. M. Stoop
1976   S. R. Allen
1980   R. G. Stevens
1983   B. E. Simmonds
1984   R. H. Renold
1988   N. Bett

Sussex Coaches

1946–48   H. P. Chaplin
1948–52   E. P. Hendren
1953–60   Jas Langridge
1961–64   G. Cox (jnr)
1965–69   J. H. Parks
1970–76   L. J. Lenham
1977–78   A. Buss

1979–86	S. J. Storey		
1987	J. M. Parks, I. Thomson, J. A. Snow		
1988	J. A. Jameson		

Sussex Scorers

1839–94	No record	1976	Mrs C. Spencer
1895–1914	W. H. Edwards		W. Sinfield
1919–39	E. H. Killick		Miss W. Wimbush
1946–51	W. R. Locke		S. J. Hicks
1952	J. F. Burt	1977	W. S. Denman
1953–73	F. G. Washer	1977–81	C. G. A. Saulez
1973–76	W. S. Denman	1982–88	L. V. Chandler

YEAR	CAPTAIN	CH'SHIP POSITION	LEADING BATSMEN	LEADING BOWLERS	WICKET-KEEPER	DEBUT
1839	Various		G.L. Langdon E. Napper	W. Lillywhite J. Dean	T. Box	G. Daniels G. Pescott M. Ewen
1840	C.G. Taylor and Match Managers		J. Hodson T. Box	"	"	E.H. Sayres F. Haslett
1841	"		C. Hawkins G. Millyard	"	"	J. Hodson
1842	"		C.G. Taylor C. Hammond	J. Dean W. Lillywhite	"	W. Napper G. Picknell
1843	"		C. Hawkins C. Hammond	W. Lillywhite J. Dean	"	R. Picknell E. Bushby
1844	"		T. Box E. Bushby	J. Dean W. Lillywhite	"	G. Barton
1845	"		G. Picknell E. Napper	G. Picknell J. Dean	"	G. W. King J. Wisden
1846	"		T. Box C.G. Taylor	J. Dean J. Wisden	"	H.M. Curteis
1847	E. Napper		T. Box J. Wisden	J. Wisden J. Dean	"	C.H. Causden J. Challen
1848	"		J. Wisden T. Box	J. Wisden J. Hodson	"	H. Osborn W. Humphrey
1849	"		G. Picknell E. Bushby	J. Wisden J. Dean	"	W. Evershed W. Randall
1850	"		J. Dean J. Wisden	J. Wisden J. Hodson	"	A. Smith J. Penikett
1851	"		John Lillywhite G. Brown	J. Wisden J. Dean	"	James Lillywhite J.G. Paine
1852	"		G. Brown E. Bushby	"	"	A. Haygarth J. Hyde
1853	"		John Lillywhite J. Wisden	"	"	E. Tredcroft J. Isted
1854	"		"	"	"	J.H. Hale

YEAR	CAPTAIN	CH'SHIP POSITION	LEADING BATSMEN	LEADING BOWLERS	WICKET-KEEPER	DEBUT
1855	"		"	"	"	H.L. Nicholson G. Wells
1856	"		"	John Lillywhite J. Wisden	"	H.G. Phillpott Earl of Winterton
1857	"		"	J. Wisden J. Dean	C.H. Ellis	J. Sams S. Coppinger G. Hooker
1858	"		J. Southerton J. Wisden	H. Stubberfield John Lillywhite J. Wisden	"	J. Pagden W.L. Sherwin
1859	"		G. Wells E. Napper C.H. Ellis	H. Stubberfield H. Stubberfield	"	C.G. Wynch E.B. Fawcett
1860	"		E. Napper C.H. Ellis	J. Wisden G. Wells H. Stubberfield	"	D.R. Onslow F.F. Thomas
1861	"		John Lillywhite	J. Payne J. Wisden	"	J. Payne G. Knight
1862	"		W. Hodson C.H. Ellis	James Lillywhite (jnr) H. Stubberfield	"	R. Fillery S.A. Leigh
1863	J.H. Hale		C.H. Ellis W. Hodson	C.H. Ellis H. Stubberfield	C.H. Ellis G. Wells	A.G. Chapman Viscount Turnour
1864	J.H. Hale and C.H. Smith		James Lillywhite (jnr) C.H. Ellis	James Lillywhite (jnr) C.H. Ellis	"	C.H. Smith
1865	J.H. Hale		C.H. Smith G. Wells	James Lillywhite (jnr) G. Figg	"	C. Payne G. Figg
1866	C.H. Smith "		James Lillywhite (jnr) John Lillywhite	James Lillywhite (jnr) C.H. Ellis	"	H. Charlwood H. Killick
1867	B. Stent G. Ashby F. Stocken		C. Payne H. Charlwood	J. Southerton James Lillywhite (jnr)C.H. Ellis	G. Knight C.H. Ellis G. Wells	J. Dean (jnr) G.C. Ewbank Hon F.G. Pelham
1868	" "		James Lillywhite (jnr)C.H. Ellis H. Charlwood	James Lillywhite (jnr) J. Southerton	C.H. Ellis G. Knight	W. Greenhill H. Phillips

266

YEAR	CAPTAIN	CH'SHIP POSITION	LEADING BATSMEN	LEADING BOWLERS	WICKET-KEEPER	DEBUT
1869	C.H. Smith G. Ashby F. Stocken		H. Charlwood James Lillywhite (jnr)	" "	G. Knight H. Phillips	A.A. Reed F. Charlwood
1870	C.H. Smith		H. Charlwood A.A. Reed	J. Southerton James Lillywhite (jnr)	H. Phillips	J.M. Mare J.M. Cotterill W.A. Humphreys
1871	"		H. Charlwood	"	"	J. Phillips J. Hodson
1872	"		H. Charlwood J.M. Mare	"	"	C.E. Jeffery
1873	C.H. Smith	8th	J.M. Cotterill G.E. Jeffery	James Lillywhite (jnr) R. Fillery	"	Rev. F.F.J. Greenfield C. Sharp
1874	C.H. Smith and J.M. Cotterill	8th	H. Charlwood R. Fillery	"	"	C. Howard A. Smith
1875	J.M. Cotterill	2nd	J.M. Cotterill L. Winslow	"	"	A.W. Anstruther L. Winslow
1876	Rev. F.J. Greenfield	6th	H. Charlwood F.J. Greenfield	"	"	J. Hide C.A. Brown
1877	"	Last	J.M. Mare F.J. Greenfield	"	"	R.T. Ellis M.P. Lucas
1878	"	Last	J. Phillips A.W. Anstruther	F.J. Greenfield J. Hide	"	W.A. Bettesworth H. Whitfeld
1879	C, Sharp and H. Whitfeld	4th	C. Howard H. Phillips	James Lillywhite (jnr) C. Sharp	"	E.J. McCormick A.W.B. Sclater
1880	R.T. Ellis	6th	R.T. Ellis H. Charlwood	James Lillywhite (jnr) J. Juniper	"	J. Juniper F.M. Lucas
1881	Rev. F.J. Greenfield	8th	W.A. Bettesworth R.T. Ellis	James Lillywhite (jnr) W.A. Bettesworth	"	W. Blackman W. Newham
1882	Rev. F.J. Greenfield	Last	W. Newham A.H. Trevor H. Whitfeld	A. Hide J. Juniper W. Humphreys J. Lillywhite	"	A. Hide C.A. Smith

YEAR	CAPTAIN	CH'SHIP POSITION	LEADING BATSMEN	LEADING BOWLERS	WICKET-KEEPER	DEBUT
1883	H. Whitfeld	Last	H. Whitfeld W. Newham G.N. Wyatt	J. Hide J. Juniper W. Humphreys W. Tester	H. Phillips	G. Brann G.N. Wyatt
1884	"	6th	W. Newham W. Blackman H. Whitfeld	W. Humphreys A. Hide W. Blackman	"	W. Quaife
1885	G.N. Wyatt	Last	F.M. Lucas W. Newham W. Humphreys	J. Juniper A. Hide C.A. Smith	"	W.H. Andrews Dr. W.G. Heaseman Rev. C.J.M. Godfrey
1886	F.M. Lucas	8th	F.M. Lucas F.F. Thomas W. Humphreys	W. Humphreys G. Bean J. Hide	"	G. Bean F.F.Thomas (Lord Hillingdon) H. Tebay
1887	C.A. Smith	8th	W. Quaife W. Newham F.F. Thomas	C.A. Smith A. Hide W. Humphreys	H. Phillips W.H. Dudney	F.W. Tate G.L. Wilson W.H. Dudney
1888	"	Last	W. Newham E.J.M. McCormick W. Humphreys	A. Hide F.W. Tate E.J.M. McCormick	H. Phillips	J. Major F.H. Gresson
1889	W. Newham	Last	W. Newham J. Hide J. Major	C.J.M. Godfrey J. Major W. Humphreys	H. Phillips W.H. Dudney T. Mayes	T. Mayes
1890	C.A. Smith	Last	W. Quaife W.H. Andrews J. Hide	C.J.M. Godfrey A. Hide G. Bean	H. Phillips H.R. Butt	H.R. Butt F. Parris
1891	W. Newham	7th	G. Bean W. Humphrey C.A. Smith	C.A. Smith F.W. Tate W. Humphreys	H.R. Butt H. Phillips	F.W. Marlow A. Hilton
1892	"	Last	G. Brann W. Newham W.G. Heasman	J. Hide W. Humphreys F.W. Tate	H.R. Butt	F.H. Gutteridge H. Love A.W.F. Somerset

YEAR	CAPTAIN	CH'SHIP POSITION	LEADING BATSMEN	LEADING BOWLERS	WICKET-KEEPER	DEBUT
1893	W.L. Murdoch	7th	W.L. Murdoch G. Bean G. Brann	W. Humphreys G. Bean F.W. Tate	"	E.H. Killick J. Lowe W.L. Murdoch
1894	"	8th	F.W. Marlow W. Newham W.G. Heasman	A. Shaw F. Parris J. Lowe	H.R. Butt G.H.A. Arlington	G.H.A. Arlington C.B. Fry Lt. Col. J.C.Hartley A. Shaw
1895	"	11th	K.S. Ranjitsinhji G. Brann W. Newham	J.C. Hartley F.W. Tate A. Hilton	H.R. Butt	J. Bean A. Collins G.R. Cox K.S. Ranjitsinhji
1896	"	Last	K.S. Ranjitsinhji W. Newham C.B. Fry	F.W. Tate F. Parris C.B. Fry	"	J. Vine
1897	"	6th	K.S. Ranjitsinhji G. Brann W.L. Murdoch	C.H.G. Bland K.S. Ranjitsinhji J.C. Hartley	H.R. Butt G.H.A. Arlington	C.H.G. Bland
1898	"	9th	C.B. Fry P.H. Latham G. Brann	F.W. Tate J. Bean C.H.G. Bland	H.R. Butt	W. Humphreys (jnr) P.H. Latham C.L.A. Smith L. De Montezuma
1899	W.L. Murdoch and K.S. Ranjitsinhji	5th	K.S. Ranjitsinhji C.B.Fry P.H. Latham	F.W. Tate C.H.G. Bland C.B. Fry	H.R. Butt R.W. Fox	
1900	K.S.Ranjitsinhji	3rd	K.S.Ranjitsinhji C.B. Fry E.H. Killick	K.O. Goldie F.W. Tate F.H. Gresson	H.R. Butt	K.O. Goldie A.E. Relf
1901	"	4th	C.B. Fry K.S. Ranjitsinhji G. Brann	F.W. Tate A.E. Relf J. Vine		A. Cordingley K.R.B. Fry C. Clarke
1902	"	2nd	K.S. Ranjitsinhji	F.W. Tate		R.B. Heygate

YEAR	CAPTAIN	CH'SHIP POSITION	LEADING BATSMEN	LEADING BOWLERS	WICKET-KEEPER	DEBUT
1903	"	2nd	C.B. Fry J. Vine	A.E. Relf G.R. Cox	"	H.J. Heygate G. Leach R.A. Young
1904	C.B. Fry	6th	C.B. Fry K.S. Ranjitsinhji E.H. Killick J. Vine	A.E. Relf G.R. Cox F.W. Tate F.W. Tate	"	E.B. Dwyer J. Seymour E.G. Read
1905	"	3rd	C.B. Fry J. Vine A.E. Relf E.H. Killick	G.R. Cox A.E. Relf G.R. Cox E.H. Killick	R. Relf	P. Cartwright H.P. Chaplin
1906	C.B. Fry C.L.A. Smith	10th	E.H. Killick A.E. Relf G.R. Cox	A.E. Relf A.E. Relf E.B. Dwyer	"	H.L. Sims J.W.W. Nason R.A. Young
1907	C.B. Fry	13th	C.B. Fry J. Vine	G.R. Cox G.R. Cox	"	J.G.C. Scott J.H. Vincett G.S. Whitfield
1908	C.B. Fry	5th	K.P. Goldie K.S. Ranjitsinhji J. Vine E.H. Killick	J. Vine A.E. Relf A.E. Relf G.R. Cox	H.R. Butt R.A. Young	A.C.G. Luther W.H. Ramsbotham H.E. Trevor
1909	C.L.A. Smith	4th	R.A. Young R. Relf R.B. Heygate	E.H. Killick A.E. Relf G. Leach J.H. Vincett	H.R. Butt R.A. Young	V.W.C. Jupp J.K. Matthews G. Street
1910	H.P. Chaplin	7th	R. Relf R.B. Heygate H.P. Chaplin	E.H. Killick A.E. Relf G. Leach	H.R. Butt G. Street	P.G.H. Fender C.L. Tudor J.L.S. Vidler
1911	"	13th	J. Vine A.E. Relf	J. Vine A.E. Relf	H.R. Butt A.H. Lang	A. Charlwood B.H. Holloway W.J. Holloway
1912	W.L. Murdoch	10th	C.L.A. Smith K.S. Ranjitsinhji	G.R. Cox G.R. Cox	H.R. Butt	E.C. Baker

YEAR	CAPTAIN	CH'SHIP POSITION	LEADING BATSMEN	LEADING BOWLERS	WICKET-KEEPER	DEBUT
	and K.S. Ranjitsinhji		J. Vine R. Relf	A.E. Relf J. Vine	A.H. Lang G. Street	E.H. Bowley E.H. Relf M.W. Tate
1913	"	7th	A.E. Relf H.L. Wilson J. Vine	N.J. Holloway A.E. Relf G.R. Cox	G. Street	H.L. Wilson
1914	"	6th	R. Relf A.E. Relf V.W.C. Jupp	V.W.C. Jupp R. Relf G.R. Cox	"	M.F.S. Jewell H.S. Malik A.J. Wilson
1915 1916 1917 1918	"					L. Williams W.G.M. Sarel J. Mercer Rev F.R. Browne
1919	H.L. Wilson	11th	J. Vine A.E. Relf V.W.C. Jupp	G.R. Cox A.E. Relf H.E. Roberts	R.A. Miller L. Williams P.V. Williams	C.H. Gibson A.H.H. Gilligan F.D. Jenner R.A.T. Miller
1920	"	6th	R.A. Young J. Vine E.H. Bowley V.W.C. Jupp	G.R. Cox V.W.C. Jupp H.E. Roberts A.E. Relf	G. Street	A.E.R. Gilligan K.A. Higgs
1921	"	9th	V.W.C. Jupp A.E. Relf E.H. Bowley	G.R. Cox V.W.C. Jupp M.W. Tate	G. Street R.A. Young	W.L. Cornford T.E. Frazer Sir A.A. Saunders A.F. Wensley
1922	A.E.R. Gilligan	9th	E.H. Bowley A.E.R. Gilligan M.W. Tate	M.W. Tate A.E.R. Gilligan H.E. Roberts G.R. Cox	G. Street	T.E.R. Cook E.L. Harris A.J. Holmes Col A.C. Watson

271

YEAR	CAPTAIN	CH'SHIP LEADING POSITIONBATSMEN		LEADING BOWLERS	WICKET-KEEPER	DEBUT
1923	"	6th	E.H. Bowley M.W. Tate A.E.R. Gilligan	M.W. Tate A.E.R. Gilligan G.R. Cox	"	
1924	"	10th	M.W. Tate E.H. Bowley H.L. Wilson	M.W. Tate A.E.R. Gilligan G.R. Cox	W. Cornford	K.S. Duleepsinhji G.S. Grimston Jas Langridge J.H. Parks
1925	"	13th	E.H. Bowley M.W. Tate Col A.C. Watson	M.W. Tate A.F. Wensley G.R. Cox	"	R.L. Holdsworth R.A. Hollingdale J.H. Naumann L.C.R. Isherwood
1926	"	10th	K.S. Duleepsinhji M.W. Tate A.E.R. Gilligan	M.W. Tate G.R. Cox A.E.R. Gilligan	"	J. Eaton H.W. Parks
1927	"	10th	E.H. Bowley T.E.R. Cook M.W. Tate	M.W. Tate E.H. Bowley J.H. Parks	"	D. Richards J.C. Wagener
1928	"	7th	K.S. Duleepsinhji E.H. Bowley Jas Langridge	M.W. Tate E.H. Bowley Jas Langridge	"	G.A.K. Collins H.E. Hammond John Langridge G.S. Pearce K.A. Sellar
1929	"	5th	" " "	M.W. Tate J.H. Parks Jas Langridge	"	
1930	A.H.H. Gilligan	7th	K.S. Duleepsinhji H.W. Parks T.E.R. Cook	M.W. Tate Jas Langridge E.H. Bowley	"	A.G. Pelham
1931	K.S. Duleepsinhji	4th	K.S. Duleepsinhji E.H. Bowley H.W. Parks	M.W. Tate Jas Langridge A.F. Wensley	"	J. Cornford G. Cox (jnr) R.S.G. Scott
1932	"	2nd	K.S. Duleepsinhji	M.W. Tate	"	A. Melville

YEAR	CAPTAIN	CH'SHIP POSITION	LEADING BATSMEN	LEADING BOWLERS	WICKET-KEEPER	DEBUT
1933	R.S.G. Scott	2nd	H.W. Parks Jas Langridge T.E.R. Cook John Langridge	Jas Langridge R.S.G. Scott	"	H.W. Greenwood
1934	A. Melville	2nd	Jas Langridge T.E.R. Cook J.H. Parks John Langridge	Jas Langridge M.W. Tate J. Cornford M.W. Tate G. Pearce	"	J. Nye
1935	"	7th	A. Melville H.W. Parks John Langridge	A.F. Wensley Jas Langridge M.W. Tate J.H. Parks	"	C. Oakes A. Tuppin
1936	A.J. Holmes	14th	Jas Langridge H.W. Parks	M.W. Tate J.H. Parks	"	B.L. Cummings R.G. Hunt R.G. Stainton D.J. Wood
1937	"	5th	J.H. Parks J.H. Parks John Langridge Jas Langridge	H.E. Hammond Jas Langridge J.H. Parks H.E. Hammond	"	H.T. Bartlett S.C. Griffith J. Oakes
1938	"	8th	H.T. Bartlett John Langridge Jas Langridge	J. Cornford J.H. Parks D.J. Wood	"	J. Duffield D.J. Smith
1939	"	10th	Jas Langridge John Langridge G. Cox (jnr)	Jas Langridge J.H. Parks J. Nye	W. Cornford S.C. Griffith	
1946	S.C. Griffiths	Last	H.W. Parks G. Cox (jnr) Jas Langridge John Langridge	Jas Langridge P.A.D. Carey D.J. Wood C. Oakes	S.C. Griffith	P.D.S. Blake P.A.D. Carey E.E. Harrison D.V. Smith
1947	H.T. Bartlett	9th	John Langridge James Langridge H.W. Parks	J. Cornford P.A.D. Carey G. Cox (jnr)	"	A.P. Doggart G.P. Hurst A.S.M. Oakman

YEAR	CAPTAIN	CH'SHIP POSITION	LEADING BATSMEN	LEADING BOWLERS	WICKET-KEEPER	DEBUT
1948	"	16th	G. Cox (jnr) James Langridge John Langridge C. Oakes H.W. Parks	J. Nye A.E. James C. Oakes Jas Langridge J. Wood	S.C. Griffith R.T. Webb	D.S. Sheppard G.H.G. Doggart A.E. James R.T. Webb C.E. Winn
1949	"	13th	John Langridge G. Cox (jnr) Jas Langridge C. Oakes	J. Cornford Jas Langridge D.J. Wood C. Oakes	"	J.M. Parks G. Potter K.G. Suttle
1950	James Langridge	13th	G. Cox (jnr) John Langridge James Langridge D.V. Smith	G. Cox (jnr) Jas Langridge C. Oakes J.H. Cornford	R.T. Webb	D.L. Bates
1951	"	10th	D.S. Sheppard John Langridge James Langridge	A.E. James A.S.M. Oakman D.J. Wood	"	R.G. Marlar
1952	"	13th	K.G. Suttle John Langridge G. Cox (jnr) Jas Langridge	R.G. Marlar D.J. Wood A.S.M. Oakman A.E. James	"	D.J. Foreman A.K.K. Lawrence N.I. Thomson
1953	D.S. Sheppard	2nd	D.S. Sheppard K.G. Suttle J.M. Parks G. Cox (jnr)	N.I. Thomson A.S.M. Oakman A.E. James R.G. Marlar	"	
1954	G.H.G. Doggart	9th	D.S. Sheppard J.M. Parks G. Cox (jnr) G.H.G. Doggart	N.I. Thomson A.E. James A.S.M. Oakman R.G. Marlar	"	D.N. Mantell
1955	R.G. Marlar	4th	J.M. Parks A.S.M. Oakman K.G. Suttle G. Cox (jnr)	D.V. Smith R.G. Marlar A.E. James N.I. Thomson	"	R.H. Willson

YEAR	CAPTAIN	CH'SHIP POSITION	LEADING BATSMEN	LEADING BOWLERS	WICKET-KEEPER	DEBUT
1956	"	9th	J.M. Parks A.S.M. Oakman D.V. Smith K.G. Suttle	K.G. Suttle N.I. Thomson R.G. Marlar D.V. Smith	"	D. Manville D.J. Semmence L.J. Lenham D.A. Stripp
1957	"	10th	D.V. Smith J.M. Parks K.G. Suttle L.J. Lenham	N.I. Thomson A.E. James R.G. Marlar D.L. Bates	R.T. Webb D.N. Mantell	R.V. Bell E.R. Dexter R.J. Langridge Nawab of Pataudi
1958	"	13th	K.G. Suttle J.M. Parks A.S.M. Oakman D.V. Smith	N.I. Thomson R.G. Marlar D.L. Bates A.E. James	R.T. Webb D.N. Mantell J.M. Parks	A. Buss D.J. Mordaunt
1959	"	15th	J.M. Parks E.R. Dexter K.G. Suttle D.V. Smith	N.I. Thomson A. Buss A.E. James E.R. Dexter	J.M.Parks R.T. Webb	D.J. Preston
1960	E.R. Dexter	4th	E.R. Dexter J.M. Parks K.G. Suttle A.S.M. Oakman	N.I. Thomson D.L. Bates R.V. Bell A. Buss	" "	F.R. Pountain C.B. Howland
1961	"	8th	D.V. Smith J.M. Parks A.S.M. Oakman L.J. Lenham	N.I. Thomson D.L. Bates E.R. Dexter K.G. Suttle	J.M. Parks T. Gunn	M. Buss R.H. Thomson T. Gunn P. Ledden J.A. Snow R.H.C. Waters
1962	"	12th	E.R. Dexter K.G. Suttle A.S.M. Oakman L.J. Lenham	E.R. Dexter N.I. Thomson D.L. Bates R.V. Bell	J.M. Parks M.G. Griffith	M.G. Griffith
1963	"	4th	J.M. Parks E.R. Dexter	A.S.M. Oakman N.I. Thomson	J.M. Parks T. Gunn	

YEAR	CAPTAIN	CH'SHIP POSITION	LEADING BATSMEN	LEADING BOWLERS	WICKET-KEEPER	DEBUT
1964	"	9th	K.G. Suttle L.J. Lenham J.M. Parks E.R. Dexter K.G. Suttle G.C. Cooper	A. Buss D.L. Bates N.I. Thomson J.A. Snow A. Buss R.V. Bell	J.M. Parks M.G. Griffith T. Gunn	
1965	"	16th	E.R. Dexter J.M. Parks K.G. Suttle Nawab of Pataudi	J.A. Snow A. Buss N.I. Thomson A.S.M. Oakman	J.M. Parks M.G. Griffith T. Gunn	P.J. Graves
1966	Nawab of Pataudi	10th	K.G. Suttle J.M. Parks A.S.M. Oakman L.J. Lenham	J.A. Snow A. Buss D.L. Bates A.S.M. Oakman	J.M. Parks T. Gunn M.G. Griffith	A.A. Jones H. Newton
1967	J.M. Parks	13th	K.G. Suttle J.M. Parks M.G. Griffith A.W. Greig	J.A. Snow A. Buss A.W. Greig D.L. Bates	J.M. Parks M.G. Griffith T. Gunn	A.W. Greig E. Lewis T.B. Racionzer
1968	J.M. Parks and M.G. Griffith	17th	G.C. Cooper K.G. Suttle A.W. Greig M.A. Buss	A.A. Jones J.A. Snow A. Buss M.A. Buss	J.M. Parks M.G. Griffith	G.A. Greenidge
1969	M.G. Griffith	7th	J.M. Parks M.A. Buss K.G. Suttle A.W. Greig	J.A. Snow A.W. Greig M.A. Buss D.L. Bates	J.M. Parks A.W. Mansell	J. Spencer A.W. Mansell J. Clarke E. Solkar
1970	"	9th	J.M. Parks M.A. Buss G.A. Greenidge P.J. Graves	A. Buss A.W. Greig J.A. Snow M.A. Buss	" "	J. Denman R.N.P. Smyth J.R.T. Barclay
1971	"	11th	M.G. Griffith R.M. Prideaux	A.W. Greig M.A. Buss	" "	R.M. Prideaux U.C. Joshi

276

YEAR	CAPTAIN	CH'SHIP POSITION	LEADING BATSMEN	LEADING BOWLERS	WICKET-KEEPER	DEBUT
1972	"	16th	J.M. Parks A.W. Greig R.M. Prideaux J.M. Parks M.G. Griffith G.A. Greenidge	J. Spencer U.C. Joshi J.A. Snow A.W. Greig M.A. Buss U.C. Joshi	J.M. Parks	C.P. Phillipson J.D. Morley A.A. Henderson
1973	A.W. Greig	15th	G.A. Greenidge R.M. Prideaux P.J. Graves J.D. Morley	J.A. Snow A.W. Greig M.A. Buss U.C. Joshi	A.W. Mansell M.G. Griffith	R.P.T. Marshall M.J.J. Faber
1974	"	13th	P.J. Graves G.A. Greenidge M.G. Griffith M.J.J. Faber	J.A. Snow J. Spencer M.A. Buss A.W. Greig	A.W. Mansell	J.J. Groome C.E. Waller R.G.L. Cheatle G.D. Mendis N. Wisdom S.J. Hoadley A.E.W. Parsons S.J. Still
1975	"	Last	A.W. Greig M.J.J. Faber P.J. Graves A.E.W. Parsons	J.A. Snow C.P. Phillipson A.W. Greig J. Spencer	A.W. Mansell G.D. Mendis	A.N.C. Wadey Javed Miandad
1976	"	10th	R.D.V. Knight P.J. Graves M.A. Buss	J.R.T. Barclay J. Spencer J.A. Snow	A. Long	A. Long R.D.V. Knight P.W.G. Parker
1977	"	8th	J.R.T. Barclay Javed Miandad J.R.T. Barclay R.D.V. Knight G.D. Mendis	C.E. Waller Imran Khan A.W. Greig J. Spencer J.A. Snow	"	K.C. Wessels Imran Khan
1978	A. Long	9th	Imran Khan P.W.G. Parker G.D. Mendis J.R.T. Barclay	C.E. Waller G.G. Arnold J. Spencer Imran Khan	A. Long T.J. Head	T.J. Head S.P. Hoadley S.J. Storey K.B. Smith G.G. Arnold A.C.S. Pigott

YEAR	CAPTAIN	CH'SHIP POSITION	LEADING BATSMEN	LEADING BOWLERS	WICKET-KEEPER	DEBUT
1979	"	4th	K.C. Wessels P.W.G. Parker Imran Khan J.R.T. Barclay	Imran Khan G.G. Arnold R.G.L. Cheatle J.R.T. Barclay	" "	C.M. Wells
1980	"	4th	K.C. Wessells C.M. Wells P.W.G. Parker Imran Khan G.D. Mendis	Imran Khan G.S. Le Roux J.R.T. Barclay G.G. Arnold C.E. Waller	" "	T.D. Booth-Jones A. Willows J.R.P. Heath I.A. Greig
1981	J.R.T. Barclay	2nd	P.W.G. Parker G.D. Mendis Imran Khan I.A. Greig J.R.T. Barclay	G.S. Le Roux I.A. Greig Imran Khan G.G. Arnold	I.J. Gould	I.J. Gould A.N. Jones A.P. Wells A.M. Green
1982	"	8th	A.M. Green C.M. Wells G.S. Le Roux G.D. Mendis	Imran Khan G.S. Le Roux I.A. Greig A.C.S. Pigott C.E. Waller	I.J. Gould D.J. Smith	R.S. Cowan D.J. Smith
1983	"	11th	Imran Khan G.D. Mendis I.J. Gould A.P. Wells C.M. Wells	Imran Khan G.S. Le Roux A.C.S. Pigott D.A. Reeve C.E. Waller	" "	D.K. Standing D.A. Reeve
1984	"	6th	C.M. Wells P.W.G. Parker G.D. Mendis A.P. Wells	G.S. Le Roux C.E. Waller C.M. Wells D.A. Reeve	" "	D.J. Wood
1985	"	7th	Imran Khan G.D. Mendis A.M. Green	Imran Khan G.S. Le Roux D.A. Reeve	I.J. Gould P. Moores	P. Moores N.J. Lenham I.C. Waring

YEAR	CAPTAIN	CH'SHIP POSITION	LEADING BATSMEN	LEADING BOWLERS	WICKET-KEEPER	DEBUT
1986	"	14th	C.M. Wells Imran Khan A.C.S. Pigott P.W.G. Parker C.M. Wells A.Wells A.M. Green	Imran Khan D.A. Reeve A.C.S. Pigott A.N. Jones C.M. Wells	I.J. Gould P. Moores M.P. Speight	R.I. Alikhan A.M. Bredin C.S. Mays A.M. Babington A.M.G. Scott
1987	I.J. Gould	Last	C.M. Wells D.A. Reeve G.S. Le Roux	G.S. Le Roux C.M. Wells D.A. Reeve	" " "	K. Greenfield P.A.W. Heseltine S.J.S. Kimber S.D. Miles M.W. Pringle C.I.O. Ricketts I.C. Waring
1988	P.W.G. Parker	16th	P.W.G. Parker A.P. Wells I.J. Gould	Imran Khan A.C.S. Pigott R.A. Bunting	" " "	A.R. Clarke R.A. Bunting N.J. Falkner J.W. Hall

Sussex Results in Refuge Assurance League & John Player Special League 1969–1988

	P	W	L	T	NR
Derbyshire	20	12	7	–	1
Essex	20	8	10	1	1
Glamorgan	20	13	2	1	4
Gloucestershire	20	8	10	–	2
Hampshire	20	7	11	–	2
Kent	20	3	12	–	5
Lancashire	20	11	7	–	2
Leicestershire	20	9	5	1	5
Middlesex	20	9	10	–	1
Northamptonshire	20	10	9	–	1
Nottinghamshire	20	7	12	–	1
Somerset	20	10	10	–	–
Surrey	20	9	7	–	4
Warwickshire	20	9	9	–	2
Worcestershire	20	9	10	–	1
Yorkshire	20	11	6	–	3
	320	145	137	3	35

Natwest Bank Trophy
(including Gillette Cup, 1963-1980)

Match Results:

	First Played	M.	Won	Lost
Cumberland	1987	1	1	0
Derbyshire	1968	5	2	3
Devon	1984	1	1	0
Durham	1964	1	1	0
Essex	1970	2	1	1
Glamorgan	1980	3	2	1
Gloucestershire	1968	5	2	3
Hampshire	1967	1	1	0
Ireland	1983	2	2	0
Kent	1963	5	4	1
Lancashire	1970	3	2	1
Leicestershire	1969	1	1	0
Middlesex	1965	4	2	2
Northamptonshire	1963	4	3	1
Nottinghamshire	1975	4	2	2
Somerset	1964	5	2	3
Staffordshire	1978	1	1	0
Suffolk	1978	4	4	0
Surrey	1964	2	2	0
Warwickshire	1964	5	3	2
Worcestershire	1963	6	4	2
Yorkshire	1963	3	3	0
		68	46	22

Cup Winners: 1963, 1964, 1978, 1986
Finalists:
1968, 1970, 1973
Semi-Finalists: 1967, 1969, 1979, 1980

281

The Benson & Hedges Cup 1972–1988

	First Played	M.	Won	Lost
Cambridge University	1974	1	1	0
Derbyshire	1982	1	1	0
Essex	1972	11	2	9
Glamorgan	1980	4	3	1
Gloucestershire	1980	2	2	0
Hampshire	1981	3	2	1
Kent	1972	11	4	7
Leicestershire	1978	2	1	1
Middlesex	1972	9	2	7
Minor Counties	1980	4	4	0
Minor Counties (East)	1978	1	1	0
Minor Counties (South)	1975	1	1	0
Northamptonshire	1978	2	1	1
Nottinghamshire	1977	1	1	0
Oxford & Cambridge Universities	1976	4	4	0
Somerset	1978	5	2	3
Surrey	1972	11	7	4
Yorkshire	1972	3	0	3
		76	39	37

Position in Refuge Assurance/John Player Special League

YEAR	POSITION	P	W	L	T	NR	PTS
1969	17TH	16	3	11	–	2	14
1970	17TH	16	3	10	–	3	15
1971	7TH	16	8	8	–	–	32
1972	15TH	16	5	8	–	3	23
1973	7TH	16	7	7	–	2	30
1974	6TH	16	8	6	1	1	36
1975	11TH	16	6	9	–	1	26
1976	3RD	16	10	6	–	–	40
1977	4TH	16	9	6	–	1	38
1978	8TH	16	6	7	–	3	30
1979	12TH	16	6	10	–	–	24
1980	9TH	16	6	6	–	4	32
1981	5TH	16	8	5	–	3	38
1982	1ST	16	14	1	–	1	58
1983	4TH	16	9	5	–	2	40
1984	3RD	16	9	4	–	3	42
1985	2ND	16	10	5	–	1	42
1986	4TH	16	10	6	–	–	40
1987	14TH	16	4	8	–	4	24
1988	15TH	16	4	9	2	1	22
		320	145	137	3	35	646

NOTE: POINTS SCORING SYSTEM FOR "NO RESULT" ALTERED IN 1974. EACH
TEAM ALLOCATED 2 POINTS INSTEAD OF 1 AS IN 1969 TO 1973 INCLUSIVE

Analysis of Results of Every First-Class Match: 1839-1988

FIRST PLAYED	OPPONENTS	PLAYED	WON	LOST	DRAWN	TIE	ABND
1880	Derbyshire	114	38	31	43	–	2
1897	Essex	137	35	43	58	1	–
1921	Glamorgan	99	33	22	44	–	–
1872	Gloucestershire	189	65	57	63	–	4
1864	Hampshire	182	68	48	65	1	–
1839	Kent	273	86	109	76	1	1
1869	Lancashire	171	38	68	62	–	3
1900	Leicestershire	123	45	29	49	–	–
1864	Middlesex	176	34	80	60	–	2
1905	Northamptonshire	108	35	33	39	–	1
1840	Nottinghamshire	179	37	75	67	–	–
1892	Somerset	150	62	36	50	1	1
1849	Surrey	237	35	113	88	–	1
1905	Warwickshire	113	33	35	44	1	–
1899	Worcestershire	126	50	33	43	–	–
1864	Yorkshire	172	25	78	67	–	2
1858	Manchester	1	1	–	–	–	–
1839	M.C.C.	79	33	41	5	–	–
1885	Cambridge Univ.	110	52	24	34	–	–
1890	Oxford Univ.	60	27	16	16	–	1
1929	Wales	1	–	–	1	–	–
1854	United England	1	–	–	–	–	–
1878	Australians	31	2	15	14	–	–
1911	Indians	7	3	1	3	–	–
1927	New Zealanders	8	–	4	4	–	–
1954	Pakistanis	6	1	1	4	–	–
1904	South Africans	11	1	4	5	–	1
1979	Sri Lankans	3	1	·	2	–	–
1923	West Indians	9	2	4	3	–	–
1852	All England XI	1	–	–	1	–	–
1970	Jamaicans	1	–	1	–	–	–
1897	Philadelphians	1	–	1	–	–	–
1967	Rest of World	1	–	–	1	–	–
1932	South Americans	1	–	–	1	–	–
1985	Zimbabweans	1	–	1	–	–	–
		2882	842	1004	1012	5	19

284

A Century in Each Innings

G. Brann	(1)	105 & 101 v Kent (Hove	1892
G.H.G. Doggart	(1)	140 & 105 v Oxford Univ. (The Parks)..............	1954
K.S. Duleepsinhji	(2)	115 & 246 v Kent (Hastings)	1929
		116 & 102* v Middlesex (Lord's).......................	1930
C.B. Fry	(4)	108 & 123* v Middlesex (Hove)	1898
		125 & 229 v Surrey (Hove)	1900
		138 & 101* v Kent (Hove)	1903
		156 & 106 v M.C.C. (Lord's)	1905
John Langridge	(2)	115 & 129 v Lancashire (Old Trafford)	1949
		146 & 146* v Derbyshire (Worthing)..................	1949
G.D. Mendis	(1)	103 & 100* v Lancashire (Hastings)	1985
H.W. Parks	(1)	114* & 105* v Essex (Leyton)	1933
J.M. Parks	(1)	101 & 100* v Worcestershire (Worcester)	1957
K.S. Ranjitsinhji	(1)	100 & 125 v Yorkshire (Hove)	1896
K.G. Suttle	(1)	112 & 120 v Cambridge Univ. (Horsham)..........	1971

NOTE: K.S. RANJITSINHJI SCORED BOTH HIS CENTURIES ON THE SAME DAY –
THE ONLY INSTANCE IN FIRST-CLASS CRICKET.

Highest Individual Innings for County

SCORE	BATSMAN	OPPONENTS	VENUE	YEAR
333	K.S. Duleepsinhji	Northamptonshire	Hove	1930
285*	K.S. Ranjitsinhji	Somerset	Taunton	1901
283	E.H. Bowley	Middlesex	Hove	1933
280*	E.H. Bowley	Gloucestershire	Hove	1929
278	T.E.R. Cook	Hampshire	Hove	1930
275	K.S. Ranjitsinhji	Leicestershire	Leicester	1900
272*	R.R. Relf	Worcestershire	Eastbourne	1909
260	K.S. Ranjitsinhji	M.C.C.	Lord's	1897
254	K.C. Wessels	Middlesex	Hove	1980
250*	John Langridge	Glamorgan	Hove	1933

Most Catches in a Match

NO.	PLAYER	OPPONENTS	VENUE	YEAR
7	A.F. Wensley	Surrey	Horsham	1934
7	John Langridge	Somerset	Taunton	1950
7	A.S.M. Oakman	Glamorgan	Worthing	1958
7	G.C. Cooper	Nottinghamshire	Hove	1961

Most Catches in a Season

NO.	PLAYER	YEAR	NO.	PLAYER	YEAR
69	John Langridge	1955	57	A.S.M. Oakham	1958
59	John Langridge	1933	52	John Langridge	1934
58	John Langridge	1950	52	A.S.M. Oakham	1959

Most Dismissals in a Match

NO.	CT.	ST.	WICKET-KEEPER	OPPONENTS	VENUE	YEAR
10	5	5	H. Phillips	Surrey	The Oval	1872
8	3	5	H. Phillips	Kent	Hove	1884
8	8	–	H.R. Butt	Kent	Tonbridge	1899
8	8	–	H.R. Butt	Somerset	Hove	1900
8	7	1	G. Street	Worcestershire	Hastings	1923
8	4	4	W. Cornford	Worcestershire	Worcester	1928
8	8	–	R.T. Webb	Somerset	Hove	1960
8	8	–	A. Long	West Indians	Hove	1976
8	8	–	A. Long	Kent	Hove	1976

Most Dismissals in a Season

NO.	CT.	ST.	WICKET-KEEPER	YEAR
95	69	26	G. Street	1923
90	84	6	J.M. Parks	1959
81	77	4	J.M. Parks	1961
71	62	9	A. Long	1976
68	62	6	J.M. Parks	1963
68	62	6	I.J. Gould	1984
65	41	24	R.T. Webb	1955

100 Wickets in a Season

13 times:	M.W. Tate
12 times:	N.I. Thomson
9 times:	A.E. Refl
5 times:	G. Cox, Snr., F.W. Tate, A.F. Wensley
4 times:	James Langridge
3 times:	D.L. Bates, A. Buss*, C.H.G. Bland

Twice:	A.E.R. Gilligan, A.E. James, V.W.C. Jupp, R.G. Marlar, J.A. Snow
Once:	A. Hide, W. Humphreys, E.H. Killick, G. Leach, J. Nye, J.H. Parks, J. Vine, D.J. Wood

---

* The last season was in 1967.

'The Double' – 1000 runs and 100 wickets in a season

7 times:	M.W. Tate
6 times:	A.E. Relf
4 times:	James Langridge
Twice:	V.W.C. Jupp
Once:	E.H. Killick, J.H. Parks, J. Vine, A.F. Wensley

In all First-Class Cricket in 1937, J.H. Parks scored 3003 runs and took
101 wickets, a feat, never equalled.

100 runs and 10 wickets in a match:

E.R. Dexter	(113, 6–63 and 4–46) v Kent (Tunbridge Wells)	1962
E.R. Dexter	(27 and 94, 7–38 and 3–58) v Surrey (The Oval)	1962
C.B. Fry	(89 and 65, 5–81 and 5–66) v Nottinghamshire (Trent Bridge)	1896
I.A. Greig	(118*, 6–75 and 4–57) v Hampshire (Hove)	1981
V.W.C. Jupp	(102 and 33* 6–61 and 6–78) v Essex (Colchester)	1921
James Langridge	(13 and 103, 7–58 and 4·66) v Glamorgan (Swansea)	1929
A.E. Relf	(103* and 8–41 and 7–36) v Leicestershire (Hove)	1912
M.W. Tate	(90 and 35, 5–48 and 6–42) v Oxford University (Hove)	1920
M.W. Tate	(101, 6–52 and 4·43) v Hampshire (Portsmouth)	1927
J. Vine	(86 and 54, 2–45 and 8–68) v Oxford University (Eastbourne)	1906

287

All Ten Wickets in an Innings

C.H.G. Bland	(25.2–0–48–10) v Kent (Tonbridge)	1899
N.I. Thomson	(34.2–19–49–10) v Warwickshire (Worthing	1964

Hat-Tricks

A.M. Babington	(1)	v Gloucestershire (Bristol)	1986
W. Blackman	(1)	v Surrey (Hove)	1881
A. Buss	(2)	v Cambridge University (Fenner's)	1965
		v Derbyshire (Hove)	1965
P.A.D. Carey	(1)	v Glamorgan (Hove)	1947
C.H. Ellis	(1)	v Kent (Hove)	1862
A.E.R. Gilligan	(1)	v Surrey (The Oval)	1923
H.E. Hammond	(1)	v Warwickshire (Hove)	1946
W. Humphreys	(2)	v Australians (Hove)	1880
		v Australians (Hove)	1884
V.W.C. Jupp	(3)	v Surrey (The Oval)	1911
		v Essex (Hove)	1919
		v Essex (Leyton)	1921
Imran Khan	(1)	v Warwickshire (Edgbaston)	1983
James Langridge	(1)	v Derbyshire (Derby)	1939
G.S. Le Roux	(1)	v Warwickshire (Hove)	1981
A.S.M. Oakman	(1)	v Somerset (Hove)	1952
A.C.S. Pigott	(1)	v Surrey (Hove)	1978
A.E. Relf	(1)	v Worcestershire (Hove)	1902
D.V. Smith	(1)	v Cambridge University (Fenner's)	1958
F.W. Tate	(1)	v Surrey (The Oval)	1901
M.W. Tate	(2)	v Middlesex (Lord's)	1926
		v Northamptonshire (Peterborough)	1934
A.F. Wensley	(1)	v Middlesex (Lord's)	1935

1000 Runs in a Season

20 Times:	James Langridge
18 times:	J.M. Parks (2000–3)
17 times:	John Langridge (2000–10); K.G. Suttle (2000–1)
15 times:	E.H. Bowley (2000–4)
14 times:	H.W. Parks (2000–1); J. Vine
13 times:	G. Cox, jnr. (2000–1)
12 times:	J.H. Parks (2000–1)
10 times:	T.E.R. Cook (2000–1); M.W. Tate; E.H. Killick
9 times:	C.B. Fry (2000–4); A.S.M. Oakman (2000–1)
8 times:	K.S. Ranjitsinhji (2000–4); A.E. Relf; D.V. Smith
6 times:	L.J. Lenham (2000–1); G.D. Mendis; P.W.G. Parker; R.R. Relf
5 times:	E.R. Dexter; K.S. Duleepsinhji (2000–2); G.A. Greenidge; C. Oakes, C.M. Wells
4 times:	M.A. Buss; H.P. Chaplin; H.T. Bartlett; P.J. Graves; A.W. Greig; R.J. Langridge; H.L. Wilson
3 times:	J.R.T. Barclay; G.C. Cooper; A.M. Green; A.H.H. Gilligan; V.W.C. Jupp; D.S. Sheppard (2000–1); A.P. Wells; A.F. Wensley

Twice:	G. Brann; R.B. Heygate; A.J. Holmes; Imran Khan; A. Melville; W.J. Murdoch; W. Newham; R.M. Prideaux; K.C. Wessels
Once:	G. Bean- G.H.G. Doggart; G. Cox, Snr.; M.J.J. Faber; P.G.H. Fender; R.D.V. Knight; G. Leach; Javed Miandad; Nawab of Pataudi; J. Oakes; W. Quaife; C.L.A. Smith

Centuries for the County

76	John Langridge	14	C. Oakes	4	J. Hide
68	C.B. Fry	13	G.H.G. Doggart	3	M.J.J. Faber
58	K.S. Ranjitsinhji	13	G.A. Greenidge	3	K.O. Goldie
50	G. Cox, jnr.	13	Imran Khan	3	R.B. Heygate
49	K.G. Suttle	12	A. Melville	3	P.H. Latham
46	E.H. Bowley	10	P.J. Graves	3	F.M. Lucas
42	H.W. Parks	10	K.C. Wessels	3	G.L. Wilson
42	J.M. Parks	9	J.R.T. Barclay	2	H.R.J. Charlwood
39	James Langridge	9	H.T. Bartlett	2	G.C. Cooper
35	K.S.Duleepsinhji	9	G. Bean	2	G. Cox, snr.
32	T.E.R. Cook	9	M.A. Buss	2	R.T. Ellis
32	P.W.G. Parker	8	A.E.R. Gilligan	2	P.G.H. Fender
32	J. Vine	8	A.P. Wells	2	I.J. Gould
27	D.S. Sheppard	8	A.F. Wensley	2	F.F.J. Greenfield
26	E.R. Dexter	7	A.M. Green	2	S.C. Griffith
24	G. Brann	7	L.J. Lenham	2	K.A. Higgs
22	E.H. Killick	7	Javed Miandad	2	R.L. Holdsworth
22	G.D. Mendis	6	H.P. Chaplin	2	R.D.V. Knight
22	A.E. Relf	6	A.J. Holmes	2	A.H. Lang
22	R.R. Relf	6	F.W. Marlow	2	G. Leach
20	A.S.M. Oakman	6	W.L. Murdoch	2	Jas. Lillywhite
18	W. Newham	6	R.A. Young	2	John Lillywhite
18	M.W. Tate	5	M.G. Griffith	2	J.D. Morley
18	C.M. Wells	5	R.J. Langridge	2	J. Oakes
17	D.V. Smith	5	R.M. Prideaux	2	W. Quaife
14	A.W. Greig	5	H.L. Wilson	2	R.S.G. Scott
14	V.W.C. Jupp	4	I.A. Greig	2	C.L.A. Smith
				2	J. Wisden

The following have each socred one century

P. Cartwright, A. Collins, J.M. Cotterill, R. Fillery, D.J. Foreman, A.H.H. Gilligan, H.W. Greenwood, F.H. Guttridge, H.E. Hammond, J.R.P. Heath, S.P. Hoadley, C. Howard, W.A. Humphreys, N.J. Lenham, M.P. Lucas, J. Major, W.J. Malden, H.S. Malik, G. Osbaldeston, A.E.W. Parsons, Nawab of Pataudi, C. Payne, H. Phillips, A.C.S. Pigott, D.A. Reeve, H.E. Roberts, W.G.M. Sarel, J.G.C. Scott, K.A. Sellar, D.J. Semmence, H.L. Simms, G.A. Stannard, G.B. Street, C.G. Taylor, W.A. Tester, A.H. Trevor, C.L. St.J. Tudor, A.C. Watson, L. Williams, R.H. Willson, A.K. Wilson, L.F. Winslow, G.N. Wyatt

Sussex Career Records 1839–1988

NAME	YEARS	INNS	NOT OUT	RUNS	H.S.	AV.	RUNS	WKTS	AV.	BB	C/ST
P.W. Adams	1922	2	1	2	1*	2.00					0/1
R.I. Alikhan	1986-88	81	7	1038	98	26.18	95	2	47.50	2/19	27
W.H. Andrews	1888-92	69	5	864	67	13.29	1	0			27
J.P. Anscombe	1862-66	5	1	7	2	1.75					1/3
A.W. Anstruther	1875-78	14	2	136	37	11.33	12	0		–	
G.G. Arnold	1978-82	81	19	746	51	12.03	4290	194	22.11	7/44	21
G.H.A. Arlington	1894-98	50	0	614	73	12.28	36	1	36.00	1/13	27/3
A.M. Babington	1986-	44	17	146	16	5.40	2874	85	33.81	4/18	14
E.C. Baker	1912-19	14	3	123	17	11.18	613	14	43.79	4/77	2
J.R.T. Barclay	1970-86	442	43	9419	119	23.60	9526	313	30.43	6/61	209
J.C. Barley	1908	2	0	1	1	0.50					2
E. Barnett	1841	6	0	30	9	5.00					2
H.T. Bartlett	1937-49	247	24	7074	157	31.72	187	7	26.71	1/0	52
J.N. Bartlett	1946-50	11	4	36	11*	5.14	271	2	135.50	1/43	6
G. Barton	1839-56	53	6	350	34	7.45					12
H. Barton	1857	2	1	2	2*	2.00					1
D.L. Bates	1950-71	358	157	1525	37*	7.59	22776	880	25.33	8/51	118
G. Bean	1886-98	365	15	7326	186	20.93	6357	232	27.40	8/29	120
J. Bean	1895-1903	57	4	453	46	8.55	841	35	24.03	5/34	27
B.F. Beard	1899	2	0	4	4	2.00	9	0			1
Sir W.F.W. Becher	1939	5	0	48	20	9.60					
W. Beecham	1857	2	0	3	2	1.50					
R.V. Bell	1957-64	227	52	1533	53*	8.76	10583	375	28.22	8/54	145
G. Bennett	1843	2	0	0	0	0.00					
R. Bennett	1860	2	0	3	3	1.50					1/1
W.A. Bettesworth	1878-83	41	2	707	77	18.13	924	36	25.67	5/66	11
A. Blaber	1890-94	3	1	29	28*	14.50	68	1	68.00	1/32	
A. Blackman	1881-87	25	1	287	73	11.96	237	5	47.40	2/44	5
W. Blackman	1881-84	65	7	1070	89	18.45	1883	87	21.64	7/86	21

NAME	YEARS	INNS	NOT OUT	RUNS	H.S.	A.V.	RUNS	WKTS	AV.	BEST SCORING	C/ST
P.D.S. Blake	1946-51	38	5	619	77	18.76	14	0			12
C.H.G. Bland	1897-1904	188	35	991	59	6.48	13388	553	24.21	10/48	80
T.E. Bourdillon	1919	2	0	28	21	14.00					
V.E. Bourdillon	1919	6	0	15	7	2.50					
T.D. Booth-Jones	1980-81	44	1	934	95	21.72					8
E.H. Bowley	1912-34	773	40	25439	283	34.71	17137	667	25.69	9/114	321
T. Box	1839-56	172	18	2246	79	14.58	55	5(+3)	11.00	5/45	91/43
A. Brackpool	1880	2	0	2	2	1.00	62	1	62.00	1/62	
H.R. Brand	1860-67	4	0	16	9	4.00					2
G. Brann	1883-1905	447	38	10858	161	26.55	2963	67	44.22	5/73	135/2
A.M. Bredin	1986	6	2	26	8*	6.50	385	7	55.00	2/50	1
*J. Broadbridge	1840	5	1	21	10*	5.25		(1)		1/?	
A.J. Brook	1873	1	0	10	10	10.00	26	0			
C.A. Brown	1876-78	20	5	137	26	9.13	576	25	23.04	7/58	10
G.G. Brown	1851-58	66	9	772	86	13.54	330	19	17.36	5/25	12
J. Brown	1890	4	0	31	19	7.75	26	0			
T.C. Brown	1890	12	1	142	38	12.91	161	1	161.00	1/38	3
C.R. Browne	1913-19	5	0	24	9	4.80	36	0	-		1
F.B.R. Browne	1919-32	60	21	224	26*	5.74	3195	136	23.49	7/62	18
G.F. Browne	1864	2	0	11	11	5.50					
G.N. Brownrigg	1921-22	5	2	26	11	8.67	103	4	25.75	4/31	2
H.R. Budgen	1886-92	20	4	120	32	7.50	19	0			6
R.A. Bunting	1988-	21	5	96	17*	6.00	1320	41	32.19	5/44	2
T.J. Burchell	1905-19	4	2	13	6*	6.50					8/1
C.T. Burgess	1919	2	0	2	1	1.00	39	3	13.00	3/39	
G. le R. Burnham	1914	1	0	0	0	0.00					
E. Bushby	1843-54	90	10	1103	86	13.79	20	0			20
A. Buss	1958-74	405	75	4250	33	12.83	23442	938	24.99	8/23	129
M.A. Buss	1961-78	517	47	11286	159	24.01	13999	481	29.10	7/58	215
C.F. Butcher	1893-96	12	0	36	13	3.00	355	9	39.44	3/107	1
H.R. Butt	1890-1912	753	217	7049	96	13.15	33	0			905/260
J.A.S. Butt	1923	2	0	10	8	5.00					

NAME	YEARS	INNS	NOT OUT	RUNS	H.S.	A.V.	RUNS	WKTS	A.V.	BEST SCORING	C/ST
K.R.M. Carlisle	1927-28	4	0	55	34	13.75					2
A. Carpenter	1853-57	7	1	20	14	3.33	26	0			3
C.W. Carpenter	1868	4	0	27	11	6.75					1
P. Cartwright	1905-22	134	7	2463	101	19.39	547	16	34.19	3/29	36
R.G. Caryer	1922	2	0	12	7	6.00	13	0			
E. Cawston	1928-31	11	0	80	32	7.27	142	4	35.50	3/38	7
J. Challen snr	1847-49	7	1	42	15	7.00					3
*J. Challen jnr	1848-57	35	0	323	37	9.23	118	8(+15)	14.75	4/?	9
H.P. Chaplin	1905-14	280	25	6230	213*	24.43	370	8	46.25	3/47	59
A.G. Chapman	1861-63	6	0	65	33	10.83	86	4	21.50	3/52	
A.E. Charlwood	1911-14	17	2	165	34	11.00					1
C.B. Charlwood	1866-69	5	0	40	15	8.00					6
C.A. Charlwood	1890	6	1	44	23*	8.80					3
H.R.J. Charlwood	1865-82	229	14	4862	123	22.61	89	4	22.25	2/12	65
R.G. Cheatle	1974-79	31	9	276	49	12.55	2409	77	31.29	6/32	43
A.G.F. Clark	1886	2	0	1	1	0.50	19	0			
A.R. Clarke	1988-	32	8	337	68	14.04	1650	44	37.50	5/60	7
C. Clarke	1902	4	2	17	10	8.50	122	1	122.00	1/56	2
C.C. Clarke	1947	6	1	31	11	6.20					
J.M. Clarke	1969	2	0	0	0	0.00					1
W. Clarke	1854	2	1	9	7	9.00	103	6	17.17	4/35	
R.D. Cochrane	1913	1	0	6	6	6.00	37	2	18.50	2/37	
G.L. Cogger	1954-57	8	1	12	5	1.71	286	7	40.86	3/20	5
P. Coles	1885	8	1	52	14	7.42					2
A. Collins	1895-1902	89	18	1812	102	25.52	1656	36	46.00	5/61	29
H.F. Collins	1923	2	0	27	27	13.50	33	0			
G.A. Collins	1939	2	0	10	17	9.50					1
G.A.K. Collins	1928-34	70	11	1050	90	17.79					16
J.H. Comber	1885	6	1	28	8	5.60	20	0			
T.E.R. Cook	1922-37	729	65	20176	278	30.39	2880	80	36.00	5/24	169/1
G.C. Cooper	1955-69	407	56	8134	142	23.17	3677	100	36.77	5/13	149
S. Coppinger	1857-61	15	1	121	43	8.64					1

NAME	YEARS	INNS	NOT OUT	RUNS	H.S.	A.V.	RUNS	WKTS	AV.	BEST	C/ST SCORING
A. Cordingley	1901-05	14	5	47	24*	5.22	546	16	34.12	5/22	9
J.H. Cornford	1931-52	397	145	1352	34	5.36	26934	1019	26.43	9/53	114
W.L. Cornford	1921-47	634	207	6430	82	15.06	45	0			651/334
G.E. Cotterill	1869-74	15	0	214	48	14.27	15	0			2
G.H. Cotterill	1886-90	16	0	161	26	10.06	90	2	45.00	3/59	4
J.M. Cotterill	1870-88	48	2	1328	191	28.87	214	6	35.67	2/44	13
R.S. Cowan	1982-83	12	1	172	50	15.64	61	0			3
G. Cox jnr	1931-60	740	57	22687	234*	33.22	5889	191	30.83	6/125	136
G.R. Cox snr	1895-1928	953	192	14354	167*	18.86	41334	1810	22.84	9/50	535
C.D. Crofts	1840	2	0	0	0	0.00					1
B.L. Cumming	1936-38	25	1	475	57	19.79	41	2	20.50	2/19	7
H. Curteis	1873	1	0	25	25	25.00					
H.M. Curteis	1846-60	75	18	416	29	7.30					7
R.M. Curteis	1873-78	15	1	101	41	7.21					5
T.H.W. Curtis	1912	2	0	3	2	1.50					
G.B. Cuthbertson	1920	2	0	2	1	1.00					
G. Daniels	1839	2	0	20	13	10.00					
R.F.H.Darwall-Smith	1946	9	1	91	25	11.38	386	11	35.09	4/72	1
J.G. Davey	1869-73	8	3	66	32	13.20					6
W.W. Davidson	1948-51	6	1	21	7	4.20					12/1
P. Havelock-Davies	1914	1	1	0	0*		26	2	13.00	2/26	
D. Dean	1871	3	0	8	6	2.67					1
*J. Dean	1839-60	190	24	1887	69	11.37	3.92189(+262)		16.89	8/38	14
J. Dean jnr	1862-66	22	4	220	39*	12.22	23	1	23.00	1/13	5
M.C. Dempsey	1919	3	0	5	4	1.66					1
J. Denman	1970-73	65	20	713	50*	15.84	3065	70	43.79	5/45	26
J.A. Dew	1947	3	0	51	29	17.00					1/1
E.R. Dexter	1957-68	238	22	8827	203	40.87	5699	218	26.14	7/24	116
P.A.H.Dobree-Carey	1946-48	64	12	690	96	13.27	3635	115	31.61	6/80	16
A.P. Doggart	1947-51	16	3	228	43	17.54	41	2	20.50	2/8	2
G.H.G. Doggart	1948-61	253	17	6716	162*	28.46	826	20	41.30	2/4	157

NAME	YEARS	INNS	NOT OUT	RUNS	H.S.	A.V.	RUNS	WKTS	A.V.	BEST	C/ST SCORING
C.G.W. Dowling	1911-13	8	0	123	46	15.38	19	1	19.00	1/19	4
W.H. Dudney	1887-93	54	4	694	97	13.88					33/6
J. Duffield	1938-47	23	6	263	60*	15.47	1043	29	35.97	5/38	3
K.S. Duleepsinhji	1924-32	187	9	9178	333	51.56	444	5	88.80	1/21	162
W. Dummer	1869	6	2	60	35*	15.00	43	0			3
P.R. Dunkels	1972	1	1	3	3*		122	3	40.67	2/60	
J.E.B.B.P.Q.C. Dwyer	1904-09	92	9	986	63*	11.88	5002	179	27.94	9/35	21
W. Eager	1854	2	0	4	4	2.00					
N.J. Eaton	1926-46	52	8	465	44	10.57	5	0			52/29
C.H.M. Ebden	1904	5	1	47	22	11.75					1
H.I.P. Edwards	1908	2	0	22	15	11.00					
H.R. Edwards	1885	2	0	0	0	0.00					
C.H. Ellis	1856-68	110	8	1576	83	15.45	2071	96	21.57	8/96	83/32
R.T. Ellis	1877-87	125	7	2329	103	19.74	68	0			27
C.R. Etheridge	1896-1901	5	2	22	17*	7.33	251	3	83.66	1/105	1
W. Evershed	1849	2	1	3	3*	3.00					2
C.C. Ewbank	1867-79	6	0	63	23	10.50					4
*M. Ewen	1839-43	11	2	61	23	6.78		(+3)		1/?	4
M.J.J. Faber	1973-76	104	5	2347	176	23.71	66	1	66.00	1/11	30
N.J. Falkner	1988-	14	0	232	55	16.57					4
E.B. Fawcett	1860-63	18	0	145	19	8.06	305	16	19.06	6/57	7
P.G.H. Fender	1910-13	85	6	1813	133*	22.95	1586	50	31.72	6/98	32
G. Figg	1865-66	17	6	77	26*	7.00	702	38	18.47	6/42	7
R. Fillery	1872-79	174	23	2420	105	16.03	5628	297	18.95	7/24	80
C.D. Fisher	1898-1903	26	1	299	80	11.96	151	4	37.75	2/8	6
M.N.R.P. Fitzgerald	1864	1	0	8	8	8.00					1
C.D.B. Fletcher	1979	-	-	-	-	51	1	51.00		1/35	-
J. Flowers	1905	3	0	9	5	3.00	59	0			
*G.H.W. Ewbank	1857-60	8	1	9	6	1.28	4	0			1
D.J. Foreman	1952-67	194	21	3159	104	18.26	273	9	30.33	4/64	120
R.W. Fox	1896-1900	11	3	28	9*	3.50					9/2

NAME	YEARS	INNS	NOT OUT	RUNS	H.S.	A.V.	RUNS	WKTS	AV.	BEST SCORING	C/ST
W. Francis	1877-79	13	1	83	17	6.92					5
J.E. Frazer	1921-24	41	0	495	43	12.07					5
H.T. Frere	1868	2	0	38	22	19.00	30	0			
C.B. Fry	1894-1908	388	25	20626	244	56.82	2714	86	31.56	5/46	143
K.R.B. Fry	1901-02	6	0	136	88	22.67					3
C.H. Gausden	1847-51	9	2	41	17	5.86					3
D.M.W. Gay	1949	2	0	5	5	2.50	76	3	25.33	3/40	1
D. Geare	1840	3	1	5	3*	2.50					2
F. Gibb	1890	19	7	41	8	3.42	550	9	61.11	2/140	2
W. Gibbs	1864-65	7	3	42	18	10.50	180	7	25.71	3/49	2
C.H. Gibson	1919-26	40	11	414	54	14.28	1672	37	45.18	4/36	53
D. Gilbert	1851-57	9	0	28	8	3.11	90	4	22.50	3/55	2
W. Gilbert	1879	2	0	5	5	2.50	14	3	4.67	3/14	1
A.E.R. Gilligan	1920-32	361	30	6712	144	20.28	13389	637	21.02	8/25	129
A.H.H. Gilligan	1919-31	477	30	7829	143	17.51	3812	114	33.44	4/13	111
C.J.M. Godfrey	1885-92	20	5	134	20	8.93	446	19	23.47	5/22	5
K.O. Goldie	1900-11	101	5	2272	140	23.67	2056	59	34.85	5/80	69/2
G. Goldsmith	1878	4	3	6	3*	6.00	60	1	60.00	1/38	2
F.S. Gough-Calthorpe	1911-12	3	0	11	11	3.67	12	0			
A.L. Gorringe	1905	6	0	46	15	7.67					
H.M. Gorringe	1920	4	1	49	29	16.33					1
I.J. Gould	1981-	217	39	5161	111	28.99	304	4	76.00	2/48	320/33
T.J.D. Grant	1946	2	0	6	6	3.00					1
P.J. Graves	1965-80	463	48	10734	148	25.87	415	6	69.17	3/75	198
A.M. Green	1980-	256	16	6890	179	28.70	1821	37	49.21	6/82	77
C.E. Green	1869	2	0	67	43	33.50	12	0			
F.F.J. Greenfield	1873-83	115	2	1885	126	16.68	1688	89	18.96	7/26	61
K.M. Greenfield	1987-	4	0	34	18	8.50					2
W. Greenhill	1868	4	0	24	15	6.00					2
G.A. Greenidge	1968-75	283	16	7629	172	28.57	444	5	88.80	2/62	84
H.W. Greenwood	1933-36	30	2	670	115	23.93	6	0			4

NAME	YEARS	INNS	NOT OUT	RUNS	H.S.	A.V.	RUNS	WKTS	AV.	BEST SCORING	C/ST
H.V. Gregory	1960	2	0	18	14	9.00	46	;			
A.W. Greig	1966-78	358	21	9528	226	28.27	14541	509	28.57	8/25	188
I. A. Greig	1980-85	137	20	3155	147*	26.96	7090	254	27.91	7/43	76
F.H. Gresson	1887-1901	34	3	384	46	12.39	457	16	28.56	5/50	13
R.G. Grevett	1939	2	0	0	0	0.00					
W.S.G. Grevett	1922	2	0	13	9	6.50					
M.G. Griffith	1962-74	386	85	7533	188	25.03	24	0			196/6
S.C. Griffith	1937-54	194	16	2991	111	16.80	23	0			187/39
G.S. Grimston	1924-30	31	4	502	61	18.59	234	6	39.00	5/40	8
J.J. Groome	1974-78	74	3	1120	86	15.37	0	0			19
G.G.S. Grundy	1880	4	0	45	20	11.25					
T.R. Gunn	1961-68	54	19	179	19*	5.11					109/4
F.H.Guttridge	1892-95	88	4	984	114	11.71	2736	96	28.50	7/35	27
I.E. Hale	1946	5	0	27	10	5.40	47	1	47.00	1/28	1
J.H. Hale	1853-65	67	1	783	61	11.86					27/1
J.K. Hall	1960	2	1	1	1*	1.00	65	3	21.67	3/47	1
W.F. Hall	1874	2	0	19	18	9.50	57	1	57.00	1/57	1
*C.J. Hammond	1841-54	74	7	932	92	13.91	4	0(2)	–	2/?	14
E. Hammond	1870	8	1	16	5	2.29					2
H.E. Hammond	1928-46	267	40	4251	103*	18.73	12290	428	28.71	8/76	170
H.E.S. Harben	1919	8	2	126	34	21.00	36	0			1
K. Harding	1928	6	1	91	55*	18.20					
E.L.J. Harris	1922-24	15	1	208	51*	14.86	59	3	19.67	213	3
S.S. Harris	1919	5	1	52	17*	13.00					
A.M. Harrison	1913	4	0	32	14	8.00					2
E.E. Harrison	1946-47	17	5	120	23	10.00	495	17	29.29	2/28	3
J.C. Hartley	1895-98	51	4	349	38	7.43	2612	89	29.35	6/85	14
H. Hartley-Smith	1889	2	0	10	10	5.00					2/1
F. Haslett	1841	2	0	3	3	1.50					1
*C. Hawkins	1839-44	50	3	568	95	12.00		(1)			22/1
A. Haygarth	1848-60	4	0	13	11	3.25				1/?	1
T.J. Head	1976-81	26	6	335	52*	16.75					54/6

NAME	YEARS	INNS	NOT OUT	RUNS	H.S.	A.V.	RUNS	WKTS	AV.	BEST SCORING	C/ST
W.G. Heasman	1885-95	26	0	566	66	21.77	46	0			7
J.R.P. Heath	1980-85	31	4	611	101*	22.63	58	0			6
G.F. Helm	1860	2	1	5	4	5.00	33	2	16.50	2/33	1
A.A. Henderson	1972	2	0	11	9	5.50	132	5	26.40	3/65	
P.A.W. Heseltine	1978-8	20	3	186	26	10.94	1069	22	48.59	2/33	3
H.J. Heygate	1903-19	11	1	252	80	25.00					
R.B. Heygate	1902-11	106	10	2730	136	28.44	102	4	25.50	2/21	38
A. Hide	1882-90	192	39	1107	45	7.24	7598	398	19.09	7/44	72
J.B. Hide	1876-93	286	19	4408	173	16.51	8781	404	21.74	8/47	101
K.A. Higgs	1920-27	69	3	1693	111	25.65	131	4	32.75	2/15	21
A. Hilton	1891-95	37	9	182	28	6.50	2284	89	25.66	7/47	17
S.J. Hoadley	1975-76	13	2	202	58	18.36	22	0			3
S.P. Hoadley	1978-79	19	0	329	112	17.32					5
A. Hoare	1869-73	4	0	38	21	9.50	37	1	37.00	1/37	1
C.J. Hoare	1885	2	1	12	8	12.00	28	0			
H.N. Hoare	1853-54	4	3	8	5*	8.00					
A. Hobgen	1872-73	5	1	31	12	7.75	25	2	12.50	2/22	1
*J. Hodson	1839-54	82	15	522	44	7.79	425	29(+59)	14.65	8/?	39
W. Hodson	1860-63	28	6	450	50	20.45	30	0			6
H. Holden	1853	1	0	0	0	0.00					1
R.L. Holdsworth	1925-29	64	10	1255	154	23.24	28	0			14
S. Hollands	1887-93	21	0	154	21	7.33					6
R.A. Hollingdale	1925-30	113	35	1062	57	13.61	2579	81	31.54	5/23	37
B.H. Holloway	1911-14	14	2	232	58*	19.33					4
N.J. Holloway	1911-25	102	32	589	55	8.41	5105	211	24.19	8/99	18
W.O. Holloway	1890	2	0	11	11	5.50	12	0			1
A.J. Holmes	1922-39	311	23	6110	133*	21.22	354	8	44.25	1/2	118
J.R.R. Holmes	1950-1	2	0	13	13	6.50					6/1
R.A.A. Holt	1938-39	7	1	60	30	10.00					1
G.S. Hooker	1857-59	6	3	35	17	11.67	146	15	9.73	5/32	1
C. Horwood	1864-65	4	1	23	12*	7.67					3
C. Howard	1874-82	37	3	583	106	17.15	8	0			6

NAME	YEARS	INNS	NOT OUT	RUNS	H.S.	A.V.	RUNS	WKTS	AV.	BEST SCORING	C/ST
R.G.D. Howell	1900	1	0	7	7	7.00					
C.B. Howland	1960	6	0	108	59	18.00					
A. Huggett	1883-85	5	1	14	5*	3.50	10	0			
G.T. Humphreys	1869-86	60	7	545	58	10.28					21/3
W.A. Humphreys	1871-96	440	80	5806	117	15.61	14138	682	20.73	8/83	191
W.A. Humphreys, jnr	1898-1900	20	6	81	27	5.79	1353	48	28.19	5/107	9
W.J. Humphry	1848-54	14	1	76	30	5.84	5	0			2
R.G. Hunt	1936-47	20	1	333	66	17.53	98	1	98.00	1/44	3
G.T. Hurst	1947-49	13	4	27	9	3.00	760	28	27.14	6/80	
*J. Hyde	1852	9	2	20	7	2.86	65	2(+2)	32.50	2/?	4
H.M. Hyndman	1864-65	14	1	270	62	20.77					3
Imran Khan	1977-88	210	41	7216	167	42.69	8119	407	19.94	8/34	29
L.C.R. Isherwood	1925-27	49	2	787	75*	16.74	24	1	24.00	1/16	11
J. Isted	1853	3	0	5	4	1.66	65	4	16.25	3/50	2
S.T. Jagger	1931	3	1	26	13*	13.00	121	1	1121.00	1/41	1
A.E. James	1948-61	414	135	3411	63*	12.23	22841	843	27.09	9/60	111
Javed Miandad	1976-79	67	11	2511	162	44.84	941	22	42.78	4/10	47
G.E. Jeffery	1872-74	25	1	358	47	14.92	186	3	62.00	1/11	10
F.D. Jenner	1919-21	50	1	595	55	12.14	66	2	33.00	2/34	9
M.F.S. Jewell	1914-19	9	0	106	50	11.78	182	4	45.50	2/64	2
A.A. Jones	1966-69	21	4	46	13	2.71	1188	47	25.28	8/25	1
A.N. Jones	1981-86	42	17	278	35	11.12	2845	93	30.59	5/29	10
U.C. Joshi	1970-74	92	35	514	28	9.02	5984	177	33.81	6/38	31
R.H. Juckes	1924	1	0	1	1	1.00					
J.W. Juniper	1880-85	97	24	490	31	6.71	3623	184	19.69	7/24	20
V.W.C. Jupp	1909-22	294	39	7452	217*	29.22	7868	351	22.41	7/38	78
P.A. Kelland	1951-53	3	1	17	11	8.50	131	1	1131.00	1/51	1
J.H. Kelsey	1902	1	0	1	1	1.00					
C.M. Kennedy	1872-79	40	6	272	37	8.00					6
R.W. Kentfield	1894-96	4	0	10	4	2.50	138	8	17.25	6/45	
R.G. Kenward	1903	5	0	23	21	4.60					
A. Killick	1866	1	0	0	0	0.00					1

NAME	YEARS	INNS	NOT OUT	RUNS	H.S.	A.V.	RUNS	WKTS	AV.	BEST	SCORING C/ST
E.H. Killick	1892-1913	752	52	18539	200	26.48	19765	723	27.34	7/10	182
H. Killick	1866-72	72	5	957	78	14.28	219	6	36.50	3/37	22
S.J.S. Kimber	1987-	16	6	215	54	21.50	911	19	47.94	3.34	4
G.L. King	1880-81	10	0	112	29	11.20					2
G.W. King	1842-54	30	5	166	25	6.64					4
H.R. Kirby	1911	2	0	9	7	4.50					
P.N. Kirsten	1975	1	0	31	31	31.00					
G. Kirsten	1853	2	0	17	11	8.50					
G. Knight	1860-74	24	4	125	21	6.25	43	1	43.00	1/25	8/11
R.D.V. Knight	1976-77	75	6	2112	165*	30.61	1405	29	48.45	4/46	24
F.H. Knott	1926	2	1	10	8*	10.00					
W.L. Knowles	1905	2	0	66	37	33.00					1
P.G. Laker	1948-49	2	1	14	8*	14.00	70	0			1
R.E. Lambert	1904	1	0	17	17	17.00					1
A.H. Lang	1911-13	25	3	566	141	25.73					11/8
G.L. Langdon	1839-42	15	1	130	38	9.28					7
Jas Langridge	1924-53	955	142	28894	167	35.54	31634	1416	22.34	9/34	345
J.G. Langridge	1928-55	972	66	34152	250*	37.70	1848	44	42.00	3/15	776
R.J. Langridge	1957-71	383	28	8143	137*	22.94	81	0			186
P.H. Latham	1898-1906	63	5	1602	172	27.62	36	1	36.00	1/0	21
A.A.K. Lawrence	1952-56	44	7	632	63*	17.08	40	1	40.00	1/14	28
G. Leach	1903-14	350	42	5788	113*	18.79	11528	413	27.91	8/48	106
P.R.V. Ledden	1961-67	56	6	756	88	15.12	338	8	42.25	5/43	18
G.W. Lees	1951	1	0	1	1	1.00					
S.A. Leigh	1862-66	16	2	155	42	11.07	5	0			3
L.J. Lenham	1956-70	539	50	12796	191*	26.16	306	6	51.00	2/24	110
N.J. Lenham	1984-	83	12	1907	104*	26.85	510	12	42.50	4/85	20
G.S. Le Roux	1978-87	156	39	3341	83	28.55	9114	393	23.19	8/107	38
E.J. Lewis	1967-69	125	18	1318	80	12.32	5334	188	28.37	6/43	77
*F.W. Lillywhite	1839-53	48	10	265	42*	6.97	278	22(+168)	12.64	8/?	15
*Jas Lillywhite	1850-60	29	5	160	33	6.67	324	21(+5)	15.43	3/11	7
Jas Lillywhite jnr	1862-83	277	33	3627	126*	14.86	12862	855	15.04	9/29	68

299

NAME	YEARS	INNS	NOT OUT	RUNS	H.S.	A.V.	RUNS	WKTS	AV.	BEST	C/ST SCORING
*John Lillywhite	1850-69	175	12	3102	138	19.03	1425	121(+3)	11.78	8/54	45
A. Long	1976-80	123	40	1689	60	20.35	2	0			216/21
H. Love	1892-93	10	1	110	30	12.22	7	0			3
R. Lowe	1893-94	24	7	180	34*	10.59	578	22	26.27	4/26	5
C.E. Lucas	1906-08	5	0	53	22	10.60	20	1	20.00	1/13	2
C.J. Lucas	1880-82	16	2	189	38	13.50	107	4	26.75	3/17	7
F.M. Lucas	1880-87	30	3	985	215*	36.48	22	0			8
M.P. Lucas	1877-90	43	2	837	131	20.41	249	7	35.57	3/35	17
E.P.H. Lulham	1894	2	0	6	5	3.00	25	3	8.33	3/25	
A.C.G. Luther	1908	13	2	145	33	13.18					6
G.H. Lynn	1872-73	13	0	128	25	9.85	8	1	8.00	1/8	1
J. Major	1888-89	22	2	359	106	17.95	53	3	17.67	2/10	2
W.J. Malden	1920-22	34	1	593	100	17.97					12
Hardit Singh Malik	1914-21	15	0	373	106	24.87					3
A.W. Mansell	1969-75	93	21	1098	72*	15.25					108/7
D.N. Mantell	1954-58	31	6	150	34	6.00					28/2
D.W. Manville	1956	5	0	13	8	2.60					1
J.M. Mare	1870-78	47	3	616	97	14.00					9
R.G. Marlar	1951-68	303	50	2576	64	10.18	17918	740	24.21	9/46	110
F.W. Marlow	1891-1904	368	23	7600	155	22.03	196	4	49.00	2/18	56
R.P.T. Marshall	1973-78	37	15	315	37	14.32	1927	49	39.33	4/37	6
W.H. Mason	1839-42	10	0	66	38	6.60					
J.K. Mathews	1920-30	61	4	778	78	13.65	98	0			11
K.P.A. Mathews	1950-51	4	1	102	51	34.00					1
H.E. Mawle	1896	1	0	0	0	0.00					
T. Mayes	1889	12	3	51	15	5.67					11/3
C.S. Mays	1986	6	2	19	8*	4.75	706	13	54.30	3/77	2
E.J.McCormick	1880-90	84	3	1228	73	15.16	330	9	36.67	2/36	21
A.J.T. McGaw	1928	3	0	34	23	11.33					1
W. Mechen	1876-79	8	0	43	20	5.38					7
R.H. Medhurst	1948	3	2	17	15*	17.00	233	3	77.67	1/11	1
A. Melville	1932-36	132	7	4952	152	39.62	1365	38	35.92	5/17	65

300

NAME	YEARS	INNS	NOT OUT	RUNS	H.S.	A.V.	RUNS	WKTS	AV.	BEST	C/ST
											SCORING
G.D. Mendis	1974-85	354	32	11272	209*	35.01	76	1	76.00	1/65	89/1
J. Mercer	1919-21	17	3	74	13	5.29	637	18	35.39	4/46	5
W.N. Mercer	1948-56	3	1	40	24	20.00	72	3	24.00	2/2	
E. Miller	1878	2	0	2	1	1.00	7	0			
W.H. Millard	1879-80	8	0	54	26	6.75	44	2	22.00	2/32	3
R.A.T. Miller	1919	22	2	191	39	9.55					10/10
*G. Millyard	1839-42	33	1	224	29	7.00				3/?	7
R.S. Minton	1919	2	0	24	24	12.00		(12)			
H. Mitchell	1882-91	14	3	44	9	4.00	355	19	18.68	5/35	
W.H. Mitchell	1886	4	0	8	4	2.00					
De Z.L. Montezuma	1898	14	4	271	80*	27.10	12	0			2
-. Moody	1843	2	0	3	3	1.50	5	0			1
P. Moores	1985-	48	4	780	97*	17.72	6	0			49/3
D.J. Mordaunt	1958-60	27	3	586	96	24.42	530	19	27.89	5/42	15
J.D. Morley	1971-76	131	12	2752	127	23.13	2	0			26/1
P. Morris	1842	2	0	17	15	8.50					
H. Munnion	1877-80	3	0	0	0	0.00	28	2	14.00	2/15	1
A.J. Murdoch-Cozens	1919	7	0	124	56	17.72					
W.L. Murdoch	1893-99	249	14	5799	226	24.68	85	1	85.00	1/26	51
S.D. Myles	1987	3	1	19	18*	9.50	28	0			1
*A. Mynn	1839-47	8	0	65	23	8.12	184	11(+12)	16.73	6/?	2
*E. Napper	1839-62	174	4	1845	83*	10.85	103	4(+17)	25.75	3/?	35
W. Napper	1842-60	96	5	730	47	8.02	123	5(+4)	24.60	3/35	25
J.W.W. Nason	1906-10	32	3	539	72	18.59	29	1	29.00	1/16	13
J.H. Naumann	1925	32	1	408	74	13.16	87	2	43.50	1/12	7
S. Nazir Ali	1927	2	0	9	9	4.50	91	1	01.00	1/71	
J.H. Neal	1951	2	0	28	23	14.00					
F.C. New	1890	6	0	63	43	10.50					
A.L. Newbery	1925	6	1	58	50*	11.60					1
W. Newham	1881-1905	583	39	13739	201*	25.26	615	10	61.50	3/57	159
F. Newland	1875-79	4	1	11	7*	3.67	79	2	39.50	2/46	1
H. Newton	1966	4	2	16	16*	8.00	141	6	23.50	5/54	

NAME	YEARS	INNS	NOT OUT	RUNS	H.S.	A.V.	RUNS	WKTS	AV.	BEST SCORING	C/ST
B.E. Nicholls	1883-88	7	2	25	8	5.00	143	7	29.43	3/26	2
H.L. Nicholson	1853-55	20	1	272	34	14.31	14	0			10
J.K. Nye	1934-47	136	33	885	51	8.59	10407	304	34.23	6/95	35
C. Oakes	1935-54	468	40	10728	160	25.07	14119	449	31.45	8/147	159
J.Y. Oakes	1937-51	218	19	4410	151	22.16	6508	166	39.20	7/64	84
A.S.M. Oakman	1947-68	847	76	20117	229*	26.09	19200	703	27.31	7/39	562
W.F.T. O'Byrne	1935	2	0	34	26	17.00					1
D.R. Onslow	1860-69	12	0	75	16	6.25	82	6	13.66	5/28	2
H. Osborn	1848-60	6	0	17	7	2.83	14	1	14.00	1/14	1
J.W. Pagden	1858	2	0	1	1	0.50					2
J.G. Paine	1851-59	8	1	84	47	12.00					3
P.W.G. Parker	1976-	416	59	12679	181	35.51	253	5	50.60	2/21	177
H.W. Parks	1926-48	740	97	21692	200*	33.73	705	13	54.23	2/37	195
J.H. Parks	1924-39	702	60	19720	197	30.72	21292	795	26.78	7/17	302
J.M. Parks	1949-72	948	138	29138	205*	35.97	1700	42	40.48	3/23	872/65
G. Parr	1853-54	4	0	31	24	7.75					2
F. Parris	1890-1900	177	24	2222	77	14.52	7539	291	25.91	8/28	59
A.E.W. Parsons	1974-75	41	2	1020	141	26.15	4	0			11
Nawab of Pataudi	1957-70	150	13	3054	101	22.29	43	0			68
E.P. Pattenden	1874-75	5	1	6	3*	1.50	33	0			1
A. Payne	1880-86	32	4	274	42	9.79	18	0			6
C. Payne	1858-70	92	13	1572	137	19.90	100	5	20.00	3/13	37
G.S. Payne	1869	2	0	4	4	2.00	7	0			1
J.S. Payne	1861	4	1	3	2	1.00	120	12	10.00	8/73	1
R. Payne	1853-66	12	0	81	28	6.75	50	3	16.67	2/23	4
W. Payne	1877-83	31	7	180	39*	7.50	488	25	19.52	3/34	9
J.R. Peacey	1920-22	7	1	54	26	9.00					
G.S. Pearce	1928-36	79	10	1295	30	18.77	2588	89	29.08	5/34	23
W.E. Pedley	1879	4	1	45	16*	15.00	138	10	13.80	7/36	
F.G. Pelham	1865-68	14	0	283	78	20.21	348	17	20.47	5/64	7
A.G. Pelham	1930-33	14	3	67	29	6.09	507	14	36.21	4/37	7
*J. Penikett	1850-51	7	1	16	6	2.66		(1)		1/?	

NAME	YEARS	INNS	NOT OUT	RUNS	H.S.	A.V.	RUNS	WKTS	AV.	BEST	C/ST SCORING
C.M. Perkins	1884	2	1	12	11	12.00					
G. Pescott	1840	2	0	0	0	0.00					
Viscount Pevensey	1854	2	0	0	0	0.00					1
S.T. Pheasant	1971	2	1	2	2*	2.00	121	4	30.25	4/88	2
H. Phillips	1868-91	335	69	2895	111	10.88	283	14	20.21	4/33	11/183
J. Phillips	1871-86	120	38	1721	89	20.98					58
C. P. Phillipson	1870-86	226	61	3052	87	18.50	5213	153	34.07	6/56	137
H.G. Philpott	1855	2	1	11	10	11.00					
F.P.U. Pickering	1874-75	4	0	54	24	13.50	64	8	8.00	4/16	4
*G. Picknell	1842-54	107	13	1284	79	13.66	331	23(+32)	14.39	6/?	37
R. Picknell	1839-45	27	1	161	23	6.19					2
F. Pilch	1840-42	6	0	60	24	10.00					
A.C.S. Pigott	1978-	169	40	2740	104*	21.24	10794	370	29.17	7/74	70
R.G.C. Pinfield	1922	7	1	97	42*	16.17					6
C.G. Plumer	1861	2	0	0	0	0.00					1
G. Potter	1949-57	84	11	1313	88	17.99	863	19	45.42	3/29	34
F.R. Pountain	1960-65	119	16	1920	96	18.64	3054	86	35.51	5/91	43
R.M. Prideaux	1971-73	119	10	3811	170	34.96	142	3	47.33	2/13	50
D.J. Preston	1959	15	2	154	54	11.85	562	13	43.23	3/45	8
M.W. Pringle	1987-88	8	0	116	58	14.50	503	10	50.30	2/45	1
E.C. Puttock	1921	4	0	9	5	2.25					1
F.C. Quaife	1928	1	0	0	0	0.00	47	1	47.00	1/19	
W. Quaife	1884-91	170	9	3079	156*	19.12	259	8	32.38	4/35	27
T.B. Racionzer	1967-69	45	7	831	86	21.87	5	0			22
W.H. Ramsbotham	1908-10	11	0	210	56	19.09					2
W. Randall	1849	1	0	3	3	3.00					
B.M. Randolph	1856	2	0	8	4	4.00					
K.S. Ranjitsinhji	1895-1920	337	43	18594	285*	63.24	3848	112	34.36	6/109	157
J.E. Raven	1874	2	0	14	10	7.00	37	0			
F.H.H. Ravenhill	1863-67	3	0	10	7	3.33					1
T.A. Raynes	1854	13	2	69	15	6.27					4
E.G. Read	1904-06	5	0	76	44	15.20					7

NAME	YEARS	INNS	NOT OUT	RUNS	H.S.	A.V.	RUNS	WKTS	AV.	BEST	C/ST SCORING
A.A. Reed	1867-73	43	4	607	70*	15.56	389	23	16.91	5/28	17
W.B. Reed	1860	10	1	38	10*	4.22	103	2	51.50	1/8	
D.A. Reeve	1983-87	101	31	1761	119	25.16	6728	239	28.15	7/37	51
A.E. Relf	1900-21	719	54	18133	189*	27.26	33410	1594	20.96	9/95	409
E.H. Relf	1912-14	23	3	232	36	11.60	212	8	26.50	2/24	5
R.R. Relf	1905-24	495	17	13533	272*	28.31	7976	292	27.32	8/79	282
D.S. Richards	1927-35	27	5	220	23	10.00	205	1	205.00	1/8	7
C.I.O. Ricketts	1987	1	0	29	29	29.00	253	5	50.60	2/40	1
H.E. Roberts	1911-25	249	76	2302	124*	13.31	8267	342	24.17	7/32	70
J.F. Robinson	1935-36	3	0	9	5	3.00	154	8	19.25	5/47	3
M.T. Robinson	1947	2	0	4	4	2.00	157	0			
R. Robotham	1946	2	0	31	21	15.50					1
C.B. Rubie	1930	8	6	51	12	25.50					7/3
G.F. Salter	1864	2	1	19	15	19.00					1
R.K. Sampson	1886	2	0	7	5	3.50					1
J. Sams	1856	4	1	32	16	10.67	41	3	13.67	2/5	2
W.G.M. Sarel	1919-21	22	2	558	103	27.90	89	0			6
A.A. Saunders	1922-23	20	4	186	36	11.63	129	2	64.50	1/6	7
*E. Sayres	1840	2	0	0	0	0.00		(1)		1/?	
A.W.B. Sclater	1879	14	5	107	18*	11.89	687	35	19.63	7/45	12
A.M.G. Scott	1986	1	0	0	0	0.00	70	1	70.00		1
H.E. Scott	1937	4	0	19	16	4.75	118	2	59.00	1/21	
J.G.C. Scott	1907-10	6	0	154	137	25.67					2
K.B. Scott	1937	9	0	101	41	11.22	322	9	35.78	2/13	1
R.S.G. Scott	1931-34	80	8	1478	116	20.52	2147	90	23.85	5/27	42
C.E. Scott-Malden	1920	3	0	6	6	2.00	20	0			
A. Seal	1904	2	0	0	0	0.00	17	0			1
K.A. Sellar	1928	13	1	321	119	26.75					9
D.J. Semmence	1956-68	55	1	831	103	15.39	49	0			24
J. Seneschall	1882-83	10	1	26	8	2.89	274	18	15.22	6/23	1
J. Seymour	1904-07	64	10	533	49	9.87	504	15	33.60	3/1	80
A.J. Sharood	1879	-	-				51	2	25.50	2/51	80

304

NAME	YEARS	INNS	NOT OUT	RUNS	H.S.	A.V.	RUNS	WKTS	AV.	BEST	C/ST
											SCORING
C. Sharp	1873-79	31	0	345	54	11.00	214	14	15.29	6/34	10
A. Shaw	1894-95	17	9	70	16	8.75	915	56	16.34	7/34	4
A.A. Shaw	1927	1	0	6	6	6.00					4/3
D.S. Sheppard	1947-62	247	23	9545	204	42.61	51	0			123
W.L. Sherwin	1861	4	1	2	1	0.67					3
G. Shoesmith	1869-81	20	7	91	17*	7.00	467	20	23.35	5/48	5
J. Shodsmith	1871	2	1	2	2	2.00	23	1	23.00	1/23	
T.E. Shoubridge	1890	4	0	10	10	2.50	32	0			
C.H. Simmonds	1920	2	0	0	0	0.00	42	1	42.00	1/18	
H.L. Simms	1905-13	132	8	2413	126	19.46	2117	88	24.06	6/37	47
R.K. Simms	1912	2	0	5	4	2.50	64	2	32.00	1/23	
J. Skinner	1873-82	20	4	41	10	2.56	479	16	29.94	4/95	6
G.B. Sly	1953	-	-	-	-	-	29	1	29.00	1/24	1
Alfred Smith	1841-52	16	1	108	15	7.20	1084	61	17.77	7/47	2
Arthur Smith	1874-80	30	8	94	13	4.27	5004	208	24.06	7/16	7
C.A. Smith	1882-96	175	16	2315	142	14.55	206	4	51.50	2/61	51
C.H. Smith	1861-74	110	7	1700	95	16.50	585	9	65.00	1/0	44
C.L.A. Smith	1898-1911	332	36	5788	103*	19.55					147
D.J. Smith	1981-84	11	2	28	13	3.11	401	19	21.10	5/25	9
D.M. Smith	1938	10	2	55	34	6.88	8928	308	28.99	5/13	5
D.V. Smith	1946-62	596	63	15935	206*	29.90	82	1	82.00	1/82	220
H.P. Smith	1878	2	0	10	10	5.00					1
K.B. Smith	1978	8	1	90	43	12.86					1
R.N.P. Smyth	1970	5	0	42	25	8.40					
E. Snell	1927-28	3	0	13	13	4.33					1
J.A. Snow	1961-77	350	88	3828	73*	14.61	18789	883	21.28	8/87	104
W.A. Soames	1875	5	0	17	17	3.40					2
E.D. Solkar	1969	2	1	41	29*	41.00	102	3	34.00	3/69	3
A.P.F.C. Somerset	1911-19	18	2	156	33	9.75	128	5	25.60	3/27	2
A.W.F. Somerset	1892-05	9	0	69	22	7.67	37	2	18.50	2/37	2
*E. Sopp	1843-47	34	4	276	30	9.20	61	6(+1)	10.16	4/16	8
J. Southerton	1858-72	83	14	613	53	8.88	3525	269	13.10	8/68	43

NAME	YEARS	INNS	NOT OUT	RUNS	H.S.	A.V.	RUNS	WKTS	A.V.	BEST SCORING	C/ST
G. Sparkes	1875	2	0	0	0	0.00	2	1	2.00	1/2	5
M.P. Speight	1986-	15	0	279	58	18.60					64
J. Spencer	1969-80	243	64	2457	79	13.73	12599	464	27.15	6/19	17
R.G. Stainton	1936-47	76	4	1766	73	24.53	13				17
D.K. Standing	1983-88	70	10	1130	65	18.83	725	6	120.83	2/28	17
G.A. Stannard	1914-26	121	14	1437	114	13.43	724	14	51.72	4/70	15
S.J. Still	1975	2	0	6	6	3.00	42	1	42.00	1/42	
S.J. Storey	1978	23	3	331	57	16.55	235	6	39.17	3/12	7
D.A. Stripp	1956-57	20	3	183	32*	10.76	297	6	49.50	2/12	10
G.B. Street	1909-23	296	70	3781	109	16.73	66	3	22.00	3/26	304/16
H. Stubberfield	1857-74	92	25	477	40	7.11	2241	117	19.15	7/10	52
A.M. Sullivan	1901	6	2	28	16	7.00					1
K.G. Suttle	1949-72	1043	91	29375	204*	30.86	8590	260	33.04	6/64	376/2
B.L. Talbot	1947	2	0	35	25	17.50					2
F.W. Tate	1887-1905	444	144	2876	84	9.59	28054	1306	21.48	9/73	230
M.W. Tate	1912-1937	774	72	17076	203	24.32	38515	2211	17.41	9/71	226
*C.G. Taylor	1839-54	69	3	932	100*	14.12	264	14 (+42)	18.85	6/21	21
H.C. Taylor	1843	2	0	7	7	3.50					
J. Taylor	1839-40	4	0	58	40	14.50					
H. Tebay	1886-90	36	0	265	43	7.36					17
W.A. Tester	1878-88	186	7	2523	130	14.09	3652	147	24.84	5/52	47
F.F. Thomas	1860-67	18	0	89	15	4.94					6
F.F. Thomas (jnr)	1886-90	35	0	678	73	19.37					6
N.I. Thomson	1952-72	558	90	6827	77	14.59	31186	1527	20.42	10/49	123
R.H. Thomson	1961	4	0	30	21	7.50	57	3	19.00	2/14	2
A.J. Thornton	1880-81	9	2	117	33	16.71	42	1	42.00	1/30	2
J.R. Thornton	1880-83	5	0	73	29	14.60					2
P.W. Threlfall	1988						31	0			
R.J. Tillard	1949	2	0	3	3	1.50					
E. Tredcroft	1852-60	33	3	237	33	7.90	8	0			16
A.H. Trevor	1880-82	23	0	480	103	20.87	52	1	52.00	1/5	6
H.E. Trevor	1908	4	1	39	22*	13.00					

NAME	YEARS	INNS	NOT OUT	RUNS	H.S.	A.V.	RUNS	WKTS	AV.	BEST	C/ST SCORING
C.L. St.J. Tudor	1910-11	14	2	235	116	19.58					7
R.G. Tudor	1912-19	6	1	78	25*	15.60					2
A.G. Tuppin	1935-39	31	6	294	31*	11.76	1626	56	29.04	5/30	11
R.M. Turnbull	1877-79	4	0	2	2	0.50	54	2	27.00	2/23	1
Visct. Turnour	1862-67	9	1	44	27*	5.50					4/1
M. Upton	1971	1	1	2	2*		120	1	120.00	1/72	
J.L.S. Vidler	1910-19	13	0	232	40	17.84	360	14	25.71	5/33	3
J.H. Vincett	1907-19	254	48	3424	90*	16.62	8897	338	26.32	7/41	114
J. Vine	1896-1923	858	69	24120	200	30.57	17688	621	28.48	8/68	240
A.N.C. Wadey	1975	2	2	0	0*		44	1	44.00	1/44	
J.G. Wagener	1927-30	13	3	266	80*	26.60	248	4	62.00	1/13	3
L.A. Waghorn	1926-27	7	1	14	7	2.33	177	3	59.00	2/34	3
P.J. Wales	1951	2	1	38	29	38.00	13	5	2.60	3/12	1
C.E. Waller	1974-85	233	97	1298	51*	9.54	15990	531	30.11	7-61	119
I.C. Waring	1985-87	3	2	0	0*		217	3	72.33	2/76	2
D. Watson	1920	2	0	3	3	1.50					
R.H.C. Waters	1961-65	12	1	140	35*	12.73					13
A.C. Watson	1922-28	174	15	2635	111	16.57	209	5	41.80	3/46	36
R.T. Webb	1948-60	331	103	2668	49*	11.70	43	1	43.00	1/34	322/127
D.J. Weekes	1952	1	0	0	0	0.00	34				
W.B. Weighell	1868-78	25	0	207	38	8.28	75	1	75.00	1/15	5
A.P. Wells	1981-	223	37	5841	161	31.40	322	5	64.40	3/67	68
C.M. Wells	1979-	329	51	9479	203	34.09	9573	294	32.56	6/34	64
F. Wells	1839	8	0	50	22	6.25					1
F. Wells jnr	1891	2	0	7	7	3.50					
G. Wells	1854-69	140	11	2209	90	17.12	1218	67	18.18	9/105	79/13
A.F. Wensley	1922-36	552	61	9807	140	19.97	28187	1067	26.42	8/41	249/1
K.C. Wessels	1976-80	94	11	4329	254	52.16	11	0			42
G.L. Whatford	1904	2	0	21	13	10.50					
T.R. White	1928	2	0	13	9	6.50	25	0			
F.B. Whitfield	1878	2	0	1	1	0.50					
G.S. Whitfield	1908	5	2	191	71*	63.67					3

NAME	YEARS	INNS	NOT OUT	RUNS	H.S.	A.V.	RUNS	WKTS	AV.	BEST	C/ST SCORING
H. Whitfield	1878-85	71	8	1366	80	21.68	235	6	39.17	2/35	40
R.C.C. Whittaker	1927	2	1	0	0*	0.00	49	5	9.80	5/36	
G. Wilder	1905-06	12	1	147	26	13.36	26	1	26.00	1/20	1
L. Williams	1919-30	38	4	913	100*	26.85	5	0			13/3
P.V. Williams	1919	19	0	198	84	10.42					6/1
C.J. Willock	1883	2	1	14	8*	14.00	14	0			2
A. Willows	1980-82	3	1	5	4	2.50	253	8	31.62	4/33	
R.H. Willson	1955-57	29	3	395	113*	15.19	159	1	159.00	1/42	8
A.K. Wilson	1914-34	30	2	546	134	19.50	202	2	101.00	2/39	4
G.L. Wilson	1886-98	90	6	1886	174	22.45	1465	22	66.59	4/47	23
H.L. Wilson	1913-24	256	12	6138	187	25.16	1184	26	45.54	4/19	56
C.E. Winn	1948-52	22	0	358	71	16.27	9	0			8
L.O. Winslow	1875	6	0	258	124	43.00	13	0			3
O.E. Winslow	1869	10	0	207	56	20.70					1
P.L. Winslow	1949	2	0	24	16	12.00	23	0			2
*J. Wisden	1845-63	148	17	2234	148	17.05	36453	50(+230)	10.41	3/24	84
N. Wisdom	1974	2	1	35	31*	35.00	33	2	16.50	1/0	
D.J. Wood	1936-55	250	72	1304	42	7.33	18084	585	30.91	7/24	89
D.J. Wood	1984	3	1	32	15	10.66					1
E.F. Woodhams	1905	2	1	14	14*	14.00					1
K.H.C. Woodroffe	1914	3	0	3	2	1.00	146	6	24.33	6/43	1
*W. Wooller	1850	2	1	2	2	2.00		(2)		1/?	
F.J. Worger	1892	2	0	1	1	0.50					2
Winterton Earl of	1856	2	0	3	2	1.50					
A.J. Wreford-Brown	1934	2	0	17	16	8.50					
G.N. Wyatt	1883-86	70	4	1182	112	17.91	89	1	89.00	1/4	22
C.G. Wynch	1852-59	11	1	81	17	8.10	4	0			4
J.V. Young	1908	5	0	105	84	21.00	28	0			
R.A. Young	1905-25	148	9	3982	220	28.65	62	2	31.00	2/32	72/17

* NUMBERS IN PARENTHESIS IN THE BOWLING COLUMN REFER TO WICKETS TAKEN IN MATCHES FOR WHICH NO FULL BOWLING ANALYSIS WAS RECORDED.

Benefactors List

Adamson A.H. – Berkshire
Aitken J.A. – Haywards Heath
Aitken S.A. – Haywards Heath
Aitken, S.A. – Ditchling
Allen P.S. – Angmering
Allen S.R. – Shoreham-by-Sea
Ambrose G.J. – Crawley
Ambrose W.D. – Ormskirk
Apps S.C. – Brighton
Argles P.S.M. – Worthing
Atthis D.H.B. – Haywards Heath
Ayling E.W. – Southwick

Backshall A.H. – Storrington
Baker S.H. – Brighton
Baldwin R.S.L. – Worcester Park
Baldwin Mr and Mrs S.H. – Surrey
Barclays Bank PLC – Haywards Heath
Barclay J.R. – Shoreham
Barrow R.J. – Tunbridge Wells
Barrington-Smith Nigel – Lancashire
Beach R.P. – Hove
Beere, D.J. – Banbury
Beilby J.P. – Lewes
Bidgood B.A. – Hove
Boddie R.P. – Seaford
Brant E.G. – Eastbourne
Bridges S.J. – Bexley
Brierley Miss D. – Hove
Brown P.A.A. – Worthing
Byrne P.R. – Kent
Buck A.F.K. – Billingshurst
Burgess R. – Chelwood Gate
Burnell K.E. – Eastbourne
Butcher Stanley – Eastbourne
Butler J.C. – Worthing

Cama S. – Brighton
Carter R.J. – Ringmer
Carter W.K. – Eastbourne
Chapman S.J. – Hassocks
Chismon P.C. – Ipswich
Church D.J. – Slinfold
Clark B.D. – Staffordshire
Clark G.J. – Harrow
Collins L.A. – Worthing
Collinson J.W.N. – Heathfield
Corr M.J.H. – Hove
Cotter P.R. – Fulking

Cranmer Mrs A.M. – Hove
Crichton R.M. – Burgess Hill

Dadswell A.T. – Burgess Hill
Dadswell R.G. – Burgess Hill
Damen D.R. – Brighton
Dalziel P. – Goring-by-Sea
David E.N. – Shoreham-by-Sea
Dickinson D.C. – Hove
Douglas G.S. – Cowshed
Dambrell A.A. – Brighton

East Dean Motoring Centre Ld – Eastbourne
Elliott J.E. – Worthing
Elliott V.P. – Horsham
Elford P. – Kent
Endeavour Motors – Brighton
Epps N.F.S. – Hove
Everitt G.L. – Hove

Falconer Mrs A. – Nottinghamshire
Fisher S.D. – Hove
Ford C.V. – Haywards Heath
Freeman J.A. – Horsham
French Julian D. – Bristol
French Nigel R. – Liverpool
French Ronald J. – Portsmouth

Gilbert G.L. – Hove
Gilliver A.J. – Lindfield
Goodenough J.A. – Hove
Gordon P. – Hove
Gravett M.L. – Surrey
Lt. Col. W.D. Griffiths D.S.P. M.C. – Hove
Lt. Col. Grimston – Brighton

Hall F. McD – Cuckfield
Hamlet D.K. – St. Leonards-on-Sea
Harrison K.C. – Eastbourne
Haselden P.H. – London
Hawkins D.J. – Crawley
Haywood A.B. – Hassocks
Heath H.W. – Hove
Heughan G.W.K. – West Yorkshire
Hill Alan – Lindfield
Hindley M.D. and R. – Hove
Holland J.W. – Hampshire
Hollingworth H.M. – Pulborough
Horne J.A. – Portishead, Bristol

309

Huggett K.H.G. – Woolwich
Hurrell P.C. – Hastings

Col. R.C. Jackman – Hove
James J.A. and I.T. – Hitchin
Johnson A.D. – Brighton
Jones K.G. – Hassocks

Kench G.A. – London
Kidsons Chartered Accountants – Hove
Knight P. – Hastings

Laye G.J. – Eastbourne
Leadley R.M. – Henfield
Lee D.R. – Littlehampton
Levine E.I. – Hove
Lurcott, M.P.W. – Lewes

Mair R.M.R. – South Glamorgan
Mannings, F.E. – Hove
Martin B.P. – Wiltshire
McArthur S.M. – Brighton
Meek B.L. – Burgess Hill
Melton A.J.H. – Brighton
Mepham T.I.J. – Hastings
Miles G.D. – Peacehaven
Miller R.A. – Hemel Hempstead
Mills R.C. – Emsworth
Milton J.T. – Eastbourne
Mitchell M.L. – Surrey
Munson D.J. – Lewes

Napper R.G. – STeyning
Nash G.L. – Hove
Nash M.W. – Surrey
National Westminster Bank PLC – East Grinstead
Noakes M.J. – Lewes
North R.F. – Ealing

Oakes R.B. – Haywards Heath

Penfold A.A. – St. Leonards-on-Sea
Peters N.H.C. – Hove
Pilgrim Alan – Brighton
Piper J.H.E. – Hove
Preddy A.J. – Chichester

Rainbird E.D. – Bedford
Rawlinson Dr W.A.L. – Hurstpierpoint

Rice Dr David – Ringmer
Ridge K.A. – Hove
Roberts R. – East Dean
Robinson A.R. – Hove
Robson Rhodes Chartered Accountants – Crawley
Roger-Jones R.B. – Brighton
Ross J.A. – East Grinstead
Rowe B. – Hove

Scovell C.J. – Crawley
Sharp N.J.G. – Surrey
Sherman D.E. – London
Sinden I.M. – Brighton
Smith H.W. – Middlesex
Smith M.L. – Shoreham
Stapleton L.F.M. – Hove
Stefanski R.E. – Billingshurst
Summerby C.J. – Brighton

Temerlies M.S. and L.J. – Hove
Thompson M.L. – Crondall
Thompson P.A. – Kent
Tremellen M.P. – Plymouth
Tuck P.G. – Surrey
Tunnicliff J. – Bognor Regis
Tye P.A. – Worthing

Vickers D.A. – Hove
Vinen D.G. – Guildford, Surrey

Wallace C.S. – Hurstpierpoint
Walshe M.L. – Grays
Ward Lund F. – Hove
Watson E.A. – Burgess Hill
White H.J. – St. Leonards-on-Sea
Wickens R.C. – Eastbourne
Williams E.J. and Mrs R.D. – Hove
Williams R.J. – Surrey
Williamson G.E. – Kent
Wilthew J. – Tyne and Wear
Wilton D.G. – Wadhurst
Winter B.J. – Kent
Wright A.L. – Broadstairs

Youngman D.T.E. – Fernhurst

310

Index

312

313

319

320